Access to Legal Education
and the Legal Profession

Access to Legal Education and the Legal Profession

Edited by

Rajeev Dhavan
Advocate, Supreme Court, Hon. Professor, Indian Law Institute, India

Neil Kibble
Senior Lecturer in Law, South Bank Polytechnic

William Twining
Quain Professor of Jurisprudence, University College London
Chairman, Commonwealth Legal Education Association

Published in conjunction with the Commonwealth Legal Education Association

Butterworths
London and Edinburgh
1989

United Kingdom	Butterworth & Co (Publishers) Ltd, 88 Kingsway, LONDON WC2B 6AB and 4 Hill Street, EDINBURGH EH2 3JZ
Australia	Butterworths Ptd Ltd, SYDNEY, MELBOURNE, BRISBANE, ADELAIDE, PERTH, CANBERRA and HOBART
Canada	Butterworths Canada Ltd, TORONTO and VANCOUVER
Ireland	Butterworth (Ireland) Ltd, DUBLIN
New Zealand	Butterworths of New Zealand Ltd, WELLINGTON and AUCKLAND
Puerto Rico	Equity de Puerto Rico Inc, HATO REY
Singapore	Butterworth & Co (Asia) Pte Ltd, SINGAPORE
USA	Butterworth Legal Publishers, AUSTIN, Texas; BOSTON, Massachusetts; CLEARWATER, Florida (D & S Publishers); ORFORD, New Hampshire (Equity Publishing); ST PAUL, Minnesota; and SEATTLE, Washington

A CIP Catalogue record for this book is available from the British Library

ISBN 0 406 70065 6

Printed and bound by Butler & Tanner Ltd, Frome and London

Preface

The Commonwealth Legal Education Association (CLEA) is a non-governmental voluntary organisation concerned with legal education at all levels, from law in schools to continuing legal education, in all Commonwealth jurisdictions. Among its objects are to disseminate information concerning legal education and research and 'to promote and conduct research in the field of legal education'. In recent years the Association has sponsored or assisted with studies and seminars on such varied topics as localisation of legal literature, legal education for non-lawyers, the training of magistrates, law teaching clinics, research and development in respect of direct teaching of professional skills and the study of human rights. The Association is particularly concerned to stimulate research and debate on neglected but problematic topics within its remit.

This book deals with such a topic. The closely related problems of access to legal education and to the legal profession are shared to some extent by all countries and jurisdictions. They have been much debated in the United States, but have only recently begun to attract sustained attention in Commonwealth countries.

What constitutes a problem of access, how it is perceived and what are considered to be feasible and appropriate responses vary not only according to the history and social and economic conditions of a given country and the nature of its legal profession and its educational system, but also according to the values and political commitment of individuals. Some patterns and trends are replicated throughout most of the Commonwealth. For example, most law students and lawyers are recruited from the upper and middle classes, and the proportion of women entering legal education has increased markedly in nearly all countries in the past fifteen to twenty years. But what constitutes a problem of access, what priority it should be given, and what measures are likely to be acceptable and feasible in a given context not only differ from place to place, but will also be the subject of differing views in particular places.

The purpose of this book is to explore issues relating to access in selected Commonwealth countries in order to draw attention to the problems, to clarify issues and to provide a context in which information, perceptions and experiences from different countries can usefully be exchanged. This is an exploratory study designed to provide information, suggest perspectives and disseminate ideas with the hope that this can provide a starting-point for local investigation and debate about problems of access in very different contexts. It does not purport to be a full-scale comparative study, still less does it presume to make general recommendations or advocate a particular strategy. While the contributors are generally in favour of extending access – about which there is not surprisingly a broad consensus – they present a variety of opinions and perspectives on particular topics such as aptitude testing, 'reverse discrimination' and affirmative action, the aims of legal education, the actual and potential roles of lawyers in society, and the desirability or otherwise of trying to regulate numbers of law students and of lawyers.

The book is organised as follows: the first four chapters deal with general topics. William Twining, using the device of a fictional report on a mythical jurisdiction, suggests some concepts, questions and perspectives for diagnosing problems of access in any jurisdiction. In the second chapter, Oliver Fulton reviews the experiences of alternative policies adopted in different higher education systems at different times. In more critical vein, two American lawyers, Leora Mosston and Terence Cannon, discuss exclusionary practices and the dangers of aptitude testing respectively. The next nine chapters are studies of the problems of access to legal education and the legal profession in particular countries or jurisdictions.

All of the authors of these 'local' papers are legal educators writing about their own country from first-hand experience; they were asked to address certain issues, but were otherwise free to express their own interpretations and opinions. These country studies not only illustrate the variety of experiences and situations in different places, but also the potentially controversial nature of many of the issues relating to access. There follows a paper on a relatively neglected topic that is becoming increasingly important: international mobility of lawyers. Campbell McLachlan explores the issues and makes the case for strengthening Commonwealth co-operation in this area.

In the last chapter Rajeev Dhavan picks out some general themes from the particular contributions, puts the whole subject in a broader perspective and raises some sceptical questions about the enterprise. Finally the appendices contain a general bibliography and selection of materials that are intended to serve as concrete examples of particular matters that have been discussed in the book, such as admissions policies, the presentation of statistics broken down by gender and ethnic grouping, and descriptions of access courses. These are again offered not as models, but rather as materials for critical examination and debate in different contexts.

This book is closely related to two other projects. Shortly before we went to press the first two volumes of a major Comparative Study of Legal Professions were published: *Lawyers in Society: The Common Law World* edited by Richard Abel and Philip Lewis (University of California Press, 1988) and *The Legal Profession in England and Wales* by Richard Abel (Basil Blackwell, 1988). We have only been able to draw on the findings to a limited extent, but we have benefited from informal collaboration and advice from Richard Abel and Philip Lewis. Their volumes set the issues of access in the context of general studies of legal professions; we hope that this book complements their important study by dealing with a particular configuration of issues in more detail.

This book is also closely related to another project connected with legal education and sponsored by CLEA. *Learning Lawyers' Skills*, edited by Neil Gold, Karl Mackie and William Twining, is published simultaneously by Butterworths as a companion volume. It attempts to take stock of the state of development of direct teaching of professional legal skills in the Commonwealth by presenting an edited selection of examples of course materials and exercises used in practical training in different jurisdictions, accompanied by a critical commentary. This is another rapidly changing area of legal education and training. Taken together, we hope that these two volumes will stimulate interest and new insights into important aspects of the Who, the How and the Why of legal education throughout the Commonwealth.

RD
NK
WLT
1988

Acknowledgments

We wish to thank the Commonwealth Foundation for financial support; the Commonwealth Legal Education Association and the Commonwealth Institute for Legal Education and Training (Windsor, Ontario) for assistance with publication costs. We thank the American Bar Association Section on Legal Education, the Law School Admission Council, the University of London and the University of Windsor for permission to reproduce copyright material.

Many individuals gave invaluable assistance during the course of the project. In addition to the contributors, we are particularly grateful to Richard Abel, Richard Karegyesa, Maurice Kogan, Philip Lewis, Linda Martin, Jeremy Pope, James P White and Gordon Woodman for invaluable help and advice. We wish to thank Butterworths Publishers for their patience and foresight, and Margaret Rogers, Secretary of CLEA, for her constant support and encouragement.

RD
NK
WLT

Contents

Preface   v
Acknowledgments   ix
List of contributors   xiii

1   Access to legal education and the legal profession: a Commonwealth
    perspective   1
    William Twining

2   Access to higher education: a review of alternative policies   39
    Oliver Fulton

3   Legal education for a changed world: an American perspective   55
    Leora Mosston

4   Admission tests for law school: some cautionary remarks   78
    Terence M Cannon

5   Access to legal education in Australia   85
    David Weisbrot

6   Access to legal education and the profession in Canada   114
    Brian Mazer

7   Access to legal eduction and the legal professional in England   132
    Neil Kibble

8   Access to legal education and the legal profession in India   162
    S P Sathe

9   Access to legal education and the legal profession in Jamaica   174
    Selina Goulbourne

10 Access to legal education and the legal profession in Northern
    Ireland   190
    Desmond Greer

11 Access to legal education and the legal profession in Scotland   217
    Alan Paterson

12   Access to legal education and the legal profession in Zambia   234
Chuma Himonga and Chaloka Beyani

13   Access to legal education and the legal profession in Zimbabwe   245
Reg Austin

14   Legal practitioner mobility in the Commonwealth   258
Campbell McLachlan

15   Legal education as restrictive practice: a sceptical view   273
Rajeev Dhavan

Appendices   303
  I   Admission bulletin of the Faculty of Law of the University of
         Windsor   305
 II   Survey of minority group students enrolled in JD programmes in
         approval law schools   312
III   Cautionary policies concerning use of the LSAT and LSDAS   316
IV   A part-time Access Course – University of London, Department of
         Extra-Mural Studies Certificate in Legal Method, *Course Handbook 1988–
         89* (extracts)   321
  V   A Full-time Access Course – Vauxhall College of Further
         Education/South Bank Polytechnic Law Access Course, *Course Handbook
         1988–89* (edited extracts)   323

Select bibliography   325
Symposia   336
Government Reports/Official Reports   337
Bibliographies   338

INDEX   339

List of contributors

William Twining
University College,
London, England

Oliver Fulton
Institute for Research and Development in Post-Compulsory Education,
Lancaster University,
Lancaster, England

Leora Mosston
Greenberg Center for Legal Education & Urban Policy,
New York, USA

Terence M Cannon
Greenberg Centre for Legal Education & Urban Policy,
New York, USA

David Weisbrot
University of New South Wales Law School,
Sydney, Australia

Brian Mazer
Windsor Law School,
Ontario, Canada

Neil Kibble
South Bank Polytechnic,
London, England

S P Sathe
ILS Law College,
Pune, India

Selina Goulbourne
Council of Legal Education,
London, England

Desmond Greer
The Queen's University,
Belfast, Northern Ireland

Alan Paterson
Strathclyde University,
Glasgow, Scotland

Chuma Himonga & Chaloka Beyani
University of Zambia,
Lusaka, Zambia

Reg Austin
University of Zimbabwe,
Harare, Zimbabwe

Campbell McLachlan
New Zealand Solicitor, Herbert Smith, (Solicitors),
London, England

Rajeev Dhavan
Advocate, Supreme Court of India, Hon. Professor, Indian Law Institute,
Delhi, India

1 Access to legal education and the legal profession: a Commonwealth perspective*

William Twining†

Introduction

Once upon a time the Law Faculty of the University of Xanadu, tired of perpetually debating curriculum, decided to turn their attention to Admissions.[1] They started by analysing who their students were; this did not take long as they already knew that they were much of a muchness. So they resolved to take on the broader question of who were not their students.

We seem to have a problem of Access, said the Dean, over 90% of our student body are drawn from only 5% of the population.

Educational institutions should not try to solve society's problems, said the Sub-Dean.

There is no problem, said the Vice-Dean, we have never had any complaints.

There is no problem, said the Admissions Tutor, we are prohibited by law from discriminating on grounds of gender, colour or religion and we select solely on the basis of the school-leaving examination.

Last year's survey showed no correlation whatsoever between school-leaving results and degree performance.

There used to be a problem about women, but now they represent 45% of our intake: the problem is solved.

The problem is not solved: it is merely postponed to a later stage in the process. Women still suffer discrimination in apprenticeship, employment and

* This is a revised and extended version of the annual Access to Justice Lecture, delivered at the University of Windsor on 2nd April 1986 and published in (1987) 7 Windsor Yearbook of Access to Justice 157–208. I am grateful to many people for help with this paper. Most of them are acknowledged in the first published version. A select bibliography on access to legal education and the legal profession is appended at the end of this book. For the sake of brevity, items listed in the bibliography are cited in the following form: Goodlad (1984). Other references are given in full.
† Quain Professor of Jurisprudence, University College, London and Chairman, Commonwealth Legal Education Association.

I have set the discussion in the mythical jurisdiction of Xanadu with a view to making the presentation more concrete and more provocative. Xanadu is a composite with many familiar features. Far from being presented as typical, it is designed to bring out some of the great variety of circumstances and problems relating to access in different jurisdictions of the Commonwealth. Constructing a mythical country frees one from both the incubus of data and expatriate inhibition. But the main purpose is to invite my audience to engage actively in the comparative method: by comparing and contrasting the position in your own jurisdiction with each circumstance in Xanadu, the nature of problems of access and prospects for effective action in your own country may be clarified in the context of a quite simple framework for analysis and comparison.

promotion. Anyway 80% of the women applicants are from the Northern middle class.

We get very few Southerners; but that is not our fault: they just don't apply.

Of course we have a problem: our student body should be broadly representative of the population at large.

That is not the problem: our student body should represent the best potential practitioners.

That is elitist: everyone should have an equal opportunity to enter law school.

We have a near-monopoly over entry to the legal profession: at present we prefer academic high-flyers many of whom probably won't practise to sound men who would be the backbone of the profession. We should only admit those who intend to practise.

We are not a trade school.

We should try to get the best and the brightest.

Ask not who is the best; rather ask who is most likely to learn the most.

Ask not who will take the most, but rather who will contribute the most to our intellectual community.

It is in our interest to favour the children of the rich.

Admission by auction would maximise revenue.

Admission by lottery is the most efficient and objective method of selection.

There is a problem, but it is insoluble.

There are plenty of solutions: for example mature student entry.

I am against reverse discrimination.

That is not discrimination: our mature students do as well as 18-year-olds and they both learn and teach more.

If the South continues to feel that it does not get its fair share of places in the education system we shall have a civil war.

We should have quotas: 50% women; 30% Northerners; 85% rural; 90% working class and so on.

No. What we need is variety: let us have two policemen; two convicted felons; two divorcees; two single parents; two married men; a trade unionist; a managing Director and a foreign diplomat.

If you want variety, why not admit mainly foreign students?

At least we should look to the experience of other countries for models or success stories.

No country in the world has solved the problem of access: there are no success stories.

Eventually the Oldest Member spoke up: 'None of us know what we are talking about: Let us consult an expert.' 'There are no experts', howled his colleagues. 'Then let us make one by appointing him', he replied. That is how, without any prior expertise, I came to write the report from which the following extracts are taken.

Whose problem?

Under what circumstances is it true to say that a problem of access exists? Obviously this depends largely on the standpoint and values that are adopted. For example, from the standpoint of an individual who wishes to study law or become a lawyer any obstacle between him/her and these goals represents part of their problem of access. And she may feel aggrieved if it seems that the barriers are artificially high or irrelevant or unnecessary or unfair in some way. For example an applicant may resent any of the following:

(i) a strict limit on numbers at one or more stages of legal education or training or qualification;
(ii) negative discrimination, direct or indirect, against him/her as an individual or against members of a class or group to which he/she belongs;
(iii) positive discrimination in favour of some other class or group;
(iv) arbitrary or biased selection, treatment or certification at any stage;
(v) a longer minimum period of education, training, apprenticeship or limited practice than seems justifiable according to agreed criteria of minimum 'competence', if such exist;
(vi) an arbitrary academic standard for professional qualification;[2]
(vii) restrictions on upward or lateral mobility that seem unnecessary or unfair or unduly rigid;
(viii) barriers that result from structural features of the economic, social or educational system rather than specifically from the organisation of legal education or the legal profession;
(ix) absence of a 'second chance' to remedy a failure or poor result at a particular stage;

and so on.

To what extent such grievances in fact exist and to what extent they are remediable depends very largely on circumstances. To what extent others will sympathise with such grievances or feel that they are justified is, of course, a matter of evaluation in the given context.

From the standpoint of those who control different stages or routes – the various gatekeepers – some of these matters will be of direct concern; but others will be felt to be outside their control or jurisdiction. For example, in formulating an admissions policy for a particular law school, criteria of admission and selection, and efforts at recruitment, must take account of the pool of actual and potential applicants from whom their students can be realistically recruited and selected. They cannot take on full responsibility for all prior and subsequent stages in the process.[3] And at times different gatekeepers may be at odds with each other.

I propose to look at problems of access from a different standpoint, that is from the perspective of the system as a whole where the concern is to devise workable *general* strategies for improving access to legal education and the legal profession in a given jurisdiction. My concern is to suggest a way of diagnosing the problem from this point of view in different contexts and of considering the range of possible strategies and devices that might be employed at different points in the system.[4] Where power over the total process is dispersed, an important factor is likely to be the willingness or otherwise of each of the gatekeepers to co-operate with others in tackling the problem.

From this perspective, the extent and nature of actual grievances, the existence of particular barriers to access and the attitudes, interests and circumstances of particular gatekeepers are all relevant. But in so far as we are concerned with describing, analysing and improving existing systems in respect of access, we need to adopt a broader perspective and a longer time-frame than those of individual applicants or particular gatekeepers. We may also need to take into account additional factors that may be marginal or irrelevant to these particular participants.

In diagnosing the problem, we need first to look at the following, in the broad context of the particular society under consideration: politico-economic factors, such as the state of economic development, existing power structures and dominant ideologies; sectarianism, racism, sexism and other forms of prejudice; the demography of the country; the education system and, in particular, the organisation, scale and financing of tertiary education; national policies concerning such matters as language, educational opportunity, and the delivery of legal services; the nature of the legal profession in both private and public sectors and the social functions – both manifest and latent – of law schools. Above all, in diagnosing the 'problem' and considering possible strategies and particular measures, the whole discussion needs to be set firmly in the particular historical context. Our concern is with feasible policy, not with Utopia.

Since 'Xanadu' is an explicitly heuristic device, it would be artificial to present a very detailed historical scenario, but it may be useful at this point to present some elementary 'facts': The country of Xanadu is an artificial construct from a series of recognisable types: independent ex-colony; politically stable (a mildly socialist democratic government); a fragile mixed economy; per capita income of say 300 pounds (US $500) per annum; ethnically varied, multicultural and multilingual, its population of 8–10 million is divided unequally between the South (mainly Muslim and local religion) and the much smaller, predominantly Christian, North; its legal system is also plural (national consitution and legislation; customary law, Islamic law and received common law) with the language and traditions of the common law presently being the dominant influence on the legal profession. This is distributed almost equally between public sector lawyers (including a career judiciary) and private practitioners (advocates) who are members of a fused profession. The education system is largely government-run, with a few private and mission schools. There is a single national university with a Law Faculty that was established in 1962; five years ago a private law college was set up in response to market demand and, after a struggle, its degree has been recognised as fulfilling the academic stage of qualification for practise. Foreign exchange difficulties have made study abroad increasingly difficult especially for lawyers. Perhaps the single most important feature is that there is a single stream method of qualifying as a lawyer whether in the private or public sector. Almost without exception the route is national school-leaving certificate, local three-year law degree (at 18 +), one year's professional training succeeded by a Bar examination, two years' apprenticeship (with an advocate or in the public service) followed by two years' restricted practice, before an advocate can practise on his or her own – a total of six to eight years post-18.

Diagnosis

One quite simple way of diagnosing the problem in a given jurisdiction is to set up a model of the different stages through which a potential law student or lawyer must pass and to ask four sets of questions of each point in the process:

(i) What are the barriers to progress beyond this stage? Do the barriers operate against members of disadvantaged groups?
(ii) Who controls entry and exit at this stage?
(iii) From the point of view of the individual: By what means might each barrier be surmounted or circumnavigated?
(iv) From the point of view of the gatekeepers and of those concerned with general strategy: What are acceptable and feasible means of eliminating or mitigating or circumnavigating the barriers or easing the passage of individual members of disadvantaged groups in the interests of improved access?

In order to simplify the presentation I propose to make some working distinctions, not all of which are of general application. First, taking birth as the baseline, it is useful to distinguish between stages and barriers that a potential recruit must pass through to come within range of being eligible for admission, and stages and barriers that confront actual applicants, students and aspirants in the process leading towards professional status. In Xanadu the line can be drawn at about the 17th birthday. For the sake of simplicity I shall treat all the factors that serve to eliminate potential recruits before that stage as falling outside the purview of this report, whether these be accidents of birth, filtering out of the school system, premature specialisation or career choice, linguistic deprivation or whatever.[5] Again, in order to simplify matters, I shall confine my analysis to the point in the process when the recruit to the legal profession becomes fully qualified to practise on his/her own – while recognising that some barriers to access or progress may be as great or greater at later stages in his/her career. This study is limited to initial qualification.

In analysing a given situation it is useful to make a number of working distinctions, most of which are familiar.[6] We need to distinguish:

(i) between *selection* among applicants and active *recruitment* of applicants;
(ii) between *minimum standards* of entry or eligibility and *criteria of selection* in situations of competition;
(iii) between competition for *any* place and competition for *more desirable* places (eg in an elite law school or a prestigious law firm);
(iv) between *selection* on entry to higher education and *certification* at the end of the educational process;
(v) between *certification* for practice (has the candidate satisfied certain academic tests and training requirements?) and *evaluation* of professional competence;
(vi) between *direct* (or intentional) and *indirect discrimination* (both in a negative sense) and between '*reverse discrimination*' and other kinds of '*positive action*';
(vii) between criteria of selection which involve *preferential* treatment and those that are *different* without being discriminatory.

In respect of admissions to an educational programme, we need to distinguish between such questions as: is the candidate likely to *complete* the course; to *excel*; to *benefit*; and to *contribute* to this institution or the community at large? One can, for example, benefit from a course that one fails to complete and excel in a course from which one has learned little or nothing, perhaps because one is overqualified for it; and one can excel in a course to which one has contributed nothing.

Two distinctions are particularly important for our purposes. First, we need to differentiate between selective and mass systems of higher education, including legal education.[7] At one extreme, applicants compete for a strictly limited number of places in a single institution which aspires to provide intensive, high quality education for the chosen few. At the other pole, there is no *numerus clausus* (or quota) and anyone who satisfies some minimal criteria, eg passing a national school-leaving examination, is entitled to a place. Large scale systems are often characterised by very large classes, poor facilities, high failure rates and very formalised instruction. In such contexts the legal education system sometimes serves as a dumping-ground for surplus demand for higher education, along with other subjects that are perceived by politicians and administrators to involve low costs.[8]

A second distinction is between single and multiple routes of entry. In England, for example, it was for a long time possible to qualify as a solicitor either solely through a combination of apprenticeship plus professional examinations, *or* after obtaining a law degree that exempted holders from the first part of the professional examinations, *or* after obtaining a degree in a subject other than law. Although in recent years there has been a strong trend towards all-graduate entry, there is still provision for qualification by graduates with degrees in subjects other than law. This is a route followed by a significant minority of candidates. There is also a good deal of variety in the types of degree available (full-time; part-time; external; mixed degrees eg law and language; law and sociology; and sandwich courses). All these provide a degree of flexibility, especially for late developers, mature students, and people who decide that they wish to become lawyers at a relatively late stage in their education. At the other extreme stand systems in which there is only a single route of entry, typically involving a whole series of barriers or filters, at any one of which a candidate's opportunity to become a lawyer may be irrevocably destroyed.

Partly because it is a small country, partly for reasons of historical contingency, Xanadu is very near to the ideal type of a system with a single route of entry. With almost no exceptions, anyone who wishes to qualify as a lawyer has to pass through a uniform series of stages, each of which may result in the elimination or filtering out of a potential aspirant, often with no further chance of re-entry. Thus in reverse order, before being allowed to practise as a sole practitioner, a lawyer must have been employed in legal work in government or in private practice for two years after qualification as an advocate; by no means all those who qualify as advocates obtain employment of a kind that satisfies this requirement. In order to qualify as an advocate a graduate has to complete two years of apprenticeship after passing bar examinations; the failure rate in the bar examinations is quite high and candidates are allowed to resit only once; by no means all those who pass manage to obtain places as trainee advocates (the equivalent of articles or pupillage in the English system). In order to take the bar examination one must have attended full-time for one year at the professional law school, for which there is intense competition for a limited number of places. Until recently holders of certain foreign law degrees or professional qualifications were eligible for direct entry to the professional school. But pressure from local law graduates has led to a considerable narrowing of this provision and, in any event, opportunities to study law abroad have declined to almost nothing in recent years. For all practical purposes, an intending lawyer must obtain second class honours in the local law degree from one of two institutions. There is in fact a significant wastage rate, by failure in examinations and otherwise, especially in the less highly regarded private law school; this is despite the fact that only about 30% of all applicants obtain a place in one of these institutions. This figure is misleading on its own, because it is well-known that only those who perform well above average in the national school-leaving examination have a chance of being accepted, and so many do not bother to apply. Also, although those who have specialised in science at school are theoretically eligible, few apply and even fewer are selected. The school system is itself a pyramid, from which students are filtered out at every stage. In theory there is universal primary education, but it is estimated that in some rural areas as many as 30% of children never in fact complete primary school.

The aspiring lawyer has to pass through a series of gates or filters, each of which is controlled by a largely autonomous authority. The highly selective school system is controlled largely by, or through, the Ministry of Education; entrance to and exit from the two local law schools are controlled by the University and the private Law College respectively, each of which is largely autonomous. Formal qualification for the legal profession is controlled by a Council of Legal Education, on which the judiciary and the two law schools are represented, but which has a majority of private practitioners. Selection for places for apprentices and for limited practice is almost entirely controlled by employers; these include local law firms, the Ministry of Justice and various other institutions in the public sector, including the larger municipal councils. Thus, as in many other countries, control over access is split among several different authorities in such a way that the diffusion of power tends to make life harder rather than easier for the aspirant: at each stage in the process he or she has to please a different gatekeeper.

Xanadu, therefore, corresponds very closely to an extreme 'ideal type' of single stream entry which has the following characteristics:

(i) The education system is a monolithic pyramid with many students eliminated at every stage.

(ii) Progression at nearly every stage depends on success in competition for a limited number of places.

(iii) There are few second chances for those who failed in such competition.

(iv) Career choice for law (for those who have such a choice) generally has to be made in theory by the age of 18, in practice for most by 16, when the decision has to be made whether to specialise in Science or Arts.[9] Most people never reach a point where such choices are open to them at all.

(v) Except for minimal provision for mature student entry to university, and the residue of recognition of foreign qualifications, there are no alternative routes of entry to the legal profession.

(vi) All intending lawyers, including those who are destined for the judiciary or the public service, have first to qualify as private practitioners. At first sight this looks like postponement of specialisation, but it can be argued that much of the training at the professional stage is irrelevant to public sector work.[10] It does not follow from this that the best solution is to stream people earlier.

(vii) The gatekeepers at each stage and the criteria they use are significantly different, which does not mean to say that they do not have some shared biases.

(viii) There are no special programmes of remedial education and few second chances within the system of legal education and training.

Other jurisdictions deviate from the model in significant respects, though few even approximate to the ideal type which represents the polar opposite; for example, a jurisdiction which has the following features:

(i)   progression depends on satisfying minimum criteria of eligibility rather than selection in competition (no *numerus clausus*);
(ii) multiple routes of entry to higher education and to the legal profession;
(iii) active recruitment, encouragement and support of members of disadvantaged groups;
(iv) second chances at each stage within each route;
(v)   specialisation and career choices are deferred;
(vi) generous provision for occupational mobility (eg transfer from one occupation to another);
(vii) generous or partial recognition of foreign qualifications;
(viii) special programmes for remedial or accelerated education;
(ix) a co-ordinated strategy for dealing with problems of access.

Why should we be concerned? Are legal education and membership of the legal profession social goods?

According to Jeremy Bentham the interests of lawyers are in constant opposition to the interests of the community.[11] In a single work he likened them to leeches, sharks, cuttle-fish, poisoners, idolators, dog-trainers, savages, slave-dealers, swindlers, lottery-keepers, spiders, depredators, tinkers, shoe-makers and fish-wives ... to mention only a few.[12] Without making too fine a point of it, one might infer from this that Bentham did not think that membership of the legal profession is self-evidently a social good. Indeed, one might reasonably infer that utility dictates reducing rather than extending opportunity to join such a band of swindlers, cuttle-fish and spiders.

Bentham was not merely, or even mainly, echoing familiar quips about the unpopularity of lawyers. He was putting forward a serious argument, though some think that he rather spoiled his case by over-indulgence in invective. Before dismissing him out of hand it is useful to consider his thesis, if only because it provides a convenient peg on which to hang some preliminary points.

First, Bentham's polemic against the legal profession was part of an impassioned plea for simplifying the law and the administration of justice by freeing it from all artificial technicality. For him justice under the law involved enforcement of rights with a minimum of vexation, expense or delay. The law needed to be simple, clear and genuinely accessible to all. He saw nearly all complexity and technicality as obfuscations attributable to the sinister interests of judges and lawyers ('Judge and Co').[13] Whatever we think of his argument as a whole, it serves as a reminder that increasing access to legal education and the legal profession does not necessarily increase access to justice. In some circumstances it may have the opposite tendency.

Secondly, Bentham was, of course, attacking the legal profession and the judiciary as it was organised in his day. In his ideal polity salaried judges would have a pivotal role and there would even be a limited place for professional lawyers in both private and public sectors. Legal education both for specialists and the public at large would be an important aspect of access to information about law. Rather than hanging all lawyers, let us hang three points on this peg:

(a) not all lawyers are private practitioners;[14]
(b) access to legal education may raise different issues from access to the legal profession;
(c) any rational strategy for increasing access to the legal profession needs to address questions about what kinds of lawyers such a strategy is intended to encourage: more of the same? law-trained people who might be expected to perform a variety of roles significantly different from those traditionally ascribed to barristers and solicitors? possibly even people who by their membership would transform the nature of the legal profession from within? Questions about who should be lawyers are inseparable from questions about what lawyers are or might be for. Similarly questions about who are or should be law students are intimately connected with questions about what kind of legal education they want or need or are likely to get.

All of these considerations apply to Xanadu. Thus, as in many other Commonwealth countries, lawyers working in the public sector – as judges, in central and local government, in public enterprise – outnumber those in private practice. Our concern here is with access to the legal profession in this broad sense.

There is, however, a complicating factor. At present anyone who wishes to qualify as a 'lawyer' in Xanadu has to qualify as an advocate, even if he/she intends to pursue a career in the public service or the judiciary.[15] This requirement has been a matter of public controversy, partly because of the existence of a career judiciary on the French model. It is beyond my terms of reference to consider this complex matter in detail; however it is relevant to point out that while the present position undoubtedly facilitates mobility between public and private sector legal occupations, it provides an extra, somewhat artificial barrier to becoming a lawyer in the public service. As commentators have pointed out, there is much criticism of the Bar examinations as an instrument for preparing or certifying a person as a competent advocate; these examinations place a strong emphasis on knowledge rather than skill and on knowledge of private law and, in particular, on a limited range of transactions which are mainly of importance to business and to middle class individuals (conveyancing, probate, commercial sales, matrimonial, accident compensation and bankruptcy). Some of these matters are of marginal relevance to intending magistrates and public sector lawyers. Some of the implications of this will be considered below. Here it is worth making the general point that problems of access to the legal profession in a broad sense look quite different in jurisdictions with a single generalist qualification, common to all lawyers, from jurisdictions with streamed routes of entry of one kind or another.

My terms of reference make it clear that increasing access to the legal profession in this broad sense is *assumed* to be socially desirable. There is not a consensus as to the reasons for this. Some support the policy as part of a wider concern with *access to justice*; others are concerned with educational and occupational *opportunity* for disadvantaged *individuals*; yet others with increasing *representation* of disadvantaged or minority groups or classes; some maintain that *the Bar should broadly reflect the composition of society* at large.[16] Advocates of *increased social mobility* are interested in facilitating entry for older people, both the educationally deprived and members of other professions or occupations who wish to transfer. There are also supporters of much greater *cross-jurisdictional reciprocity* in respect of recognition of foreign or external qualifications.[17]

These reasons (access to justice, individual opportunity, group representation, balance or pluralism within the profession and mobility between occupations and jurisdictions) are different. To some extent they reflect broader ideological views. They interact in complex ways. Of course they are not necessarily mutually exclusive, but the different concerns are often in competition with each other. In order to simplify my analysis I shall interpret my terms of reference as being based on the assumption that in Xanadu the highest priority favoured by those responsible for policy is increasing representation of various *groups*, especially women, Southerners and Muslims, but that this has to be fitted within the broader policy of improving both individual educational opportunity and access to justice.

Developmental relevance and the numbers game

I have said that it is assumed that increasing access to the legal profession is socially desirable. This needs to be qualified in two ways: First, there has been a long-running debate about the 'developmental relevance' of law and lawyers.[18] In many countries, including Xanadu, legal education and training is almost entirely financed from public funds.[19] As in many countries at this stage of development there is an acute shortage of 'high level manpower'. Accordingly questions have been asked especially by the Treasury, manpower planners and donors of foreign aid, about the priority to be given to legal education and training in the education budget and about the desirability of having strict manpower planning in respect of lawyers.

In theory there is a close connection between the two. Historically the reality has been very different. In the immediate post-independence period an attempt was made to set rigid quotas in all subjects in tertiary education on the basis of a national manpower plan that was regularly revised. To start with the target for lawyers was set so low that it would not have been possible to justify a local law school.

The story is a quite interesting variant on a common pattern: the 1960 manpower plan set an initial target of 5 new lawyers by 1975, rising to 15 by 1985. This represented approximately 1% of the anticipated intake into tertiary education. Thus the manpower planners decreed that only one lawyer should be produced every 3 years for the first fifteen years after independence; thereafter the rate of production would be permitted to treble to one per year. These targets could be achieved by sending students abroad to study law. What actually happened was very different: in 1962 a local law school was set up in response to pressure from politicians, many of whom were lawyers. The first intake was 25; when a second (private) law school was established in 1970 in response to strong market demand, this time mainly from middle class parents, the university law school intake had already risen to 60. In addition, for about a decade starting in the early 1960s, a substantial number of individuals went abroad to study law: some were privately financed, but many more were on scholarships from foreign governments of varying political and legal complexion. Most, but not all, returned home after obtaining one or more legal qualifications of even more diverse provenance. By 1985 the population of law-trained personnel had risen to 1500, exactly 100 times the original 1960 projection. This repeated, in (only slightly) more dramatic form than elsewhere, a very widespread (possibly the predominant) pattern in former British dependencies in the post-colonial period.[20] At about the same time an independent professional school was established to provide one year's full-time postgraduate training for law graduates. The establishment of such a programme was recommended, by a team of foreign experts, on what is known as the 'Gower' model that was originally instituted in Nigeria and then was widely imitated in the Commonwealth, including in the three jurisdictions of the United Kingdom.[21] Contrary to their recommendation the Law School was entirely separate from the University and because of this was lucky to receive any financial support from government. This added to the cost of formal legal education and training, but not to the overall numbers of those qualifying. In fact it served as a brake on numbers both by having a quota of places and because it provided another financial disincentive.

What explains this phenomenon of the popularity of law? It is a complex matter and, pending further research, we cannot be sure of the answers. However, some factors are reasonably clear. First, even more than in other sectors of tertiary education, recruitment to particular disciplines was almost entirely demand-led, despite the efforts of the planners. Law was extremely popular, and remained so, with only minor fluctuations. This seems to have been an extremely widespread pattern internationally.[22] Secondly, the man-power planners underestimated the output of the secondary schools and the availability of foreign aid for education in the first decade after independence. They also made some elementary errors about Law, in particular equating law graduates with practising lawyers and practising lawyers with private practitioners.[23] In fact, here as elsewhere, the law degree served as a multi-functional feeder to a variety of occupations and more lawyers (ie advocates) found employment in the public sector than in private practice.

There was also a political dimension: an uneasy alliance of law teachers, leaders of the Bar, senior judges and middle class parents exploited the planners' errors from a mixture of motives: the law teachers needed students; the bar wished to develop 'critical mass'; many of the older generation of legally qualified people remembered that the colonial regime had restricted access to legal education for fear that it would be a breeding ground for politics, as indeed it was; students from diverse backgrounds and middle class parents saw the Law as financially attractive; and an international 'Law-and-Development' lobby articulated the case for the developmental relevance of law with great fervour and mixed success.

About 1970 the Law Society reversed gear and started complaining of 'overcrowding', but with conspicuous ambivalence and no success at all. They were too late. The lawyer factories were in full production sustained by their own momentum, by self-interest and by continuing public demand. Today the rate of production is considerably higher than the national birthrate. If current trends continue it will take until AD 3050 until there are more lawyers than people in Xanadu. According to a recent projection, the United States is due to reach that happy state of affairs considerably earlier despite the recent fall in law school applications.[24]

Of course, manpower planners and governments concerned with public expenditure are not the only parties who have been interested in control of numbers. Legal educators have regularly seen size of classes as a major factor in determining the nature and quality of legal education: large law schools may provide more opportunities for offering a variety of options but, more significantly, large classes and mass legal education are nearly always seen to be in conflict with high standards. Again, 'overcrowding' of the Bar has been a recurrent concern of practitioners and their professional associations at different times in various countries. This is a surprisingly neglected topic in the comparative study of legal professions. It is too large and complex to consider in detail here, but it may be illuminating to highlight a few examples in the literature: For example, there is a quite extensive literature on debates about 'overcrowding' in the United States in the 1930s.[25] At the height of the controversy leading academics, such as Karl Llewellyn and Lloyd Garrison, pointed out that complaints about overcrowding coexisted with significant unmet needs for legal services.[26] The problem was that there was strong competition for one sector of the market for the delivery of services to elite groups, but neglect of the needs of much of the rest of the population. Such arguments have been echoed in recent years in various parts of the Commonwealth.

Two of the more sustained attempts to analyse the problem of numbers are worth mentioning: one in New South Wales in 1979 (Bowen Report), the other in Ontario in 1981–82.[27] Both reached no firm conclusions on the control of numbers in the context of quite sharp disagreements. The NSW Enquiry vaguely recommended that the Law Society 'should give serious attention to the need to reduce the number of people embarking on legal education with regard to the capacity of the community to utilise their training', but significantly failed to specify any particular measures.[28] More candidly, the Ontario Report concluded, after much controversy, that 'if in fact there was overproduction, there was little that could or should be done about it'.[29] Calls for quotas or other overt limits on numbers have been rejected in Canada, the United Kingdom, several European countries and many American jurisdictions.[30] Perhaps this is because the idea is seen to be incompatible with a free market ideology or with the notion of a liberal profession or because of a genuine concern not to limit access or because other brakes on numbers (eg excluding non-citizens, shortage of places in educational institutions or for apprentices or allowing the market to take its toll after admission) are seen to be as effective and more acceptable.

As we have seen, in Xanadu the production of law graduates has greatly exceeded the projections of planners or the expectations of anyone. It would be comforting to suggest that, given this boom in the production of law-trained persons, there is no serious problem of access to legal education and the profession. I would not have been invited to undertake this exercise if there had been no perceived problem and my impression is that there probably is one. This is a bit puzzling, for prima facie the single best way of improving access is to increase student numbers and reduce competition for places. It is difficult to fathom the extent and nature of the problem because here, as elsewhere, reliable information is strikingly patchy; experience elsewhere suggests that the compilation and interpretation of adequate statistics, especially statistics based on race, is both difficult and controversial. We have a fair idea of the social demography of the Bar, but not of lawyers in the public sector and even less information about law graduates not engaged in legal work. We know fairly accurately the composition of the present law student body in the Law Faculty and the private Law College. We can guess that nearly all of the diminishing numbers of those who are studying abroad (or have studied law abroad in recent years) have been privately financed (mainly by affluent parents), for one of the minor victories of the manpower planners has been that it is against government policy to award scholarships for law at either undergraduate or postgraduate level.[31] We can also make a rough estimate of the breakdown of applicants to the Xanadu Law Faculty: 45% women; 80% class I and II; 90% Northerners; a clear majority urban; only a handful of overseas students. On the whole, these figures are reflected in the composition of the student body, except that the percentage of Southerners and mature students is higher, suggesting a slight element of indirect positive discrimination in selection.

Some of these figures may be useful as a basis for looking in detail at particular barriers to access, for example in university admissions, but much more is needed if a serious attempt is to be made to analyse such matters as the recruitment of mature students (how large is the pool?) or broader issues such as alleged overcrowding. Compilation of such statistics has sometimes been resisted on the ground that they would serve to perpetuate existing divisions or provide data that may help discrimination. However, it is my impression that there is a significant international trend in opinion favouring compilation of statistics about particular categories of people – by race, gender, class etc – for the benefit of the disadvantaged.[32]

Barriers and obstacles

A systematic analysis of the problem of access in a given jurisdiction would need to consider each of the points of entry and exit in a total process which may involve several different routes. Some barriers – such as finance, language, inadequate schooling, may pervade the whole process; others such as overt discriminatory hiring practices or unfair admissions criteria or shortage of apprenticeship places may operate at some points only. For example, the fact that nearly 50% of Xanadu law students today are now women does not mean that there are no gender-related problems regarding access in Xanadu: very few southern women reach law school; women encounter both direct and indirect discrimination and other barriers at later stages of the process – and, indeed, many of them move out of the system in anticipation of such barriers.

In the time available, I can only look briefly at four examples of barriers that are particularly important, but seem to operate in different ways in different contexts: language; the length of period of qualification; negative discrimination; and opposition to positive action.[33]

Obstacles to access

(a) Language

In almost all societies language is a major factor influencing opportunity; in multi-lingual societies the problems can be both acute and complex. A recent study on Sri Lanka by Mark Cooray provides a graphic illustration of some of the problems in relation to law.[34] In Sri Lanka the mother tongue (swabasha) for the bulk of the population was either Sinhala or Tamil, but the language of administration between 1858 and 1970 was English. Until 1970:

the legal profession was closed to the vast majority of the people of the country who did not possess a western education. Legal education was in English and therefore it was open to that class which had been educated in English. The degree of knowledge of English which was required of a person who wished to proceed to higher education and legal studies could only be obtained by attending one of the good English schools, and almost all such schools were situated in the principal towns. Thus in effect the legal profession was open only to those living in urban areas whose parents could afford to send them to English schools. The English schools prior to 1945 were fee-levying. Social class was not necessarily a barrier to an English education, but economic circumstances and residence in non-urban areas [were].[35]

Even after the introduction of free education, those who came from affluent backgrounds, went to fee-paying schools and spoke English at home, had an overwhelming advantage.

After 1945 political pressure for a national language switchover began to mount. The pressure came particularly from the Sinhalese majority who had three main objectives: '(i) Equality of opportunity in education for all classes; (ii) Equality of opportunity in obtaining employment; (iii) Gradual resurgence of Sinhala culture and development of the language.'[36]

A language switchover began to be implemented in 1945, but it was not until 1970 that teaching of Law in *swabasha* was introduced in the University of Ceylon. Cooray documents in fascinating detail the politics, law and logistical difficulties of this change. Not surprisingly, a rearguard action to preserve the use of English was fought by some law teachers and members of the legal profession. They argued that English was the language of law in the courts and the legislature and, with greater force, that there were almost no books and materials on law in *swabasha*.[37] These arguments were in part valid, for as Cooray points out, in the circumstances a switch to *swabasha* in legal education inevitably meant a lowering of standards, 'at least temporarily if not permanently', especially because of the problem of literature.[38] But they also used delaying tactics and their resistance resulted in almost complete unpreparedness when the inevitable switch came. The battle depicted by Cooray involved what was perceived as a tension between what he calls 'the educational ethic' and 'the socialist ethic'.[39] One side argued for the maintenance of standards at all costs; the other side pointed out that legal education in English effectively excluded 94% of those who qualified for admission to the Arts stream in the university; since this was essentially the only route of entry to the legal profession, it excluded the vast bulk of the population from the chance of becoming lawyers. A political choice had to be made and in Sri Lanka 'the socialist ethic' prevailed.

In other countries similar choices have to be made but, of course, it is not only socialists who support national language policies and increased opportunity. In 1975 the ILC *Report on Legal Education in a Changing World* noted the importance and complexity of language as a factor in legal education and observed:

> The greater challenge to legal educators comes through the adoption of a local language as the medium of instruction. This has been happening in a number of countries recently. Some Indian law schools now teach in Hindi; in Sri Lanka there are now three streams, Sinhala, Tamil and English; in the Sudan much of the teaching is in Arabic, and it is intended that instruction in Ethiopia and Tanzania will eventually be in the Amharic and Swahili languages, respectively. In Indonesia the law schools have for a number of years now taught in Bahasa Indonesia. The switch in the language of instruction is generally part of a wider national policy to change the language of the legal system and of education.

There can be various reasons for such policy – the local language may be intended to be used as a vehicle for national unity (Tanzania, Indonesia); it may be a manifestation of nationalism (Sudan); it may be used in effect to reallocate resources or to undermine the dominant position of one ethnic group (especially in plural societies). But in each case there is a further important consideration – a legal system which operates in a language which is not understood by the majority of the citizens may fail to inspire confidence in its fairness. The parties to a litigation may fail to understand the proceedings (even more so than in other countries). Countries which are striving towards models of popular participation in the machinery of justice find the use of the local language to be an essential preliminary.[40]

The ILC Report noted how very little attention had been devoted to the relationship between law, education and national language. This is still true today. Mark Cooray's work is a shining exception that could serve as a model for further studies. In the present context Sri Lanka is a particularly interesting case study because the national language switchover was largely motivated by concern for educational and occupational opportunity.

However, the particular situation of Xanadu is rather different from that in Sri Lanka and, sadly, there is almost no reliable information about the relationship between language and access to legal education and the legal profession – a critical gap in our knowledge. Xanadu is a multi-lingual society; there are said to be over fifty indigenous languages, but there is no indigenous *lingua franca*. There are several official languages, but English in practice dominates. English is still the main language of secondary and tertiary education, but it is being rapidly displaced in the schools by instruction in the main vernaculars. The time will come when this inevitably will affect legal education. The situation in Xanadu is different from Sri Lanka in important aspects – for example, customary law is probably much more important in Xanadu – but at least three general lessons can be extracted from Cooray's study: first, research on the relationship between law and language in multi-lingual societies is feasible and deserves a high priority; secondly, legal educators need to prepare the ground carefully and well in advance for a switch in the medium of instruction. This raises particularly acute problems in respect of legal literature.[41] Where, as in Xanadu, the language of education in schools is changing, this inevitably will have important implications for legal education. Thirdly, in this respect as in others, there is perceived to be a tension between concern for high standards and concern for access.[42] Difficult choices have to be made and such choices are inevitably political.

(b) Length of period of full qualification

Another point at which there is regular tension between access and standards is the length of the period of legal education and training in law. In order to make approximate trans-national comparisons it is convenient to take the standard base-line as 18 and to include in the total process all formal requirements for education, training, apprenticeship, internship and restrictions on solo practice, since all of these have a direct bearing on access. There is, of course, a great divergence in the standard routes of entry. Canada follows a pattern rather similar to the United States. In England the law degree is a first degree, but only represents the fist (or academic) stage of a three stage system of training. An intending solicitor, for example, has to take a full-time twelve-month course in a professional law school, pass a stiff final examination and then do two years articles – followed by five years of continuing legal education. On the other hand, one does not need a law degree at all in order to qualify and a significant number of Arts and Science graduates become barristers or solicitors by a different route. In India the traditional pattern has been a three-year BA, followed by a three-year LLB with no Bar exams or apprenticeship. But it is now proposed to collapse this into a five-year LLB.[43]

Despite great divergences, it is possible to venture a few general observations. First, in the past fifteen to twenty years there has been a near-universal international trend towards graduate entry to the legal profession, with law degrees being the normal and in most countries a necessary academic qualification.

Secondly, variations in the length of the total minimum period for qualification for full practice are not as great as is sometimes supposed. Thus it is almost unknown for someone to be allowed to 'hang out a shingle' as a sole practitioner below the age of 23; yet in very few countries does the minimum period extend beyond 27. The greatest differences in formal requirements relate to the differences between jurisdictions in the emphasis placed on general education, formal legal education and formal apprenticeship or internship. Of course, the actual pre-qualification careers of intending lawyers are much more varied than the minimum requirements suggest. For example, many American students spend four years over their undergraduate degree, a significant number 'intermit' or do postgraduate work or have a period of judicial clerkship or decide to qualify as lawyers when they are much older than 18 – and the point at which making such a decision becomes crucial varies considerably between and even within systems.

Thirdly, almost nothing is known about the relationship between access and different patterns of qualification. However, on the basis of particular studies of access, backed by commonsense impressions, it is possible to formulate a general hypothesis: in almost all countries, the longer the period required (in practice) for qualification, the more access is reduced for less privileged members of society. This hypothesis needs to be tested and refined in different contexts. But there are good reasons (some backed by research) for believing that it is generally true.[44] For example, even in systems in which there is relatively generous financial support for legal education and training, these provisions very rarely remove all the economic barriers to qualification for the less well-off. This extends far beyond problems of fees, accommodation, books, vacation living etc to the economic expectations and needs of the families and dependants of students from poor backgrounds. Besides direct economic barriers, there may be significant cultural, social and other disincentives inherent in a prolonged period of education and training – and one would expect these to vary quite considerably from place to place.

The length of the period of qualification is another area in which there seems to be a regular tension between concern for high standards (what Cooray calls the educational ethic) and concern about access. I have to acknowledge that in several jurisdictions in which Law has been a first degree I have regularly supported moves to extend (or maintain) the length of first degrees in law from three to four years (and, in one instance, to five years). In the process of thinking about access, I have become much more aware of the close connections between the length of education and barriers to access. Yet my enthusiasm for four-year under-graduate degrees in Law (and, for mixed multi-disciplinary degrees) has been tempered, but by no means extinguished. How can this be justified? A simple answer is as follows: first, in the circumstances of the United Kingdom there are overwhelming educational arguments in favour of four-year degrees in Law. The strength of the purely *educational* case is not diminished by the argument concerning access. Indeed, in respect of some categories of disadvantaged students (eg those with a poor command of the language of instruction), the case may be stronger. It is quite misleading to suggest that a concern for educational excellence is intrinsically elitist. As a teacher of law I believe in aspiring towards excellence. This does not involve indifference to problems of educational opportunity, but it does create a dilemma. Secondly, in all the contexts in which I have supported four year degrees, there have been multiple routes of entry to the legal profession. Thirdly, support for the opportunity to spend four years over a law degree is not incompatible with support for one year conversion courses or two, three or even five-year pro-grammes in certain circumstances. I would not favour many four-year law degrees in the USA, for example.

(c) Discrimination

The Constitution and laws of Xanadu forbid discrimination in employment, education and most sectors of public life on grounds of religion, sex, race, ethnic origin or, in certain particular cases, age. Anti-discrimination legislation relating to race and sex has recently been extended to cover 'indirect' as well as 'direct' (or intentional) discrimination, along the lines of modern British legislation.[45] Preferential treatment, generally in favour of under-represented groups, is permitted in certain limited spheres (including admission to edu-cational institutions), but is normally not required.[46] The exact scope of these latter provisions is a matter of uncertainty. It is clearly narrower than the kind of mandatory scheme that exists in India.[47]

The framework of anti-discrimination laws cannot be written off as merely 'paper rules'. Since Independence successive governments have proclaimed an egalitarian ideology and have made genuine efforts to try to enforce anti-discrimination legislation, especially in respect of race and sex, and to promote anti-discrimination policies and practices, especially in public sector employ-ment and institutions. There have been some modest programmes of positive action, but almost none so far that relate directly to legal education and the legal profession.

Despite genuine attempts over a long period to tackle problems of under-representation and discrimination, it is openly acknowledged that the reality falls far short of the aspiration. The situation in legal education and the legal profession broadly reflects general patterns in society at large. The great bulk of the existing legal profession originally came from urban, middle class backgrounds. Southerners, women, Muslims, rural communities, the urban working-class, and some religious and ethnic minorities are hardly represented at all. This pattern is largely repeated in legal education, except that the number of women law students has increased rapidly (to about 45%); but, as we have seen, nearly all of these are drawn from the urban middle class.

There is widespread acknowledgement that there is a serious 'problem' and that it is directly rooted in fundamental problems of poverty, underdevelopment, cultural diversity and political conflict. Not surprisingly, there are sharp disagreements about the precise nature of the problem, its causes and what, if anything, should be done to tackle it. These disagreements reflect profound differences in ideology, expectations and material interests. In Xanadu some of the most passionate public debates have recently centred around the related topics of discrimination, reverse discrimination and affirmative action. This is a minefield where both angels and outside 'experts' fear to tread. All that I shall attempt here is to try to clarify some key concepts and to comment briefly on some of the more accessible literature from elsewhere, notably the United States and India. These concepts, it is hoped, may be helpful in eliminating some unnecessary disagreements; the admittedly selective comments on the American and Indian experiences are intended to serve as a reminder that one needs to be discriminating in looking to foreign experience and 'solutions' for guidance.

I suggested earlier that it is useful to distinguish between direct (or intentional) and indirect discrimination (both in a negative sense) and different kinds of positive or preferential treatment; and between reverse discrimination and other forms of 'positive action'.[48] These concepts need to be elucidated and related to other standard terms in common use, such as 'institutional discrimination' and various 'isms' that carry a strong condemnatory charge, such as 'sexism', 'racism', 'sectarianism', and 'tribalism'. The present purpose is to produce a reasonably clear and workable vocabulary rather than to explore in depth some of the complexities and refinements that are inevitably associated with them.

It is probably fair to say that lawyers have contributed a good deal to the development of a more precise and less emotionally laden vocabulary in this area.[49] However, what is needed here is a usable vocabulary for analysis of problems of principles and policy in different national contexts, shorn of the technical refinements associated with specific legal doctrines in particular jurisdictions. In this regard, some of the Anglo-American legal vocabulary is suggestive, but is not entirely appropriate for present purposes. What follows is an attempt to sketch the outline for a simple and admittedly crude lexicon of concepts for diagnosis and prescription of access problems in widely differing contexts.

As a start, it is useful to distinguish between two spheres of morality:[50] *individual* morality is concerned with the rightness, or more broadly, the goodness of individual actions. Moral principles, in this sense, are concerned with guiding and evaluating the conduct of individual actors. *Social or political morality*, on the other hand, is concerned with guiding and evaluating choices, decisions and actions made by or on behalf of groups, institutions, or a whole community. This reflects Bentham's classic distinction between the principles of morals (how ought I to behave?) and of legislation (on what principles(s) ought the legislator to decide?).[51] In the present context, we are concerned directly with political morality and only indirectly with individual morality, for we are concerned with devising and evaluating strategies for dealing with a perceived problem on behalf of the community as a whole.

The concept of 'morality' in this usage is directly related to concepts of choice, responsibility, and action. It focusses on the choices and actions of responsible actors or agents and falls within the sphere of 'the philosophy of action'. However, in considering a perceived problem of maldistribution and inequality we may need to go beyond the sphere of the philosophy of action to include evaluation of states of affairs, which may or may not be blamed on any human agency. This involves switching attention from the choices and responsibilities of actors to the interests, needs and concerns of victims.[52] From the point of view of victims of disastrous events or situations it may be of secondary importance, or even of indifference, whether their plight is attributable to human agency or to other factors, such as chance or historical contingency or Acts of God. The primary concern of a starving person is to obtain food, not to find a scapegoat for his/her situation. Similarly radical inequalities of distribution of goods in society represent a bad state of affairs independently of the extent to which it is possible to attribute blame for the situation on individual or collective human agencies.[53]

It follows from this that it is important to distinguish between past-directed and future-directed 'responsibility': a human agency may be held 'responsible'[R1] for the occurrence of an event or situation that has occurred for any one of a number of reasons – for example, in lawyers' terminology, because of intention, recklessness, negligence, omission or on some notion of strict liability. Or a human agency may be 'responsible'[R2] for taking future action to try to remedy or compensate for an undesirable state of affairs independently of how this is thought to have come about. For example, many governments, groups and individuals feel that they have a duty to succour victims of natural as well as man-made disasters.[54]

In countries such as the United States and the United Kingdom, discussions of problems of access have been to a striking extent agent-oriented. Public debate and even legislation has tended to be conducted largely in terms of words like 'discrimination', 'prejudice', 'racism', 'sexism', which focus attention more on the attitudes and behaviour of powerful individuals, groups and institutions rather than on the interests, needs and aspirations of those who have suffered. As discussion has become more sophisticated, some of these terms have been extended to cover behaviour and situations for which agents are held responsible[R1] even though their attitudes and conduct are not necessarily morally reprehensible. Thus, for example, the concept of 'discrimination' was originally restricted to intentional acts of unjustified unfavourable treatment of others. Over time it became accepted that this was too narrow, not only because intention was difficult to prove, but also because many examples of unfavourable treatment were recognised to result from structures and practices which were not attributable to deliberate intent to discriminate. Accordingly, following American models, the British Sex Discrimination Act 1975 and the Race Relations Act 1976 were extended to cover 'indirect discrimination' which required those subject to the legislation, such as employers, to adopt criteria and procedures which took into account prior existing disadvantages and the effects of such practices on the opportunities and interests of racial minorities and women. While this represented a significant enlargement of the scope of the legislation, the focus remained on 'how the distribution was arrived at rather than the outcome'.[55]

Such agent-oriented perspectives may be appropriate in legislation establishing tortious or criminal liability, especially in countries in which past and present prejudice are major factors in the situation. However, a victim-oriented perspective and language may be more appropriate to a country like Xanadu in which racial (though not sexual) prejudice is almost certainly only a minor contributing factor to what is widely recognised to be a situation involving radical maldistribution of opportunity and of the particular spheres of access with which we are concerned. If one were looking for scapegoats the facts of geography, natural disaster, centuries of conflict and the policies of former colonial rulers would no doubt be prime candidates. But our task is to try to ameliorate a bad situation, whatever its causes, rather than merely to allocate blame. We are concerned with devising positive and realistic measures (including allocating responsibility[R2], for the future and only incidentally in attributing blame for the past. For this purpose, the language of distributive justice, utility and positive action is more useful than that of moral culpability.

There are, however, two contexts in which inter-related notions such as discrimination are important. First, although Xanadu is a remarkably tolerant and friendly society, it would be foolish to assert that prejudice and unfair discrimination are unknown. So far as racial prejudice is concerned, it is fair to say that the legislation and the machinery that exists for its implementation are the most that can be hoped for in the circumstances. The problems of sexual equality in a multicultural society, with a large Muslim population, are too complex and delicate to be dealt with in this paper. Suffice to say that successive governments have consistently proclaimed their commitment to principles of sexual equality and such proclamations are broadly reflected in the Constitution and laws of the country.[56] To sum up: direct and indirect discrimination has probably contributed less to the existence of a problem of access in Xanadu than in some other countries and a fairly standard range of anti-discrimination measures has already been implemented.

(d) Opposition to positive action

A second context in which an agent-oriented vocabulary is clearly relevant and in need of clarification is in the area commonly referred to as 'affirmative action'. Here again the Anglo-American debates may obscure as much as they illuminate. Such terms as 'affirmative action', 'preferential treatment', 'positive action' and 'reverse discrimination' have been used in a variety of different senses. In the context of local debates some have become associated with specific measures that have aroused strong opposition. As a preliminary to considering the acceptability of different measures, it is useful to construct a working vocabulary.

It is helpful to have a broad general term that refers to all measures specifically designed to address the kinds of problems with which we are here concerned. Because the term 'affirmative action' has over time acquired some rather specific associations, let us substitute the less familiar 'positive action'. This is both broad and vague and so we need to distinguish between different species within the genus.

Adapting a useful set of working distinctions recently suggested by Christopher McCrudden in the context of employment,[57] let us differentiate five species of positive action as follows:

(i) *Direct preferential treatment,* such as quotas or goals in admissions, which explicitly discriminate in favour of particular groups as such at the expense of identifiable groups and individuals in situations of competition or scarcity. This is nearest to the standard case of 'reverse discrimination'.[58]

(ii) *Indirect preferential treatment,* for example criteria for selection which in practice have the effect of benefiting members of disadvantaged groups at the expense of others, but without using criteria which explicitly refer to those groups.[59] For example, reserving a quota of places for 'the unemployed in Handsworth', where it can be shown that the vast majority of those eligible will be blacks. This is the converse of 'indirect discrimination' as used, for example, in British anti-discrimination law.

(iii) *Anti-discrimination measures*, directed at specific practices and acts of direct and indirect discrimination; for example, prohibitions on unfavourable treatment in such areas as employment and education in modern legislation in many Commonwealth jurisdictions.[60]

(iv) *Functional preferential treatment*, that is measures which explicitly resort to criteria normally associated with disadvantage, such as race or sex, because these criteria are claimed to be functionally relevant to the situation concerned.[61] For example, prescribing that women will be preferred to men, or blacks to whites, as performers for parts portraying women (or blacks). Or, having a quota or goal for members of minority groups in admission to law school on the grounds that the educational programme will benefit by the presence of members of these groups. Such provisions are only clear examples of 'positive action' when they are introduced for the primary purpose of furthering positive action.

(v) *Non-preferential positive action.* This is a residual category covering all forms of positive action not falling under (i)–(iv).[62] Typically these will arise in situations where there is no direct competition in respect of a finite 'cake' of resources. For example, access courses, remedial teaching or encouraging members of disadvantaged groups to apply. Here more resources may be allocated to the disadvantaged than to others on the basis of need, but within a framework in which formal criteria of eligibility, selection or certification remain standard.

These are only 'ideal types' and rather vague ones at that. However, they are useful as a way of making broad differentiations between types of positive action that may meet opposition in particular contexts. For example, in England 'direct preferential treatment' is a matter of continuing controversy; 'indirect preferential treatment' has not attracted much opposition, perhaps because it has not been a focus of attention; anti-discrimination measures have, over time, become a broadly accepted aspect of the order of things, whereas it is probably fair to say that categories (iv) and (v) have been relatively uncontroversial. In the Xanadu Law School the term 'reverse discrimination' has been applied indiscriminately to admissions quotas, and mature student entry and, even on one occasion, to the allocation of funds to visits to schools in a part of the country from which no law students had previously been recruited. Such examples differ both in respect of the kinds of arguments that are relevant to justifying (or opposing) particular measures and in relation to their general acceptability in practice in a given context. In Xanadu, for example, public controversy has been most acute in respect of quotas for admission to University. This is a clear example of direct preferential treatment, which is, not surprisingly, the area in which opposition to positive action tends to be most virulent and to be supported by the most plausible arguments. Accordingly it is worth looking more clearly at opposition to direct preferential treatment, as the most problematic kind of positive action.

Direct preferential treatment

In the English-speaking world debates about such policies in respect of admission to professional schools have been both stimulated and dominated by the controversy surrounding the American cases of *DeFunis, Bakke, et al.*[63] It is, of course, an enormous advantage to be able to draw on the rich and sophisticated literature that has developed around this controversy. However, one needs to sound a note of caution in the present context.

The most obvious point is that the terms of the debate were established in the context of American culture at a particular point in history.[64] For example, the ideological frame of reference did not accommodate the kinds of state socialism that would form the context of such a debate in say India or Sri Lanka or Tanzania. Secondly, the central issues in the American cases concerned the legality and legitimacy of certain kinds of provision for direct preferential treatment (notably racial quotas and differential criteria of selection). In some countries there is no doubt at all that such provisions are permitted by law and this not only in countries that have few or no anti-discrimination laws; in some, as in India, such provisions have been legally *mandated*.[65] In such contexts the main focus of controversy is as likely to be on the general costs and benefits and effectiveness of such provisions and policies as on problems of detailed implementation. Again, most of the leading American cases concerned competition for places in a limited number of relatively prestigious institutions in an educational context characterised by an extraordinary heirarchy of institutional prestige, on the one hand, and varied educational opportunity on the other. I am told that at no time since 1945 has there been an absolute shortage of law school places in the United States (medical schools may be different) and that, if one includes unaccredited schools, by and large the number of places in all law schools exceeds the demand from applicants who satisfy some minimal criteria of entry.[66] Bakke and DeFunis, for example, were not fighting for an opportunity to qualify at all, but for the right to compete for a place in relatively prestigious institutions on the basis of 'merit' alone.[67] The focal point of the American legal debates has been an opportunity to enter elite institutions and to have access to the higher echelons of a stratified profession. Whatever the imperfections of the American system of education, by and large the disadvantaged seem to have more chances of obtaining some legal education than in most other countries (but, again, India may be an exception).

In many countries there is intense competition to have *any* opportunity to study law or become a lawyer. For example, in Xanadu, someone who fails to obtain a place in one of the two local law schools is with minor exceptions denied *any* chance of obtaining a law degree or of qualifying for practice. On the other hand in some countries large scale legal education has been one of the dumping grounds for surplus demand for higher education.[68] Anyone with minimal educational qualifications can study law but very few are destined to reap much economic or social advantage by doing so.

Furthermore in interpreting the American situation it is difficult for the outsider to discern what was the likely impact of the *Bakke* line of decisions (in so far as it permitted certain kinds of affirmative action) and how far this has anything to do with figures concerning participation rates in legal education by women and members of certain minorities. For example, the extensive figures published by the ABA Section on Legal Education in 1984 suggest that between 1971 and 1984 minority enrolments in ABA approved schools doubled and the number of women increased by a factor of five.[69] It seems rather unlikely that programmes involving direct preferential treatment of the kind that were at issue in *Bakke* directly account for more than a small proportion of these increases. Other, less controversial measures, such as anti-discrimination rules and policies and non-preferential positive action programmes, together with much broader social trends and changes in the climate of opinion are probably more important.[70] Moreover these figures only relate to ABA approved schools; yet in some American States it is possible to obtain a law degree and to qualify to practise as a lawyer in non-approved schools.

A second caveat about the American literature relates to the level of abstraction of the debate. American constitutional litigation is known for its tendency to convert fundamental philosophical questions into legal issues. One reason for the intense academic interest generated internationally by *Bakke et al* is that the topic of 'reverse discrimination' is philosophically interesting. In the process of justifying direct preferential treatment utilitarians may be found to be committed to justifying all kinds of discrimination. Can an egalitarian justify unequal treatment to further a long-term goal of equality? Do not measures which constrain benefits in the pursuit of policy smack of coercion of individuals and curtailment of rights? As Richard Tur puts it: 'Any practice which can simultaneously embarrass the utilitarian, confound the egalitarian and challenge political individualism is worthy of study in its own right.'[71]

The philosophical issues raised by direct preferential treatment are intellectually interesting and of some practical importance. However, they are not the only examples of positive action that have aroused opposition. Moreover, in many countries the problems are so acute that over-concern with philosophical niceties may inhibit effective action by sowing confusion. If in a particular country over 90% of the population is effectively excluded from access to certain kinds of educational and occupational opportunity, it is not difficult to transcend philosophical differences to reach a broad consensus that something is badly wrong. The main issue is not whether, but how? Thus some measures such as opening up multiple routes of entry or investing more in remedial or second chance education or in scholarships may win widespread support from people of quite different political and philosophical persuasions. So too, in extreme circumstances, exceptional measures may be widely accepted, some of which might be considered unjustified in other contexts. Philosophical clarity need not inhibit positive action: rather it can provide a basis for devising coherent strategies and, by differentiating between different kinds of positive action, it may help to reduce unnecessary controversy.

The notion of 'reverse discrimination', as an example of direct preferential treatment, implies deviation from a system purporting to apply uniform conditions of merit; it presupposes three conditions:

(i) That fair competition involves all candiates competing according to a single set of criteria of selection on merit;

(ii) That these criteria are in fact good indicators of 'merit' in that either
   (a) the criteria are good predictors of relevant future performance (potential)
   or
   (b) the critiera are reliable indicators of either intelligence or past achievement or experience that deserves to be rewarded by success in this competition;[72]

(iii) That the competition is in practice fair to all applicants.[73]

A sceptic might suggest that none of these criteria is satisfied in Xanadu. There is no good reason for suggesting that a uniform test of admission is appropriate for candidates drawn from such diverse backgrounds: for example the language of the schools and the school-leaving examinations is different in the North and the South, and educators despair of making confident comparisons of these examinations as tests of academic 'excellence', given the radically different traditions of the two school systems.[73] Mature students are selected by yet other criteria which are different, but their performance in law school examinations suggests that these criteria are at least as good predictors of this kind of performance as the school-leaving examination. It is misleading to say that this type of mature student entry is an example of 'reverse discrimination', ie direct preferential treatment. In this context, it merely provides alternative criteria of selection which are considered to be equally valid.

The sceptic can go on to doubt that selection of school-leavers is in fact made on 'merit': the school-leaving examinations are acknowledged to be unreliable indicators of first year performance in law school;[74] they are even less reliable in respect of final degree results;[75] being largely tests of memory (especially in the South) they may be better indicators of likely success in Bar examinations, but that is mere speculation. There is no evidence at all that they have any claim to be predictors of likely success in legal practice; nor are these examinations highly regarded as tests of 'intelligence' or capacity for clear thought. They make no claim to be indicators of such qualities as honesty, compassion and commitment to democratic ideals of law and justice, that Chief Justice Dickson of Canada has recently suggested should weigh heavily in training and selecting future lawyers.[76] No use is made here of legal aptitude testing (on which more later). Accordingly, as in most Commonwealth countries, it is arguable that there is no baseline of 'merit' from which a policy of 'reverse discrimination' could be said to deviate.

The sceptic could go on to point out that the standard complaint against direct preferential treatment is that meritorious candidates are denied opportunity despite their success in a fair competition. But it is generally acknowledged that to obtain the same result in the school-leaving examination there is no uniformity in the number of barriers each candidate has had to surmount (nor in the amount of assistance he or she has received). In this view the educational rat-race is an obstacle course with a variable number of obstacles and aids for each candidate. It can hardly be said to be a fair competition. A variant of this argument is advanced by Katherine O'Donovan: arguments against reverse discrimination as advanced by whites, men etc are based on denial of equal opportunity to them. But where there have been past disadvantages, minority or women applicants typically have not had equal opportunity themselves, taking birth as the base-line.[77]

It may be objected that the sceptic has overstated her case: because existing criteria of selection fall short of perfection, it does not follow that they are completely unmeritorious as tests of 'merit'. If one accepts 'merit' as the most important, or at least an important, criterion of selection the question is not: 'are existing criteria perfect?' but: 'are they the best available?' In practice, some of the factors mentioned by the sceptic are taken into account in admission, admittedly in a rough and ready way (for example that some candidates have had to surmount more barriers than others). To suggest that school-leaving examinations (or other academic records) are useless as indicators of past academic excellence or future potential, is greatly to overstate the case.

How reliable and useful they are varies according to circumstances. The American LSAT, whatever its limitations, is a subtle and flexible instrument; it is carefully monitored and is capable of continuous refinement, adjustment and improvement on the basis of extensive data.[78] English 'A' levels are much less reliable predictors of performance in law school, but nevertheless they serve to eliminate large numbers of clearly unsuitable or indolent candidates who would not satisfy either the 'benefit' or 'success' entry standards.[79] As for fairness, it can be pointed out that national examinations and aptitude tests at least provide public, external criteria, known in advance by candidates, and which are more relevant and less arbitrary than lotteries and other random mechanisms favoured by some.[80] Without such criteria admissions processes would be susceptible to allegations of corruption or abuse or arbitrariness.

Even if one accepts some or all of these objections as valid, they by no means completely dispose of the sceptic's thesis. In particular, it is worth stressing (i) that by no means all admissions criteria other than past academic record or aptitude tests are examples of 'reverse discrimination'; (ii) that standard arguments against direct positive action are weakened in so far as particular criteria of alleged 'merit' are shown to be deficient in one way or another; (iii) that the 'fairness' of a particular competition is also a relative matter and (iv) that access can often be increased by means of other kinds of positive action in admissions (eg remedial education; taking account of past circumstances in assessing 'merit' either as desert or predictor; pursuing the goal of a diverse educational community).

India: a case study

A recent article by Jill Cottrell on Legal Education in India (as it was in 1983) highlights some features of the Indian scene that contrast quite sharply with the situation in North America and England.[81]

Indian legal education is, not surprisingly, vast and complex. As in North America, law degrees are postgraduate, although there are moves to change this. The three-year LLB is both a necessary and a sufficient qualification for practice. There are no Bar examinations, no formal requirements for apprenticeship, and no longer any requirements for limited practice. India presents a striking example of mass legal education. Nearly 350 institutions offer legal education to nearly 150,000 law students. In some places, there is a policy of 'unlimited admissions regardless of merit'.[82] Standards are very variable; classes tend to be large; staff/student ratios range from 50/1 to 150/1;[83] the students tend to be very poorly motivated and, in some places, they are both restless and powerful; cheating is endemic in some institutions; the curriculum is largely dictated by the profession, yet over 90% of law graduates do not enter practice. The overall impression given to the outsider is that neither the institutions themselves nor governments (state and central) nor the profession is able to exercise much control over numbers, standards or even orderly conduct of classes and examinations. There are some centres of excellence, and some have degrees of high standing, but Cottrell reports that much legal education is described by one law teacher as 'a refuge for the unemployed and the rejects from the science and technical courses'.[84] On the other hand it offers to many what may be a last chance of upward mobility. Thus despite the requirement of a first degree before starting the study of law, access to legal education is not as acute a problem as in many countries, at least for those who have reached the tertiary level of education. Nor is formal admission to practice. It has been estimated that only between 5% and 10% of law graduates enter practice, many of them because of lack of a more attractive alternative.[85]

Over the years energetic efforts have been made by the Bar Council of India, by many institutions and individual law teachers to exert stronger control over legal education and to improve its quality. Recently the main focus has been on a scheme to substitute a five-year degree in law, starting at 18+, for the present 3+3 (Arts followed by Law) pattern. The objects of this proposal are to reduce the scale and improve the quality of legal education by increasing student motivation, controlling numbers, cutting the period of formal education post-18 by a year, encouraging a broader approach to the study of law and greatly strengthening quality control. The proposals have received a mixed reaction and it remains to be seen to what extent they will be implemented with what results.

At first sight this looks like yet another example of the conflict between Access and Excellence. In many ways it is. But this tension can exhibit itself in complex ways: undoubtedly the reduction of numbers and the imposition of higher standards will reduce access, but it is access to a system of legal education that may not offer very much increased opportunity to the vast majority of its students. One of the main objectives of the scheme is to increase student motivation; yet the effect of making law degrees full-time will be to eliminate part-time, evening courses that are said to contain more highly motivated students, many of whom are drawn from underprivileged backgrounds.[86]

The proposal is also seen as an example of the leaders of the profession abdicating responsibility by seeking to exercise control only indirectly:

> There is some criticism of the role of the Bar Council itself. Some teachers have expressed resentment at what they see as the autocracy of the Council – though this is not a widespread reaction, possibly because the LLB degree has been for so long structured by the demands of the profession. There is a feeling that the Bar is expecting the universities to do its dirty work for it. The profession wants to achieve two things: a reduction in the number of entrants to the profession and a raising of the standard of education of those who do not enter. In theory these could be achieved by the profession's raising its own gateways to practice – by requiring the passing of professional examinations set by itself, or by running its own professionally oriented post-graduate courses, or by an apprenticeship requirement – and each of these approaches has its advocates among university teachers. But the Bar Council feels it lacks the capacity to administer and enforce any such restrictive devices and is in effect saying to the universities: 'You build the gateway – to our specification.'[87]

Galanter's study

As I suggested above, in recent years perceptions of the nature of the problems of access to legal education have been strongly influenced by the extended debates surrounding the American cases of *DeFunis* and *Bakke*.[88] As so often happens, American constitutional litigation has stimulated profound and searching analysis of fundamental issues. But some tough questions have to be asked about the relevance of this debate to other countries. Conversely, one may ask: have not the American debates been too sharply focussed on some rather narrow issues and have they not been unduly parochial and isolationist? For example, on one interpretation, the *Bakke* case presents an inconclusive answer to some highly specific questions about selection for elite professional schools.[89]

For non-Americans, trying to make sense of the American literature can be as perplexing as it is seductive. The issues seem universal, yet they are posed and imbedded in their own unique context. One striking feature of that literature is that it almost never refers to experience outside the United States. A major step away from this isolationism has been taken by the publication of Marc Galanter's monumental work, *Competing Equalities*.[90] This is a detailed study of the vast and bold Indian system of 'compensatory discrimination', in which preferential treatment in respect of such matters as legislative representation, the public service, education and employment has been required by law. I cannot attempt to do justice to this superb work here, nor can I explore some of the (minor) reservations that I have about it.[91] But, it is worth pointing out that it raises a host of questions that are worth asking, and which may have been relatively neglected in the familiar American debates, at least by lawyers. Galanter shifts the focus of attention from questions about the legitimacy of positive discrimination to questions about implementation, especially legal implementation. For example, given such a policy, who exactly should be the beneficiaries? What sorts of benefits should be included with what priorities? Can individuals leave or enter a beneficial class through marriage, conversion, or economic success or failure? On the basis of what criteria should quotas be set? What are the economic constraints and consequences of such provisions? What rights, if any, should be recognised for those excluded from beneficial treatment? What are the political implications of the very real sense of grievance that such programmes tend to generate? What are the broader political implications of such programmes? What are the global costs and benefits of such a strategy? Can any coherent rationale be articulated for compensatory discrimination? What differences does it really make to the overall position of the disadvantaged groups? and so on.[92]

Because the Indian Constitution and legal system have been directly influenced by the common law and by some American ideas and because it is by an American scholar, Galanter's study will no doubt have more direct resonance for many American readers than some other accounts of Commonwealth experience. The context of the problem may be exotic, but the response and Galanter's interpretation have echoes in American experience. Conversely, to an Englishman, some aspects of the Indian approach to the problems and Galanter's treatment of it seem remarkably American, not least in the way in which some problems of access have been transformed into legal issues and have been the subject of litigation. In my own country, and I suspect in the great majority of other Commonwealth jurisdictions, it seems strange to perceive Law and the courts as having such a significant role to play in addressing problems of access. This, too, raises a host of fascinating questions that cannot be pursued here.

Thus it is extremely difficult to judge how much direct relevance the American debates and Galanter's work have to diagnosing the problem of formulating access strategies in the very different circumstances of my own country and of Xanadu. In Xanadu preferential treatment is neither required nor prohibited. Following Ronald Dworkin, who is at his most persuasive on this issue, positive discrimination is justified if it is directed towards increasing the participation of minorities in certain professions.[93] Applicants to professional schools do not have a right to a place nor a right to be considered on the basis of a single set of criteria based on academic 'merit'. It is one thing to treat people as equals, it is another to treat them equally.[94] Such positive discrimination does not violate rights, but it can involve costs, including costs for those who are meant to benefit. In India, for example, Galanter characterises the overall story as 'A costly success'[95]: These costs include:

(i) a sense of grievance on the part of disappointed applicants and others who consider themselves to have been harmed by the practice;

(ii) a loss of respect, and possibly of self-respect, for beneficiaries who are perceived not to have won a place on 'merit';

(iii) disputes, possibly litigation, about the legitimacy of a particular programme or some specific aspect of it;

(iv) uncertainty about application of criteria;

(v) rigidity leading to absurd results and invidious decisions when rigid criteria or fixed quotas are instituted; accusations of corruption or favouritism where more flexible arrangements are prescribed;

(vi) if formal criteria of positive discrimination are based on race or caste, it is claimed that this may have the effect of perpetuating the very divisions and categories that are under attack;

(vii) by no means all programmes of positive discrimination have been successful in practice in significantly increasing opportunities for disadvantaged groups.

Given the social and economic costs of programmes of positive discrimination it is always worth considering whether the same goals may be furthered as well by other means. Yet the symbolic significance of such measures also needs to be taken into account. Galanter is careful to emphasise that 'no single big lesson' can be drawn from the Indian experience;[96] he points to many ironies, vagaries and inconsistencies in the system; but he concludes that the benefits of this bold experiment outweigh the costs and that the system he describes is 'more congenial in practice than in theory'.[97] As a recent article in the Harvard Law Review suggests, this fascinating study has considerable potential relevance and resonance for those concerned with the subject of access in very different contexts.[98]

Access versus excellence?

A recurrent theme of the literature that I have cited and of some parts of this paper is that there seems to be a regular tension between Access and Excellence.[99] Cooray presents the debate in Sri Lanka as a conflict between the Socialist and the Educationist ethic.[100] In that debate both sides acknowledged that a rapid switchover from English to *swabasha* in legal education would almost inevitably result in a lowering of standards, at least for a period. It was a price that the socialists were prepared to pay. Conversely it is acknowledged in India that most measures currently being advocated for improving the quality of legal education will involve some restrictions on access.[101] Those of us who have advocated four-year degrees for most undergraduate law students in England recognise that an extra year means an additional financial and psychological barrier for most students. In the United States some historians of the legal profession have attributed an alleged decline in the American bar to its democratisation during the Jacksonian period.[102] Again the debates about accreditation and homogenisation of American law schools in the 20s and 30s were often depicted as a direct conflict between standards and opportunity.

I hope that I have made it clear that I think that all such interpretations are too simple. Modern historians doubt whether the Jacksonians made much impact on the quality or role of the American Bar generally.[103] They probably hastened the demise of apprenticeship; yet ironically this method of qualifying has probably offered better prospects of upward mobility in some jurisdictions, at least to some groups, than institutionalized legal education. And as for India: What real opportunities are in fact offered to their students by many of the non-elite programmes that are under attack?

However, the theme is too persistent for one to be able to ignore the question: are Access and Excellence inherently incompatible? I personally find this question worrying because I both believe in increasing access and as a teacher and educator I am committed to the idea of excellence. I do believe that they are compatible in principle and practice, though I readily acknowledge that in particular contexts they can give rise to acute dilemmas and conflicts. So let me conclude by justifying this belief.

To begin with let us ask: excellence in respect of what? To me excellence in legal education relates to the quality of learning and excellence in legal practice to the scope and quality of services offered to clients and to the community. The best educational experience is the one in which one learns most about something that is worth learning. The best educational institution is one in which students best learn worthwhile things. An excellent legal profession is one which delivers needed services well to the whole community.[104]

It is easy to lose sight of these simple ideas. For example, there are many well-documented instances in history where the rhetoric of excellence of 'standards' has cloaked other interests and motives.[105] When a legal profession fights to raise entry standards the primary concern may be to enhance the prestige and status of the group as part of the process of 'professionalisation' or to reduce competition by restricting numbers or to improve its public image or as part of a power struggle with government or the law schools. These motives may be mixed in with a genuine concern for the quality of the services offered by the profession to its clientele. Even so, in this context it is always worth asking: the quality of which services *to whom*? For sometimes the standards are being raised in the interests of one sector of the potential clientele at the expense of the rest.

Academics are at least as vulnerable to such charges of hypocrisy or self-deception. Take, for example, the claim that a law school selects students on the basis of 'merit'. Such claims are not universally false, but we have seen that there are several strategies of scepticism in respect of such claims.

(i) A particular test of 'merit' may be:
   (a) unreliable as an indicator of past academic performance;
   (b) a poor predictor of academic performance in law school;
   (c) a poor predictor of or largely irrelevant to professional competence;
   (d) discriminatory or otherwise unfair to some types of candidate.
(ii) Many competitive tests are not governed by rules that make the competition fair.

(iii) Where a test of merit is both reliable and relevant to future performance, it could be used as a pre-test to exempt people who already have the skills or knowledge that the course in question is designed to develop. Yet such tests are sometimes used in practice to select people for an education that they do not need.

(iv) In practice methods of testing and selection for admission to law school and to practice are governed, perhaps inevitably, as much by administrative convenience as by genuine concern for 'merit'.

Merit claims cannot be dismissed entirely, but they always deserve scrutiny. Similarly with talk about 'excellence'. When my colleagues boast that our institution attracts 'good students', they may mean students who have performed better than others in one or more tests of 'merit' or who are good examinees or people who are already well-educated or professionally or economically ambitious or well-connected or stimulating or interesting to have around. Whatever the attractions or otherwise of some of these qualities they are conceptually different from the notion of excellence in education that is used here.

In many countries law schools perform functions of selection, elimination, certification, career guidance, placement and control of numbers. They often offer security, prestige, fun and freedom to the faculty. These are not necessarily bad or wrong, but they are incidental to the enterprise of education. At its heart education is not about status or prestige or winning competitions or certification or selection or placement or entertainment; it should be about learning (whether for its own sake or for some other end). Above all one should not confuse excellence resulting from opportunity to learn or to perform a useful social role with prestige by association. If one keeps this clearly in mind the tensions between access and excellence can, at least to some extent, be dissolved.

There is a fundamental and obvious reason for rejecting the idea that conflicts between access and excellence are inevitable. If extending access means broadening the pool of talent from which law students and lawyers are recruited, it would be paradoxical to maintain that this must lead to a general lowering of standards. Whatever the ideological fine-tuning of particular access strategies, surely part of the motive force is the idea that potential talent is being wasted. Whether one emphasises individual opportunity or social equality or group representation or the general welfare, increasing access is generally favoured because of a basic faith in some potential for excellence and the rejection of the idea that the disadvantaged are inferior. To assert this as an article of faith need not blind one to the formidable constraints, the complexities and the acute dilemmas that have to be confronted in particular contexts.

Most practical measures will involve costs, including sometimes short-term sacrifices of excellence or standards. But it is surely a denial of faith in human nature shared by people of many different religious and political persuasions to suggest that increasing opportunity for the development of talent will necessarily be inimical to excellence in legal education and legal practice.

Conclusion

The primary purpose of this essay has been to raise some questions and suggest some concepts that may be pertinent to analysing practical problems of access in different contexts. It precedes rather than reports on some detailed investigations. However, it may be useful to suggest a few tentative hypotheses and conclusions arising from this preliminary inquiry.

(1) Access to legal education and the legal profession is part of a much broader problem of access to education and to elite occupations. There are some major barriers which are effectively beyond the control of those who are in a position to do something about the legal sector: for example, accidents of birth; what happens in the school system; many aspects of economic, social and linguistic disadvantage. Nevertheless, Whose responsible for that sector have a duty to try to mitigate the effects of such barriers.

(2) What specific measures have much hope of making a significant impact depends very largely on context. However, it is worth offering a few tentative hypotheses:

(a) A general policy of flexibility in respect of routes of entry and occupational mobility is likely to provide the most effective way of surmounting or circumnavigating barriers to access. For example:

(i) multiple routes of entry;
(ii) avoidance of premature specialization;
(iii) generous provision for mature entry, external qualifications and lateral mobility;
(iv) the provision of second chances at every stage.

(b) Systematic diagnosis and monitoring of the barriers to access in a given jurisdiction depend on adequate information, including regular statistics concerning potentially disadvantaged classes.

(c) Intensive remedial education targeted directly at the needs of particular groups that have suffered educational disadvantage offers one of the most promising avenues of improving access. Remedial education can be general or specialised; this can be offered either pre-law or within legal education. The costs tend to be high, the numbers affected small, but there is ground for thinking that measures, such as the American CLEO programme and the specialised access courses that are beginning to develop in England, can be remarkably cost-effective.[107]

(d) Law school admission policies that include:

(i) multiple, alternative criteria of admission and selection;
(ii) positive recruitment programmes aimed both at attracting applicants from particular groups (eg mature students from particular localities) and overcoming psychological barriers to applying;
(iii) communication of full information about admissions policies and selection criteria to all potential applicants.

(e) Financial assistance that takes account of the total economic situation of those in need of help.

(f) In multi-lingual societies, sensitivity to the importance of language in respect of admission, instruction, and examination and of available literature must be a high priority, often requiring long-range planning and considerable adjustments in teaching.

(g) Aptitude testing validated in respect of disadvantaged groups can be an efficient and more objective method of selection than many other methods which are more likely to be biased in favour of more privileged groups (eg interviews, certain kinds of examination). However, the very advantages of such tests may lead to their over-use; for example, when uniform tests are used to eliminate law school applicants who might have the potential to be competent lawyers.[108]

(3) My personal view is there is nothing wrong in principle in employing positive action, or even direct preferential treatment, in selection for education or training to further an important social purpose. As the Indian experience shows, such provisions can give rise to extremely complex, often intractable, problems of implementation; they almost invariably give rise to deeply felt grievances and other social costs. Whether the benefits outweigh the costs in a given context will often involve difficult and contentious issues of political judgement.

(4) Attempts artificially to control numbers at the point of entry to the profession rarely succeed in the long-term and tend to operate to the detriment of the disadvantaged.

(5) There is often a perceived tension between Access and standards of Excellence, at least in the short-term. However, it is a fallacy to assert that increasing the pool of talent from which law students and lawyers are recruited necessarily involves a 'lowering of standards'. In the long term improved access is the ally, not the enemy, of excellence.

(6) Problems of access are complex and intractable. They tend to be context specific. Nevertheless there is much to be gained from looking at these problems from an international perspective and pooling experience of problems and attempted responses. Commonwealth countries can learn a great deal from the American experience as well as from each other; it may be that looking at the experience of other Commonwealth countries may suggest some new perspectives on your own situation.

NOTES

[1] For prior reports from Xanadu see William Twining 'Taking Facts Seriously' (1984) 34 Jo Legal Education 22; 'Keeping Up to Date in Xanadu' Seventh Commonwealth Law Conference, Hong Kong, *In What Can We Place Our Trust: Libraries, Textbooks, Software or Intuition* (1983) 235–40; 'Theory in the Law Curriculum' (with Neil MacCormick) in William Twining (ed) *Legal Theory and Common Law* (Oxford: Blackwell, 1986) 238–54.

[2] Eg the requirement of second class honours in one's first degree as a condition of admission to the Bar, introduced in England by the Senate of the Inns of Court in 1981, taking effect in 1983. Discussed Soc Pub Tchs Law Newsletter (Summer 1985) 4–5.

[3] For a powerful plea that higher education institutions should acknowledge a share of the responsibility for low participation rates of some groups, see Neil Kibble 'Race, Class and Access to Legal Education' (1986). See also Chapter 7, below. Accidents of birth are often the biggest single factor affecting equality of opportunity. In Sri Lanka, for example, up to 1970 it was estimated that approximately 94% of the population were effectively excluded from university legal education and hence entry to the legal profession by virtue of competitive entry based on academic standards, in particular a stringent English language requirement. (Cooray, 1985. Discussed below.) In most countries one's chances of reaching university are to a large extent pre-determined at birth (or before) given that gender, colour, class, geographical location and family background are all likely to be significant factors in determining one's life chances, especially in the educational system. For certain purposes, for example in devising practical ways of improving access, it may be sensible for the gatekeepers in the system, such

as law school admissions tutors and those who control entry to the practising profession, to take a later baseline for analysis. For example, in Xanadu it may be sensible to concentrate on increasing recruitment from those who left school after 16 and to recognise that it may not be practicable for an access policy to do much for those who have been eliminated at an early stage. But if one is to take the notion of opportunity seriously it is important to recognise that for the vast majority of the population in most countries the opportunity to study law or to qualify as a lawyer has effectively been lost at an earlier stage.

If we are serious about educational opportunity or increasing representation of certain groups we need much more information, some of which will be hard to come by. For example, it is clear that at birth large sectors of the population have almost no chance of becoming lawyers because almost none will go beyond primary school and even fewer will, under present arrangements, reach university. Those concerned with law can do very little about this. But even in areas where policies of increasing access might have a reasonable chance of making a difference, reliable information is hard to come by. Suppose, for example, that the Xanadu Law Faculty were to decide to try to treble its intake of mature students, especially Southerners. How could it work out a realistic medium-term policy without a great deal of information about the pool of possible recruits, and cultural and other factors affecting the demand for law?

[4] My terms of reference prescribe that I have to advise the Law Faculty (and no-one else) about the problem. Other interested parties have kindly agreed to help me, but have made it clear that in return they do not wish gratuitous advice from a foreign academic. This at least helps to clarify my role: what I shall try to do in this report is to suggest a general approach to analyzing problems of access to legal education and the legal profession in any common law country; I shall suggest questions to be asked and factors to be considered in devising a general strategy for improving such access, and I shall draw attention to some relevant experience and literature, but it is beyond my brief to make specific recommendations. My job is to intellectualise the problem: it is for locals to contextualise it, and to try to reach agreement on a common strategy. This, given the diffusion of power, is a highly political matter.

[5] Legal education and training in Xanadu broadly approximates to jurisdictions that have adopted the 'Gower' model of legal education and training. This was pioneered in Nigeria in the early nineteen-sixties, consolidated in England after the Ormrod Report on Legal Education in 1971 and adopted, with several variants, in many Commonwealth jurisdictions, Perhaps the most significant divergencies from the Xanadu pattern of legal education and training are as follows: (a) a requirement of a first degree or a minimum period of undergraduate study, before entry to law school (eg Canada, Australia); (b) no formal provision for apprenticeship (eg Nigeria, most Australian states); (c) multiple routes of entry to the profession (eg non-graduate, non-law degree entry), as in England and Wales: (d) provisions for qualification through external degrees and other forms of distance learning. On variations between systems see *Legal Education in a Changing World,* International Legal Center, New York (1975) ch II (hereafter ILC 1975).

[6] Several of those distinctions are elaborated in Oliver Fulton 'Overview of Access and Recruitment to the Professions' in Goodlad (1984) ch 7. On 'discrimination' and 'preferential treatment', see below pp 17 ff, 20 ff.

[7] See ILC (1975) paras 68–71.

[8] Prima facie the absence of quotas remains one of the main barriers to access. However, as the authors of *Legal Education in a Changing World* (1975) have argued, such systems of legal education may be quite dysfunctional in respect of both the legal system and more basic manpower objectives. Furthermore, because of high failure rates and graduate unemployment, they offer only the illusion of increased economic opportunity for most of the students:

> In the deliberations of our committee and in reports presented to us, this point has been strongly argued, and we sketch here a model of a large scale system which may produce these bad effects. The description may be overtaken, but it is set forth to offer a critical perspective, often lacking in thinking about legal education. Thus it is argued that in some systems the university law school is required – or under heavy pressure – to admit and educate masses of students: the law school is run 'on the cheap'; student-teacher ratios are high, and teaching demands are heavy; there are long-established, 'received', venerated beliefs about law as an academic discipline and how to teach it: and these orthodoxies are reinforced by the way law teachers are recruited, prepared and used in the system; the dynamics of higher education work to maintain the law school as a 'dumping ground' institution for students who are not law-oriented and are, in fact, seeking a general, broad education as preparation for useful lives in their society and for work in any non-specialist employment currently available. But the institution does not help its graduates to become easily employable. Law is taught to masses of students in a formal, traditional, didactic way; neither the discipline nor the curricula are adapted to the environment: the methods

used do not emphasise active student participation in problem-solving and the development of other skills (eg, communication) – rather they emphasise the retention of information, much of which may be of marginal relevance to their future careers or intellectual interests; student apathy towards the education offered, and discontent with the system which provides it, run high. (ILC (1975) para 136)

[9] School-leavers 'specializing' in Science are eligible for admission to the Xanadu Law school, but only a small number apply. Of course, one needs to distinguish between points in time at which opportunity to become a lawyer is effectively eliminated and the point(s) in time at which one is effectively committed to becoming a lawyer. Even in countries where occupational mobility is restricted, the latter points tend to occur significantly later.

[10] Some students in the professional school complain that the curriculum and Bar examinations are too heavily oriented towards the needs of sole practitioners and small practices. The official response is that this is the best way of trying to ensure minimum competence of those entering practice, that specialisation at this stage would be premature, and that large organisations in both private and public sectors should be able to provide further training 'in house'.

More generally it has been argued, in the context of professional education in the United Kingdom, that short of massive social change 'the only hope of changing [existing patterns of differential access] in a progressive direction ... is to attempt major changes not just in entry criteria but in the structure of higher education (for which the only irresistible lever available to governments may be finance) ... Probably the best general recipe is simply to delay choice by delaying specialisation.' (Fulton in Goodlad (1984) at 89). Part of the thinking behind this is that systems of professional qualification that require early specialisation or are inflexible in similar ways tend to operate to the detriment of the underprivileged.

[11] Eg J Bentham 4 *The Works of Jeremy Bentham*, Bowring ed (New York: Russell and Russell, 1962) 495. In this passage, Bentham qualifies his generalisation with the phrase 'with very inconsiderable exceptions'.

[12] J Bentham *Rationale of Judicial Evidence*, J S Mill ed (London, 1827), passim. Bentham's vituperations against lawyers in this work were usefully assembled by William Empson in a review of the 'Rationale' 48 Edinburgh Rev 457, 473–82.

[13] See generally, W Twining *Theories of Evidence: Bentham and Wigmore* (London: Weidenfeld and Nicolson, 1985) ch 2.

[14] For a critique of the 'private practitioner' image on the development of legal education in Anglo-phonic Africa in the 1960s see Twining (1966) and Gower (1967) at 132–34.

[15] Gower (1967) ch 3.

[16] Traditionally the profession has been recruited almost entirely from urban, middle-class males. Recently the proportion of women recruits has risen fast, but most of them come from the same social background as their brethren. In other respects lawyers in both public and private sectors are unrepresentative in terms of class, religion and geography.

[17] Eg Symposium on 'Freedom of Movement in the Commonwealth Legal Profession' (contributions by Linda Spedding, Campbell McLachlan and John Hamilton *The Commonwealth Lawyer*, vol I, No 2, 7–39 (1986) and chapter 14, below.

[18] Eg International Legal Center, *Law and Development* (New York, 1974). A recent example is Keith Patchett (1987).

[19] It is estimated that in Xanadu approximately 50% of the total income of private practitioners is derived from public funds. In countries with more developed systems of legal aid or in which private practitioners regularly act as prosecutors the percentage is significantly higher.

[20] Eg Twining (1966); ILC (1975) paras 135–39; J S Bainbridge *The Study and Teaching of Law in Africa* (South Hackensack N J: Rothman, 1972) ch 1; JCN Paul and WL Twining *Legal Education and Training at UBLS, Inter-University Council, 1971* (Botswana, Lesotho and Swaziland).

[21] Supra note 5.

[22] This phenomenon has received surprisingly little attention and deserves further study.

[23] Supra note 14.

[24] Unwarranted extrapolation from figures in Frank T Read *Demand for Legal Education into the Twenty-First Century*, paper presented to the ABA section on Legal Education (London, July, 1985).

[25] For a useful review, see J Willard Hurst *The Growth of American Law: The Law Makers* (Boston: Little, Brown & Co, 1950) 255, 314–17, see generally R Abel and P Lewis (1988).

[26] L Garrison et al 'The Economics of the Legal Profession,' ABA, Chicago, 1938. K Llewellyn 'The Bar Specialises – With What Results?' 167 Annals 177 (1933); and 'The Bar's Troubles and Poultices – and Cures?' 5 Law and Contemp Problems 104 (1938), reprinted *Jurisprudence* (Chicago: U of Chicago Press, 1962) 343.

[27] *Legal Education in New South Wales* (Bowen Report) (NSW: Government Printer, 1979); Law Society of Upper Canada 'The Report of the Special Committee on Numbers of Lawyers'

(1983) 17 LSUC Gazette 222. See further, T C Colchester 'Views on the Numbers Game from the Sidelines: The New South Wales and Ontario Enquiries' 37 CLEA Newsletter (1984). See further below chapters 5 and 6.

28 Colchester (1984) 2.

29 Ibid, 3. The final resolution by the Law Society of Upper Canada is of interest: The Law Society of Upper Canada is concerned by evidence that the increasing number of lawyers in private practice in Ontario may adversely affect the quality of legal services in this province but considers that it would be inappropriate for it to limit admission to the profession arbitrarily.

Accordingly the Society resolves:

1. that the society confer with the appropriate government ministries and with the universities in Ontario which have approved law faculties, to review the number of seats available in their first years;
2. that the Law Society in co-operation with the universities bring to the attention of existing and prospective students the financial difficulties confronting many lawyers at the present time;
3. that the Bar Admission Course and the Continuing Legal Education Departments make special efforts to prepare students and practitioners for the financial and other pressures they are likely to encounter, so that they can better cope with these pressures;
4. that the Society, in co-operation with the law schools, do as much as possible to facilitate employment of law graduates and members of the Society in careers other than private practice by:
   (a) preparing them for such alternative careers and bringing these to their attention;
   (b) permitting law graduates to delay their entry into the Bar Admission Course for a period of up to ten years instead of five as at present, to enable them to find places in other careers; and
   (c) providing such services as are already being provided by the alumni programmes at Osgoode Hall Law School and at the University of Western Ontario Law Faculty to encourage prospective employers in the public and private sectors to recognise the value to them of employing law graduates in administrative, managerial and other capacities. In addition the Society should support agencies to help place lawyers in industry.
5. that the profession be advised that a proper level of service provided to clients must, at all times, be maintained, regardless of economic circumstances; as a corollary, members should avoid placing themselves in a position where their financial arrangements preclude the maintenance of such service. (1983) LSUC Gazette 240–41.

30 Information supplied by Richard Abel.
31 Cf Patchett (1986).
32 On controversies about collecting such data in India see Galanter (1984) passim (index under census). The American Bar Association, Section on Legal Education and Admissions to the Bar complies and publishes statistics on women and minorities in individual law schools. On the United Kingdom, see, for example, *Education for All* (Report of the Committee of Inquiry into the Education of Children from Ethnic Minority Groups (The Swann Report) (Cmnd 9453, 1985) 173–76, 600–61 et passim. On some ways of presenting such statistics see the Appendix below at pp 312 ff.
33 Other barriers and obstacles are considered in the papers in this volume, especially chapter 3 (Mosston), 4 (Cannon), 7 (Kibble) and 15 (Dhavan).
34 Cooray (1985). See also the same author in Twining and Uglow (eds), 1982, ch 12.
35 Ibid, 147–8.
36 Ibid, 49. On the position of the Tamil minority, see especially 41–43.
37 Ibid, 122–25.
38 Ibid, 124.
39 Ibid, 124.
40 ILC (1975) para 247. This passage is in certain respects out-dated on some points of detail, but the general argument still holds. For example, on India see Cottrell (1986).
41 See generally Twining and Uglow (eds) (1982).
42 See further below, pp 28 ff.
43 Cottrell (1986). See now Sathe, ch 8, below.
44 See generally Fulton (ed), 1983. Jill Cottrell points out that India may provide a counter-example: 'In some states it has been remarkably easy to enter the legal profession, although it takes a long time. The new (10 + 2 + 5) scheme, which is shorter, is part of a strategy designed to restrict access.' (Cottrell, private communication).

36   Access to legal education and the legal profession: Commonwealth

45 L Lustgarten *Legal Control of Racial Discrimination* (London: MacMillan, 1980); D Pannick *Sex Discrimination Law* (Oxford: Clarendon, 1985).
46 On 'preferential treatment' see above pp 20–21.
47 Above p 26.
48 Above pp 20 ff.
49 On the uses of 'persuasive definition' in the Anglo-American context see McCrudden (1985). Implicit in the thesis presented here is the assumption that a fairly sharp distinction needs to be drawn between diagnosis of 'the problem' and prescription of feasible strategies for action. Strongly emotive terms and 'persuasive definitions' may have a role to play in promoting particular policies, but tend to be unhelpful in diagnosis.
50 See further W Twining 'Torture and Philosophy' Procs of the Aristotelian Society, Supplementary Vol LII, 1978, 143 at 144–47; and 'Academic Law and Legal Philosophy: The Significance of Herbert Hart' 95 LQR 557, 571–73. See further, J L Mackie *Ethics: Inventing Right and Wrong* (London: Penguin, 1977).
51 J Bentham *An Introduction to the Principles of Morals and Legislation,* J H Burns and H L A Hart eds (London: Athlone Press, 1970). The significance of this distinction between morals and legislation within utilitarian theory is explored by A J Ayer in 'The Principle of Utility' *Philosophical Essays* (London: MacMillan, 1963), 254 et seq.
52 The arguments for and against three different rationales for affirmative action (compensatory justice; distributive justice; and social utility) are usefully explored in Myrl L Duncan (1982). However, the analysis is rather too rooted in the agent-oriented vocabulary of 'discrimination', 'affirmative action', 'treatment' etc. What is suggested here is that the rationales of distributive justice and social utility are more clearly articulated in victim-oriented terms that treat the past behaviour of agents as merely contingent factors that may have contributed to a greater or lesser extent to the existence of 'the problem' in different contexts.
53 Some of the conceptual difficulties about the scope of 'morality' are explored in debates about 'moral luck'; eg Bernard Williams and Thomas Nagel in Procs Aristotelian Soc, Supp Vol L, 1976.
54 Compare the analogous shifts in recent writings from fault based notions of liability in tort to a broader notion of compensation for accident caused by human agents to a yet broader concern with all kinds of misfortune, including disease. *Atiyah's Accidents, Compensation and the Law* Peter Cane 4th ed (London: Weidenfeld & Nicolson, 1987); Jane Stapleton *Disease and the Compensation Debate* (Oxford: Clarendon, 1986).
55 McCrudden (1985) 84.
56 Some non-legislative anti-discrimination measures, such as explicit non-discriminatory admissions criteria and voluntary codes of practice in respect of selection, promotion etc in employment have yet to be implemented.
57 I am grateful to Christopher McCrudden for help with this section. See especially, McCrudden (1985) and (1986). The vocabulary adopted is slightly different from that suggested by McCrudden, who was writing with specific reference to discrimination in employment. The distinctions are almost identical and the main thesis that many objections to 'reverse discrimination' do not apply to other forms of positive action is the same.
58 Direct preferential treatment includes situations where factors such as race, gender, locality are used as a sole criterion, or as one of several relevant factors, or to 'break ties'. If the more emotive term 'reverse discrimination' is applied to all of these, it is important to recognise that arguments for and against such measures need to take account of these different species.
59 This is slightly wider than McCrudden's 'facially neutral but purposively inclusionary policies', op cit 57, in that it includes all measures that have such effects whether or not this is their primary purpose.
60 Cf McCrudden, op cit, on 'Eradicating discrimination', 223.
61 This is approximately equivalent to McCrudden's 'Redefining "merit",' ibid, 225.
62 This includes, but is wider than, McCrudden's 'outreach programmes', ibid, 223–24.
63 DeFunis v Odegaard 82 Wash 2d 11, 507 P 2d 1169 (1973), treated as moot 416 US 312 (1974). *Regents of the University of California v Bakke* 438 US 265 (1978). See references in Select bibliography under M Cohen *et al*, R. Dworkin, O Fiss, A Goldman, B Gross, S Guest and A Milne, and R Tur. Gross (1978) and Goldman (1979) containing useful bibliographies of the earlier literature.
64 On some alleged parallel between the Indian and American experience see A Blumrosen 'Some Thoughts on Affirmative Action There and in India: Galanter's *Competing Equalities*' (ABF Res J, 1986) 653.
65 Galanter (1984) categorises the Indian provisions as 'compensatory discrimination', because 'it does not blink at the fact that some are left out, that we are dealing with something more than a benign process of inclusion. At least where scarce resources are distributed, it employs

a principle of selection that is akin to the old discrimination' (2–3). However, he acknowledges that there are also 'non-discrimination and general welfare themes' in the Indian policies (ibid, 3).

[66] Eg Clyde Summers in University of Toledo L Rev Symposium (1970) 383. Confirmed by R Stevens (private communication). In 1985–86 American law schools were concerned about a fall in law school applications.

[67] On different interpretations of the precise nature of such claims, see R Dworkin (1985) 298–99. As Dworkin points out, '[t]here is no combination of abilities and skills and traits that constitutes "merit" in the abstract' (299).

[68] ILC (1975) paras 68–71.

[69] ABA (1985) 66–68.

[70] However, Stevens (1983) 245–47, suggests that CLEO and other 'headstart programmes' for minority students played a major role in the increase of minority enrolments in law schools between 1969–79.

[71] Tur (1983) 271.

[72] On 'Merit', supra n 67.

[73] Cf alleged cultural biases in law school admission tests.

[74] Eg Lee (1984) on A levels in England.

[75] Defenders of aptitude testing are prepared to acknowledges that little is known about the relations between test scores and long-term performance. Eg Jennek Brittel and William B Schroder state: 'Far too little research using broader and longer-range measures of success has been done. In part, this unsatisfactory state of affairs is attributable to the lack of agreed upon indicators of success in college or success in life, and to the fact that research in this field is costly and difficult. Admissions testing is, however, vulnerable to the criticism that too little is known about the relationship of test scores to college and career success.' 'College Admissions Testing in the United States' in *International Council for Educational Development* (1978). The Australian experience of aptitude testing, for example in Queensland, may be at least as relevant to some Commonwealth countries as the American.

In most Commonwealth countries, with the exception of Canada, almost no use is made of aptitude testing in law. One argument put forward, in its favour, is the converse of the US criticism: viz that some educationally disadvantaged candidates may have a better chance through selection through aptitude testing than through their academic record, especially if the latter is based – as happens in many countries – on a uniform national examination. The core of American criticism of the LSAT seems to be that, at least in its present form, it is used as a means of eliminating large numbers of candidates who might turn out to be capable of becoming competent lawyers. The core of the objections relate to the test (which may have class, ethnic or other biases) and to its use as a condition for qualifying for law school. It seems that, even if these criticisms of the LSAT are sustained – which is a matter of controversy – they are not fundamental objections to aptitude testing in general, which has great potential in increasing access, not least in providing certain kinds of short-cuts. (See further n 78, below).

[76] Chief Justice Brian Dickson (1986). In another context Chief Justice Dickson has written: 'The primary goal of legal education should be to train for the legal profession people who are, first, honest; second, compassionate; third, knowledgeable about the law; and fourth, committed to the rule of law and justice in our democratic society.' Introduction to the *Canadian Law Schools Admission Handbook* (1986). In the context the author makes it clear that legal education prepares people for a variety of other careers.

[77] K O'Donovan 'Affirmative Action' in Guest and Milne (1985) 77, 79.

[78] See LSAC Research Studies (1959–83). The most common charge against the American LSAT relates to alleged racial or cultural biases (eg David M White, 1981). See further below chapters 3 and 4. My personal view is that aptitude tests can both promote and restrict access, depending on how they are designed *and* used.

[79] Dee (1984) and Kibble (1986) both acknowledge this.

[80] Eg Duncan Kennedy's 'Utopian Proposal': 'There should be a test designed to establish minimal skills for legal practice and then a lottery for admission to the school: there should be quotas within the lottery for women, minorities and working class students. There should be a national publicity campaign about our goal of modifying the social composition of the bar.' *Legal Education and the Reproduction of Hierarchy: A Polemic Against the System* (Cambridge, Mass: Afar, 1983) 121–122.

[81] Cottrell (1986). Cottrell's article was based largely on material collected in 1983. This section does not take account of developments since then. On India generally see chapter 8, below.

[82] Ibid, 6. Citing a report on Uttar Pradesh.

[83] Ibid, 11.

[84] Ibid, 7 (quoting S K Agrawala).

[85] Ibid, 12.
[86] Ibid, 12.
[87] Ibid, 22–3. By 1989 several institution, including the newly established National Law School of India at Bangalore, had introduced five-year degrees.
[88] Eg the discussions in Guest and Milne (1985), McCrudden (1986) and reviews of Galanter (1984) cited below at n 91.
[89] R Dworkin (1985) ch 15.
[90] Galanter (1984).
[91] See reviews by J Cottrell (1985) 34 ICLQ 658; J D M Derrett (1985) Jo Commonwealth and Comparative Politics 272: R Dhavan (1985) Law and Policy; Lance Liebman (1985) 98 Harv L Rev 1679; R Meister (1985) Wisc L Rev 937.
[92] See Cottrell, op cit n 91.
[93] R Dworkin (1977) ch 9, (1985) chs 14–16.
[94] R Dworkin (1977) 1, 227.
[95] Galanter 563.
[96] Ibid, 563.
[97] Ibid, 567.
[98] Liebman, op cit n 91.
[99] The locus classicus is Gardner (1961).
[100] Op cit, 122–25.
[101] Cottrell (1986).
[102] Eg Charles Warren *A History of the American Bar*, (Boston: Little, Brown & Co, 1911); A H Chroust *The Rise of the Legal Profession in America* (Norman: U of Oklahoma Press, 1965).
[103] Eg Robert Stevens (1983) ch 1.
[104] To assert that the primary function of law schools is to provide opportunities for learning does not involve a denial of the point that they also play a role (which varies from place to place) in selecting and certifying individuals for legal practice. All too often, in practice, the educational function is subordinated to these other, secondary, functions.
[105] See generally, Stevens (1983). On the tendency to confuse academic standards and quality in university education, see Eric Ashby *Universities: British, Indian, African* (London: Weidenfeld and Nicolson, 1966) 237–38, 259–60.
[106] Cf military training, in which pre-testing of skill in rifle-shooting may exempt (or even disqualify) individuals from particular aspects of training. In so far as many 'legal skills' represent applications in a particular context of more general intellectual or human skills, many of those who enter legal education need little or no training in such skills, whereas this may be a prime need for others. In view of the fact that much skills training tends to be labour-intensive and expensive, this is a matter of considerable potential significance for professional legal training.
[107] On Law Access Courses in England see Kibble (1986). On CLEO, see University of Toledo Law Review symposium (1970); Stevens (1983) 245; and chapters 3 and 6 below.
[108] On the dangers of some kinds of aptitude tests and their possible misuse see below ch 5.

2 Access to higher education: a review of alternative policies

Oliver Fulton[*]

Introduction

This paper is about policies for access to higher education, and through it to professional occupations; and in particular about the feasibility and effectiveness of various policies for improving access for 'under-represented groups', as the current North American phraseology has it. As Twining (chapter 1) shows, entry to higher education constitutes only one of the possible hurdles for the potential entrant to a profession (the others are professional examinations, apprenticeships, and first employment or success in self-employment). But as a degree becomes increasingly crucial for more professions in more countries, selection for higher education plays a more and more dominant role.

It is, in fact, a key characteristic of the professions in modern societies that their first line of control, of both the number and the characteristics of their entrants, is achieved through universities or other higher education institutions, which are (typically) formally independent of the professions themselves. In the case of law, 'everywhere', (Abel, 1988, 'the university has become the dominant institution ... The profession has relinquished control to the universities and the state that supports them.' But this attributes too much deliberation to the profession concerned. In truth its 'use' of universities is in line with the near-universal process by which the responsibility of selection or sorting for differentiated employment has moved from the labour market to the education system. Most papers in this collection treat the legal profession as a special case. My purpose here is to set it in its broader context.

Some critics would argue that the transfer of the tasks of regulation and selection from the professions to higher education is largely cosmetic and inconsequential: that the professions and the staff of university professional schools are so closely connected that the interests of the profession are bound to predominate. In fact this is not necessarily the case. It is true that higher education is the object of broad social processes, notable among them the growth and transformation of the professions, and the latter's utilisation of higher education in what Larson (1977) calls 'the professional project'. But outside the Soviet Union and countries which have borrowed from it, most higher education institutions are not 'monotechnic': they cater for a wide range of professions and occupations whose needs and expectations are not identical. The admissions procedures of a university law school or department cannot be explained as simply a reflection of the needs of that profession: they are developed in multi-purpose institutions with a range of constituencies to

[*] Institute for Research and Development in Post-Compulsory Education.

respond to, and they are subject to the constraints that apply to higher education as a whole.

It is commonly argued that modern societies grant monopoly privileges to the professions in exchange for two perceived attributes: first, their expertise and secondly, their fairness in selecting new entrants. It is, then, a reasonable interpretation of the events of the hundred years or so up to the 1960s that higher education took over the responsibility for entry control precisely because it was seen as a provider and guarantor of these two aspects. Suspicions that the professions were using illegitimate criteria for admission (such as nepotism, self-perpetuation, restraint of competition) were defused in the late nineteenth century by the growing commitment of the modern university to academic values: of which the two most strongly espoused were expertise and fair, interpreted as meritocratic, competition.[1] In more recent years the criteria for fairness have been challenged, to an extent that now threatens public trust in higher education also. This is the consequence not so much of a new failure by higher education to live up to its proclaimed values – although it may not always do so, this is certainly nothing new – but of the visible persistence of social inequality in higher education and the professions. The apparent consequences of meritocracy have begun to suggest that the two values of equity and expertise may not be fully compatible, and indeed may dictate policies that pull in opposite directions. In what follows I shall trace the shifting patterns of academic and public understanding and of political pressure, show how these have led to a series of changing policies, and discuss the latter's achievements and drawbacks.

Inequality of participation identified

In one sense or another, the awareness of potential social inequality is as old as higher education; even the medieval and Renaissance universities provided scholarships to give poor students access not only to academic study but also to proto-professional careers. But it was in the nineteenth century that the issue of equity helped the universities to a gradual transformation from their eighteenth-century role as places for the socialisation of those already marked out by birth, wealth or patronage for elite careers, to one as places for selection on merit and training in newly necessary skills. An essential partner in this transformation was the rise of secondary education, with preparation for higher education as one of its first tasks. It then became possible to use expertise – that is, the possession of learned academic capacities and knowledge – as the measure of fitness not only for entry to a professional career but also for admission to higher education. And such was the success of the 'professional project' that the linked functions of meritocratic selection and training were little questioned or scrutinised in the first half of the twentieth century: the rise of examination-based entry procedures for higher education, and of scientific and other forms of expertise in the professions, provided ample justification for this new role.

In most countries political awareness of de facto inequalities in access to higher education increased sharply in the early 1960s, with the advent of educational 'planning' and the new information systems which made it possible. Systematic studies by OECD and many of its member countries, and by the World Bank, showed that in nation after nation women, the children the children of working-class parents, children from rural, inner-city or other-wise deprived regions or communities, and children of ethnic minorities were not represented in student populations in the same proportions (and generally the differences were very substantial) as their proportions of the relevant age group in the population at large. Psychologists demonstrated that there was potential for greater achievement among these 'under-represented' groups; sociologists offered explanations, with implications for possible remedies, for 'under-achievement'; while economists provided in human capital theory a further justification for policies designed to enhance the social utilisation of scarce talent.

Equality of opportunity

Within higher education, the first response to this 'discovery' was to assert or reassert a strong commitment to 'equality of opportunity', on the assumption that the inequality resulted from failure to adhere to equitable principles for access. If so, it ought to be possible to reduce it by ensuring that every *qualified applicant* for higher education had an equal chance of admission, regardless of any other characteristics. The terms 'qualified' and 'applicant' both beg certain questions: but at the time, this commitment met with wide approval. Essentially, it had three components: the removal of discrimination, the assurance of financial aid, and the provision of an adequate number of places to accommodate all qualified applicants.

(a) Removal of discrimination

The first element of equal opportunity is straightforward: it prescribes equality of treatment by higher education itself at the moment of application – or to be more precise, that applicants may be treated unequally, but only in respect of *academic* qualities which have a direct bearing on their likely capacity to benefit from their chosen course. No other personal or ascriptive characteristics are relevant.

This had not necessarily been normal practice: many institutions were still using ascriptive criteria, amongst others, for selection. There was, no doubt, some covert and prejudiced discrimination, though probably less than in the pre-war period. And some institutions, especially small, selective ones, used ascriptive characteristics to create what they called a 'balanced' entry – with a potential for discriminatory abuse. But many others discriminated unapologetically, especially in terms of gender and age, on actuarial grounds – in the belief that persons with certain characteristics were less likely to complete, or alternatively to make use of, their degrees.[2] Discrimination was often for-malised, and consisted of an outright ban, quotas in numbers or proportions from specific groups, or the requirement from them of a higher standard for entry. But there was certainly also informal discrimination, operating through the uncodified but generally approved preferences of the responsible staff – and easily blurring into unfounded prejudice. Because of its informality, out-siders could only detect it by statistical methods; and it has clearly been harder to outlaw than formal procedures which simply required a change in administrative practice.

In many countries this kind of discrimination has been abandoned since the 1960s, except perhaps in regard to 'balance' and age. (Of course, 'balance' can be used in a 'progressive' direction – that is, to the advantage of under-represented groups – as well as against them. This and the issue of older students are discussed later.) Political pressures have made most kinds of actuarial discrimination as illegitimate as that based on prejudice and stereo-type. The process began in the United States during and after the civil rights movement, and followed quickly in most other OECD countries; developing countries too began to consider the same issues as power and influence shifted in the post-colonial period. In some cases students and staff led the opposition, citing the incompatibility of ascriptive discrimination with academic values, and it was outlawed by the institutions in response to these internal pressure groups; while others responded to direct pressure from excluded groups outside. In many countries, however, the latter worked through national channels, challenging institutional behaviour in the courts, or even obtaining new civil-rights legislation that outlawed discrimination generally. However, such chal-lenges have been more effective for some categories than others. For example, gender and age are easy to define and monitor, whereas the definition of ethnicity may well be more controversial, and there can be great resistance to monitoring it; and while social class may be suitable for statistical monitoring, it is not, except in Marxist societies, normally a legally-defined attribute for policy eligibility. Furthermore, whereas state-controlled universities and colleges can be instructed to amend their behaviour, and others in receipt of state finance can be subjected to conditional funding, those with a tradition, and still more a legal right, of autonomy may need to be persuaded.

But, to turn prescriptive, there is no question that any attempt by institutions or departments to improve the flow of students from specified under-rep-resented groups must *begin* by examining whether any directly discriminatory policies or practices exist; and by asking if apparently rational claims are actually camouflaging unacceptable prejudice. And any formal changes that result need to be followed by checking on informal signals (for instance in publicity materials) which may still imply that discrimination exists. Not to discriminate among applicants is one thing: it is harder to persuade the unconvinced to apply.

(b) Financial aid

At the same time as discrimination was being tackled, an equally important second pillar of equal opportunity was the provision of financial support, to help and encourage those who were now no longer to be excluded. Institutions have always sought ways to keep down their costs, both in tuition fees and in the living costs of attendance: traditionally they built up private endowments in order to recruit and support poor but able students. But it is only more recently that student subsidy has become an area for government action. There are, however, a number of policy choices or dilemmas if such subsidies are to have a broadly progressive effect – that is, to benefit mainly or exclusively lower-income students.

For here too we find exemplified the potential conflict between fairness and excellence: to what extent is the basis for subsidies or scholarships to be financial need or academic merit? Institutions may prefer to attract very able students with academic scholarships – and the recipients will certainly not correspond exactly to those in greatest financial need. Many governments assume that all students are both meritorious and needy, and – in the cause of investment in education as well as equal opportunity – provide assistance in the form of general grants to reduce or eliminate tuition fees. But this too is fiscally regressive: much of the subsidy goes straight to the economically privileged, since under-represented groups tend to drop out of school well before college-entry age – and often for financial reasons. The alternative (though most systems use a combination of methods) is to give means-tested support directly to students. But there is still a tendency for upward drift to take place. In the United States, largely because of the exceptional political leverage of their parents, most middle-income students have become eligible for federal support which was originally intended for low-income students only; in Britain, too, there is a steady pressure (not, however, successful of late) to abolish means-testing for student grants. Countries with subsidised loan schemes, too, find it hard to restrict them to poorer students. In general, as the age of majority falls while students' ages rise, parental means-testing has come to seem increasingly unreasonable.

Thus all attempts to direct funds to those with greatest financial need tend to be diluted by a large number of others who fall into whatever categories are devised; subsidy or support schemes turn out not only less progressive but more expensive than was originally hoped. And cost considerations in their turn lead either to per capita reductions in direct student support or to the introduction of unattractive loan schemes, each of which may deter marginal candidates. There is a need, therefore, for widely publicised, carefully means-tested support schemes – including either outright grants or subsidised loans with attractive repayment arrangements – to be available *from the minimum leaving age onwards*. Low tuition fees are also important, especially for older or first-generation students who may not want to take on a substantial cost even if loans are available.

(c) Expansion as a remedy

The third pillar of equal opportunity, which was also adopted in most countries in the 1960s, was the expansion of the total supply of places in higher education. There were many other compelling reasons for expansion, including sharp increases in private demand, and economists' newfound faith in human capital theory for national economic development. But expansion was widely supported on the plausible-seeming assumption that it would provide extra space in higher education for those at present under-represented – and without any sacrifice by anyone else. 'Prima facie', as Twining puts it, 'the single best way of increasing access is to increase student numbers and reduce the competition for places.' Both the OECD and national policy-makers based their case for expansion largely on equal opportunity grounds, arguing that current reforms of secondary education would reduce social inequalities in qualifying for university entrance, so that places would be needed for the increasing number of female, working-class, rural and (they later added) ethnic minority students who would shortly be applying for them. Once again, this argument was correct as far as it went: it is far harder to change the composition of a student body by removing those 'over-represented' than by making room for new entrants; but it was a necessary rather than sufficient condition for change. And even at this time there was considerable debate about whether what was needed was simply an expansion of existing institutions which had up till that point proved to be de facto socially biased, or whether new and different institutions might do a better job of recruiting under-represented groups.[3]

Equality of opportunity policies assessed

These policies were a necessary first step towards greater social equality in higher education. Without the abolition of discrimination and the availability of adequate numbers of student places and funds to support them, it is imposs- ible to imagine a system which avoids gross social bias – though it may still be possible for such a system to permit a limited amount of 'sponsored mobility' in which some more or less token representatives of under-represented groups are admitted – and then, quite likely, heavily socialised out of their allegiance to or connection with the groups from which they came. The question is, however, whether equal opportunity policies are adequate to stimulate or even satisfy the aspirations of previously excluded groups, still less to achieve any kind of equality of outcomes. In the 1960s it was generally believed that they would be. This belief rested on the fundamental assumption that the supply of talent, and therefore the capacity to benefit from higher education, were equally distributed across all social strata, however defined: if one could only provide the opportunities, there was every reason to hope for much greater equality of participation, and even, optimistically, that inequality could be virtually eliminated. The great attraction of this combination of policies was that they seemed to reconcile political and economic imperatives, to satisfy rising expectations and maximise the use of scarce talent, while preserving the two ideological planks of the professions' claims to privilege: their monopoly of expertise and their openness to the deserving. Both were to be ensured by meritocratic access procedures, operated at a safe distance by unimpeachably equitable universities and colleges.

However, the results have been mixed at best. In most industrialised coun- tries (both OECD and centrally planned) and in some developing countries as well, the proportion of *women* entering undergraduate courses in higher education has risen, in some cases reaching parity with that of men. On the other hand, the proportion from other under-represented social groups has generally changed much less. In the words of OECD (1981) 'no ... [member countries] ... have come anywhere near the kind of equality of achievement which would make expenditure on higher education economically redis- tributive or even neutral.' This seems particularly true for elite institutions such as full or research universities, about which we generally know most – and on which, of course, expenditure is highest.

As a result, it became customary in many countries by the mid- to late 1970s to approach equity in higher education in a tone of despairing 'realism', often simply asserting that policies for equality had 'failed'. This is a serious over- simplification. But there is no denying the OECD statement above. There are two main, and probably equally unanticipated reasons. The first is that a chief effect of expansion is to change the relationship of higher education qualifications to the labour market. Whereas, in small 'elite' systems, attendance was genuinely optional for many middle-class children, unless they aspired to a quite limited range of professional occupations (and sometimes even then), as systems expanded a degree became a virtual necessity if they were to retain middle-class status. These children (who increasingly included women) naturally began to exercise their opportunity of attendance, and largely because of their greater success at secondary school, they ended up at the head of the queue of new entrants, well above the other groups whom the expansion had been intended to help. If 'elite' systems provide open opportunities for the middle class and limited opportunities for others, 'mass' systems convert the middle-class opportunity to a requirement while doing little for the rest of the population. In any case, neither the steps just described nor widespread attempts to reform secondary education have succeeded in outweighing the combination of social, cultural and economic pressures which reduce the likelihood of members of under-represented social or ethnic groups even aspiring to, let alone applying for, a place in higher education. In some countries application rates from such groups actually declined during the 1970s;[4] and in others short-term gains were not sustained.[5]

But the new doubts about equal opportunity policies were not just a product of continuing inequality: they also stemmed from two other sources, of which the first was the changing economic climate. To the governments of the 1960s, the political attractiveness of expansion was clear. As in many other areas of social policy, increased expenditure and increased opportunity promised to satisfy rising expectations at apparently small cost to anyone – apart from the direct economic costs, which looked to be an excellent national investment, and were paid for by growing national wealth. In recent years, however, we have rediscovered the acute problems of 'zero-sum' policies, in which new opportunities for the under-privileged involve visible costs for those previously advantaged. Indeed, there is a new danger. It is now sometimes suggested that if expansion failed to produce greater equality, then it could be ended or reversed without increasing inequality. But the assumption that the last entrants (ie the more marginally-motivated middle-class students) would also be the first to leave is certainly wrong; it is much more likely to be those with marginal academic qualifications who will be squeezed out – and these tend to be the socially disadvantaged.

It is not only economic difficulties that have increased the political stakes; greater understanding of social processes has corroded public acceptance of 'meritocratic' policies. The main spotlight is on the processes of secondary schooling. The well-documented social biases in its outcomes are now viewed as inevitable. Structural reforms have done little for those they were chiefly designed to help: at best they have encouraged the process, just described, whereby first school-leaving qualifications and then degrees have become the norm for middle-class children.

Attention has also turned back to higher education. The disappointing results of equal opportunity policies (not only for student populations but also for staff appointments) have led to the development, though by no means the general acceptance, of the concept of 'institutional' sexism, racism, etc to describe the cumulative effects of practices which, while apparently fair in themselves, appear to have unfair results in the aggregate. Entry criteria have been one of the key examples. The critique began at lower levels of education, with the complaint that standardised tests of achievement *and* aptitude were 'culturally biased' in favour of white, male, middle-class students. In the

United States the argument was applied directly to the national college-entrance tests, and similar questions were raised about European school-leaving qualifications. These criticisms were reinforced by research on student performance in higher education, which undermined the usual justifications for using standardised entry qualifications. In courses of many different kinds it has become clear that the normal entry criteria are in general very moderately correlated with students' achievements on exit. This weakness makes the competitive use of academic criteria quite problematic; indeed it fuels the suspicion that an alleged meritocracy based on academic achievement simply substitutes a more socially acceptable form of elite self-recruitment for outright selection by ascriptive criteria.

Alternative entry criteria

It is therefore only logical to tackle this problem by moving away from traditional entry criteria, or indeed conventional methods for applying them. There are essentially three kinds of admission for higher education: *competitive* or selective admissions, in which a limited supply of places is awarded to selected applicants in order of their 'merit' on entry or pre-entry tests; *qualifying* admissions, in which all those who reach a set minimum mark are entitled to a higher education place, subject only to administrative, not competitive requirements (eg redirecting later applicants from oversubscribed courses); and *open* admissions in which anyone may enrol regardless of previous educational achievement (in practice these commonly apply a minimum age requirement): examples are Swedish higher education in general, the Open University or the London External LLB in Britain and most community college systems in the United States. These categories are related to Trow's well-known divisions of elite, mass and universal systems of higher education: competitive admissions ensure an elite system, unless underpinned by other institutions with more open policies; qualifying admissions have led irresistibly to mass systems, even if not originally intended to do so; and only open admissions can support universal access.

The national 'mix' of institutions of different 'standards', defined by their admissions procedures, derives from a mixture of social, political and academic pressures. In many countries it has a long history; others have made it a central plank in a more recent 'framework' or 'master plan' for higher education. In all cases it is the object of political attention. But it is not purely political: it also represents statements about the kind of higher education that goes on in institutions of each type. Places with qualified admissions can assume a certain minimum standard of common curricular experience; while those with competitive admissions generally have a higher standard, which they themselves can control directly – subject to their market position. Each will have a different view of the relevance of alternative criteria to the curriculum and style of teaching that they can provide. It is all too easy, and common, for selective institutions to refuse to consider unconventionally qualified candidates because their teaching 'standards' do not permit it; and in the light of the low correlations between entry and exit performance it is certainly reasonable to ask them for more flexibility. But any course which depends on a level of previous knowledge or aptitude in its entrants needs to be satisfied of its existence: it does no service to under-represented students to admit them, only to have them fail. This is not to say, however, that such courses should never change their assumptions: a refusal to do so is one of the best indirect methods of preserving the status quo.

Different considerations apply in different cases. In open systems the chief problem in ensuring adequate representation from different groups will not be admission but recruitment[6]. Each of the other two systems depends on the success of secondary education in bringing candidates from different social groups to a certain standard. But there are still different ways of measuring this standard. These can be summarised in three choices: between previous achievement and 'aptitude', or potential to benefit; between criterion-based and norm-based assessment; and between assessment which is based within secondary schools and wider or national tests.

The achievement/aptitude dilemma is simply described. Achievement tests measure accomplishments in a predefined syllabus; aptitude tests are standardised, quasi-psychometric tests, which claim to measure potential, regardless of past experience. There is, unfortunately, no such thing as a coaching-proof aptitude test; but they may reduce the social bias inherent in achievement examinations, which clearly favour candidates from schools with better teaching standards and resources. However, past achievement is the natural first choice for admission to those courses which build directly on earlier learning. It guarantees to the admitting institution that it will not need to provide remedial or elementary teaching, which is unpopular with staff and costly in resources. But these advantages mainly apply when the pre-entry course involves specialisation in the same subject. Where entrants change their discipline at university level, or where high school achievement tests are broad rather than narrowly-focused, the arguments are weaker; even in highly-specialised systems the predictive value of achievement tests is often surprisingly low, and aptitude tests can produce roughly similar – that is, equally low – correlations, though subjects certainly vary. And even though no one has devised coaching-proof – or culture-fair – aptitude tests, blanket testing with aptitude measures always reveals substantial numbers of people, disproportionately from under-represented groups, with the capacity to benefit from higher education but who would not qualify by achievement measures. There is, therefore, as most North American institutions now agree, a good case for using both types in combination, setting minimum acceptable thresholds for either achievement *or* aptitude – or a more complex algorithm of the two. There is also a strong case for permitting a range of alternative achievement measures. The introduction of a technical baccalaureat in France, and of examinations of vocational instead of academic achievements in England, have each allowed for somewhat more diversity in the mix of entrants.

'Criterion referenced' marking defines a series of accomplishments which will constitute success in an examination, regardless of how many people possess them at a given session; 'norm referencing' awards passes by ranking candidates in relation to their fellows. Whereas there may sometimes be an academic logic in using achievement rather than aptitude tests, norm-referenced testing has only administrative convenience to commend it. Any institution with a fixed capacity will find it useful to rank its applicants, and take as many as it can from the top down. But given what we know about both social bias and low predictive value, this is unfair and wasteful of potential talent. It would be a more valid use of test scores (of either kind) to set a lower threshold at the point below which students would be expected to have difficulty, and then to use other criteria to select from the resulting pool. The fact that this is rarely done owes something to convenience, but probably more to a concern with the status indicated by an institution's drawing power for highly able students, and also to worries about public legitimacy: intuitively, meritocratic competition looks more defensible. In his chapter, Twining discusses the philosophical defence of using non-academic criteria, and I describe some of the practical alternatives in the next section. However, one possibility deserves mentioning here, since it is essentially neutral and non-preferential: that is to use a lottery to select among candidates all of whom are thought to be perfectly acceptable. The Netherlands was, I think, the first country to do so for entries to medicine and other severely over-subscribed courses; but lotteries have also been suggested for admissions to law schools in North America. Early experience suggests that they are not popular: for a once-in-a-lifetime event such as college attendance people seem to prefer disappointment to uncertainty. In principle, however, they are a neat solution. It is even feasible to construct weighted lotteries so that the most able candidates, those who have persevered for several years, or any other category desired, have a greater chance of success.

Another, more popular solution is to retain achievement testing, but to allow it to be done by individual secondary schools, rather than national or regional examining bodies. There are two conflicting strands in current educational policy: on one hand the proponents of 'excellence' favour national testing systems that claim reliability and accountability, in the hope that they will compel higher standards; on the other, there is the movement towards individualised, 'student-centred' teaching and assessment, which emphasises particularised measurement at the level of individual schools. Pedagogically, there is little contest – students learn better and are more highly motivated under the latter system unless expectations in their schools are truly appalling. And school-based assessment has the great advantage of ranking children against their local peers, who are likely to face the same combination of advantages and disadvantages at home. But it is not only the supporters of accountability and those concerned with 'falling standards' who like centralised assessment: for understandable reasons, higher education too generally prefers standardised, normed examinations. But given all the inequalities that exist between schools and localities, equity would certainly be better served by allowing each school, within broad guidelines, to select its own recommended candidates for higher education, as some European countries do. However, in most places this degree of trust does not exist.[7]

Clearly only those students who can benefit from a given type of higher education should be admitted to it – and depending on an institution's expectations, difficult problems may arise about the gap between theoretical potential and adequate preparation. But if they are to improve the social balance in higher education by reducing the advantages provided by extra resources, at home or at school, admissions procedures must allow for a mixture of alternative criteria: aptitude tests as well as or instead of achievement examinations; school-based as well as national-standard assessment; and especially threshold, criterion-referenced assessment, not competitive norms. To provide a range of alternative benchmarks for applicants to meet is bound to complicate the processes of filling limited places and forecasting demand for the future. But it will certainly lead to a more diverse student population, with advantages for the institution itself, as well as for the otherwise rejected applicants.

From 'weak' to 'strong' equality: equality of results

However desirable diversified entry criteria may be, they will not prevent (and have not) calls for more radical steps, and in particular, a shift from a 'weak' equality of *opportunity* to a 'stronger' conception of equality of *outcomes*. If taken literally, this means that equity is to be judged not by the way in which institutions respond to applicants for their places, but by whether or not the social balance among entering students meets agreed criteria; of which the simplest is that the proportion from under-represented groups should cor-respond to these groups' proportions in the population at large. Given different application as well as qualification rates, this may well imply not only different treatment on application but special recruitment policies as well. But as far as applications are concerned, the logical implication of a full-fledged 'strong equality' policy is to use different criteria and procedures for different groups, depending on whether they are under- or over-represented. The ideas discussed above may well improve the situation substantially, but it is inescapable that, contrary to the letter of Policy 1 (non-discrimination), admissions staff may find themselves, instead of turning a consciously blind eye to ascriptive charac-teristics, paying renewed attention to them. If so, ascription will again be used for discrimination, though in reverse.

Twining (chapter 1) suggests several justifications for attempting to equalise results, all of which have much to commend them. Possibly the most attractive to academics is the hypothesis that the capacity to benefit from higher edu-cation is, if latently, equally distributed in different groups of the population. An advantage of this view is that it cuts through the arguments about causality. In this way one can argue for compensatory or positive discrimination without needing to accuse one's institution of sexism, racism etc. In the United States, for instance, many people who would reject these charges still agree that higher education is an entirely appropriate instrument for rectifying inequalities elsewhere in society, and indeed that as the key allocator of life chances it is essential for democracy that it do so.

It would be wrong to imply that these arguments are generally accepted. Certainly accusations of sexism or racism, however softened by naming them 'institutional' and thoughtless rather than the deliberate acts of individuals, are still hotly denied. From time to time evidence is offered (though it cannot possibly be conclusive) to suggest that academic potential may not be randomly distributed in the population; or it may be argued that social inequalities are partly a product of an unequally distributed taste or distaste for higher education – a perfectly natural feeling which it is not the business of the state or its agencies to combat. And even if the basic political point is accepted, the consequences of radical policies are disputed. The evidence of low correlations between entry and exit scores seems counter-intuitive to most academics. Both the institutions of higher education and their political supporters or mentors need a great deal of reassurance that those for whom exceptional treatment is designed can in fact benefit from it, let alone reach results as high as those who would otherwise have been admitted in their places.

One useful method to soften the resistance is operated by a number of American universities. It is to use conventional criteria for the majority of admissions, but to retain a small pool of places (generally less than 10%) for which conventional measures will not be applied. These 'special admissions' places can be used for a number of different categories, including not only those for whom a wider social case can be made, but also those with particular talents who do not meet all the normal entry criteria.[8] By creating a separate pool, they suggest that rather than competing in a 'rigged' competition, these candidates are in a separate competition altogether; this seems to be more acceptable, even if the pool's small size limits its effectiveness.

There are, however, several other possibilities. These include 'affirmative action', targets or quotas for admission of particular groups, and 'positive discrimination'. By affirmative action American universities and colleges usually mean a coherent set of policies designed to encourage and recruit members of targeted groups, including publicity campaigns, mutual school-university visits for familiarisation and advance recruitment, special scholarships, advance-preparation and tutoring programmes and so on. For any group whose aspirations are lower than their potential, this kind of programme has a vital part to play. Although it may involve modest extra expenditure in favour of targeted groups, it is usually seen as compatible with strictly equal opportunity at the moment of application. The difficulty for those who cling to the letter of non-discrimination comes when it blurs into 'positive' measures which clearly favour the disadvantaged. By these I mean explicit decisions to require a lower standard on whatever entry tests are used. Of course at an individual level this has long been common practice in selective institutions: most admissions authorities have traditionally sought to achieve a 'balanced' intake. All that is new, arguably, is that the kinds of qualities sought are changed; but there is no denying that to demote academic criteria in selective systems where they are the normal currency of competition, or to prescribe lower thresholds for a minority in selective or qualifying systems, is troubling to many academics. It may too, in some countries, run foul of anti-discrimination statutes.

The distinction between affirmative action and positive discrimination can be paralleled by the differences between 'targets' for minority admissions and firm 'quotas'. An institution that adopts targets is making a public declaration of aspiration or intent, which does not, however, bind it to any particular means of achieving its goal. The target can be read by members of the relevant group as encouraging where previously they might have expected prejudicial treatment; and if set reasonably high, it provides a firm benchmark against which actual achievements can be measured. A quota, on the other hand is fixed in advance, and implies that separate methods or standards of admission will be used for different groups, in order to reach the planned intakes. By definition it will be more certainly effective than a target, at least up to the point of admission; but it is also likely to create considerably more resistance, and if it does not allow for adjustment to the supply of applicants, it runs the risk of admitting severely underqualified students, and in turn confirming prejudices about the differences in ability between minority and majority groups.

Once again, a careful combination of policies is likely to be most effective. Recruitment efforts, on the lines of 'affirmative action', are essential. But except in cases of quite marginal under-representation they will hardly be enough on their own. Any institution which is serious about an active policy to improve its social balance needs targets for self-monitoring purposes; and should seriously consider either earmarked quotas or at least a pool of special admission places. If this pool is large enough, it can be surprisingly effective, and serve to disarm opposition by maintaining 'normal' procedures for the majority of admissions – though there is a danger that 'special admissions students', if identifiable, may feel themselves stigmatised. Whatever 'positive' policies are used, they need to be accompanied by a careful concern for the preparation *and retention* of those who are exceptionally admitted; and they need to be applied on a wide scale, not just in token, socially-concerned departments or institutions.

Policies for older students

In a sense, older candidates might seem a group with a less deserving claim to special treatment than the other groups discussed here: unlike the others, they have all once belonged to the majority category of young people and should have had their chance of access. But there are a number of reasons why they deserve special consideration. The simplest is generational inequality. As participation rates have risen over the past twenty or thirty years, each new cohort of eighteen-year-olds has had greater opportunities of access than its predecessors. Almost everywhere in the world, anyone over forty in 1987 will have faced far more severe competition when he or she was eighteen than those now reaching that age. But there is also a connection between age and membership of other under-represented groups. Women's participation, for example, has only recently begun to approach that of men; and because of different life-cycle expectations, to exclude students in their thirties and forties mainly means excluding 'women returners'. For other groups different processes have similar effects. The socially disadvantaged whose secondary schooling was truncated or inadequate either take longer than middle-class children to obtain the necessary qualifications for higher education entry, or enter the labour force early, and fail to obtain them at all. So any policies which favour younger entrants increase the disadvantage of those from under-represented groups.

For these reasons alone it is right not only to avoid discriminating against older applicants, but to make 'affirmative' efforts to recruit them. But we can go well beyond this. Evidence from many different systems shows that in most subjects older students perform remarkably well in higher education, making up in motivation and maturity for any lack of paper qualifications. In other words, standard entry tests designed for younger applicants are much less useful as predictors of adults' success – and many systems recognise this, some going so far as to offer open access to adults while still requiring qualifications from younger students – and without noticeably higher failure rates. This is not always true; less qualified adults do find difficulty in some sequential courses where entrants are expected to bring a good knowledge of a subject with them. Here they need appropriate counselling, and remedial or preparatory courses. But the general case for flexible and even open entry is strong.[9]

Access to what?

I suggested earlier that, whether or not the professions have willingly 'relinquished' it, higher education has taken over the primary task of selection from them. It is certainly true that most major professions are now inaccessible without a degree in most countries, and that improving access to higher education is therefore a necessary first step for improving access to the professions. But it is by no means automatically sufficient to bring about change in the professions themselves, whose own selection procedures constitute further 'gatekeepers' from which the debate over access to higher education may distract attention. In this context we should remember that higher education is never a homogeneous entity. Martin Trow has pointed out that mass systems generally provide space for the elite functions of higher education to continue within them – either in whole institutions or in particular subject areas. In other words, the arrival of mass higher education, which connects higher education more closely with the whole range of middle-class jobs, does not necessarily weaken the elite institutions' connection with elite jobs – indeed it may actually strengthen and give legitimacy to it. There is a serious danger that policies for improving access may fudge this issue by implying that access to *any* degree is sufficient for equity purposes. Unfortunately, a single institution which adopts more flexible access policies on its own may well alter its status position for the worse; one of the defining characteristics of an elite institution, as the name implies and the staff frequently insist, is the rigour of its selection policy. But as North American policy has recognised, if affirmative action is desirable, it is as much so, or even more, at elite institutions as at those with open access. Some of the former may argue that under-qualified students should go to those institutions with most experience in teaching them. Aside from the fact that many elite colleges have considerable experience of under-qualified students, albeit from a different social milieu, this will in fact deny under-represented students the chance of access not only to elite education but to the careers which it alone can lead to.

Retention in higher education

This concern with graduates' opportunities suggests a further caveat. It cannot be assumed that access to higher education guarantees success, even within the degree programme itself. Conventional entry qualifications may well be only very moderately correlated with the likelihood of success; and some groups, notably older students, make up in other qualities for the lack of precisely tailored and certified preparation for their course. Nevertheless, admitting students who fall well below the standard normally required for entry is obviously dangerous, and 'specially admitted' students who find themselves floundering are understandably inclined to drop out rather than persist in a failing struggle. Two of the main tasks of selectors in any kind of programme which moves away from strict meritocratic criteria are first, to satisfy themselves that the students have the capacity, with suitable help, to succeed; and secondly to diagnose and arrange for the help that will be necessary. Systems vary considerably in the ways in which they may provide this, whether it is academically remedial or socially and psychologically supportive. At one extreme, where courses are designed to build on a considerable amount of specialisation before entry, it may be a sensible practice to provide 'special access' or preparatory courses which the selected students must take *before* entry, so that by the time they join other undergraduates they are on an academic par with them. The main difficulty with this procedure – adopted with some success in Britain, for example – is that 'access students' take up to one year longer to graduate, at considerable cost (and disincentive) to themselves and/or the state. The obvious alternative is to admit special action students in the normal way, and provide whatever extra monitoring, social and remedial support is necessary as they progress through their first year, or even longer. This is easier to arrange in systems which only expect a low level of preparation in subject specialisms on entry, so that exceptionally admitted students are not grossly handicapped; and which also operate a unit-credit course structure, so that it is easy to insert extra or alternative classes without over-burdening students' timetables (Fulton and Rothblatt, 1987). However, despite these cautions, it should be emphasised that even in highly selective institutions, most of the students admitted under special procedures are nevertheless perfectly well qualified at a threshold level to cope with the demands of their course: they simply are not the most highly prepared and highly selected members of their elite class.

Conclusion

In the end, the policy decisions that are taken – at national or regional level, by whole institutions, by departments or by individual academic staff – will be the product of a mixture of moral, political and economic concerns. On the political level, changes in access policies range from, at one extreme, serious attempts to incorporate new groups into leading institutions and hence provide them with access to elite positions in society, to symbolic gestures – quite possibly worthless if the labour market still makes its traditional distinctions – or attempts to pacify the group concerned by co-opting or even controlling a few leaders. These changes (and refusals to change) are decided on in response to the weight of pressures from different interest groups – the under-represented and their spokespersons on one hand, and a variable array of people who profit from the status quo on the other. In the middle, academic staff, who hold much of the power in their own hands, are frequently divided, weighing their traditional concerns for meritocracy, for status, for the kind of teaching to which they are accustomed, against the search for new roles, for a fresh supply of students and so on. Their own moral values will differ on the nature of academic imperatives: equity and competition, institutional freedom versus social responsiveness. And behind all these is the question of cost. On a narrow level, equality of opportunity and progressive student support schemes are not only justifiable but desirable, to improve the utilisation of scarce talent. But they are investments for the medium term which may conflict with short-run economy. 'Stronger' forms of equality may find it even harder to demonstrate their economic efficiency. In particular, efficiency considerations may seem to run counter to the recommendation that policies for equality belong in all institutions, not just the least selective. My own view is that an adequate assessment even of the narrow economic advantages, let alone the broad social and political benefits of greater equality would tilt the balance firmly in its favour. But this case still needs to be made.

NOTES

[1] See Burton J Bledstein (1976) 'The Culture of Professionalism' chs 6–8 for a description of the process in the United States.
[2] This was probably most common in medical schools, which frequently rejected well-qualified

women and older students on the grounds that medical training was so expensive that cost-benefit calculations were essential: young male students were expected to return the highest number of working years to their investment.

[3] For example community colleges in the United States, or more explicitly vocational or technical colleges in Europe.

[4] Working-class males in Britain, for example.

[5] Eg Afro-Americans in the United States.

[6] But even here there will be concerns about entrants' capacity to benefit: most 'open' admissions systems have counselling procedures to half-close the door to over-optimistic applicants – or at least to divert them to more appropriate courses.

[7] In California, for example, where the state's Master Plan states that the 'top 12.5%' and 'top 30%' 'of high school graduates' may enter, respectively, the University and State University systems, these percentages are not applied to each school on its own: they are translated into statewide norms and end up in wide variations in the proportions going on from different schools.

[8] The oldest example in the United States is of athletes, but other examples might be musicians, the children of staff or alumni, or any other characteristic which the college or university may feel would be an asset justifying exceptional treatment – including of course social need.

[9] Here one of the most interesting experiments is the system, first developed in the United States, of giving academic credit for experience outside academic settings – experience gained either in the workplace or, for example, in child-rearing, voluntary activities in the community and so on. If appropriately and carefully assessed and examined, these can both provide useful guides to adults' capacities and suitability for a course and, by exempting them from part of the required coursework, give them an additional incentive to apply.

3   Legal education for a changed world: an American perspective

*Leora Mosston**

Introductory note

Historically, Anglo-American legal traditions have mirrored not only the social and economic values of the societies in which they function, but also law has defined the status of participants in the society and has influenced the way in which participants experience and perceive their relations with others.[1] Who is permitted to practice and mould the direction of legal interpretation and law-making has pervasive impact on the directions of a society. Entry to legal education and completion to qualification to enter the profession affect not only who become lawyers and judges but how members of a society perceive their possibilities of experiencing legal and social equity in the courts, legislative bodies and electoral positions.[2]

Throughout the history of the United States all Afro-Americans, all Native Americans, and all women have been affected by legal definitions rendering them inferior before the law, denying them access to the most basic rights of citizenship, miring them in subordinate relationships in the economic sector and denying them absolutely, for most of the nation's history, access to political power.

The law has not only placed these groups in inferior relationships to the society but has specifically authorised and legitimised their debasement.[3] Racism has been an integral part of American practice and law since the first day the Europeans reached the New World. Admission to legal education and the practice of law has similarly been affected by racist exclusion. This chapter will trace the development of the barriers erected and consider some of the conditions which still obtain and which affect the admissions and survival of people of colour and from low economic status in law school and in the legal profession.

* Director (Acting), Max and Filomen M Greenberg Center for Legal Education & Urban Policy, City College of The City University of New York; Adjunct Professor of Law, CUNY Law School at Queens. BS, MS, City College of The City University of New York, JD Rutgers Law School, Newark, New Jersey.

Racism and gender exclusion under US law

Twenty years after Columbus reached the New World, African Negroes, trans-
ported by Spanish, Dutch and Portuguese traders, were arriving in the Caribbean
Islands. Almost all came as slaves. By 1600, there were more than half a million
slaves in the Western Hemisphere.

In Colonial America, the first Negroes landed at Jamestown in August, 1619.
Within 40 years, Negroes had become a group apart, separated from the rest of
the population by custom and law. Treated as servants for life, forbidden to
intermarry with whites, deprived of their African traditions and dispersed among
Southern plantations, American Negroes lost tribal, regional and family ties.

Through massive importation, their numbers increased rapidly. By 1776, some
500,000 Negroes were held in slavery and indentured servitude in the United
States. Nearly one of every six persons in the country was a slave.[4]

Absolutely every aspect of the new society; law, religion, education, politics,
and human connection, was infused with racist and sexist doctrines. Eleven
years after the Declaration of Independence (1776) announced 'all men are
created equal' the male white property-owner citizens of the new nation
experienced neither logical nor moral difficulty in adopting a constitution that
sanctioned chattel slavery based upon race and colour and decreed that persons
of colour who were held in bondage should be counted as three-fifths of a
'person', Indians and women being excluded from rights and responsibilities
absolutely.[5]

Slavery is not mentioned in the constitution until after the Civil War, women
never, even in the amendment that attempts to reverse their exclusion from
full participation in the political life of the society.[6]

The task of eliminating the overt manifestations of racism and sexism from
statutory and decisional law has absorbed lawyers, judges and advocacy groups
for over one hundred years.[7]

Access to higher education of substantial segments of this society became a
rallying point of unity in the late 1960s coincident with the national movements
for equal opportunity for all excluded groups. The black civil rights movements
perfected the legal, political and social strategies that could not be ignored
and which focussed national attention.[8]

The quest for inclusion in higher educational institutions is particularly
sharp[9] in respect to legal education[10] which has been the gateway for so many
from mean origins in US society to positions of economic and political power.[11]
This discussion of the inclusion and exclusion of applicants to the privileges of
legal education and the legal profession is informed by presumptions about
the effects of race, gender and economic class not only on admissions practices
and procedures historically and contemporaneously but also on the rites of
passage required for entry into the legal profession.[12]

To make their case consistent, these opponents (of change in access to legal
education will) ... have to explain what 'merit' has been possessed by those
professionals who have enjoyed the rewards of restrictive rules of entry to their
professions (eg lawyers and doctors); by businessmen, bankers and brokers who
were privileged by virtue of coming from an acceptable social background; public
employees who belonged to the right ethnic group in the right place at the right
time; craftsmen whose acceptance by a trade union has been contingent on their
recommendation by members of their own family; and academics who through
most of their careers have engaged in neither productive scholarship nor innovative teaching but have rather been 'good old boys' expertly mimicking the values
of their superiors.[13]

This paper will provide a short history of access to the practice of law and to legal education in the United States from the perspectives described above, will discuss the existence and implications of contemporary barriers to legal education and will briefly discuss the Urban Legal Studies Program of the Max E and Filomen M Greenberg Center for Legal Education and Urban Policy of The City College of New York, a model of inclusion[14] with which I have had the opportunity to work for most of its years of existence.

Colonial and revolutionary period

Education for the legal profession in the United States has reflected the competing pull between 'aristocratic' (old world) and 'equalitarian' (new world) directions.[15]

The colonists from England established the first court system in the New World. For example, the first court in New Jersey was established in 1661 and the first legislatures of the Provinces of West New Jersey and East New Jersey established court systems in 1681 and 1682 respectively.[16]

Popular feelings about lawyers prior to the American Revolution were extremely hostile. Lawyers in practice were viewed as pettifoggers and petty court officials who encouraged litigation. Lawyers in the colonies were apparently not trained or bound by discernible ethical standards and appeared to be so lacking in public respect or confidence that many colonies passed statutes forbidding the practice of law and establishing the right of individuals to represent themselves.[17]

Puritan and Quaker settlers in particular had suffered bitterly from the administration of the laws of their English motherland and viewed lawyers as feudal and tyrannical – an aristocratic self-perpetuating class who represented the interests of the hereditary ruling class in a legal system that used death and transportation as primary remedies to control the traditionally oppressed lower classes of England.[18]

In the simple colonial agrarian society it must have seemed possible for a common man to manage his own legal affairs with a remembrance of the English common law, common sense and faith in the Bible.

> There were few among those who practised in the courts or sat on the bench that made any pretence at legal training. There was no requirement of special training for leave to practise in the courts, and the capable men of every community appeared in the courts, in such litigation as the parties could not manage for themselves.[19]

But complex societal changes in the colonies which preceded the 1776 Declaration of Independence from England, made such simplicity difficult. As the population grew, relationships became more complex. Statutory prohibitions on practice were lifted. New England lawyers formed local and county Bar associations and set and enforced standards of competence and ethical conduct.

By 1770, as the course of legal study became fixed and the Bar association became more efficient in its organisation and assured of its power, it established very rigid rules and fixed the requirements for apprentice study for those seeking admission to practice as lawyers. The lawyer had taken his place with the physician and the clergyman as community leaders.[20] Lawyers ranked at the top of the colonial gentry. Lawyers restricted to the middle and upper-classes were, at the time of the American Revolution, about to become a hereditary profession in Virginia, South Carolina, New York and Massachusetts.[21]

The climate of the American Revolution, fostering politically militant egalitarianism and an innovative spirit of individualism and optimism particularly disfavoured the incumbent legal profession. Lawyers, traditionally conservative,[22] generally supported the Tories thereby increasing popular hostility against them. The crisis caused by the dislocation of the economy during the Revolution also nourished hostility toward lawyers seeking to collect debts and to foreclose property. In New England law libraries were burned and many lawyers fled to Canada and England.[23]

Post revolutionary period

The practice of law has been the common route to political power in the United States from the earliest days.[24] The values of Jacksonian democracy which viewed exclusive hereditary class privileges as interfering with the rights of the common white man and the increasingly powerful philosophy of laissez-faire capitalism rejected the self-perpetuating class aspects of the Bar and the legal profession and sought entry to this gateway to political power. The legal profession as a special class enjoying the exclusive privilege of practice was placed under public control.[25]

Within two generations, the popularly elected legislatures of all the new states drastically reduced, and in some cases, eliminated stringent educational requirements and supervision of competence for access to the legal profession. Clerkship terms were reduced and examination systems became minimal.

> In a few states a prescribed period of preparation survived, but in the majority the only educational test came to be the ability to pass a Bar examination. In most instances this became a mere farce; and in four states even this test was abandoned, proof of good moral character being the only requisite for admission to practice ... It was generally assumed without question that a single process of admission, no more rigorous than democratic ideals permit, was to yield the general privilege of engaging in any kind of legal practice.[26]

Egalitarians had routed the aristocrats from controlling the legal profession for the first time in modern history. White upwardly mobile men from humble origins had general access to entry to the legal profession without regard to their ancestry. This protection of the individual rights of ambitious practitioners led to serious abuse of clients after the Civil War. Incompetent and corrupt lawyers stimulated public demand for reform.[27] By the 1870s state and local Bar associations began forming and the American Bar Association (ABA), intended to be a watchdog, was founded in 1879 as an all-white institution which it remained until the social protest movements of the 1960s.[28]

The powerful Committee on Legal Education and Admissions to the Bar of the ABA was established to monitor and set standards for the profession. It took more than thirty years before the first standards of a high school diploma and three years of law school were adopted. The struggle over their adoption was another round in the struggle between the aristocrats who were proponents of the standards and the egalitarians who made the 'Abe Lincoln' argument that a man of modest means should not be deprived of the privilege of practice because he could not afford a formal education.[29] The egalitarians lost though even their apprenticeship model seemed costly and beyond the means of most.[30]

The establishment in the early nineteenth century of formal legal education as a precondition for entry to the profession fixed the orientation and composition of the profession until the 1960s. The struggle between the worldly advocates of the apprenticeship system and the scholarly school men was settled. In the early nineteenth century the school men became ascendant. Formal legal education then struggled with the decision whether to adopt the English (Inns of Court) method of education or the continental (liberal university) method. The issue was decided in favour of a narrow professional curriculum like the one developed at the Litchfield School and later adapted to the setting at Harvard University.[31] For half a century the school men ran law schools nearly like monasteries.[32]

However, the struggle for social and economic justice in the courtrooms and public forums of the United States and the view of law as an integral part of society rather than a self-contained system placed inexorable pressure on the academy to examine traditional academic notions of qualification, admission practices and policies. The increased use of eligibility measures such as the Law School Admissions Test (LSAT) on those segments of the population, particularly black people, Latinos, Native Americans and women historically excluded from the profession continues to be the target for popular and, increasingly, academic criticism.[33]

Current law school admissions and the composition of the profession

Black and Latin women and men began seeking entry to legal education in more than token numbers in the late 1960s and early 1970s,[34] in the wake of the enactment of the Civil Rights Act of 1964 and the subsequent promulgation of Executive Order 11246.[35]

In a society that allocates more of its decisions, political debates and concerns to courts and lawyers than any other nation, entry to the legal profession is seen as the route to political office and public decision-making as well as a method of ensuring greater equity of treatment in courts by those who perceive the courtroom as the route to changing social and political power relationships as well as a lucrative source of income.[36]

An extraordinary interest in law school generally during the recent period is demonstrated in the research of the Law School Admission Council (LSAC)[37] and other researchers.[38] Both black people and women were among those who attempted to enter the bastions of law school, hitherto almost exclusively white and male.[39] According to the Carnegie Report, between 1966 and 1976, the number of persons taking the Law School Admission Test (LSAT) increased almost 200% from 44,905 to 133,609[40] while the number of first-year places in all schools grew by only 62%. This phenomenal increase shifted the focus of the law school admissions process from the elimination of grossly unqualified applicants from a small to moderate-sized pool of white middle-class males with a range of academic qualifications to making selections from a far more diverse pool of applicants.[41] Examinations of undergraduate grade point averages and scores on the LSAT, a standardised test developed in 1948 to help screen the markedly increased number of law school applicants following the 1939–45 war[42] were, by 1968, essentially the two academic indicia being used by most law schools to select from this vastly increased pool.[43]

It must have seemed more feasible to beleaguered law school admissions officers to look at applicants' 'numbers' on paper applications than to follow Dean Wigmore's suggestion that the best way to determine aptitude for the study of law was to see what a 'boy' could do during his first year of legal studies.[44] Notwithstanding Wigmore's profound scepticism of the ability of a single test to prove aptitude for the study of law,[45] law schools in ever greater numbers relied on 'scores' to sift through these applicants for grossly insufficient law school places.

> For example, 50,793 persons took the LSAT in 1967–68. In 1971–72 the corresponding number was 121,871, an *increase of 140%* in four years. Over the same period of time, however, the number of first year law students *increased by only 47%*, from 25,746 in 1967–68 to 37,742 in 1971–72.[46]

The Scholastic Aptitude Test (SAT), the first standardised educational test of its kind was developed in 1925 to screen applicants seeking admission to a small elite group of universities in the eastern part of the United States, including Columbia and Princeton.[47] The Medical College Admission Test (MCAT) followed in 1946 and the LSAT in 1948. The first year the LSAT was administered, only 18 law schools required its scores for admission.[48]

The reader is referred to the most current *Law School Admission Test, Law School Data Assembly Service Information Book* for their analysis of current test composition and the weighted grading system they use.[49]

Elsewhere one of my colleagues has written on the perils of the LSAT[50] as a primary measure of an applicant's potential for success and a career in law school.

One Director of Law School Admissions provides an interesting cautionary tale.

> A few short decades ago my predecessors in admissions at Yale Law School had to scramble annually to get enough live bodies to fill the seats available. The admissions task was simply to determine if an individual applicant possessed the necessary academic credentials to get by. Drumming up enough interest in the law was the problem. Stories are legion about latecomers getting into law school by appearing at the door at registration time with the requisite fee. One such case was a young man named Byron White. We know him today as an Associate Justice of the United States Supreme Court. Justice White, at an alumni meeting a few years ago, delighted in telling of the casualness with which he was admitted late. Today no such casual late admissions could occur.[51]

Beginning in the 1970s, many people expressed concern about the apparent inability of professional schools to accept white male majority applicants whose credentials would have been considered excellent in previous years.[52] In 1975 approximately 83,000 applicants sought law school admissions for 39,038 first-year places available in ABA-approved law schools. Notwithstanding allegedly changed social priorities, few of those increased numbers admitted were minorities[53] in the subsequent years of maximum applications.[54] The proportions did not change as can be seen below.

In the years discussed above, the overall US population of citizens is calculated at 214,159,000. 11.6% Black; 6.5% Hispanic; 1% Asian; 0.3% Native

Law School Enrolment

Total Law School Enrolment 1976–1979
1976–77 117,451; *1977–78* 118,557; *1978–79* 121,606

	1978–79	*1977–78*	*1976–77*
Black Enrolment			
Black Americans	5,350	5,304	5,503
Percent of total	4.4%	4.5%	4.6%
Hispanic	2,758	2,547	2,375
Percent of total	2.3%	2.1%	2.0%
Asian/Pacific Islander	1,424	1,382	1,324
Percent of total	1.1%	1.1%	1.1%
Native Americans/Alaskans	390	363	301
Percent of total	.3%	.3%	.2%
Non-minority Enrolment			
Total	111,684	108,961	107,948
Percent of total	92%	92%	92%

Source: James P White, 'Minority Group JD and LLB Candidates Enrolled in Approved Law Schools – 1971 Through 1978 – Minority Group JD and LLB Degrees Awarded 1977–78', American Bar Association Memo QS 7879-15 (Memorandum to Deans of ABA-Approved Law Schools, Chicago, 30 April 1979).[55]

American. These essentially inaccurate[56] data certainly underestimate the minority populations then or now (1988) in the United States.[56]

According to recent (1986–1987) statistics although 12% of 1968 law school graduates are classified as minorities, Blacks are reported to make up only 4.78% of law students enrolled for 1986–87 (compare *1976–1979* supra).[57]

Women's law school admissions

While the population of the United States has almost doubled since the 1930s, the number of all lawyers has more than tripled since 1960 going from 205, 515 to 678,000 in 1984. In 1951, women comprised 2.5% of all lawyers (5,500). By 1984 there were 83,000 women lawyers who were 12.8% of the total.[59] But note that in 1960 the Bureau of Census counted 2,575 'non-white' lawyers (1.3%).[60] In 1984, after the number of all lawyers are reported to have tripled only 2.6% black and 2.0% Hispanic lawyers are reported.[61]

Moreover, notwithstanding the apparent absolute increases in the number of women and minorities in the profession, traditionally disparate relations between income and race and gender continue.

After close to twenty years of efforts to close the gap between minority-culture persons in the legal professions there is an apparent continued under-representation of people of colour while the numbers of white women have increased markedly.

In fact, a 1978 survey of minority lawyers in California shows a *decrease* in the percentage of minority lawyers since 1970 despite an increase in the absolute numbers of all lawyers between 1970 and 1975. In 1970 there were 1,473 minority lawyers in California, constituting 5.6% of all lawyers. In 1975,

Income by Race, Sex and Age in 1979 of Lawyers and Judges

	35–44 Yrs old		45–54 Yrs old	
	Number	*Mean annual earnings*	*Number*	*Mean annual earnings*
White male	108,135	$46,632	68,988	$54,981
Black male	2,337	29,930	1,314	39,322
White female	11,147	20,285	4,915	20,768
Black female	755	18,493	338	19,242

Source: 1980 Census of Population, US Dept of Commerce and Bureau of the Census (May 1984), pp 301, 342.

1,696 minority attorneys represented only 3.8% of the total lawyer population in California.[62]

One issue that must be considered is why so few black and brown women and men have been able to squeeze past the first barrier to access to law school: The Law School Admissions Test[63] and after admissions, what conditions prevail in schools so that so few complete to qualification to the profession?

Racially and culturally biased testing

In the early twentieth century, when masses of white immigrants were living in poverty, facing an alien culture, and struggling to unionise, they too had test results which showed most of them to be mentally defective. Although test performance undoubtedly depended upon familiarity with American language and culture, the dominant interpretation of the First World War army data stressed that recent immigrants from southern and Eastern Europe had performed poorly because they were members of inferior races (sic) – Jews, Alpines, and Slavs, as opposed to Nordics who were superior. The correlation between test scores and the number of years lived in America was explained by the fact that most of the earlier immigrants were from northern Europe and Great Britain while most of the recent ones were not. Carl Brigham, the primary author of this interpretation, received acclaim in psychology journals, influenced congressional debates over immigration restriction, and later came to head the College Entrance Examination Board.[64]

Testing as a mirror of a society's biases and prejudices is clearly not a recent phenomenon. In recent years there has been marked concern expressed by organisations representing black and Hispanic people in the society.

The NAACP expressed such concern in a presentation to the US Congress in 1979:

We appreciate the opportunity to appear before you to share the NAACP's views on the important issue of testing and how it affects Blacks and other minorities. I must share with the committee the grave concern the NAACP has regarding the wholesale use and misuse of standardised tests and the disproportionate impact such testing has on our constituents.

For four years I was the NAACP's National Director for Education Programs and had occasion to work closely with all of our units on education issues, confer with many educational officials at all levels and officials of the major testing companies on the consequences of ability grouping practiced by whole educational systems which results in racial isolation, the enforcement of stereotypes, the labelling of children and the reinforcement of feelings of inferiority which can lead to a third class education.

From the cradle to the grave, there has been an increasing reliance in this country on the use of an assortment of standardised tests to screen, select, admit, reject, to classify, stratify, track, license or certify. Such subjective dependence on 'objective' tools makes it possible, and even attractive, in some quarters, to use tests inequitably in ways which preclude a segment of the population from reaching the heights of it aspirations and realising its potential. The accelerated widescale use of standard tests limiting access of Blacks and other minorities to institutions of higher education led to the mandate by the NAACP's 65th Annual National Convention to its national office to call upon the Association of Black Psychologists and the College Entrance Examination Board to assert leadership in addressing themselves to the issue of standardised testing and the misuse thereof.

In 1972 the NAACP adopted a convention resolution calling for a moratorium on standardised tests until after other suitable and non-biased criteria for measuring pupil progress and teaching accountability have been devised.[65]

Designed with the intention of indicating a competency to study law, the LSAT has become, intentionally or not, an exclusionary device which has a disproportionate impact on the disadvantaged[66] and on racial and ethnic minorities.[67] Clearly alternates to its use as a predictor must be employed. In addition to Dean Wigmore's reservation about single standard standardised tests, discussed earlier, Justice William Douglas' observations in his opinion in *Defunis v Odegaard*[68] should be considered.

> The answers the student can give to multiple-choice questions are limited by the creativity and intelligence of the testmaker. ... If he (the testmaker) is strong-minded, non-conformist, unusual, original or creative – as so many of the truly important people are – he must stifle his impulses and conform as best he can to the norms that the multiple-choice testers set up [at 328].

Justice Douglas continues by saying '(t)*he tests do not have the value that their deceptively precise scoring system suggests* ... (T)here are many relevant factors, such as motivation, cultural backgrounds of specific minorities that the test cannot measure and they must inevitably impair its value as a predictor.' (*Defunis*, supra at n 68 at 329.)

Law schools which intend to change the racial and economic composition of their student bodies must

> ... re-examine the larger issues of admissions, questioning the divine-like assumption that only numerical indices measure 'quality' or 'merit' or potential for performance in the trenches of a profession. And we must pierce the cost-benefit analysis which rationalises over-reliance on them. We must clarify admissions discussion with contextual analysis of fundamental policies.[69]

Cognitive factors alone (academic performance at previous educational institutions, and LSAT or other standardised scores), should not be the narrow bases upon which law school admissions stand. Just as institutions of higher learning have used a variety of factors including whether parents or relatives are alumni/ae or are potential or actual donors to schools,[70] other indices such as whether an applicant adds to the development of a diverse and representative student population can be evaluated concurrently with academic criteria. These factors should include, race, gender, socio-economic status, geographic

origins and political orientation.[71] Other non-academic characteristics that
should be given probative weight to enrich the law school community are bilingualism, demonstrable community-service experience and maturity. Each
of these factors can be given quantitative weight in admissions decisions if the
policy decisions have been made that it is in the interests of society and
professional education that those who enter the society's leadership must
experience a society's diversity before their narrow view hardens into bigotry.
The argument is generally made that society has a duty to educate people of
promise from all walks of life. Law schools and policymakers that support that
view must consider its implications to all phases of qualification including staff
composition and law school curricula and teaching styles.[72]

This author would also like to encourage the view that all western societies
built on European expansionist ideologies of, at least, the past four hundred
years must examine the institutions that have evolved in these societies and,
most particularly, legal institutions.

Schools of legal education might begin considering if they are producing
graduates who are prepared to function in the year 2000 in a world of changing
demographics, greater international intimacy, shrinking resources and shifting
bases of political power. Will high scores on the LSAT help select lawyers who
can develop creative solutions to the problems of the broad range of economic
and social problems that must be solved in a changing world if we are to
survive? Much more than half the people of the world are from origins that
have been excluded from that power, people whose human and social needs
have been ignored and who have lost faith in the capacity of institutions in
the Anglo-American tradition to secure justice for them.

> Society needs to think once again about the kind of equality it would prefer and
> about the desired relation between productivity, social status, and standard of
> living. Most of all, it needs to distinguish between education as preparation for
> service to society, education as preparation to get more out of living, and education
> as a means of certifying social status.[73]

The decision to change admissions criteria will inevitably be a catalyst for
other changes.[74] The next section describes the Urban Legal Studies Program
which was developed to implement an alternate vision of higher education
flowing from institutional commitments to serve society. One of these obligations is that learning should include as many representatives of those formerly
excluded from legal education and the legal profession. Changes must be
considered in every phase of the process; including teaching, counselling and
curriculum development.

The Urban Legal Studies Program: theory into practice

In 1975, the City College of New York established a unique experiment in
legal education: The Urban Legal Studies Program which is designed to
increase inclusion of diverse students into legal education and the profession
with as little attrition as possible.

The Urban Legal Studies Program (ULS) initially taught and administered
by the City College and New York Law School is presently in affiliation with
CUNY Law School at Queens College. It provides a six-year course of study
leading to the BA–JD degrees and focuses on the practice of law in an urban

environment. Its goals include the education of highly qualified, committed professionals who use their skills as advocates for the underserved.[75] Coordination of the ULS Program is maintained by the Center for Legal Education and Urban Policy of the City College of New York[76] in association with the programme's law school partner, CUNY Law School at Queens.[77]

Each year since 1975, through a special and competitive application process, to be discussed below, up to thirty students are selected for admission to the programme.[78]

Students who are accepted into the Urban Legal Studies Program and intend to be eligible for admission to CUNY Law School at Queens after the completion of three years are required to have completed 96 credits at City College from three approved categories of courses in addition to satisfying each individual's college-wide requirements. The Urban Legal Studies Major consists of three categories of courses plus individual university-wide requirements (foreign languages, maths and possibly other basic skills development): liberal arts honours; required law and law-related courses; and urban selections.

Liberal arts honours

The liberal arts honours programme provides learning opportunities and challenges in traditional academic studies through enriched introductory courses. Liberal arts honours students are required to complete up to thirty credits (but no less than twenty-eight) in each of three divisional areas: the Social Sciences, Humanities, and Natural Sciences.

Urban Legal Studies required Law and Law-related Courses

First Year	*Spring Semester*
First Year	
Introduction to Law and Legal Process I	*Introduction to Law and Legal Process II*
Introduction to Legal Writing	*Logical Thinking and Writing*
Second Year	
Constitution Law I	*Constitutional Law II*
Law school course equivalent	Law School course equivalent
Third Year	
Criminal Law	*Family Law*
Law School course equivalent	Law School course equivalent

AND   A clinical internship MUST be taken for a stipend or credit *after* the successful completion of *Legal Research* and before Law School admission – *4 credits or $400.00*

Students are assigned to work under the supervision of a lawyer or sitting judge.

Urban selections

ULS students must select seven (7) courses from advanced electives in the Social Sciences and Humanities including, but not limited to: Political Science, Anthropology, Economics, Sociology, Psychology, History, Philosophy, Area Studies, Black Studies, Jewish Studies, Latin American and Caribbean studies, Women's Studies, and Asian Studies.

These courses are inter-disciplinary and are intended to clarify the social, cultural, economic and political conditions which, of necessity, affect the work of the urban lawyer. They encourage an examination of institutions which affect powerless segments of the society – and they provide the analytic tools needed for developing creative perspectives and contributions to the fundamental problems of the urban situation which can include social as well as legal alternatives.

The curriculum approaches and teaching methods of the required two semesters of *Introduction to Law and Legal Process, Introduction to Legal Writing* and *Logical Thinking and Writing* have been developed since the inception of the programme to address the collective and individual needs of ULS students on the threshold of the study of law. The entire new ULS class attends together for the first year beginning the process of development of personal respect, academic support systems, and loyalty to each other as through study and analysis students explore their cultural differences and experiential diversity. This process helps develop the group sense which stimulates intellectual and personal confidence, and educational growth.

Over the thirteen years of the programme's existence, the ULS student population has reflected the range of racial, ethnic and economic diversity characteristic of the College and the City after which it is named.[79] Numerical demographics aside, ULS first-year students can range in age from fifteen to fifty-five, can have attended school recently as new high school graduates or have not been at any school since they dropped out years earlier; they may be bilingual and recent immigrants or may have never left the borough of their births except on infrequent family outings. They may be single parents, spouses, gay or straight, community activists through secular or church based groups, graduates of elite New York City public high schools, or be recipients of hard-earned General Education Equivalency Diplomas (GED) taken long after they dropped out of school. They may be veterans of the military, military reservists through conviction or financial need, non-violent disciples of Reverend Martin Luther King, Jr or Gandhi, or supporters of armed struggle by the African National Congress and the PLO in their struggles for national liberation. They may be Muslims, Christians, Jews, Buddhists or Mystics, devout or atheist.

In the first months of their entry into the programme, their primary commonality includes the ability to read and write at least at the 12th grade level as indicated by standardised skills assessment tests and an articulated personal commitment to use the law and legal profession as a means of social change and amelioration, however construed.

The entwined intellectual purposes of the first-year ULS required courses are to appraise and test the capacity of each student's individual readiness for the intellectual processes required for legal reasoning, logical thinking and the theoretical demands of higher education; to advise and involve the student in a plan of oral, written and visual learning which consolidates the student's accomplishments and competencies and improves the intellectual and personal areas which need strengthening; to develop the intellectual habits of problem-solving and the identification of relevant and irrelevant issues; to develop the skills of logical oral persuasion and public poise; to develop and hone writing skills which enable students to write logically as a separate but related process from thinking logically; and ultimately, to build respect, among and between students and teachers, for diversity, difference, and the heuristic search for academic understanding which occurs at individual rates of speed.

Syllabi and teaching approaches to students have evolved from the past twelve years of analysing ULS students' academic performance at the college level and in law school at staff and teaching retreats and meetings which evaluate how effective various teaching methodologies are for realising academic and social goals with students.[80]

Mentors and role models

In 1978, when the Urban Legal Studies Program and the Max and Filomen M Greenberg Center for Legal Education and Urban Policy were only three-years-old and before any ULS student had entered law school, the Charles H Revson Foundation granted the first three years of funding to the centre to select 24 outstanding public interest lawyers and other professionals – eight each year – to work with the programme. These first Fellows, all of whom were part-time, taught special courses, supervised ULS interns off campus, clinical placements in legal service agencies, law offices, and community.

An underlying presumption of the Revson Program is that the fellowships should provide special opportunities for renewal and reflection by hardworking urban lawyers who have experienced struggles similar to those ULS students face. They also serve as role models, mentors and teachers for Urban Legal Studies students. That intention has been more than realised over the past years. During their tenure, Fellows have completed law journal articles, books and plays, considered career changes, become parents, taken advanced degrees, established or become more active in community based legal assistance projects and other organisations with a public interest focus, ascended to the bench, become law professors at other institutions and become ULS Program partisans affecting legal education institutions in the United States and the United Kingdom.

Perhaps most important to the ULS community, every year since 1979 when the first Fellows began, close personal relationships have been forged between ULS students and Fellows which continue long past the actual term of the Fellowship. ULS students and alumni/ae are working in past Fellows' law offices, have become close personal friends and colleagues with Fellows, have worked together on joint projects including electoral campaigns and legal challenges on behalf of under-represented constituencies (tenants, welfare recipients, the old, the homeless and the young) and have initiated academic projects.[81]

In 1981, after an independent evaluation of the programme by then NYU Law Professor John Costonis, the Revson Foundation provided funds for another three years. This grant, recognising the need to provide staff continuity and time for experimentation with the innovative ULS curriculum, provided funding for three more years supporting three non-renewable part-time fellowships for each year, and two full-time renewable fellowships. In 1985, the Revson Foundation provided another three-year grant, the first year of which provided funding for two full-time Fellows, and three part-time Fellows and the last two years' support for four part-time Fellows, one of whom was responsible for ULS internships and clinical work. The Foundation also sponsored the Charles H Revson Urban Law and Policy Lecture Series. The inaugural lecture of the series was given by Professor Derrick A Bell, Jr in November 1985 in observance of the Tenth Anniversary of the establishment of the Urban Legal Studies Program, the second by Professor Kader Asmal, Senior Lecturer in Law, Trinity College, Dublin. The third will be held in the Fall of 1988 to which a distinguished woman jurist will be invited.

In 1988, the Revson Foundation provided another three-year grant to support three Fellows to continue the innovative development of the programme and a fourth to edit the past years of unique curriculum developed by Fellows with the intention of a publication to be completed in 1991.

The Revson Fellowship Program has made an incalculable contribution to the centre and the Urban Legal Studies Program. Most importantly, perhaps, Fellows are also unique models for ULS students. In addition to the intellectual energy generated by the addition to the community each year of Fellows who are immersed in struggles in the public interest and who bring to their teaching and every other contact their experiences and passion for the use of law as an instrument of social change, we have benefited from their contributions to curricular innovations which merge legal, conceptual, and societal issues in unique ways. Some of these courses, developed and refined by Revson Fellows have become part of the permanent Urban Legal Studies curriculum. Revson Fellows Donna Lieberman and Terence Cannon who served first as part-time Fellows and then as full-time staff have been particularly influential in the development of this first-year curriculum.

These first-year courses are taught in a coordinated fashion between those teaching legal process, legal writing and legal reasoning and they focus on analysis of fact patterns, the recognition of evidence, the use and evaluation of analogy, syllogistic reasoning, the uncovering of logical contradiction and fallacies utilising cases and law-related materials and issues.[82]

Students who successfully complete the first year of the programme are expected to have the capacity to read casebooks, analyse (brief) cases and have conscious awareness of their verbal and written areas of strength and weakness and strategies to address these needs. They also have developed a sense of community.

Students who stay on after the first year of the programme will most certainly complete their BA degree and will probably continue to law school and if they enter law school, they will complete it successfully.[83]

Upon successful completion of the three years of the undergraduate curriculum, students may enter the cooperating law school. The BA degree is awarded at the end of the fourth year of the programme (the first year of law school) and the JD at the end of the sixth or the student may continue on for a fourth year to completion of the BA.

One of the original goals of the programme was to test the assumption that seven years of post-secondary education were not essential to the preparation of a competent lawyer; that six years would be adequate, and considerably less expensive, while content and quality of education would not be sacrificed.

A number of very competent lawyers prepared in the Urban Legal Studies

Program can attest to the validity of this assumption. However, some ULS students choose to stay at City College for a fourth year so they may inquire more deeply into subject matters to which they have been introduced by the integrated ULS curriculum.[84] Therefore, some students have deferred admission to law school so they might take additional courses in, for example, Literature, International Studies, Political Science, Women's Studies, Mathematics, Theatre, Creative Writing, Russian, and other languages and to study abroad (Japan, China and Zimbabwe) for a final undergraduate year. One of the serendipitous results of the programme has been the emergence of scholarly interests in a broad range of disciplines in addition to law and society in students whose preparatory education had been limited to the public high schools they had attended.[85]

Another presumption of the ULS Program, evolved from our experiences is that intellectual range like cultural diversity is an essential element in the development of excellent public interest practitioners who return to their communities to practise or who serve the society in other ways.

ULS recruitment: selection and admissions policies

A qualified model need not connote narrow or mechanical decision-making. Rather, it is an opportunity for schools to assign numerical weights to any set of student characteristics that are consonant with their changing institutional missions. Thus law schools may develop comprehensive, well thought-out admissions procedures responsive not only to their educational goals, but also to the moral and social responsibilities incumbent on institutions in a pluralistic society.
Brown and Morenco *Law School Admissions Study*, MALDEF (1980) at 54.

The Urban Legal Studies Program has been described in the Harvard Educational Review[86] as a 'model' for minority admissions programmes after the *Bakke*[87] decision and as a 'prototype' for the 'creation of a qualified and diverse student applicant pool for law school'.[88]

However, the ULS Program is not a minority admissions programme. In keeping with the educational and social obligations of the City College of New York which has fostered academic excellence and scholarship in students from every sector of the urban community since its founding in 1847, City College has built bridges to professional and intellectual careers, nurtured the talents of the non-affluent, non-well born and those traditionally excluded from higher education. It is a quintessential urban institution which prides itself on its cultural diversity, its symbiotic connections to the City and its responsiveness to the changing face and abiding ambition of its working class population.[89] The Urban Legal Studies Program in keeping with this accomplished academic and culturally sensitive urban tradition, vigorously seeks out and recruits potential applicants from a broad range of sources throughout the metropolitan area, in addition to the city's public and private high schools. Institutions contacted include churches, trade unions, community organisations and legal organisations such as the National Conference of Black Lawyers, Puerto Rican Legal Defence and Education Fund and the Asian American Legal Defence and Education Fund. Posters illustrated with photographs of actual students in all their diversity emphasising the possibility of a legal career in service to the urban community as a lawyer are placed throughout the city. Thousands of brochures and applications spelling out the admissions criteria are mailed out each year. ULS students speak at their former secondary schools to stimulate aspiration in young people just entering high school.

The goals of the programme to train excellent lawyers who will serve the needs of those who comprise the majority of any large urban setting – the non-affluent, the young, the old, the non-English speaking, people of colour and the ill – are emphasised. Eligible applicants must have a high school diploma, an 80 or better high school average at graduation,[90] a performance level of approximately twelfth grade or better in standardised skills assessment tests of reading and writing[91] and an expressed commitment to the goals of the programme.

Admissions decisions both to the ULS Program at City College and to CUNY Law School[92] are made about equally on the basis of academic criteria and on candidates' expressed and realised levels of commitment to use their legal skills on behalf of underrepresented urban constituencies. Commitment is appraised without reference to the applicant's academic standing by an independent evaluation of applicant's paper record: letters of recommendation and personal statements, and by individual personal interviews conducted by three members of the Admissions Committee, two faculty members and an Urban Legal Studies student in which candidates' maturity, leadership potential and integrity are evaluated during the course of an interview in which applicants discuss their extracurricular and community activities and life goals. Successful applicants must demonstrate strength in both academic and community orientation.[93]

This detailed and individualised method of selection which quantifies not only academic performance but also levels of maturity, leadership, and community involvement and responsibility has consistently produced a body of students from a broad range of experience and cultural origins, never yielding *less* than 50% people of colour, evenly divided overall among men and women whose family origins are almost exclusively from the working poor or from economically marginal and immigrant communities.[94]

ULS students tend to take a disproportionate share of academic prizes, scholarships and honours at the College and at the law schools they have attended and to create a mutually supportive environment in which they strive for academic and socially responsible excellence.

Notwithstanding the rigour of the curriculum and their daily struggles with the drugs, poverty, and societal neglect that beset their communities as well as their struggle for ordinary urban survival, ULS students accomplish and excel in the programme.[95]

Law school admissions

One of the most innovative aspects of the ULS Program apart from its orientation to preparing lawyers to serve interests and constituencies historically excluded from the benefits of the legal system and generally neglected by the majority of the legal profession, is its capacity to evaluate and prepare students for successful completion of law school and the passage of the Bar examination.[96]

Student performance in the law school level courses taught by law faculty jointly selected by the cooperating law school and the Urban Legal Studies

Program provides law schools with a reliable indicator of students' capacity to perform in law school and precludes reliance on the LSAT.[97]

Students can apply for admission to CUNY Law School[98] after they complete the special undergraduate three-year curriculum discussed above and they satisfy both university-wide and programme requirements. It is assumed that students will have achieved an overall 3.00 minimum Grade Point Average, an overall 2.00 or better average in the required law courses (assuming A = 4.00), have taken the LSAT examination, filed with the Law School Data Assembly Service (LSDAS) and have maintained a discernible commitment to law in the public interest as demonstrated by extracurricular activities, clinical and community involvement, and the students personal statement and personal interviews. Student performances in fact in the substantive law courses (Constitutional Law, Criminal Law and Procedure and Family Law) provide a far superior predictor of probable success in law school than the LSAT.[99]

Since the establishment of the programme all except two Urban Legal Studies students admitted to law school have completed the JD degree.[100] As of Spring 1988 85% of those completing law school have passed the Bar examination in at least one jurisdiction.[101]

Not all ULS students elect to attend CUNY Law School after the third year. Some continue at the College for a fourth year to satisfy undergraduate requirements and to broaden their education perspectives as discussed earlier and apply to other law schools or to CUNY. Others accelerate their undergraduate studies and apply to other law schools.[102]

Conclusion

The Urban Legal Studies Program seeks to address specifically and consciously the primary exclusionary barriers that have impeded access to the legal profession. Those barriers include LSAT as a criterion for law school success; students' prior educational and social backgrounds which encourage expectations of failure among the students themselves; cultural and social norms and attitudes in the higher educational institutions as manifested by the faculty and staff which have a dampening and chilling effect on learning by students from other social and economic strata; racial, ethnic, and gender isolation resulting from 'token' admissions of Black, Latin, Asian or other people of colour and women to learning and the destructive effect of the failure to provide teaching environments and viable role models in positions of authority and obvious competence as teachers, counsellors, staff and administrators.

The curriculum is designed to provide academic and personal support and development for students whose prior life and educational experiences have prevented them from developing the refined academic skills needed for success in higher education, in humanistic studies as well as the social sciences, and in professional legal education. It stimulates and nurtures academic and professional goals among women and men from racial, ethnic and economic backgrounds typically excluded from the practice of law and, consequently, the judiciary, legislatures, and other citadels of political power.

Within the limits of an extremely lean budget, thanks to the Revson Foundation, the programme can actively recruit lawyers from ethnic, minority, bi-lingual and poor origins, who typically have experienced their own primary struggles to enter the profession to serve as teaching staff, mentors and counsellors. They consciously create an environment that supports students more accustomed to societal neglect, indifference, and debasement. The community created enhances concepts of self-worth and professional potential, aiding not only themselves and their families but also their society and communities. The students know that their academic success at City College and at the law school constitutes a contribution to the future of this society.

It is a model of inclusion which can be modified for use in other societies committed to change the race, economic, class and gender composition of their legal profession and the judiciary.

NOTES

1   Cynthia Epstein Fuchs 'Reworking the Latent Agenda of Legal Education' (1986) 10 Nova LJ 449.
2   '... (A) law career in this society is a vital pathway to positions of power. To deny effective access to the profession is to deny totally access to judgeships and to limit severely access to government, business, and politics.' (Leo Letwin, 'Some Perspectives on Minority Access to Legal Education' (1969) Experiment and Innovation 2 (May) p 10.)
3   See for example Derrick A Bell Jr *Race, Racism and American Law* (1973) Brown and Co; Albie Sachs and Joan Hoff Wilson *Sexism and the Law* (1978) The Free Press; Kenneth M Stampp *The Civil Rights Record: Black Americans and the Law 1849–1970* (1970) Thomas Y Crowell Co; Sidney M Wilhelm 'Black Man, Red Man, White American: The Constitutional Approach to Genocide' (1969) *Catalyst* (Spring).
4   Report of National Comission on Civil Disorder 'Rejection and Protest: An Historical Sketch' (1968) 95.
5   '... Representatives and direct Taxes shall be apportioned among the several States which may be included within this Union, according to their respective Numbers, which shall be determined by adding to the whole Number of *free Persons* including those bound to Service for a Term of Years, *and excluding Indians not taxed, three fifths of all other Persons.* The actual Enumeration shall be made within three Years after the first Meeting of the Congress of the United States, and within every subsequent Term of ten Years, in such Manner as they shall by Law direct.' US Constitution, Art I, §2 (emphasis supplied).
6   AMENDMENT XIII [1865]
    SECTION 1. *Neither slavery nor involuntary servitude,* except as a punishment for crime whereof the party shall have been duly convicted, shall exist within the United States, or any place subject to their jurisdiction ... Idem (emphasis supplied).
    AMENDMENT XIV [1868]
    SECTION 1. All persons born or naturalised in the United States and subject to the jurisdiction thereof, are citizens of the United States and of the State wherein they reside. No State shall make or enforce any law which shall abridge the privileges or immunities of citizens of the United States; nor shall any State deprive any person of life, liberty, or property, without due process of law; nor deny to any person within its jurisdiction the equal protection of the laws.
    SECTION 2. Representatives shall be apportioned among the several States according to their respective numbers, counting the whole number of persons in each State, *excluding Indians not taxed.* But when *the right to vote at any election* for the choice of electors for President and Vice President of the United States, Representatives in Congress, the Executive and Judicial officers of a State or the members of the Legislature thereof, *is denied to any of the male inhabitants of such State,* being twenty-one years of age, and citizens of the United States, or in any way abridged, except for participation in rebellion or other crimes, the basis of representation therein shall be reduced in the *proportion which the number of such male citizens* shall bear to the whole *number of male citizens twenty-one years of age in such State* ... Idem (emphasis supplied).
    AMENDMENT XV [1870]
    SECTION 1. The right of citizens of the United States to vote shall not be denied or abridged by the United States or by any State on account of race, color, or previous condition of servitude ... Idem.
    AMENDMENT XIX [1920]
    The right of citizens of the United States to vote shall not be denied or abridged by the United States or by any State on account of sex. Idem.
7   See for example *Sweatt v Painter* 339 US 629 (1950) (segregated law schools, unequal in respect to specific benefits enjoyed by white students); *Brown v Board of Education* 347 US 483 (1954)

('separate but equal' doctrine as applied to education violative of Constitution); *Jones v Mayer Co* 392 US 409 (1968) (outlawing private discrimination in housing); *Loving v Virginia* 388 US 1 (1968) (declaring State antimiscegnation Statute void); *Bradwell v Illinois* 83 US (16 Wall) 130 (1873) (woman forbidden to practise law). But note that discrimination on the basis of race but not sex is forbidden by the Civil Rights Act of 1964.

8   Continuing political struggles on the rights of people of colour and women in US society are in the background of every contemporary event. Readers are referred inter alia to Barbara A Babcock et al *Sex Discrimination and the Laws: Causes and remedies* (1975) Little Brown; Bell, supra; Higgenbottham *In the Matter of Color* (1978); Zinn, Howard *A Peoples History of the United States* (1986); Van Woodward *The Strange Career of Jim Crow* (1974).

9   For a comprehensive discussion of the policy issues involved in professional school admissions, see *Selective Admissions in Higher Education* (1977) the Carnegie Council on Policy Studies in Higher Education, Jossey-Bass Inc.

10 See for example *Rutgers Law Review*, vol 24 (Fall '69); *Univ of Toledo (Ohio) Law Review*, vol 277 (Spring '70); *Rutgers Law Review*, vol 31 (Fall '79); *Duke Law Journal* April (1987); Mexican American Legal Defense and Educational Fund *Law School Admissions Study* (1980) by Brown and Marenco.

11 See discussion below.

12 Bar examinations, character investigations, and other specific rituals for admissions to the Bar in the 50 states and the District of Columbia will be discussed in a subsequent article.

13 Green, Philip 'The New Individualism' in (1981) Christianity and Crisis 41 (30 March) pp 79–80.

14 See the Urban Legal Studies Program discussed as an alternative model for non-racist and democratic inclusion in legal education in MALDEF *Law School Admissions Study*, at 54; Harvard Educational Review, 'Minority Admissions Program After Bakke' (1979) vol 49 No 3 at 313.

15 Charles E Consalus 'The Law Admission Test and the Minority Student' U Tol L Rev 1970 at 277, 501, 502.

16 E Keasbey *Courts and Lawyers of New Jersey 1661–1912* (1912).

17 C Warren *A History of the American Bar* (1911) 4–5. Of course, as discussed earlier, 'by individuals' we mean male white property owners only.

18 A Chroust *The Rise of the Legal Profession in America* (1965) at 11–12, 27. See also Roscoe Pound *The Lawyer From Antiquity to Modern Times* (1953) 132–133.

19 Keasbey, supra at 259–60.

20 Warren, supra at 18, 196, 211.

21 Chroust, supra at 85–6.

22 Some may consider conservatism a natural hazard of the legal profession.

23 Warren, supra at 214–215.

24 See inter alia, Kerner *Report of the National Advisory Commission on Civil Disorders* (1968) US Govt Printing Office (extended discussion of Black and Latino communities' rage at exclusion from powerful roles in law and politics and presence as professionals in the prosecution of young minority people accused during 1960s urban uprising).

25 A Reed *Training for the public Profession of the Law* (1921).

26 A Reed *Present-Day Law Schools in the United States and Canada* (1928) at 6–7.

27 Reed (1928), supra at 90–102.

28 The American Bar Association (ABA) was a segregated white membership organisation by law and custom from its founding until the end of the sixties.

29 A Harno *Legal Education in the United States* (1953) at 73–9 (Abe Lincoln had studied law as an apprentice and had not gone to school beyond the secondary level).

30 Warren, supra at 166. Under the apprenticeship system a young man (sic) earned nothing for three to five years. In addition, he had to pay for the privilege of clerking: a fee of one or two hundred dollars a year was common, and a famous mentor could demand as much as five hundred dollars.

31 See generally, A Chroust, Supra at n 18 and R Pound, supra at n 18.

32 Consalus, supra at n 15 at 502.

33 This discussion of legal education is primarily focussed on access to rather than the content of legal education which is certainly related, especially curriculum. For some excellent discussions on curriculum issues in legal education, the reader is referred to *Transforming Legal Education: A Symposium of Provocative Thought* (1986) Nova Law Journal, volume 10, Number 2 (Winter). This author will also be collaborating on a collection of innovative law and society curricula to be published in 1991.

34 For an excellent extended discussion of the initial experiences of minority students seeking legal education during this first wave of non-traditional people's entry to law schools see, *Univ*

of Toledo Law Review (Spring-Summer 1970); see also US Commission on Civil Rights *Towards Educational Opportunity: Affirmative Admissions Programs at Law and Medical Schools* (1978) Clearinghouse Publications 55 (June).

[35] 42 USC 2000d (1974); 3CFR §339–348 (1964–1965 comp).

[36] But see Kairys, David (ed) *The Politics of Law: A Progressive Critique* (1982) Pantheon Books. For an extended discussion from a number of perspectives of law as the 'major vehicle for maintenance of existing social and power relations by the consent or acquiescence of the lower and middle classes in a society ... characterised by domination by a very small, mainly corporatised (sic) elite', Kairys at 5.

[37] The LSAC is the legal education research and data compilation arm of the Educational Testing Service (ETS) of Princeton, New Jersey which also administers the Law School Admissions Test, hereinafter 'LSAT', to be discussed in greater detail below and elsewhere in this volume.

[38] See for example Carnegie Council on Policy Studies in Higher Education *Selective Admissions in Higher Education* (1977) hereinafter 'Carnegie Report'.

[39] For vivid descriptions of the experiences of spiritual and intellectual isolation and overt hostility experienced by black and women law students prior to 1975, see Derrick A Bell Jr 'Black Students in White Law Schools: The Ordeal and the Opportunity' (1970) U of Tol LR supra at n 15 at 536; J Otis Cochran 'The Law School's Programmatic Approach to Black Students' (1972) Howard Law Journal, vol 17 at 358 and Epstein, supra at n 1; cf Duncan Kennedy 'Legal Education as Training for Hierarchy' in Kairys *The Politics of Law*, supra at n 36 at 40. And see Richard Chused 'The Hiring and Retention of Minorities and Women on American Law School Faculties' (1988) 137 U of Pa L Rev 537.

[40] Carnegie Report at 98.

[41] Ibid at 97.

[42] Undergraduate Grade Point Averages (hereinafter UGPA) are calculated from all grades earned by a student in a college or university prior to receipt of a degree. In general, grades are awarded on a point scale with 4 equalling the best grade 'A'; 3, 'B'; 2 'C'; 'D', (the lowest passing grade). A failing grade of 'F' will generally result in a deduction from the grade point average by a formula based upon the number of credit hours for which it is taken. UGPA is, with the LSAT or other standardised tests (Graduate Record Examination, GRE, etc), the most important and common index used to define academic excellence in higher education in the United States.

[43] Carnegie Report, supra at 112.

[44] John H Wigmore 'Juristic Psychopolyemetrology – or How to Find Out Whether a Boy Has the Makings of a Lawyer' (1929) 24 Ill L Rev 463.

[45] Wigmore, supra, prophetically wrote: 'What is not to be encouraged is the premature acceptance of any particular test as dependable ... Faith in any particular test ought to wait a lengthy process of verification. We cannot afford to be too sanguine. The human mind is almost infinite in its variable individualism. The varient factors are numerous and often untraceable.' Ibid at 454, 455.

[46] Robert Lunn 'Test Bias and the Prediction of Grades in Law School', 'Reports of LSAC sponsored Research (1977) 3 vol Princeton, NJ LSAC; reprinted in (1975) 27 J Legal Ed 293–323. Emphasis supplied.

[47] Brill 'The Secrecy Behind the College Boards' (1974) New York Magazine, 7 Oct.

[48] Evans *Applications and Admissions to ABA Accredited Law Schools: An Analysis of National Data for the Class Entering in the Fall of 1976* Law School Admission Research 77–1 (1977).

[49] A free copy can be ordered from LSAC/LSAS, Box 2000, Newtown, Pennsylvania 18940–0998, USA. Special LSAT tests for admission to Canadian law schools are also available at the above address.

[50] Terence M Cannon this volume, Ch 4.

[51] James A Thomas 'Heavy Traffic on the Purple Brick Road: The Route to Law School' at p 225 in *Hurdles* (1978) (ed) Herbert S Sacks et al, Atheneum.

[52] See for example, Joel Dreyfus and Charles H Lawrence III *The Bakke Case: The Politics of Inequality* (1979) Harcourt Brace Jovanovich and Montoya infra at note 54.

[53] Ibid at 138.

[54] Robert Montoya, 'The Myth of Reverse Discrimination' (1978) Health Pathways No 3 (Sept).

[55] Absolutely accurate racial data are hard to come by but reported statistics of the census data of the US population for the period discussed in *Law School Enrolment 1976–1979* are: (1978) 214,159,000 US citizens; 11.6% or, approximately 24,839,000 Black, 6.5% or approximately 14,000,000 Hispanic origins, more than 1% or 2,090,372 Asian; (1970) .03 or 93,000 (1970) Native American. US Dept of Commerce, Bureau of Census *Statistical Abstract of the US* (Wash, DC) (1978) Government Printing Office.

[56] The 1978 census figures are certainly inaccurate in respect to persons of Latin/Hispanic origins since most categories of this census were classified as 'white' or 'black'. In addition there are no 1978 statistics for Asians or Native Americans.

[57] National Association for Law Placement (NALP) Washington, DC, February, 1987. Report quoted in *National Law Journal*, Vol 10, No 22, 8 Feb, 1988, in 'White Males Dominate Firms: Still a Long Way to Go for Women, Minorities' p 1, 48 et seq.

[58] *Statistical Abstract of the United States* 1964 at 229; 1986 at 402, US Dept of Commerce and Bureau of the Census.

[59] Barbara Curran *The Lawyer Statistical Report* (1985) American Bar Foundation, Chicago at p 10.

[60] *Statistical Abstract* (1964) p 229.

[61] *Statistical Abstract* (1986) p 402.

[62] Felicienne H Ramen 'Minority Lawyers in California: A Survey' (1978) Los Angeles Daily Journal Report 17 November.

[63] See esp Brief *Amicus Curiae for American Association of Law Schools (AALS) in Support of Petitioner* (*No 76-811*), *The Regents of the Univ of Cal v Bakke* 438 US 265 (1978). For an excellent analysis of the *Bakke* case which has had a profoundly chilling effect on the zeal and imagination with which law schools have been addressing minority admissions, see MALDEF *Law School Admissions Study*, supra esp V 'Analysis of the *Regents of the University of California v Bakke*' at p 33.

[64] Jeffrey Blum *Pseudoscience and Mental Ability* (1978) Monthly Review Press p 100.

[65] Althea T L Simmons, Director, Washington Bureau of the National Association for the Advancement of Coloured People (NAACP), statement before the Subcommittee on Elementary, Secondary and Vocational Education of the House Committee on Education and Labour on HR 3564, 'The Truth in Testing Act of 1979' and HR 4949 'The Educational Testing Act of 1979' 24 September, 1979. Testimony prepared in conjunction with Dr Anderson J Franklin, Professor of Psychology and (then) Director of the Center for Academic Skills, City College of the City University of New York. See also, publications of the Asian American Legal Defense and Education Fund, 99 Hudson Street, New York, NY 10013, Puerto Rican Legal Defense and Education Fund, 99 Hudson Street, New York, NY 10013. *Fair Test*, the publication of the National Center for Fair and Open Testing, Box 1272 Harvard Square Station, Cambridge, MA 02238, USA is particularly useful for analyses of the racist and sexist impact of all standardised tests of this type.

[66] By 'disadvantaged' I mean poor, but the term 'disadvantaged' has currency in professional life. This author prefers the plain four letter word.

[67] Allen P Sindler *Bakke, DeFunis and Minority Admissions* (1978) Longman Inc at 28.

[68] 416 US 312 (1974). In 1970, the University of Washington Law School rejected applicant Marco DeFunis, a white man whose grades and test scores rate as high or higher than those of minority applicants who had been offered admission to the school. DeFunis challenged the constitutionality of the school's admissions policy which considered minority applications separately and by different criteria and argued that the school's policies discriminated against him on the grounds of race in violation of the fourteenth amendment (qv supra at note 6) and asked for injunctive relief to compel his admission. The trial court granted his relief, the Supreme Court of Washington reversed and upheld the school's admission policies but let him remain in school. By the time the US Supreme Court heard his case on writ of certiorari, he was almost finished with law school. By *per curiam* opinion (of 5 justices) the court held the case moot under Art III, US Const and refused to hear the merits. Justices Douglas, Brennan, White and Marshall dissented. *Cf Regents of the Univ of California v Bakke* 438 US 265 (1978).

[69] Peter J Liacouras *Toward a Fair and Sensible Policy for Professional School Admission, Cross Reference* (1978) vol 1, No 5 (March-April) p 157.

[70] See MALDEF, Law School Admissions Study, supra *Table 2 Non-Cognitive Characteristics that Enter into Admissions Decisions* p 27.

[71] For example regions of the United States represented as well as urban and rural origins.

[72] Can we argue persuasively that in the Commonwealth a specific number of A levels passed (or points) is the best criterion for the study and practice of law?

[73] Lee J Cronbach 'Five Decades of Public Controversy over Mental Testing' in *System of Multicultural Pluralistic Assessment* Riverside: Univ of Cal 1977–1978; reprint from *American Psychologist* (January 1984) pp 15–41.

[74] See esp Lennox S Hinds 'The Rutgers Report: The White Law School and the Black Liberation Struggle' in *Essays to Demystify Law, Order, and the Courts* (1971) (ed) Robert Lefcourt, Vintage Books, New York and Arthur Kinoy 'The Rutgers Minority Student Program: Commitment, Experience, and the Constitution' (1976) Rutgers Law Journal 857.

[75] 'Underserved' is used here as a generally encompassing term meant to include not only the economic status of clients but also the substantive areas of law which have a substantial impact

on urban populations but which are generally not viewed as lucrative by the profession. For example, environmental issues, the legal problems of the aged, children, the mentally handicapped, abused women and children, the medically indigent, the homeless and undocumented migrants. Such representation can be provided through publicly and privately funded legal service projects or through *pro bono* projects of law offices in private practice.

76 The Center for Legal Education and Urban Policy, in addition to coordinating the ULS Program, is engaged in a programme of community and campus based activities enriching the environment in which the ULS Program functions. Such activities include, but are not limited to the development of law-related curricula for the public (state-supported) schools; the sponsorship of colloquia and seminars on legal issues open to academics, the local Harlem community and general public; and lay education and referrals on legal matters of special interest to community organisations and residents.

77 CUNY Law School, whose motto is 'Law in the Service of Human Needs', was established as part of the state supported City University of New York System in 1983. Its mission is to produce public interest lawyers, and its programme, based largely on clinics, not classes, is to teach not just law but lawyering: negotiation, counselling, advocacy and ethics. 'It is a labor-intensive enterprise, placing far greater demands on teachers than on law professors elsewhere. Its students are older and more diverse and its atmosphere is just as distinctive. The hierarchy depicted so vividly in "The Paper Chase" has been banished; everyone – professors, students and janitors – is on a first-name basis and one finds no pompous teachers nor quivering students.' Author's paraphrase from CUNY Law School at Queens College, catalogue, 1987–1988.

78 Originally conceived by then City College President Robert E Marshak and the New York Law School Dean E Donald Shapiro and developed by a joint City College/New York Law School Executive Committee made up of student representatives, faculty and administrators from both institutions. An intake of up to 50 students had been contemplated. It was clear by the time this author joined the Administration and Executive Committee in January 1977 that the academic and social demands of the programme required either more resources or fewer students.

79 As of the Fall '88 term, the ULS population of 125 students in all six years of the programme include 52% women; 40% black, 40% Hispanic and 20% Asian and white, 95% of whom must work at jobs while they attend school and 25% of whom are parents. They range in age from 16 to 45.

80 Since the Urban Legal Studies Program and the Center for Legal Education were established in 1975 coincident with a severe fiscal crisis in New York City, no permanent faculty lines were identified to the fledgling programme and a commitment was made by the college that the centre would seek private sector support for its activities and the innovative curriculum development and teaching of the programme for the first ten years of existence.

81 **Summary of gender and racial composition**

Charles H Revson Urban Legal Fellows 1979–1988				
	Asian	*Black*	*Latino*	*White*	*Total*
Male	2	14	6	7	29
Female	1	7	2	6	16
Grand total	3	21	8	13	45

82 Copies of specific Urban Legal Studies curricula including substantive law courses are available on request from the Center for Legal Education. As discussed above, the Revson Foundation has provided a three-year grant to the centre to prepare a text from the innovative legal education and substantive law and social issues curricula developed by Revson Fellows beginning in 1978. It is anticipated that the completed volume will be available in 1991.

83 ULS students, with only two exceptions, have completed the law schools to which they were admitted. Over one hundred ULS alumni/ae have entered the legal profession since 1981, the first year in which ULS students completed law school. They have consistently passed the Bar examination at rates as high or higher than the state wide average. ULS graduates are to be found in Legal Aid, Legal Services, other government services, prepaid private legal plans, private practices with *pro bono* clients and, in the main, have maintained a public interest orientation.

84 'Integrated' in this context is used to define a curriculum which considers the study of law and legal institutions as inseparable from the political, economic, and social contexts in which they function.

[85] As discussed below, many ULS students come from non-academic high schools or have GED certificates taken after they dropped out of high school.

[86] John Sexton, 'Minority Admissions Program After *Bakke*' Harvard Educational Review, Vol 49, No 3 (1979).

[87] *Regents of the University of California v Bakke* 438 US 265 (1978). Supra at n 68.

[88] Brown, Susan E and Eduardo Marenco Jr *Law School Admissions Study*. Supra at n 14 at p 54.

[89] Seven City College alumni have won the Nobel Prize. CCNY ranks fourth nationally in the total number of graduates in all disciplines who have gone on to earn the PhD degree and ranks seventh in the number of alumni/ae elected to the National Academy of Sciences.

[90] People who have not attended any school for two years or more do not have a high school Grade Point Average requirement but must satisfy all other academic and personal criteria.

[91] The immediate academic demands of the ULS Program require that students have adequate reading proficiency and some writing potential upon admission. We do not have sufficient resources to provide students with less developed skills the capacity to achieve readiness to go forward in the ULS curriculum. There is no doubt in this author's mind that given staff resources, a very effective ULS Program could be developed for those who need additional time for skills strengthening but who are both motivated and committed to study.

[92] CUNY Law School Urban Legal Studies admissions will be discussed below.

[93] Approximately one out of four ULS applicants are accepted to the ULS Program. Non-successful applicants may be counselled to reapply after a successful year at the College building up skills or referred to the College's excellent pre-law programme which is more appropriate for people who will not benefit from an accelerated programme or who have no articulated interest in the study of law in the public interest.

[94] Persons interested in receiving a sample set of admissions materials, procedures, and guidelines can write to Center for Legal Education and Urban Policy, Shepard Hall 25, City College, New York, NY 10031 USA.

[95] All City College students (and CUNY Law School students) commute daily to their homes which may require a daily trip of two hours or more, typically on mass transit. In addition, as indicated above, they frequently maintain part-time jobs and manage families as well. In general, because of deep fiscal cuts in aid, most students are eligible for minimal financial support (grants) and must augment their incomes by work and loans.

[96] Brown and Morenco *Law School Admissions Study*, supra at n 15.

[97] The LSAT discussed in more detail above, purports to predict student success in the first year of law school and is, as discussed here and elsewhere, a major impediment to the entry to law school of students from Black, Hispanic, Native American and low income origins.

[98] CUNY Law School admissions policies for all applicants consider the LSAT as one factor towards admission as is past academic performance. But 'assessment of academic ability alone will not dominate the admissions process . . . (L)ess tangible qualities that make an outstanding lawyer, including judgment, energy, initiative and the ability to work both collaboratively and independently' will also be considered. CUNY Law School at Queens College *Bulletin 1987–1988* at p 35.

[99] Assuming without conceding the predictive value of the LSAT.

[100] In 1979, one student admitted to New York Law School at the end of three years was dismissed from the law school for academic reasons. He returned to City College, completed his BA, applied to and was admitted to another New York State law school from which he graduated. As of Summer 1988, he is awaiting the results of the New York State Bar exam. Another ULS student, a police officer, who completed the undergraduate four-year programme while he served on the night shift of the NYC Transit Police Department, took a leave from law school to which he plans on returning when he retires from the police force.

[101] The percentage includes ULS alumni/ae who received their JD degrees in the years since 1981, the first year in which ULS BA/JD degree students graduated. It includes ULS alumni/ae who passed the late Winter ('88) Bar exam. We do not know if all of the remaining 15% have taken any Bar exam. It does not include those who graduated from law school in June, 1988.

[102] For example, ULS students with BA degrees have been accepted to the law schools of Harvard, New York University, Georgetown, Columbia, Rutgers, Northeastern, Emory, Howard, Washington University, Hastings School of Law, inter alia. For many who receive adequate financial aid, it is an opportunity to see the United States apart from the New York metropolitan area. Still others apply to other law schools to test themselves and then elect to go to the cooperating law school thus 'staying with the community' as one student described her decision. A few have elected to take joint degrees (as for example, JD/Masters in Public Policy, Harvard and JD Rutgers/PhD, International Studies (CUNY) to satisfy intellectual and professional interests.

4 Admission tests for law school: some cautionary remarks

*Terence M Cannon**

For the last two decades a debate over the fairness and utility of standardised testing has been intensifying in the United States. The Scholastic Aptitude Test (SAT), taken by some 1.7 million students last year and used as an entrance exam by most US colleges, has come under fire as biased against women and minorities, and has been dropped by several small but prestigious colleges. Harvard Business School no longer requires students to take the Graduate Management Admissions Test. In 1987 Johns Hopkins University Medical School stopped requiring the Medical College Admissions Test.[1]

The Law School Admission Test (LSAT), used in the admissions process of nearly every American Bar Association-approved law school in the US and in many law schools in Canada, has also undergone serious criticism. First implemented in 1948 to control the flood of law school applications from returning GI's and others enjoying post-war prosperity and opportunity, it has served since its inception to narrow the pool of applicants to US law schools. When the civil rights and women's movements produced a new wave of law school applicants from previously under-represented populations, there also arose strong demands for reform of the LSAT, based on charges of cultural bias, elitism, and invalidity. It would therefore profit Commonwealth law schools considering the introduction of an LSAT-type examination into the legal education system to consider the issues raised by the US experience of the last forty years.

Is it fair?

The current shock over the SAT comes from recent studies that show that while high school girls earn higher grade point averages than boys – including in the freshman year of college – in 1986 girls averaged 61 points lower than boys on the SAT and were therefore denied admissions, programme and scholarships on the college level.[2] Commented one education researcher, 'A test taken by 800,000 females every year that doesn't accurately predict their abilities should be illegal. If boys were getting higher grades and lower test scores, the test would be rewritten.'[3] After researchers at the Massachusetts Institute of Technology (MIT) discovered in 1987 that SAT scores consistently

* Research Associate Center for Legal Education, City College of New York.

underpredicted women's college grades, the Institute began to weigh SAT scores differently for men and women.

On the issue of racial bias, both supporters and critics of the LSAT agree on one crucial fact: minority test-takers score approximately one standard deviation lower than majority test-takers.[4] This is an order of high magnitude. In a normal population, roughly 66% of the scores on a test will lie in the range of one standard deviation on either side of the mean. A study by Joseph Gannon of Boston College showed black students scoring a mean of 110 points less on the LSAT (former 200–800 grading system) than non-minority students *who had roughly equivalent grade point averages*.[5]

Today, no reasonable scholars, testing agencies or law school administrators would claim that this occurs because minorities are less able to 'think abstractly', or are 'undereducable' or any other euphemism for being less intelligent. Those few who do so argue are at best victims of the error of reification – holding that a number produced by a test actually has some concrete existence as 'intelligence'.[6] At worst, they are racist.

Since minority test-takers do score more poorly, and since they are just as intelligent en masse as those in the majority, then there are several – sometimes seemingly contradictory – explanations for the inequality of result: (1) the LSAT is culturally biased; (2) the LSAT is objective and therefore simply replicates the existing class and race biases of society and the educational system; (3) the LSAT can be coached, usually for a high fee, unaffordable by minority and working-class students. These explanations are not mutually exclusive.

Whether the LSAT is biased along class, race and sex lines is hotly debated. David M White of the National Conference of Black Lawyers has identified numerous LSAT questions which in his opinion demonstrate insensitivity to minority group traditions, intentionally ambiguous wording, ignorance of minority community values, assumptions contrary to those of minority group members, reinforcement of prejudicial stereotypes, and other characteristics that would lead minority test-takers to interpret answers to those questions 'wrongly'.[7] The Educational Testing Service (ETS), which created the LSAT, denies these allegations. In a letter to Mr White, Franklin R Evans, Program Research Scientist for ETS, stated,

> For many years, special efforts have been taken to eliminate any possible cultural bias in the LSAT. Minority staff members are assigned to work on the test and efforts are made to obtain a variety of outside item writers, including substantial numbers of women and minority writers. Efforts are made to include in each new test material of special interest to minorities and to women.[8]

If one reads an LSAT exam booklet as a cultural document, the world it portrays either tends toward the male, arcane and elitist or makes little effort to counter such a portrait. Choosing at random the February 1987 LSAT, for example, one finds few examples of material 'of special interest to minorities and to women'. Women's names appear in only two of the 26 problems in the Reasoning section, and then arbitrarily – without relationship to content. The only reference to 'minorities' is a logical problem written in language interpretable as racist: 'If the Tuli declare war, so will the Puki; and, if the Jambi declare war, so will the Ramki . . .'[9]

The Reading Comprehension section is yet more culturally remote. The first selection, written in dignified but unfamiliar nineteenth-century prose, concerns a literary gathering attended by Oliver Wendell Holmes and James

Russell Lowell. The second selection is a quotation from 'Glastonbury and the Holy Grail', by R F Treharne. The third is a theoretical essay on democratic government; the fourth a meditation on medicine and the scientific method. None is written in clear, concise, contemporary prose; none concerns current vital issues.

In this author's opinion, these sections are not biased because they demand specific knowledge of Lowell or Glastonbury Abbey or medicine. Instead, they handicap many students – women, minorities and working-class students in particular – because they are remote and unfamiliar in content, inaccessible in language and intimidating in tone. It is my experience as a teacher of legal writing, logical reasoning and problem-solving that students reason more quickly and confidently when they have some familiarity with the topic (not necessarily the content). I have found, for example, that an identical logical problem will be answered correctly more often when it is clothed in a familiar topic (child abuse), than an unfamiliar topic (tennis). Clearly, the student knows how to reason, but feels greater 'permission' to reason when the subject is accessible.

This is borne out in the 'Issues and Facts' section of the test, whose form is law-like (a fact pattern, a dispute, two legal-type rules, and questions that ask the test-taker to classify each question in terms of the relation of the rules to the dispute). The section opens with a statement that 'these questions do not presuppose any specific legal knowledge on your part . . .' and indeed they do not. However, students in the Urban Legal Studies Program at City College consistently score higher on this section – not because the questions require legal training, but because the language, the situations, the 'culture' of the problems are familiar and accessible. Language such as 'A teacher will not be subject to termination of contract for any classroom activity that is conducted with the prior approval of the principal' does not intimidate them. Our students are lucky in that respect; other students, not enrolled in legal studies, would be at a disadvantage.

On the other hand, culturally biased questions may not be the major cause of unequal test results. The LSAT may in fact accurately measure what it claims to measure: 'skills and knowledge typically developed over a long period of time'.[10] In this case the unequal scores reflect a history of prejudice, bigotry, discrimination, lack of opportunity, discouragement, existing social and economic deprivation – the entire socio-political system that also produces other lower 'scores': lower wages, lower educational levels, lower expectations. As the Law School Admissions Council, the administrator of the LSAT, put it in an *amicus* brief to the US Supreme Court:

> Like college grades, test scores penalise blacks not because the tests measure innate intelligence or mental capacity, but rather because they measure abilities which are taught, acquired, and developed in formal education. A different, inferior education naturally tends to produce different, inferior scores.[11]

Despite this revealing quote, it is regularly claimed by test-creators that students cannot usefully be coached – for if coaching works, then the tests do not measure academic potential, but rather the ability to take tests. Dean Whitla of Harvard, a consultant to the College Board, stated it frankly: 'If the Board's tests can regularly be beaten through coaching, then the Board itself is discredited.'[12]

Ironically, while claiming that the LSAT cannot or should not be coached, the Law School Admission Council is simultaneously leading the testing industry away from this very position.[13] Beginning in 1989, it is eliminating from its test the 'Issues and Facts' section – mentioned above as the most law-related and accessible – on the grounds that it is 'coachable'. At the same time, the LSAC is entering the multi-million dollar test-coaching industry, publishing two 'Official LSAT Sample Test' books ($14 each) and test-preparation computer software ($50–$75).

Since the LSAT is coachable, by now an incontrovertible fact, this aggravates the already existing class bias. Those who can afford $14 books, $50 computer software (plus the hardware to use it on), and $400-a-weekend commercial prep courses have an obvious advantage over those who cannot. Though I know of no statistics directly correlating income to LSAT scores, such figures do exist for the SAT, and they are indeed telling:[14]

Family Income	Average SAT
Over $50,000	982
$40,000–49,999	942
$30,000–39,999	916
$24,000–29,999	896
$18,000–23,999	866
$12,000–17,999	837
$ 6,000–11,999	794
Under $6,000	745

Is it useful?

All tests measure something. If we do not imagine that the LSAT score measures 'intelligence' or 'aptitude', what *does* it measure? In the words of its creators;

> The LSAT is designed to help law schools assess the academic ability of their applicants. It was not designed, nor is it intended to be used, to predict success in the practice of law. No study purporting to show a correlation between LSAT scores and success in the practice of law is known to LSAC/LSAS.[15]

The LSAC/LSAS makes no predictive claim for the LSAT score beyond an unimpressive correlation with first-year law school grades. Validity studies in 1986 showed that correlations between LSAT scores and first-year law school grades ranged from .20 to .66 depending on the law school. When combined with the undergraduate grade point average (UGPA), the correlation ranged from .33 to .71.[16] No predictive claim has ever been made beyond that of first-year law school grades. In fact some studies have shown that for second and third-year grades the LSAT has no greater predictive value than the UGPA.[17] Furthermore, since only those students *accepted* into law school are included in the measurement of correlation, the validity studies cannot take into account those who were not accepted, but who would have done well.

A test that only predicts – and with middling accuracy – the first-year grades of new law students raises larger questions: Is the LSAT useful to law students themselves and to potential law students? Is it useful to minorities and women? Is it useful to the legal profession? Is it useful to society at large? Perhaps most importantly: does the LSAT locate people who will be good lawyers and enable them to get a good legal education?

Undoubtedly, it locates some. Though we do not know how many students who grade well in their first year of law school go on to benefit their profession, their community and their society, it can be presumed that many will. We will never know how many students who might have performed poorly in their first year, or would have performed well despite a low score, would go on to be excellent lawyers, because the LSAT prevents most of them from entering law school in the first place.

How is it used?

Most schools use a formula to arrive at an Admission Index: $I = A (LSAT) + B (UGPA) + C$. The values of the relative weights A, B, and C are either determined by the school or suggested by the LSAS. How greatly these values differ can be seen by comparing the formulas used in the same year (1982) by Columbia Law School and Rutgers Law School:[18]

> Columbia: $I = (1.175 \times LSAT) + (10.132 \times UGPA)$
> Rutgers: $I = (.25 \times LSAT) + (2.32 \times UGPA) + 13.4544$

The influence of the LSAT score on the Admission Index 'I' is greatly diminished by the Rutgers formula, compared to the formula used by Columbia. A student with a 3.5 UGPA would increase her Columbia Index almost 12 points by scoring 30 rather than 20 on the LSAT. A similar rise in LSAT score by a Rutgers applicant would boost her Index a mere 2.5 points.

The Rutgers formula broadens the admissions pool to more women and minorities, but that raises again the central issue: if lowering the weight given the LSAT increases access to the legal profession – why have an admission test at all – unless one wishes to exclude women and minorities? Why not rely instead on grade point averages coupled with non-racist, non-sexist means of evaluating qualities vital to the legal profession, and which lead to an integrated, diverse professional membership?

Alternatives to the LSAT

The 40-year history of the LSAT is filled with attempts at reform and reformulation. The test was reorganised and rewritten in 1951, 1956, 1963 and 1970, but the most sweeping alterations came in June 1982 when the scoring system was changed from a 200–800 scale to a 10–50 scale (then later to its present 10–48 scale).

These revisions have done nothing to quiet the demand for reform, the most popular at this time being a call for the application of the 'Golden Rule' principle. Under this principle, test publishers must select those questions – within groups of equally-difficult items in the same content area – which result in the least difference in correct answer rates between majority and minority test-takers.[19]

Considerable variation is also possible in the *use* of the test results by law school. The relative weights given the LSAT score and the UGPA may be adjusted yearly. A law school may decide to use the Admission Index as a cut-off point or to establish flexible categories (Acceptable/Questionable/ Unacceptable). The written essay (ungraded) may be given any weight desired.

But much of this falls under the classification of 'tinkering'. No number of reforms can create a written standardised test that successfully compensates for social inequality in a multiracial, multiclass, multinational society. An entirely different approach is needed, one that considers qualities in a law school applicant not measurable by the LSAT or any other standardised test: enthusiasm, creativity, potential racial, sexual or ethnic contributions, motivation, concern for the community, and devotion to equal justice, to name but a few.

One model for this is the admissions process of the Urban Legal Studies (ULS) Program at City College, which gives equal weight to academic and non-academic criteria. The ULS process governs entry into a six-year accelerated programme resulting in both a bachelor's and a *juris doctor* degree. Beginning in their second year, ULS students take law-school level courses.

Applicants are first screened for minimal admissions criteria. This requires that they have high school averages of 80 or higher or college GPAs of greater than 2.8. Their applications and letters of recommendation are then numerically scored for leadership ability, self-awareness, maturity and urban legal commitment.

At a subsequent interview, interviewers (who have not had access to the academic portion of the application) question the applicant in two areas: (1) leadership ability, independence, self-awareness, maturity, judgment and social and intellectual growth, and (2) an awareness of legal and social community problems, a commitment to providing legal services where they are most needed, and an ability to relate life experiences and academic skills to broader problems or legal services in the urban community.[20]

These qualities are assigned scores by the interviewers in the team (composed of two City College faculty members and one ULS student). These figures are combined with a quantified score assigned to the written application, resulting in three pools of applicants grouped by their combined academic and non-academic scores. Applicants are then admitted in the order of their scoring, until the appropriate class size is reached.

The result of this selection process – and, of course, the six-year programme that follows – is an 85% first-time pass rate for the US Bar Examination for all ULS students who complete the programme (100% on the second try), an achievement unequalled by any law school or legal education programme in the United States.

Ultimately, the question behind the issue of whether to use admission tests or some other process of selection is – what goal do you want to achieve? Do you want to select for high first-year law school grades? For a high Bar Exam pass rate? For the inclusion of women and minorities? For prestige, and if so, by what standard of prestige? These goals are not necessarily mutually exclusive and they are achievable. It would be a pity if UK and Commonwealth law schools passed up the opportunity to develop a good selection process and became trapped into using some form of a test which *at best* accurately measures social inequities and quantifies them for administrative use in the school system.

NOTES

[1] *Fair Test Examiner* The National Center for Fair and Open Testing, Fall 1987, p 14.
[2] *Fair Test Examiner* The National Center for Fair and Open Testing, Spring 1987, p 2.
[3] Ibid.
[4] Joseph Gannon 'College Grades and LSAT Scores' in *Towards a Diversified Legal Profession* National Coalition of Black Lawyers, p 273.
[5] Ibid, p 277.
[6] For an excellent treatment of this subject, especially the errors of Cyril Burt, see Stephen Jay Gould *The Mismeasure of Man* New York, W W Norton, 1981.
[7] David M White 'An Investigation into the Validity and Cultural Bias of the Law School Admission Test' in *Towards A Diversified Legal Profession* Section D, p 132.
[8] White, p 269.
[9] LSAT Disclosure Booklet, test date 2/21/87, test form S-8ALS8.
[10] 1987–88 Law School Admission Test Law School Data Assembly Service Information Book, Law School Admission Services, Inc 1987, p 9.
[11] Brief of the LSAC in *Regents of the University of California v Bakke* 98 S Ct 2733 (1978).
[12] *Fair Test Examiner* Fall 1987, p 7.
[13] Edward A Adams 'Will Admissions Council Counteract A Change in Composition of LSAT?' The National Law Journal, 8 Feb, 1988, p 4.
[14] Ramist and Arbeiter *Profiles, College Bound Seniors, 1985* p 97.
[15] *1987–88 Law School Admission Test/Law School Data Assembly Service Information Book* Law School Admission Services, Inc 1987, p 30.
[16] Ibid.
[17] Donald E Powers, Educational Testing Service 'Predicting Law School Grades for Minority and Non-minority Students Beyond the First-Year Average' LSAC-81-1.
[18] LSAS Law School Report, Candidate Copy, 12/20/82.
[19] *Fair Test Examiner* Spring 1987, p 4.
[20] *Student Admissions Guidelines and Procedures* ULS Executive Committee, as revised Jan 1980.

Editors' Note: Statement of 'Cautionary Policies' by the Law Schools' Admissions Council is reproduced in Appendix 3 below.

5   Access to legal education in Australia

*David Weisbrot**

Modes of legal education

The legal profession in colonial Australia initially was composed of lawyers who had qualified in Great Britain or Ireland, or had taken their articles in Australia and passed a professional examination.[1] Law faculties emerged in the second half of the nineteenth century at Melbourne University (1857), Adelaide University (1876) and Sydney University (1890).[2] Apprenticeship remained a major mode of qualification well into the second half of the twentieth century, however, especially in New South Wales and Queensland.

In 1964, a review of higher education in Australia found that although the great majority of lawyers in most states were university graduates, only 50 per cent of barristers and 59 per cent of solicitors in New South Wales and 71 per cent of solicitors in Queensland had law degrees.[3] It was not until 1968 that yearly admissions to practice throughout Australia tipped in favour of university graduates, and not until the late 1970s that university-trained lawyers in New South Wales clearly overshadowed those admitted by apprenticeship.[4] While apprenticeship has been the main route of entry to most occupations in Australia, Law is alone among the professions in retaining this path.

In 1960, there were six university law schools in Australia – one in each state. By the mid-1970s the number had doubled, with second law schools established in Victoria and Queensland, three new law schools in New South Wales, and another established at the Australian National University in Canberra, the Australian Capital Territory (ACT). One of the law schools in each of Queensland and new South Wales was established in an Institute of Technology, the non-university half of the increasingly blurred binary divide in higher education.

Although phased out in Queensland in the 1970s, New South Wales retains another mode of entry into the legal profession through the Admission Board system. The Board, which is supervised by the Supreme Court, runs a programme of lectures at night and periodic examinations. Progress through this part-time course is slow and haphazard. Only about half of the 3000 enrolled students appear to be 'active' at any given time; less than one-quarter proceed through the course and receive a certificate with the minimum number of examination attempts; and a large proportion do not complete the course.[5]

Many students who would previously have attempted to qualify through

* Associate Professor of Law, University of New South Wales.

the Admission Board system are now attracted to the part-time or extension degree courses available at a number of tertiary institutions. Indeed, the law schools at the New South Wales and Queensland Institutes of Technology cater almost exclusively for part-time students, and after Macquarie University's law extension programme was established Admission Board examination sittings in the country areas of New South Wales declined dramatically. These programmes all reserve a significant number of places for persons with legally-related employment experience, such as those working as law clerks or in the magisterial services or justice department bureaucracies.[6]

Some states still offer limited opportunities to qualify for admission through apprenticeship. In Tasmania, a person who has served for five years as an articled clerk may be admitted after examination.[7] In Western Australia there is an equivalent admission procedure for articled clerks as well as special procedure for more experienced clerks.[8] New South Wales began to phase out entry through articles in 1968 and effectively closed it off in 1975.[9]

Numbers of lawyers

Undoubtedly, the most central empirical fact in the development of the modern Australian legal profession is the explosion of numbers over the past two decades. While numbers rose only modestly between 1911 and 1947 – and actually dropped slightly between 1933 and 1947 – there was a 600 per cent increase between 1947 and 1986, with much of that coming in the last decade. (See Table 1, below.)

Table 1   Number of Australian Lawyers 1911–1986

Year	Number of Lawyers
1911	2,955
1933	4,345
1947	4,329
1961	6,636
1975	12,580
1986	26,007

Sources: Australian Bureau of Statistics Census figures for 1911–1961 and 1986; 1975 figure from Disney et al, *Lawyers* (1977) 79.

The census figure for 1986 is somewhat higher than the legal professional associations recognise, since it includes those who self-identify as lawyers even though they may not all be current holders of practising certificates. Aggregating the figures supplied by all of the professional associations, there were close to 22,000 practising lawyers in Australia in mid-1985, about ten per cent of whom practised exclusively as barristers. Nearly three-quarters of these lawyers were located in New South Wales (9,347) and Victoria (6,134). These are by far the two most populous states, but they also have the lowest population-to-lawyer ratios. Whereas the legal profession did not grow as fast as the general population in Australia for the first half of this century, the ratio of population to lawyers has fallen significantly in all states and territories over the past 15 years. Overall, the figure is now 603:1 nationally, down from 1751:1 in 1947, 1600:1 in 1968, and about 1000:1 in 1977.[10]

Law school enrolments indicate that the legal profession will continue to expand. The number of law students more than doubled between 1950 and 1965 (to 3,039), and then nearly quadrupled between 1965 and 1984 (to 11,254) before levelling off in the past few years.[11] By comparison, there were 8,907 students studying medicine in 1984. As with practising lawyers, the great majority of law students are to be found in the largest states of New South Wales and Victoria, compounding the geographic imbalance in the profession. For example, over the next five years the production of lawyers in New South Wales through all modes of legal education is likely to be two to three times higher than in Western Australia on a per capita basis.[12]

Apart from a few brief flirtations with the idea, the legal professional associations in Australia have not really sought to impose restrictive supply-control measures. Instead, the profession has turned to market-control approaches to maintain income levels in the face of increased numbers. For example, the profession has: lobbied hard to defend its monopolies over lucrative areas of work, such as conveyancing; diversified the range of services available, to include, eg, investment and tax advising; authorised advertising; and benefited from public funding or subsidy of legal aid services.

In the late 1970s and early 1980s, when the numbers of law graduates and admissions to practice reached new levels after the doubling of the number of law schools, almost all the forecasts for employment of law graduates were very pessimistic, talking in terms of 'flood' and 'over-supply'. For example, an inquiry into legal education in New South Wales in 1979 recommended consideration of the reduction of student places, and saw this as a matter of some urgency, stating that 'action to deal with an excessive output of lawyers involving a waste of resources should not wait upon definitive statistical studies proving the point conclusively.'[13] This recommendation was not implemented, and in the event the panic and projections turned out to be quite wrong, so that the Commonwealth Tertiary Education Commission (CTEC) inquiry into legal education reported in 1987 that there would be a continued demand for law graduates and a widening field of employment.[14] Notwithstanding the palpably increased anxiety among law students, recent graduates have a remarkable employment record. The Graduate Careers Council of Australia found that in the years 1983–1987, over 96 per cent of law graduates were in full-time employment within months after graduation. This record is surpassed (very fractionally) only by graduates in accounting, medicine and dentistry.[15]

One reason for the continued high rate of employment of law graduates is the increasing willingness and ability of lawyers to work outside of the traditional modes of private practice. The Commonwealth Department of Employment and Industrial Relations (DEIR) estimates that 10–15 per cent of lawyers are employed by governments, while 'surplus' law graduates 'appear to be absorbed relatively easily into generalist administrative positions'.[16] A CTEC survey of law graduates found that 25 per cent were in employment which was either 'not essentially legal', or was 'essentially legal' but not private practice or government lawyering. This included work in teaching, legal publishing and corporations.[17] Another CTEC study found that some law graduates were also well placed to move into new areas of work: 'high technology and growth in service industries will increase demand for tertiary graduates ... in the traditional professions (eg law and accountancy) with a competency in, and understanding of, new techniques.'[18] These days most law students are obliged to, or choose to, enroll in joint-degree programmes, which provide graduates with an additional qualification in arts, commerce or science and enlarge the ambit of employment opportunities.[19]

An elite profession

The Australian legal profession does not reflect the socio-economic class, ethnicity or gender composition of the society at large. The recent huge expansion in numbers has resulted in a very young profession. The other key demographic shift has been in the significant increase in the number and proportion of women lawyers. However, the social background of young lawyers is, if anything, more elite than in previous generations.

As will be detailed below, the university law schools largely cater for a very select segment of society. University law students typically come from homes which are significantly more affluent than the norm; most attended selective or elite, private secondary schools; their parents mainly have professional or management backgrounds, and many already have family connections in the legal profession.

On the other hand, the Australian legal profession has traditionally allowed entrants to qualify for admission by means other than full-time university study. Thus the Law Society of New South Wales can argue with some force that:

> traditionally it has probably been easier for people from lower socio-economic backgrounds to enter the legal profession than any of the other major professions . . .
> [A]ny person who could pass the necessary qualifying examinations [of the Admission Boards] could obtain entrance to the profession and such entrance was not confined to the sector of the community that could afford a lengthy period at University whilst not deriving any income.[20]

In the past twenty years, however, apprenticeship and other alternative modes of entry have been steadily phased out or reduced in importance, while university law schools have achieved centrality in providing legal qualifications. The levelling off of available places in the law schools coupled with increased demand has created a highly competitive situation whereby applicants in New South Wales, for example, must finish in the top five per cent of Higher School Certificate (HSC) examinees in order to be confident of admission – and must finish in the top two or three per cent to be in a position to choose among the law schools. The number of women applicants has increased greatly in the past decade and, since these women are drawn from the same social class as male students, this has had the effect of doubling the number of upper-socio-economic-class aspirants.

The shift from the 'White Australia' policy to 'Multi-culturalism' and the large influx of migrants from other than Anglo-Celtic backgrounds after the 1939–45 war has substantially affected Australian society and culture.[21] The effect on the legal profession thus far has been small, but will doubtless increase as the second generation of migrants comes of age.

Apart from data on gender and work place, demographic information on the legal profession is difficult to obtain. The professional associations and admission authorities maintain a positive disinterest in such matters. For example, the New South Wales Law Society states that it:

> does not maintain any records which would indicate the socio-economic background of its members as compared with that of the general community ...
>
> No enquiry is made as to the socio-economic background of an applicant for entrance to the profession, nor is it a relevant matter ... nevertheless the view has been expressed by many members of the profession that the legal profession does differ from the general community in terms of socio-economic background ... Whatever may be the position, the Law Society considers that the socio-economic background of members of the profession does not affect the ability of the legal profession to render legal services for all sectors of the community and does not make the profession unsympathetic to the needs of the disadvantaged sectors.[22]

Similarly, at the opening of the 1985 Australian Legal Convention, the former Chief Justice of Australia, Sir Harry Gibbs, referred to as 'heresy' the view that the courts 'should be representative of all races, sexes, classes, creeds and geographical areas ... irrespective of the merits of the individuals concerned'.[23]

With respect, while meritocratic tests have ostensibly replaced ascribed characteristics as the filter for entry into the profession (and appointment to the judiciary), matters such as gender, race and class background still exert a powerful influence on entry into and distribution within the legal profession. This has several important consequences. First, a number of commentators have challenged the assertions of the professional associations and the judiciary and argued that the elite background and commercial orientation of Australian lawyers raise doubts about whether they are able to sufficiently identify with, and adequately service the needs of, disadvantaged persons.[24]

Second, there is evidence in Australia (and overseas) of a certain amount of social tracking within the profession, with factors of race, class and gender partly determining career paths.[25] Third, the social background of lawyers and judges means that there is an inevitable infusion of upper-middle-class values into the legal system and legal ideology.[26] Finally, the important social role accorded to lawyers and judges, with the accompanying power and influence in the political and economic spheres, is largely reserved for persons of elite background despite professed commitments to egalitarianism and meritocracy.

Age and experience

Students who enter university directly from, or soon after, high school account for the great majority of Australian law students. A survey of students entering seven law schools in 1986 found that between 65–78 per cent of entrants were twenty years of age or younger, except at Macquarie University (49%) and the New South Wales Institute of Technology (now the University of Technology, Sydney – 21%),[27] which especially cater for extension and part-time students, respectively.

Most Australian law students do a 'combined' law degree programme, which couples LLB studies with degree studies in another discipline (such as arts, commerce or science), and which normally takes at least five years to complete. The average time to complete at the University of New South Wales, where most students are required to do a combined degree, is nearly six years.[28]

If we add six months for the post-graduate legal training course or a year or two of articles, the typical entrant into professional practice is about 25-years-old. However, it is still possible in some universities for a student to commence at 17 or 18, do a three year 'straight' LLB degree, and then proceed to be admitted as a barrister before they turn 21.

There are many persons who delay entry into university, or interrupt their law studies, or enter through special 'mature age' admission programmes, or undertake their studies on a part-time basis, or come to law studies after having commenced another career. The proportion of older students has jumped significantly in the past decade. A 1976 survey of four law schools found that only nine per cent of new entrants were over 26-years-old; by 1986, this figure (at the seven law schools surveyed) increased to 21 per cent. At Macquarie, 40 per cent of entrants in 1986 were over 26, and at the Institute the majority (52%) were over 26 and 71 per cent were over 23-years-old,[29] the current, designated 'mature age' borderline. The increase is most likely attributable to the removal of all tertiary tuition fees by the Whitlam government in 1974. Students in the Admission Board course in New South Wales typically are in full-time employment, often in the public service, and are usually considerably older than university law students when they qualify for admission.[30]

With the doubling of the number of law schools since the mid-1960s and the consequently large increase in the annual output of law graduates, as well as the decline of Admission Board and apprenticeship programmes, the average age of the profession has fallen steadily for the past twenty years. For most of this century, the majority of Australian lawyers were over 40 years of age, and nearly a third were over 50.[31] However, in late 1987 about three-quarters of all solicitors in New South Wales were in the 25–44 age groups,[32] with the median age down in the thirties.[33]

Survey studies in New South Wales and Victoria indicate that the Bar has a somewhat older profile than the solicitors' branch.[34] It is not surprising that in a divided profession, with barristers reliant upon reputation and contacts among solicitors in order to get work, the Bar would be the 'senior branch' in terms of age and experience.

The relatively recent entry of women into the practising profession in significant numbers is reflected in the different age profiles of men and women lawyers. For example, in New South Wales in 1988, 68 per cent of active women solicitors were under 35 years of age, as against 37 per cent of male solicitors. Twenty-nine per cent of women solicitors were aged between 35 and 54, and only three per cent of women solicitors were over 55 years old; for male solicitors the figures are 52 and 11 per cent, respectively.[35]

Young and recently admitted solicitors tend to practice as employees rather than as principals (that is, partners or sole practitioners), and may be required to do so by the terms of their initially restricted practising certificates. By contrast, in the 35–39 year old group of New South Wales solicitors in 1987, principals outnumbered employed solicitors by five to one; in the 50–54 age group, principals outnumbered employees by 17 to one.[36]

Gender

It has been true in Australia, as elsewhere, that for some time now there have been 'as many women employed in the general provision of legal services as there are men. However, while men occupy the lucrative and prestige-carrying sectors of legal work, women are employed to do the secretarial and reception work.'[37] Until this century, women have been formally excluded from most western legal professions, and informal quotas and other impediments to entry into the profession persisted until quite recently. Exclusion of women was not justified on the basis of any supposed incapacity for legal practice by individual female applicants for admission, but rather on the basis of 'maintaining professional standards' generally. That is, the exclusion was premised on the supposed incompatibility of femaleness with professionalism. The attributes or ascribed characteristics of professionalism were seen to be co-extensive with notional middle-class male features: intellectual detachment, emotional uninvolvement and so on. Thus,

> The profession, like clubs and elite schools, were not simply institutions from which women happened to be absent. Their maleness became part of their character, so that the admission of women was seen as not merely adding to their numbers or introducing some novelty, but as threatening the very identity of the institutions themselves.[38]

In Australia the position slowly began to change early in this century.[39] Victoria was the first to remove (by legislation) the legal bar to the admission of women, in 1903, followed by Tasmania (1904), Queensland (1905) and South Australia (1911). New South Wales did not remove the gender bar until 1918,[40] although this was one year earlier than in England, and Western Australia followed later in 1923. The first woman actually admitted to practice law in New South Wales was Ada Evans in 1921, who had led the fight for women's rights to practice since her graduation from Sydney University Law School in 1902. Having gained admission after all those years, Ms Evans declined to practice, feeling that her legal knowledge and skills had become stale.[41]

Only a few women were admitted to practice each decade until the 1950s, with the significant changes in the number of women lawyers and law students beginning in the 1960s. From that time, not only has the number of women in law increased markedly, but also the proportion of women in the profession. For example, between 1976 and 1981 there was a 28 per cent increase in the number of male solicitors in New South Wales, while there was a 165 per cent increase in the number of women solicitors,[42] which nearly doubled the overall proportion of women. Starting from such a disadvantage, however, it will be several more years before women lawyers reach the 20 per cent mark nationally.

More details are available about the growth patterns of women in the local legal professions in Australia. Table 3, below, indicates the rapid, recent changes in New South Wales. The figures are similar across the states. For example, women were three per cent of legal practitioners in Western Australia in 1952, and 14 per cent in 1984, including five per cent of the separate Bar.[43]

The increase in the number of women lawyers is, of course, a flow-on from the number of women studying law, and enrolments of women have risen sharply over the past twenty years in Australia. Women comprised only 11.4 per cent of Australian university law students in 1960, 12.4 per cent in 1968,

Table 2   Women Lawyers in Australia

Year	No of Women Lawyers	% of All Lawyers
1911	6	0.2
1933	49	1.1
1947	109	2.6
1971	618	6.0
1986	4,473	17.2

Sources: Australian Bureau of Statistics national census figures.

22.1 per cent in 1974, 29.1 per cent in 1977,[44] 33.3 per cent in 1980, and 41 per cent in 1984.[45] This latter figure is precisely the same as for women in university studies generally,[46] and is higher than many other professional faculties, most notably engineering.[47]

Table 3   'Active' Women Lawyers in New South Wales

Year	No of Women Solicitors	% of All Solicitors	No of Women Barristers	% of All Barristers
1911	0	0	0	0
1940	—	—	2	0.7
1950	15	1.0	—	—
1955	—	—	1	0.3
1958	65	3.0	—	—
1965	—	—	9	2.0
1969	161	5.0	—	—
1975	304	6.0	15	3.0
1981	—	—	43	5.0
1984	1,056	13.7	78	7.0
1988	1,941	19.9	87	8.0

Sources: 1911 census; 1950–1975 from Disney et al, *Lawyers* (1977) 188; 1981–1987 from the NSW Law Society, Bar Association and Women Lawyers' Association.

There is some evidence that a relatively larger proportion of women do not complete their legal studies. At the University of New South Wales, for example, the discontinuation ratio is 100 women for every 70 men students, and the corollary is that graduation rates favour men by about the same factor.[48] While this indicates that more social and institutional support may be necessary for women students, most women do go on to graduate and obtain professional qualifications, with less 'wastage' than is reported in some other countries.[49] In the four graduating classes between December 1983 and June 1985 of the New South Wales College of Law, which is the post-graduate training centre for persons seeking admission as solicitors, the average percentage of women was 35 per cent.[50]

While all of the above figures clearly indicate that the feminisation of the Australian legal profession is one of the most important developments of the modern profession, the increased proportion of women apparently will not affect class composition. Studies in Australia,[51] and overseas, demonstrate clearly and consistently that 'women are drawn, even more than men, from professional and managerial families with large incomes and high levels of parental education.'[52] The spouses of women lawyers are also far more likely to be high status professionals or managers than the spouses of male lawyers.[53]

The most comprehensive survey to date of the place of women in the Australian legal profession was that conducted by Hetherton in Victoria.[54] Briefly, she found that: (1) there was a major inequality between men and women lawyers with respect to income, with the median income of women just over half that of men. Even the upper quarter of women was well below the male median. Only three per cent of women were in the high income range, compared with 21 per cent of men, while 23 per cent of women were in the lowest income range, compared with eight per cent of men.[55] (2) There was a significantly different occupational profile between male and female lawyers. There were relatively few women barristers or partners in law firms, and a much higher proportion of women were employed solicitors.[56] (3) There were substantial differences in the types of matters handled. Women were markedly concentrated in family law and probate, strongly under-represented in commercial law, company law and criminal law, and somewhat under-represented in taxation and estate planning, personal injury and litigation (other than family law litigation).[57]

Recent statistics from the professional associations in other states also bear out the differentiation in the occupational profile (and, perforce, prestige and income) of men and women lawyers. For example, women lawyers in New South Wales and Western Australia make up only a small percentage of barristers, partners in law firms and sole practitioners, and tend to work as employed lawyers, whether in private practice, government or industry. Put another way, while nearly half of male solicitors in private practice in New South Wales are partners and only 27.6 per cent are employed, only 12.6 per cent of women solicitors are partners and fully three-quarters are employed.[58] Another recent survey found that women represented only 3.7 per cent of partners in Tasmania, 9.7 per cent of partners in Victoria, 11.3 per cent of partners in the ACT and 5.9 per cent of partners in the Northern Territory.[59]

The position among the big corporate law firms is similar. Only 4 of 64 partners in Minter Ellison in June 1987 were women (6.3%); 5 of 150 partners (3.3%) in The Australian Legal Group (which includes Allen Allen & Hemsley in Sydney, Arthur Robinson & Hedderwicks in Melbourne, and other firms in Brisbane, Adelaide and Perth); 10 of 132 partners in Freehill, Hollingdale & Page (7.6%); 6 of 67 partners in Phillips Fox (9%); and 4 of 117 partners in Mallesons Stephen Jacques (3.4%).[60]

Overall it is still true in Australia,[61] as elsewhere, that a disproportionate number of women lawyers do stereotyped 'women's work': family law, probate, juvenile law, government and legal aid work. This is occasioned by a complex of factors, including: cultural stereotypes and role assignments about women's interests and abilities which operate on both employers and women lawyers themselves; the greater availability of certain types of work; idealism; pragmatism, in terms of seeking flexibility in working hours and arrangements; and expectations of fairer treatment in the public sector. The ironic reality of women's work experiences in law is that while disadvantaged, women lawyers as a group come much closer than men to actually living up to the service ideals of the profession.

While the great increase in numbers in recent years will inevitably result in a somewhat larger proportion of women partners, barristers, judges and professors, structural barriers to advancement – some broadly social, others peculiar to the legal profession – will prevent time alone from producing gender equality.

A national survey of recent Australian law graduates found that 35 per cent of women respondents reported that their gender was a disadvantage in finding work, and 33 per cent said being a woman was a disadvantage in day-to-day legal work. About nine per cent of women felt that their gender was an advantage. Only one per cent of men felt disadvantaged in either respect because of their gender.[62] In 1986, the report of an official task force in New York on gender bias in the courts found that bias against women lawyers and litigants was 'a pervasive problem … women uniquely, disproportionately, and with unacceptable frequency must endure a climate of condescension, indifference and hostility.'[63] Given the current and historic dominance of men in public and private sector lawyering and academia, including the extent to which legal culture and style reflects male culture and style,[64] women lawyers also often report feelings of social isolation and difficulties in finding 'professional mentors' who can provide guidance and assistance in shaping and advancing their careers.[65] Client acceptance is sometimes also a problem and, as has already been mentioned, women lawyers tend to cluster in areas of practice (such as family law) that restrict advancement in the large, corporate law firms and at the Bar.

The key problem, however, is coping with the demands of both professional practice and family care responsibilities, which still mostly fall to women whatever their occupation.[66] For women lawyers with children there are multiple practical problems, such as the very limited availability of satisfactory part-time work, inadequate child care services, pressures to limit the taking of full maternity leave and other leaves of absence, and so on. As Dixon and Davies have stated:

> The legal profession generally, while in theory accepting of women on equal terms with men, sees childrearing as an individual female practitioner's problem, rather than one affecting the profession as a whole, and does not actively seek solutions to the conflict between the demands of career and family for the benefit of all married practitioners with children.[67]

Religion

There are few formal links between legal and religious institutions or personnel in Australia. One of the current Justices of the High Court of Australia, Sir Ronald Wilson, has recently become President of the Uniting Church of Australia. Despite some speculation that he would step down from the Bench to concentrate on his new Church position,[68] he has chosen to continue in both capacities for the present.

A relatively recent survey of New South Wales lawyers indicated that the religious profile of the legal profession closely followed that of the general community (see Table 4, below). Only Jews are substantially over-represented in the survey (by about six times per capita), but given the small numbers involved and the margins for error, not a great deal can be concluded from this. However, it is very likely the case in Australia, as in the United States and elsewhere, that a career in law 'remains disproportionately attractive to members of minority religions, perhaps because it promises upward mobility to the children of small businessmen, for whom other routes remain less accessible'.[69] Protestant lawyers generally were less inclined to describe themselves as 'practising' their religion than Catholic or Jewish lawyers.[70]

Table 4   Religion of New South Wales Lawyers, 1978

Religious grouping	Percent of lawyers	Percent in community
Church of England or Anglican	33.0	33.9
Catholic	30.0	30.7
Methodist, Uniting or Presbyterian	16.0	12.8
Jewish	3.1	0.5
No Religion	11.0	9.6
Other	6.9	12.5

Sources: For lawyers, R Tomasic 'Typifying Lawyers' (1980 PhD thesis, UNSW) at 187, Table 1; for general population, New South Wales Year Book No 69 (1985) 53.

Race and ethnicity

Australia has a significantly less homogeneous population than 40 years ago. In 1981, persons born outside of Australia were 21 per cent of the population, compared with ten per cent in 1947. However, over 87 per cent of the population were either born in Australia or in the United Kingdom, Ireland or New Zealand.[71] The current multicultural policies involving greater migration from non-Anglo-Celtic Europe and Asia have only been in place for the past decade or so, but have had an impact on popular culture well in excess of actual numbers, perhaps because of the concentration of migrants in several of the large cities.[72]

The Aboriginal and Torres Strait Islander population in the 1981 census was about 160,000, or one per cent of the national total. It is only in the Northern Territory that Aborigines still comprise a substantial (25%) percentage of the small population; in no state does the Aboriginal community exceed a few per cent of the total population.[73] However, in the 1986 census, the Aboriginal and Islander population rose to nearly 230,000, or 1.43 per cent of the national total. The increase cannot be accounted for by the birthrate alone, which means that much of the increase comes from Aboriginal people being more ready to identify themselves as such.

The legal professional associations and admission authorities do not keep records of race or ethnicity, and most surveys have called for country of birth rather than ethnic identification. These surveys have shown Australian lawyers overwhelmingly as Australian-born, with most of the foreign-born lawyers coming from the United Kingdom, Ireland, New Zealand or other English-speaking countries. Over 88 per cent of New South Wales lawyers were born in Australia (and nearly 80 per cent of the lawyers' fathers were Australia-born). Suburban solicitors were most likely to be foreign-born (17.5%), while country solicitors were almost all (97.8%) Australian-born.[74] These figures are similar for the Victorian profession.[75] With respect to the two major migrant groups in Victoria, a survey revealed that only 2.7 per cent of lawyers had Italian-born fathers and 0.8 per cent had Greek-born fathers, compared with

5.5 per cent and 3.4 per cent respectively of the adult male workforce generally.[76] The Pearce Committee's survey of recent law graduates also found that 87 per cent were Australian-born and another eight per cent were from other English-speaking countries.[77]

The per capita representation of migrant groups in the legal profession should continue to rise, given that participation rates in university education tend to increase with duration of residence.[78] However, the substantial changes in the post-war ethnic composition of urban Australia have not yet fully flowed through to the legal profession, much less the judiciary. A national study of the social composition of all tertiary students found that law schools had among the highest proportions of Australian-born students.[79]

Until 1975, all Australian jurisdictions required that a person be an Australian citizen or a British subject in order to be admitted to practice law. South Australia removed this requirement in that year, and New South Wales (1977) and Victoria (1978) soon followed suit.[80] However, the Commonwealth's Public Service Act now requires that most federal employees – including government lawyers – be Australian citizens.

A small number of Aboriginal lawyers have qualified, for the first time, in the past decade, assisted somewhat by special admission programmes at the University of New South Wales, Queensland University and Monash University law schools. In 1986, six Aboriginal lawyers had been admitted to practice in New South Wales, two each in Victoria and Tasmania and one each in South Australia and the Northern Territory. Because of the very small numbers and the geographic spread there is no professional association for Aboriginal lawyers, although the various branches of the Aboriginal Legal Service obviously serve as a focus.

The survey of Victorian lawyers found a correlation between race/ethnicity and the types of work performed by lawyers. Virtually all lawyers practising in the high status, high reward areas of company and commercial law were Australian-born. In the relatively newer (and therefore more open) speciality of taxation law, 25 per cent of lawyers (and 42 per cent of their fathers) were foreign-born.[81] However, this sort of correlation may have more to do with socio-economic considerations than socio-cultural ones. Law students whose parents were born overseas were less likely to attend elite private schools, and their fathers typically had less formal education and lower occupational status.[82] Migrant lawyers would also tend to lack the family and personal contacts in the profession that so many Australian-born lawyers have (see below), and thus miss out on an 'important basis of social support role models and easier access to jobs in the profession'.[83]

Even the relatively small proportion of lawyers with non-British antecedents has excited concern among the most conservative elements of the profession. In a 1977 submission to the New South Wales Law Reform Commission, the late Francis C Hutley, then a Supreme Court judge, wrote:

> The immediate effect of World War II was to open up the legal profession to groups who had no historical connection with the professions. [This occasioned] the flooding of the profession by persons who, without either professional family association or adequate indoctrination, have acquired the often dangerous skills put into the hands of lawyers.
> If the maintenance of professional standards, particularly of integrity, which need to be above those of the general community, is of fundamental importance and it is desired to greatly increase the number of lawyers and to draw the increase from largely unrepresented classes such as the aboriginals and migrants, an

elaborate course of indoctrination will be necessary. The clan type loyalty which I understand is the basis of such aboriginal and migrant morality is fundamentally inconsistent with the individual integrity which is required of a lawyer.[84]

Confronting attitudes such as these, it is little wonder that migrants 'show an even greater sense of disillusionment with the law and with the legal profession than either the Australians or the British'.[85]

Socio-economic class

From the earliest days the professional practice of law has been associated with the upper-middle class. The variety of modes of entry into the profession did provide opportunities for 'the especially able children of the poor', in limited numbers.[86] However, the decline of the non-university avenues to admission, such as apprenticeship and examination board programmes, and the extreme competition for places at university, still make it very difficult for persons without advantaged backgrounds to enter into the profession.

A recent, detailed study of participation rates in higher education in South Australia found that students from the upper one-third of the metropolitan population in socio-economic terms were 20 times more likely to gain entry into medicine or law than students from the bottom third, and were five times more likely even to apply for admission to those faculties.[87]

In 1974, the Whitlam Labor Government abolished all tertiary tuition fees and instituted a student allowance scheme in an attempt to increase working-class participation in higher education.[88] However, follow up studies have indicated 'relatively little change in the socio-economic composition of students ... If anything the balance has shifted marginally over time in favour of those from higher socio-economic backgrounds.'[89] It is much less clear, however, whether the fee abolition experiment should be classed a failure, as the current Labor government – especially the Education Minister, John Dawkins – is so oddly insistent upon doing.[90] The participation rate of women and mature age students did increase markedly during this period, for example. Further, the decline of state-funded teacher cadetships; economic recessions and the massive reduction in youth employment opportunities; the significant rise in school retention rates and the consequent increased competition for tertiary places;[91] and the great decrease in real terms of financial assistance to tertiary students, were all important countervailing factors. Given this situation, and the con-traction of the working class as a proportion of society,[92] the abolition of fees was probably essential to maintaining the participation rate of lower income and other disadvantaged persons, which would otherwise have dropped to trace levels.

Even within the elite world of the university, 'medicine and law reflect by far the most extreme (socio-economic) discrimination levels, not only for student enrolments but also for applications.'[93] Social background also appears to play a part in predisposing some students toward legal studies. One study of Australian university students found that 'students in the science and humanities streams choose medicine and law respectively if they are from high status families, engineering or teaching if they are from lower status families.'[94]

In a survey of students entering university law schools in 1986, over 36 per cent had fathers with tertiary degrees and 20 per cent with mothers holding degrees.[95] At the same time, only about eight per cent of the total Australian workforce was qualified to at least first-degree level.[96] Law students are at least twice as likely as students in commerce, education, arts and engineering to have fathers with university degrees, and only medical students come from (slightly) better-educated family backgrounds.[97]

Similarly, lawyers are disproportionately drawn from high status occupational backgrounds. Surveys of lawyers in New South Wales[98] and Victoria[99] found that they were about four times more likely than the general population to have fathers who were in professional or managerial positions, and about one-fourth as likely to have fathers who were blue collar workers. Of the fathers of law students entering university in 1986, 42 per cent were professionals or in senior management, 30 per cent were self-employed or in lower status managerial positions, 19 per cent were in skilled trades, six per cent in unskilled trades, and three per cent in labouring or other low status positions.[100]

Considering the occupational backgrounds of lawyers' and law students' families, it is unsurprising that they are also from economically affluent backgrounds, with over one-quarter coming from the highest income category.[101] The 1986 entering student survey found that students in the part-time programme at the NSW Institute of Technology and the external programme at Macquarie University were from far less affluent families, suggesting 'that the financial barriers to full-time study of law are considerable.'[102]

A striking feature of the Australian legal profession is the extent to which there are strong 'hereditary and tribal aspects'.[103] A survey of practising lawyers in New South Wales found that about 40 per cent of barristers and 50 per cent of solicitors had legally qualified relatives, with private practitioners somewhat more likely than government or corporation employed lawyers to have other lawyers in the family.[104] A similar Victorian survey[105] found a similar pattern: nearly 40 per cent of practising lawyers had another lawyer in the family, and 13 per cent had two or more lawyer relatives (mainly spouses, brothers and uncles). Over 15 per cent had lawyer fathers, even though lawyers accounted for only about 0.3 per cent of the male workforce in Victoria. The 1986 entering law student survey also noted this correlation, but found that students in New South Wales and Victoria were somewhat more likely than students in other states to have a lawyer relative.[106] Apart from providing the proper social background and motivation for legal studies, these strong family networks provide 'an important basis of social support role models and easier access to jobs in the profession than would be available to otherwise similar potential recruits'.[107]

The type of secondary schooling received is another peculiarly telling sociographic factor in Australia, with lawyers and other upper professionals drawn heavily from elite, expensive private schools and selective public schools. Among Western democracies, only Ireland has a greater proportion of children attending private schools, although in Ireland this is mainly for religious rather than class reasons.[108] Australia also has a sizable systemic Catholic school population, but most elites are alumni of Protestant private schools (and some independent Catholic private schools).

Among those members of the national elite who were educated in Australia, 38 per cent came from private non-Catholic schools, even though such schools accounted for only nine per cent of national secondary enrolment.[109] This figure would be substantially higher except for the fact that only a small percentage of trade union leaders (6%) and Labor Party leaders (8%) attended these schools. By comparison, 56 per cent of business leaders, 47 per cent of cent of the leaders of the conservative political parties, 45 per cent of media executives, and 64 per cent of academic leaders attended private non-Catholic schools. State schools educated 73 per cent of secondary students but provided less than half the national elite. Catholic school graduates (18 per cent of the national total) are marginally under-represented (14%) among the elite.[110] The concentration of future national leaders in just a few schools is quite remarkable. Of the many hundreds of secondary schools operating in the 1930s and 1940s, 33 per cent of all future leaders attended only 17 private schools, and another ten per cent attended only five selective public schools.[111]

Attendance at one of the elite private schools not only reflects privilege, but also enhances the chance to go on to university and activates the 'old school tie' network. In a country where there is relatively little status differentiation among universities, greater affection and identification seems to be reserved for school affiliations. In 1985, all twelve directors of BHP Australia's largest company, were graduates of elite Protestant private schools, as were all of the directors of AMP, the largest insurance company, and all but one of the directors of Westpac, the largest banking corporation.[112]

Surveys of lawyers and law students over the past few decades demonstrate gross over-representation of persons with private school backgrounds, especially those from the elite independent schools. Anderson and Western's 1965 study of Australian university students[113] found that 33 per cent attended independent schools, 29 per cent Catholic schools and 32 per cent state schools. At that time, the state schools educated 73 per cent of all secondary students, while independent school enrolments accounted for only nine per cent of the national total. By comparison, only 19 per cent of engineering students came from independent schools and 57 per cent from state schools.

Another survey of students entering university in 1976 found that private school graduates were over-represented in all faculties, but especially in law and medicine.[114] Fifty-five per cent of law students attended a private secondary school (29% independent, 26% Catholic), compared with 51 per cent of medical students, 37 per cent of science students, 40 per cent of commerce students, 39 per cent of arts students, 36 per cent of engineering students and 30 per cent of education students. Surveys of lawyers in New South Wales and Victoria in that same year revealed a similar pattern, with 33 per cent of NSW and 45 per cent of Victorian lawyers coming from independent school backgrounds.[115]

Goldring's survey of students entering law schools in New South Wales, Victorian and the ACT in 1986 (and the Pearce Committee's commissioned national survey of law graduates) revealed that the position was unchanged.[116] Only 41 per cent of law school entrants were from state schools, even though 62 per cent of all Year 12 students in the preceding year were educated at state schools. Private school leaders accounted for 55 per cent of law school entrants (32 per cent independent schools, 23 per cent Catholic systemic schools), even though those schools produced only 39 per cent of that year's matriculants (26 per cent independent schools, 13 per cent Catholic systemic schools). The proportion of independent school students in Victoria was much greater than in New South Wales or the ACT. Women entrants were slightly more likely to have attended state schools.

Bradsen and Farrington's research into student selection and performance at Adelaide University's law school[117] also makes the point very strongly. In 1985, 40 per cent of all school leavers entering into Law came from only four private schools, and 78 per cent came from only 12 private or Catholic schools.

By contrast, independent schools provided only 17 per cent, and Catholic schools 16 per cent, of South Australia's matriculants in 1984, while the state school system produced 67 per cent. Even taking into account transfer students and other entrants who did not come straight from school, only 33 per cent of the entering class in 1985 had state school backgrounds.

The proportion of private school students entering law school is, if anything, likely to increase in future. An Australian Teachers' Federation report[118] says that between 1975–76 and 1985–86, private school enrolments increased by 25 per cent, which represented a six per cent drift overall from the public schools to the private schools. This was no doubt occasioned in large part by greatly increased Commonwealth funding for private schools at the same time that funding to the public schools decreased and education funding generally dropped as a proportion of the federal budget.[119] Recent studies by the New South Wales government and the Australian Bureau of Statistics have found that a much higher proportion of private school students complete their secondary education than state school students (63% vs 41.5%), and private school students were three times as likely to attend university the year after finishing school.[120]

Professional mobility is very limited in the Australian legal profession, with a high correlation between first legal job and subsequent career path, in terms of the size and location (city, suburban or country) of the first and last law firms worked for. Thus, lawyers 'seem to have limited options available to them after their first law job'.[121] Put more concretely, lawyers who start off working for small suburban or country law firms or in the public service are relatively unlikely to be able to move later to more prestigious and lucrative positions in the large, corporate law firms. Similarly, such lawyers rarely go to the Bar, and thus are most unlikely ever to be considered for the Bench, whereas the road from the big city firms to the Bar is well travelled. As already indicated, social background is an important factor in determining opportunities for and choices of first jobs, which in turn predict career patterns. Some young lawyers come to the profession with the personal and clan contacts,[122] self-confidence, financial safety net, and private sector orientation necessary to get on at the Bar and in the large corporate firms of solicitors. Thus, advantage is accumulated.[123] Those from relatively less advantaged backgrounds are more likely to seek and find work in the more socially open and more secure, but less prestigious and lucrative, areas of government and in-house corporate lawyering, or with smaller private firms, or in non-law jobs, such as management or the public service.

Access to the profession for the disadvantaged

Although there are still a number of alternative routes to legal practice available in some states, such as articled clerkships and Admission Board examinations, the university law schools are now central to professional qualification in Australia. Thus entry into the legal profession has become inextricably bound up with entry into law school.

As demonstrated above, lower socio-economic groups are substantially under-represented in the universities generally, and particularly in highly sought after upper-professional degree programmes such as Law and Medicine.[124] The abolition of fees in 1974 has not altered the socio-economic balance significantly, for reasons already discussed, but did help to improve the representation of women and mature age students in higher education.

Competition for places in the law schools is fierce, with all law schools except the University of Tasmania maintaining quotas on entry. Because of effective funding cuts, the number of places actually fell by about 200 between 1980 and 1985 while demand increased, correspondingly raising the cut-off marks for entry by school leavers. Even though there is a great deal of self-selection, based on expectations of examination scores and other factors, there were still over 20,000 applications in 1985 for about 2600 first year places in Law.[125] In South Australia in 1986, there were over 1000 first preference applicants for only 120 places in Adelaide University's first-year Law programme.[126] At Sydney University in 1987, there were over 1500 first preference applicants for 215 places in the law school.[127] In 1976, entry into any Australian law school was pretty well assured to an applicant who had finished in the top 15 per cent of school leavers; however, in 1985, entry to all law schools was limited to the top ten per cent of school leavers, and Melbourne, Sydney, Adelaide and New South Wales Universities only took the top two or three per cent.[128]

In such a competitive climate, it is not surprising that any substantial disadvantage or disability – whether socio-economic, linguistic, physical or other – would make chances of entry remote. As the Pearce Report noted, 'Persons from lower socio-economic levels apparently do not even contemplate studying law.'[129] The barriers to entry arise well before the law schools determine their admission policies, of course, since 'the most disadvantaged groups drop out of education before Year 12, the problems of the disadvantaged having more to do with what happens in the family, school and society than in the selection process.'[130] Participation in higher education by school leavers is most associated with the degree of parental encouragement, which is in turn related to socio-economic background.[131] Conversely, very few 'children of adversity' – that is, children from backgrounds involving poverty, marital discord, unstable employment history of parents, or linguistic or socio-cultural problems in schooling – proceed to Year 12 or apply to a tertiary institution.[132]

This disadvantage is well demonstrated in high school Year 12 retention rates. Australian rates generally are quite low by industrial world standards, but have risen from 34 per cent in 1975 to 48 per cent in 1986. (By comparison, Sweden's retention rate is 85 per cent, the United States 84 per cent and Japan 94 per cent). The rates vary with the type of secondary schooling. During that same period the rate at government schools increased from 28 to 42 per cent; at independent schools from 53 to 67 per cent; and at Catholic schools from 40 to 57 per cent.[133] Rates also vary between states and territories, with the Northern Territory and (19.2%) Tasmania (25.8%) doing particularly poorly and South Australia (50.2%) and the ACT (77%) doing relatively better.[134] More importantly, there are big variations between schools, based on geography, socio-economic status and selectivity. In New South Wales in 1987, the retention rate at state schools averaged 40 per cent, but at 13 schools (including the selective schools) the rate exceeded 80 per cent. At the other end, there were schools with less than 20 per cent retention, mainly in the outer Sydney suburbs and in the country.[135]

In recent years there have been strong expressions, at the governmental and institutional levels, of commitment to facilitate access to higher education by persons from disadvantaged backgrounds. In 1983, the Hawke government announced the establishment of the Participation and Equity Program (PEP), aimed at improving the prospects of disadvantaged school students. A Secondary Allowances Scheme and Disadvantaged Schools Program were also instituted. In its Report for the 1985–1987 Triennium, the Commonwealth Tertiary Education Commission affirmed its policy that:

> the student base be broadened in those professions, such as medicine and law, which are expected to serve all members of society. Aborigines, migrants and people from non-English speaking backgrounds and children from working-class backgrounds, should be given reasonable chances to enter these faculties. We expect Institutions which have highly restricted faculties to undertake an urgent review of their existing selection arrangements, with a view to providing fairer opportunities for disadvantaged groups.[136]

The Australian Law School Deans also recently committed themselves to such a policy:

> Law affects all members of the community irrespective of wealth, ethnic background, gender or any other social or individual difference. If the law is to respond to the needs of these different groups, lawyers themselves need to reflect the broadest possible social mix.[137]

Government actions – and funds – have not matched the rhetoric, however. Funding for higher education has declined 22% in real terms over the last decade, and has also declined substantially as a proportion of the federal budget and of GDP, even while the Commonwealth's investment in private secondary education has increased significantly.[138] Income support for students has been improved after a decade of decline, but the institution of an 'administration charge' of $250 in 1987 has discouraged participation, especially among mature age and part-time students.[139] The bridging courses that are essential to prepare disadvantaged students for tertiary studies have not been sufficiently funded either. The already poorly-resourced law schools have neither the funds nor the specialist staff to mount such programmes.[140] The CTEC Trennium Report, while calling for access to professional programmes, expressly avoided dealing with the question of funds for bridging courses, suggesting that such courses are within the province of the Technical and Further Education (TAFE) sector, which is a state rather than federal responsibility and is already very under-resourced.[141] The pilot SUCCEED bridging programmes at Sydney University had its federal government funding removed after only one year.[142]

One area where limited bridging and support programmes do exist, and have dramatically demonstrated their worth, is with respect to Aboriginal students. Aborigines are the most under-represented group in higher education.[143] In 1984, only 13 per cent of Aboriginal students completed their full secondary education, and only 4.1 per cent of Aboriginals have some post-secondary educational qualification, compared with 24 per cent of the total workforce. In 1985, Aborigines comprised just over one per cent of the population, but represented only 0.07 per cent of university students and 0.3 per cent of college of advanced education students.[144] Because of the small numbers of eligible persons and the history of dispossession and disadvantage, many law schools will admit Aboriginal students outside of quota restrictions. In 1987, there were 36 Aboriginal law students in Australia. The University of New South Wales, which admitted 34 Aboriginal law students between 1971 and 1985, and Monash and Queensland Universities have been most associated with special admission schemes for Aborigines.

Only Monash, however, has a bridging course to facilitate university entry, with its Monash Orientation Scheme for Aborigines (MOSA), a preparatory year programme which aims to bridge the educational and cultural gap and is particularly designed to lead to entry into Arts and Law. In 1987 there were 34 students from around Australia in the MOSA course; in 1986, four Aboriginal students entered the law school through the programme. The University of Western Australia has approved in principle the establishment of a similar programme,[145] but has not yet proceeded for financial reasons.

Because of a large private bequest (rather than government funding), the University of New South Wales was able to set up a special support programme for Aboriginal students in the law school (and others), with academic and personal counselling services, tutoring, and study facilities. Until 1986, the first year drop-out rate in the special admissions scheme for Aborigines averaged 40 per cent. In 1987, after the introduction of the support programme, twelve out of 14 Aboriginal law students (86%) successfully completed first year, which is equivalent to the results for the rest of the student body at the university.[146]

Many law schools now have provisions for special admission of a limited number of applicants from disadvantaged backgrounds, but it is still true that 'only a small percentage of entrants are selected on other than academic merit.'[147] The great majority of admittees (65%) are school leavers, who are selected almost entirely on the basis of their aggregate mark in final year examinations. This criterion has been justified as producing the academically 'best' students, being the most reliable predictor of success in law school, being easy to administer, and removing 'nepotism and influence in selection (which is no small problem for law schools)'.[148] However, this view of academic 'merit' is extremely limited and invariably results in the reproduction of social class differences.[149] A better view may be that 'the primary aim of higher education should be actually to create merit, and not merely to certify or to process those who already possess it.'[150]

A number of strategies are available, some of them already in practice in limited degrees, which could open up access to law studies and the legal profession for persons from disadvantaged backgrounds. Simply increasing the number of places available will not shift the socio-graphic profile of the student body, as the experience of the past two decades indicates. In highly selective courses such as Law and Medicine the additional places will mostly be filled with students from the same socio-economic background as those already enrolled, who now become able to gain their first preference.[151] A study conducted in South Australia[152] showed that increasing the number of first-year places at Adelaide University law school by 30 per cent would result in no appreciable change in the socio-economic composition of the incoming class in terms of gender, geographic origins (urban-rural), residence, parents' educational backgrounds, parents' occupations, and non-English speaking home environment. The proportion of students from independent private schools would have fallen slightly (from 53 to 47%), as would average parental income (from $36,600 to $35,100), but overall entrants would still be from high socio-economic status backgrounds. Only a fully-fledged 'open admissions policy' would substantially alter the class composition of law students, but would also reduce the proportion of women students from the current 52 per cent to 37 per cent.[153] In any event, such a policy is not currently acceptable.

Greater equity could be achieved in politically and academically acceptable ways, however, by diversifying teaching and admissions policies to include relatively larger proportions of mature age students, transfer students from other faculties, and part-time and external students. Most law schools already have special admission schemes for mature age students, but enrol only small numbers in this category each year.[154] There is strong evidence that admissions in this category serve an important social equity function. A recent, detailed study of mature age entrants in Australia revealed that they 'are far removed from the stereotyped "middle-class housewife", and indeed are an important part of the movement to redress the imbalance of participation of lower socio-economic groups in higher education.'[155] Over one-third of mature age entrants were early school leavers who came mainly from disadvantaged backgrounds, and used the special admission schemes as a 'second chance' to improve their education and occupational opportunities. The Pearce Committee's review of legal education in Australia endorsed mature age entry as a method to broaden the social base of law students, but expressed concern about the significantly higher drop-out rate of mature age students.[156]

Similarly, Goldring's study of the social background of Australian law students indicated that part-time and external students tended to come from less advantaged backgrounds than other law students. He concluded that 'the most practical way' of achieving broader access to legal education 'is by expanding the opportunities for part-time or distance education in law',[157] since these types of courses are often the only ones which disadvantaged students can afford (in terms of direct expenses and foregone income) to pursue. Of course, these programmes need sufficient resources to permit development of special teaching methods and materials.

While studies of equity in education have called for the preservation and expansion of such schemes,[158] mature age entry, part-time and external programmes are under threat because of increasing demand for tertiary places from school leavers, and the increasing cost of higher education. As already noted, the imposition of the relatively modest 'administrative charge' of $250 in 1987 caused part-time and external enrolments to fall by up to 15,000,[159] even though many low income earners are exempt from the charge. In the 1987–88 Budget Papers, the Commonwealth government responded to the problem of insufficient tertiary places to meet school leaver demand by increasing the 1988 intake by 5,800 'young school leavers', but providing funds for only 3,500–4,000. The government proposed that the balance 'be found by adjustment of intakes in favour of young school leavers' and away from part-time and mature age students. Such a policy ignores the differential social composition of these groups and operates against principles of equity.

Something of a compromise would involve delaying entry into law schools for most students until after one year of studies in another faculty, with entry based on tertiary results rather than on school results. The law schools in Tasmania and Western Australia have followed this approach for some time, and Adelaide has recently joined them. Most other law schools permit, but do not require, transfer from other faculties.[160] Such a scheme has two main advantages. First, the Bradsen and Farrington study of Adelaide law students found that tertiary results were a much better predictor of likely success in law studies than were school matriculation results. Even transfer students with matriculation marks far below those necessary to enter the Law Faculty on that basis were 'expected to perform just as well, if not better, than those with high matriculation marks'.[161] Equally important is the evidence that students from less advantaged backgrounds are able to 'catch up' in the first year of tertiary studies. Students from state schools, for example, may improve their relative standing by five to seven per cent, which may make the difference in reaching the quota levels in competitive faculties such as Law.[162] It is for these reasons that Adelaide changed its admissions policies from 1987, selecting students into Law after a one year preliminary general course at the university. The Pearce Committee suggested that all law schools give consideration to this selection scheme 'as the principal means of entry for law studies',[163] and the Australian Law Deans seem enthusiastic about this course of action as well.[164]

Most Australian law schools now have special admission schemes for disadvantaged students,[165] mainly established in the past few years. Sydney University, Australia's oldest, only began to consider the question of broadening access after a highly contentious debate in 1985.[166] Melbourne University established its scheme in 1985, and the University of New South Wales in early 1986. The UNSW 'ACCESS Scheme' is typical of those at other universities. About seven to ten per cent of first-year places across the university may be offered to persons who demonstrate that they have suffered disadvantage. Categories of disadvantage include non-English speaking background; disruptive family circumstances; low income; ethnicity, race and gender; geographical distance (outer suburban, rural); physical disability, and so on. However, in order to gain admission into a particular field of studies, an Access student must have an aggregate within 30 marks of the cut-off point for the quota. In other words, the effect of the scheme is to give a 30 point boost to students whose aggregates have suffered because of social disadvantage.

This has only a marginal impact in highly competitive faculties, such as Law. In 1987, the HSC aggregate required for entry into Law was 433, second only to Medicine (436) and nearly 100 points above the mark needed for general matriculation or acceptance into the Applied Science, Science, Surveying, Building, Social Work or Arts courses. Even with a 30 mark benefit, ACCESS students would have needed a higher aggregate to enter Law than was required for ordinary students to enter any course except Medicine, Computer Science or Optometry, and this is clearly well beyond the reach of students who by definition have suffered significant educational disadvantage. Accordingly, the UNSW Law School endorsed the ethos of the ACCESS Scheme, but suggested that in practice it would be necessary to defer consideration of ACCESS applicants until after one year of studies in another faculty.[167] ACCESS students interested in Law would be able to gain admission into Arts, say, with a mark as low as 328 (in 1987), and if their performance in first year was satisfactory they would be able to transfer into Law.

Higher education generally is in for the biggest shake-up since the 1960s, when the system expanded exponentially and the Commonwealth took over funding. Led on this issue by John Dawkins, the Minister for Employment, Education and Training, the federal Labor government has set about restructuring most aspects of the tertiary system, including the effective ending of the binary system (of universities and colleges), funding arrangements, staffing arrangements, and educational and research priorities. The new vision in a series of documents over a short period of time, from the Minister's 'The Challenge for Higher Education in Australia' in November 1987, the release of a government Green Paper in February 1988,[168] a report on funding through new fee and taxation plans (the Wran Report) in April 1988,[169] and finally the release of the government's White Paper on Higher Education Policy in late July 1988.

Quite apart from the general effect on teaching, research and morale in the tertiary sector, the new arrangements present a mixed bag of incentives and disincentives for greater equity in access to legal education. First, the new system calls for another major expansion of student numbers, with 20,000 new places being created in the next few years and double that by the turn of the century. However, as discussed earlier, increasing places will not in itself achieve equity goals since the pool of advantaged students is very large and has become larger with the entrance into the system of great numbers of women. Further, little of the expansion will be in Law. The Minister has on a number of occasions referred to the 'over-supply' of lawyers and doctors (without presenting evidence of this), and the White Paper specifies 'national priorities' – and therefore funding priorities and student places – in the areas of engineering (especially industrial) and technology, computer science, accounting and business management, and Asian studies. This vocationally-oriented, instrumental approach to higher education is supported in the Green Paper by numerous charts and graphs, but regrettably little in the way of compelling analysis or principle.[170] Another problem is that the newly created places appear to be earmarked for young school leavers pursuing full-time studies, freezing out mature age, part-time and external students.

Further problems are introduced by the new funding arrangements for tertiary institutions which partially rely on 'efficiency' notions and 'competition'. Specifically, the government proposes that institutions engage in competitive bidding for funding for a certain number of student places each year; in effect, these places will be auctioned off to the lowest bidder, and frills such as academic support schemes will not be viable. Similarly, the government proposes to tie a proportion of a discretionary funding allocation to institutional graduation rates, which are to be taken as a benchmark of efficiency, if not quality, in higher education. Success rates in Law are relatively high, which is unsurprising given the extremely high entry standards. In 1982, law students had success rates in their studies which exceeded the rates for the total student population in all categories: full-time (87% to 84%), part-time (79% to 75%), and external (77% to 71%).[171] However, institutions with a commitment to equity in access which enrol significant numbers of disadvantages, mature age, part-time or external students risk lower than average success rates,[172] and thus financial penalties.

Two proposed major contributions to access in the new regime are the announced expansion of student financial support schemes, and special funding for equity programmes. In 1974, when the Whitlam government abolished tertiary fees it also introduced a means-tested Tertiary Education Assistance Scheme (TEAS) for full-time students (who are citizens or permanent residents). In 1974, 79 per cent of students were eligible for TEAS, but the figure has dwindled to 42 per cent in 1988 because the means test has not been realistically adjusted. Moreover, the relative value of TEAS, or Austudy as it is now known, had declined substantially and was no longer reasonably related to maintenance costs. This problem clearly overshadowed the abolition of fees, and operated against equity goals,[173] when potential students weighed up the high direct costs of three to five years of undergraduate studies (rental and living expenses, books, transportation, and fees and charges) plus the income foregone during that period. As one study of access to higher education concluded:

> If the ideals of the Participation and Equity policy are to be realised, a greater public understanding of the economic and socio-cultural benefits to individuals and society of investing in higher education will be needed, and of the direct and indirect costs. In addition, a more rational and equitable income support scheme

for students in financial difficulty is needed. Such a policy does need to recognise that the barriers to participation are not a simple function of parental income.[174]

It is now proposed to increase the reach of income support coverage 'over the next decade ... to include at least 50 per cent of the full-time student body', and to enhance the level of support.[175] These targets do not meet the level of decline over the past decade, but nevertheless represent movement in the right direction.

The major policy improvement in the White Paper with regard to access is the proposal to make discretionary funds available to institutions contingent upon a demonstration that selection criteria have been altered in favour of disadvantaged groups, as evidenced by institutional 'educational profiles'. This will likely lead to expansion of the limited special access programmes already in existence, and validating affirmative action as an appropriate strategy for achieving social equity in tertiary selection. The extra funding would presumably be used for needed academic support services to assist the increased numbers of disadvantaged students. As the Pearce Committee review of legal education recognised, affirmative action 'is the only certain way of increasing the participation in law schools of groups perceived to be disadvantaged'.[176] However, it did not recommend this policy, anticipating that it would not be 'politically acceptable', particularly without 'full exposure of the issues of principle underlying it and appropriate parliamentary sanction'.[177] Apparently that sanction has now been granted, even if the issues have not been fully ventilated.

The White Paper avoids the question of where the funds for these two access initiatives will come from. However, running in tandem with the Green Paper–White Paper process has been a very public debate about the government's clear inclination towards a 'user-pays' approach to higher education. Although Australian Labor Party platform policy used to call for 'free' tertiary education, the Party's national conference in June 1988 replaced this with an undertaking to 'ensure that all qualified Australians will have access to a tertiary education regardless of their means'. This shift allowed for implementation of key aspects of the Wran Report, which recommended that expansion be funded by a user-pays system, with 'contributions by individual beneficiaries of higher education average around 20 per cent of course costs', payable as a tax levy after studies have ended (whether a degree was taken out or not).[178] The Report scrupulously avoids use of the politically charged word 'fees', but the tertiary tax scheme clearly amounts to a euphemistic re-institution of fees, even if the liability is payable after studies rather than before. Students would be permitted to pay the tertiary tax 'up front', and where paid by an employer the contribution would not be subject to the fringe benefits tax.[179]

Although the tertiary tax proposal has met with very strong opposition from academics, students, University Councils, parts of the trade union movement, the Left of the Labor Party and the youth wings of all four major political parties, a modified plan was approved by the Cabinet's Expenditure Review Committee (ERC) in late July 1988 and seems certain to be implemented.[180] Under the Wran plan, tax debits would be accrued at a rate of $3,000 per year for students in 'expensive' courses such as medicine, dentistry, veterinary science and agriculture; $2,500 per year for students in engineering, surveying and certain science courses; and $1,500 per year for all other courses, including Law.[181] However, the plan approved by the ERC calls for a flat charge of $1,800 per year for all courses, payable by a one-to-three per cent surtax which slides with income. The current administration charge (now $263) would be abolished. Although easier to administer, the new scheme is anomalous on its own user-pays terms. The cost per degree in Law, given the severe under-resourcing of Australian law schools, is $12,143, but law students who do five-year combined degrees will apparently be asked to re-pay $9,000. Students in engineering, medicine and veterinary science will re-pay the same amount even though their degrees cost the taxpayers $31,209, $53,393 and $69,845 respectively.[182]

In sum, the unwillingness of the Commonwealth government to maintain relative expenditure levels in higher education has forced it to seek alternative sources of revenue, most notably by placing a tax levy on graduates.[183] Earlier experience with fees and administrative charges suggests that even low levels of costs serve as a significant disincentive to participation in higher education for those disadvantaged groups which have traditionally been excluded. Whether expansion of the Austudy student financial support scheme and affirmative action admission policies will overcome this remains to be seen.

NOTES

[1] Report of the Committee of Inquiry into Legal Education in New South Wales (1979) (the 'Bowen Report') 6–9; L Martin 'From Apprenticeship to Law School: A Social History of Legal Education in Nineteenth Century New South Wales' (1986) 9 (2) UNSWLJ 111 at 113–120.

[2] Martin, ibid, at 120–143; D Derham 'Legal Education – University Education and Professional Training' (1962) 36 Australian Law Journal 209–212.

[3] Report of the Committee on the Future of Tertiary Education in Australia (1964) (the 'Martin Report') 70.

[4] Bowen Report, op cit, note 1, at 184; 'Legal Education and the Rationalisation of Law: A Tale of Two Countries' (paper presented at the Tenth World Congress of Sociology, Mexico City, August 1982) 20.

[5] Bowen Report, op cit, note 1 at 158–159 and 307.

[6] D Pearce, E Campbell and D Harding *Australian Law Schools: A Discipline Assessment for the Commonwealth Tertiary Education Commission* (1987) 472–476.

[7] Legal Practitioners Act 1959 (Tas), s 13(a)(iv).

[8] Legal Practitioners Act 1893 (WA), ss 15–16 and 19. See also the Report of the Committee of Inquiry into the Future Organisation of the Legal Profession of Western Australia (1983) (the 'Clarkson Report') 149 and 184–185.

[9] New South Wales Supreme Court, Solicitors Admission Rules 4(ddd) and (di).

[10] D Weisbrot 'The Australian Legal Profession: From Provincial Family Firms to Multinationals' in R Abel and P Lewis (eds) *Lawyers in Society – The Common Law World* (vol 1, 1988) 244 at 303, Table 6.1.

[11] Ibid at 304, Table 6.2.

[12] Ibid at 259.

[13] Bowen Report, op cit, note 1, at 61. See also C W Pincus 'Future Employment of Lawyers' (February 1980) Queensland Law Society Journal 45; and T W Beed and I G Campbell 'Supply and Demand Factors Associated with the Legal Profession in New South Wales' University of Sydney Sample Survey Centre Occasional Paper No 1 (1977) 72–73.

[14] Pearce Report, op cit, note 6, at 528.

[15] Graduate Careers Council of Australia '1986 Australian Graduates in 1987: Activities as at 30 April' (1987).

[16] DEIR Employment Prospects by Industry and Occupation (1983) 89.

[17] Pearce Report, op cit, note 6, at 24.

[18] CTEC 'Labour Market Factors Affecting Demand for Tertiary Education' (1986) para 19.

[19] Pearce Report, op cit, note 6, at 71.

[20] Law Society of New South Wales, Composition of the Profession (1978, Submission to the NSW Law Reform Commission) 14.

[21] See D Altman *Rehearsals for Change – Politics and Culture in Australia* (1980) 61–63; and J Wilton and R Bosworth *Old Worlds and New Australia – The Post-War Migration Experience* (1984).

[22] Law Society, op cit, note 20, at 14–15.

23 Reported in the *Sydney Morning Herald,* 6 August 1985, 3.

24 See, eg M Cass and R Sackville *Legal Needs of the Poor* (1975); J Fitzgerald *Poverty and the Legal Profession in Victoria* (1977); J McClintock 'Needs: Continuing Legal Education' in J Bowen and C Mitchelmore (eds) *Continuing Legal Education in the 1980s* (1981); and S Rendalls, R West and D Whitmont *The Legal Needs of Institutionalised People* (1985) 60–67.

25 M Hetherton *Victoria's Lawyers – Second Report* (1981) 34, 73 and 108–109; R Tomasic and C Bullard *Lawyers and Their Work in New South Wales* (1978) 178–181; Pearce Report, op cit, note 6, at vol 4, Appendix 5, 80–81 and 115–120; R Tomasic 'Social Organisation Amongst Australian Lawyers' (1983) 19 Australia and New Zealand Journal of Sociology 447 at 453 and 458.

26 R Cotterrell *The Sociology of Law: An Introduction* (184) 210–211.

27 J Goldring, 'An Updated Social Profile of Students Entering Law Courses' in the Pearce Report, op cit, note 6, Appendix 4, at 3.

28 Information from the University Registrar.

29 Goldring, op cit, note 27, at 3.

30 See the Pearce Report, op cit, note 6, at chapter 23. See also the Bowen Report, op cit, note 1, at 161.

31 Figures from national census reports of 1911, 1933, 1947 and 1954. For example, in 1954, 54.4 per cent of Australian lawyers were over 40, and 30.5 per cent were over 50.

32 'Age has not wearied them' (February 1988) Law Society Journal 8.

33 (August 1984) Law Society Journal 448.

34 Tomasic and Bullard, and Hetherton, op cit, note 25, at 21–22 and 11–12, respectively.

35 NSW Law Society figures on 30 June 1988. See also Hetherton, ibid at 318.

36 Loc cit, note 32.

37 A Sachs and J Wilson *Sexism and the Law* (1978) 177.

38 Ibid at 170.

39 See J Mathews 'The Changing Profile of Women in the Law' (1982) 56 Australian Law Journal 634.

40 Women's Legal Status Act 1918 (NSW). This Act also removed prohibitions on women becoming judges, magistrates, justices of the peace, and members of state parliament and local government councils.

41 Mathews, op cit, note 39.

42 Ibid.

43 J Musk 'An Overview of Women in the Legal Profession' (September 1984) Brief 6.

44 Tomasic, op cit, note 25, at 451; Mathews, op cit, note 39; and M Kirby 'The Women Are Coming' (June 1982) Australian Law News 11.

45 Pearce Report, op cit, note 6, at 451.

46 Australian Bureau of Statistics, Tertiary Education, New South Wales 1983 (1984) 15.

47 For example, at the University of New South Wales in 1987, the percentage of women entering the various faculties was as follows: Applied Science 36%; Architecture 44%; Arts 66%; Science 48%; Commerce (includes accounting) 46%; Engineering 8%; Law 48%; Medicine 40%; and Professional Studies 76% (includes social work and librarianship). See H Simpson 'Profile of New Undergraduate Students Enrolled at the University of New South Wales 1987: A Comparison with 1974' (Tertiary Education Research Centre, UNSW, Research and Development Paper No 67, September 1987) 1, Table 1.

48 Figures from the University Registrar. Cf Pearce Report, op cit, note 6, at 502, which suggests that the progression rate of women is 'normal', but uses a questionable statistical method to establish this.

49 Such as England. See Sachs and Wilson, op cit, note 37, at 176.

50 Figures obtained from the College of Law.

51 D S Anderson and J S Western 'Social Profiles of Students in Four Professions' (1970) 3(4) Quarterly Review of Australian Education 1, 20; Hetherton, op cit, note 25, at 116; and K Ziegert 'Students in Law School: Some Data on the Accumulation of Advantage' (unpublished, Sydney University Department of Jurisprudence, 1983) 9.

52 Ibid at 20.

53 B Winter 'Women Lawyers Work Harder, Are Paid Less, but They're Happy' (1983) 69 American Bar Association Journal 1384.

54 Hetherton, op cit, note 25. A summary of the report is also found in M Hetherton 'Practising Women Lawyers in Victoria – Some Survey Findings and Unanswered Questions' in P Cashman (ed) *Research and the Delivery of Legal Services* (1981) 300.

55 Ibid at 126.

56 Ibid at 116–119.

57 Ibid at 131–137.

58 Derived from Law Society statistics, December 1987. Another 25 per cent of male solicitors and 12.7 per cent of women solicitors are sole practitioners.

59 C Falls 'Unequal before the law – the long haul to partnership' *Times* on Sunday, 7 June 1987, 19.

60 Ibid.

61 Hetherton, op cit, note 25, at 131–137.

62 Pearce Report, op cit, note 6, at vol 4, Appendix 5, 115, Table 4.23.

63 (December 1, 1986) American Bar Association Journal 48, 52. Task forces on gender bias have also been established in New Jersey, Rhode Island, Arizona, Massachusetts, Illinois, Florida and California.

64 Sachs and Wilson, op cit, note 37, at 179–181.

65 L A LaMothe 'For Women Lawyers, It's Still an Uphill Climb' (September 1987) California Lawyer 8.

66 M Dixon and M Davis, 'The Legal Profession: Career Patterns and Expectations' (February 1986) 13 Brief 22, 24. This is the first part of a summary of a research project, the full results of which are in M Dixon and M Davies 'Career Patterns in the Legal Profession and Career Expectations of Male and Female Law Students in Western Australia: A Comparative Study' (University of Western Australia, 1985).

67 M Dixon and M Davies 'Career Paths in the Law – Part 2' (March 1986) 13 Brief 24, 25.

68 'High Court comes first for judge, although he will head Church' *Sydney Morning Herald,* 18 June 1985, 13.

69 R L Abel 'United States: The Contradictions of Professionalism', in R L Abel and P S C Lewis (eds) *Lawyers in Society: The Common Law World* (1988) 186 at 201.

70 R Tomasic and C Bullard, op cit, note 25, at 24.

71 R J Cameron *Year Book Australia 1985* (1985) 81.

72 For example, the 1986 census figures revealed that nearly 30 per cent of the population of Sydney was born outside Australia, with 584,000 persons born in non-English-speaking countries and 650,000 people speaking a language other than English at home. The figures are discussed in the *Sydney Morning Herald,* 7 July 1987, 3.

73 Cameron, op cit, note 71, at 82.

74 Tomasic and Bullard, op cit, note 18, at 21–23.

75 M Hetherton, *Victoria's Lawyers* (1978) 15–17.

76 Ibid at 16, Table 2.4.

77 Pearce Report, op cit, note 6, at vol 4, 20, Tables 2.4–2.5.

78 Anderson and Western, op cit, note 51, at 22.

79 D Anderson, R Boven, P J Fensham and J P Powell, *Students in Australian Higher Education: A Study of Their Social Composition Since the Abolition of Fees* (1980) 93. Law was second to Education and just ahead of Medicine in the percentage of Australian-born students. At the University of New South Wales in 1985, law students were the most Australian-born of any faculty, with 81 per cent. This compares with 71 per cent of all students, and 62 per cent in medicine, 73 per cent in architecture and 60 per cent in education.

80 See Disney et al *Lawyers* (1986) 290–291, and the Bowen Report, op cit, note 1, at 95–96.

81 Hetherton, op cit, note 25, at 34–35.

82 Ziegert, op cit, note 51, at 22–24.

83 R Tomasic 'Lawyers and Social Control – A Preliminary Inquiry' (1983) 3 Windsor Yearbook of Access to Justice 20 at 47.

84 F C Hutley, unpublished submission, 29 April 1977, at 11.

85 M Cass and R Sackville, op cit, note 24, at 88.

86 Hutley, op cit, note 84, at 10.

87 R D Linke, L M Oertel and N J M Kelsey 'Participation and Equity in Higher Education: A Preliminary Report on the Socio-economic Profile of Higher Education Students in South Australia 1974–1984' (1985) 11(3) Australian Bulletin of Labour 124, 138.

88 G Whitlam *The Whitlam Government 1972–1975* (1985) 323.

89 R D Linke, 'The Facts of the Matter – Equality: Forwards or Backwards?' (paper presented at the seminar on Access to Higher Education, at the ANU, Canberra, on 3 December 1987) 4. See also Linke et al, op cit, note 87; Anderson et al, op cit, note 79; D S Anderson and A E Vervorn *Access to Privilege: Patterns of Participation in Australian Post-Secondary Education* (1983) 129–149; and articles in (1987) 13(2) Australian Bulletin of Labour 108–125.

90 See, eg 'Dawkins questions free education's value to the poor' *Sydney Morning Herald,* 8 October 1987, 3; and 'Free tertiary education a failure, says Dawkins' *Sydney Morning Herald,* 5 May 1988, 2.

91 Linke, op cit, note 89, at 5.

92 C McGregor 'Labor excludes its own' *Sydney Morning Herald,* 6 June 1988, 15.

93 Linke et al, op cit, note 87, at 138.
94 Anderson and Western, op cit, note 51, at 24.
95 Goldring, op cit, note 27, at 7. In 1976, the figures were 28% and 11.2%, respectively.
96 'Not enough graduates, industry forum told' *Sydney Morning Herald,* 30 March 1987, 5.
97 Anderson et al, op cit, note 79, at 77.
98 Tomasic and Bullard, op cit, note 25, at 178–179.
99 M Hetherton, op cit, note 75, at 12–14.
100 Goldring, op cit, note 27, at 13, Table 16. See also Anderson et al, op cit, note 79, at 81–82. Anderson found that law students had the lowest representation of fathers who worked as manual labourers (5.9%) – somewhat lower than medical students (12.3%), considerably lower than arts students (21.3%), and far below the national figure (over 40%).
101 Anderson et al, op cit, note 79, at 87 and 92. See also Goldring, op cit, note 6, at 9–12.
102 Goldring, op cit, note 27, at 10. The income brackets of the fathers of Macquarie students divided according to whether the students were enrolled in the full-time LLB course or the external course.
103 M Sexton and L Maher *The Legal Mystique: The Role of Lawyers in Australian Society* (1982) 8.
104 Tomasic and Bullard, op cit, note 25, at 23 and 177.
105 Hetherton, op cit, note 75, at 15.
106 Goldring, op cit, note 27, at 14. See also the survey of law graduates in the Pearce Report, op cit, note 6, at volume 4, Appendix 5, 81. Twenty-seven per cent of graduates reported that they had at least one close relative in the legal profession.
107 Tomasic, op cit, note 83, at 47.
108 P Smark and J Whelan 'A Middle-Class Dilemma: How to Educate Kate and James' *Sydney Morning Herald,* 22 July 1985, 4.
109 J Higley, D Deacon and D Smart *Elites in Australia* (1979) 86.
110 Ibid.
111 Ibid at 87–88, Table 3.3.
112 Smark and Whelan, op cit, note 108.
113 D S Anderson and J S Western 'Notes on a Study of Professional Socialisation' (1967) 3 Australian and New Zealand Journal of Sociology 67, 70.
114 Anderson et al, op cit, note 79, at 124.
115 Tomasic, op cit, note 44, at 451–452.
116 Goldring, op cit, note 27, at 5–6, and the Pearce Report, op cit, note 6, at vol 4, 23–24, respectively.
117 J R Bradsen and J A Farrington 'Student selection and performance in the Faculty of Law, The University of Adelaide' (1986) 29(1) Australian Universities' Review 25 at 31. A rough residential division of Adelaide also indicated that 'the more affluent eastern/north Adelaide areas are particularly strongly represented in the Law School.' Ibid. See also C Power, F Robertson and M Baker *Access to Higher Education: Participation Equity and Policy* (CTEC, 1986) 97–103. This study was of entry (and non-entry) into higher education in South Australia in 1985, and found that law, with medicine, architecture and fine arts, stood out 'as the courses which are most elitist in terms of students' family background.' Ibid at 100. More than half of law students attended independent secondary schools (53%, and 18% Catholic) and had fathers with degrees who were professionals. The average income of law students' parents was significantly higher than in any other course, and a far greater proportion of law students (27%) were in the top income bracket (more than $50,000). Ibid at 144, Table 7.3.
118 *Trends in Commonwealth Spending in Schools,* discussed in A Suskind 'Funding to private schools up 123 pc' *Sydney Morning Herald,* 31 July 1987, 4.
119 Ibid, and see M D Kirby 'Recession, Law Reform and Education' (1983) 13 Queensland Law Society Journal 62, 68–69.
120 W Jamrozik 'Children of the State learn in private' *Sydney Morning Herald,* 31 December 1987, 3.
121 Tomasic, op cit, note 44, at 453.
122 In surveys of recent graduates carried out by the Young Lawyers Section of the Law Society of New South Wales in 1979 and 1982, respondents reported that 'friends or relatives' were among the two or three most important sources of employment. See 'Careers Survey' (August 1984) Law Society Journal 448.
123 See Ziegert, op cit, note 51.
124 Power et al, op cit, note 117, at p ii.
125 Pearce Report, op cit, note 6, at 470.
126 Bradsen and Farrington, op cit, note 117, at 25.
127 *Sydney Morning Herald,* 23 September 1987, 12.
128 Pearce Report, op cit, note 6, at 471 and 474.

[129] Ibid at 484.

[130] Power et al, op cit, note 117, at p ii.

[131] D Beswick, M Hayden and H Schofield *Evaluation of the Tertiary Assistance Scheme* (1983); and R D Linke 'Implications of Alternative Selection Procedures for Tertiary Education in Australia' (paper delivered at the Conference on A New Order for Tertiary Education in Australia, Darling Downs Institute of Advanced Education, 9–12 July 1987) 18.

[132] Power et al, op cit, note 117, at 173.

[133] Figures from the Commonwealth Schools Commission.

[134] Linke, op cit, note 131, at 3. These are 1984 figures.

[135] A Susskind 'In some schools, few pupils reach Year 12' *Sydney Morning Herald*, 20 February 1987, 1, 5.

[136] Volume 1, p 59, paras 3.77–3.78. See also chapter 3 of the Report of the Committee of Enquiry Review of Efficiency and Effectiveness in Higher Education (1986), esp at 94.

[137] Response of the Australian Law School Deans to the Higher Education Policy Discussion Paper (Green Paper) (May 1988), 5.

[138] Power et al, op cit, note 117, at 166, 170.

[139] S Marginson 'A tax on participation?' (February 1988) 7(2) Australian Society 31 at 32; M O'Callaghan 'Tertiary fee forces thousands to quit' *Sydney Morning Herald*, 11 April 1987, 3; A Susskind '$250 uni levy "crippling" for young women' *Sydney Morning Herald*, 11 March 1987, 6.

[140] Pearce Report, op cit, note 6, at 480–481.

[141] Op cit, note 136, at paras 3.79–3.81.

[142] Law Deans' Response, op cit, note 137, at 5.

[143] See eg, Power et al, op cit, note 117, at 20, 45 and 174; and Efficiency and Effectiveness Report, op cit, note 136, at 90.

[144] Figures from the CTEC.

[145] Pearce Report, op cit, note 6, at 477–478.

[146] Law Deans' Response, op cit, note 137, at 4–5.

[147] Pearce Report, op cit, note 6, at 474.

[148] Ibid at 475.

[149] Power et al, op cit, note 117, at 177.

[150] O Fulton 'Principles and Policies' in O Fulton (ed) *Access to Higher Education* (1981) 5 at 23.

[151] Power et al, op cit, note 117, at 104–113, 172 and 178; and Efficiency and Effectiveness Report, op cit, note 136, at 73–74.

[152] Power et al, op cit, note 117, at 212, Table 10.

[153] Ibid at 178 and 212, Table 10.

[154] Pearce Report, op cit, note 6, at 473.

[155] L H T West, T Hore, E G Eaton and B M Kermond *The Impact of Higher Education on Mature Age Students* (CTEC, 1986) 20.

[156] Pearce Report, op cit, note 6, at 482.

[157] Goldring, op cit, note 27, at 15–16.

[158] Power et al, op cit, note 117, at iii and 179.

[159] See note 139, above, and accompanying text.

[160] Pearce Report, op cit, note 6, at 471–472.

[161] Bradsen and Farrington, op cit, note 117, at 30.

[162] Pearce Report, op cit, note 6, at 483 and 486.

[163] Ibid at 487–488.

[164] Law Deans' Response, op cit, note 137, at 5.

[165] Pearce Report, op cit, note 6, at 473–474 and 482–483.

[166] L M Garcia '"Middle class" Sydney Uni may relent' *Sydney Morning Herald*, 9 March 1985, 4. Sydney University ultimately adopted the 'Broadway scheme', to commence in 1988, after a 'long and bitter fight' in the University Senate. The scheme is similar to the UNSW ACCESS programme described below, setting aside about ten per cent of places annually for disadvantaged students, who nevertheless must be within 30 or so marks of the cut-off point. Interestingly, most of the reportage of the establishment of the Broadway scheme focussed on the fact that reservation of places for disadvantaged students absent any increase in places overall would cause aggregate cut-off points to rise for students who apply through the normal channels. See, eg A Susskind 'New quota squeezes university vacancies' *Sydney Morning Herald*, 20 June 1987, 7.

[167] Faculty Resolution 86/9, 11 June 1986.

[168] Higher Education: A Policy Discussion Paper (1988).

[169] Report of the Committee on Higher Education Funding (the Wran Report) (1988).

[170] For six crucial commentaries on the Green Paper by leading educationists, see 'Education for what?', (February 1988) 7(2) Australian Society 25–33.

[171] Efficiency and Effectiveness Report, op cit, note 136, at 97. Success rates are defined as the 'ratio of the number of subjects/units passed in a given year to the total number of subjects/units in which students were enrolled for that year'.

[172] Ibid at 95.

[173] Ibid at 92–94.

[174] Power et al, op cit, note 117, at 167.

[175] Wran Report, op cit, note 169, Recommendations 15–20. Special study grants to Aboriginal students would also be enhanced.

[176] Pearce Report, op cit, note 6, at 485.

[177] Ibid at 483.

[178] Wran Report, op cit, note 169, Recommendations 1–6.

[179] Ibid, Recommendations 5 and 26.

[180] M Steketee 'Discount if students pay in advance' *Sydney Morning Herald*, 30 July 1988, 4.

[181] Wran Report, op cit, note 169, Recommendation 2.

[182] W Jamrozik 'What's the price of an education?' *Sydney Morning Herald*, 7 May 1988, 1.

[183] The Wran Report also considers industry levies as an additional source of revenue, but this has not been taken further. See Recommendation 22.

6 Access to legal education and the profession in Canada

*Brian M Mazer**

Introduction

The Canadian legal system is composed, by constitutional divisions, of a Civil Law system unique to Québec and Common Law systems unique to each of the other nine provinces and the two territories. Issues of legal education and the profession therefore are often unique to either the Common Law or Civil Law systems. In addition, since legislative jurisdiction over the legal profession and universities is a provincial matter, there are, particularly in Common Law Canada, variations in the regulations and rules regarding admission, curriculum, period of articles or clerkship, Bar admission, et cetera.

Québec, where the legal profession is split between notaries and the Bar, has five Law Faculties which offer courses of study leading to a civil law degree. In addition, one of those Faculties also offers a course of study for an LLB as well as a combined Civil Law-Common Law degree programme. There is also one Faculty in Ontario, at the University of Ottawa, which has both a Civil Law and a Common Law section offering separate degrees and a combined degree programme.

Each of the other provinces, except Newfoundland, Prince Edward Island, and the Northwest and Yukon Territories, have at least one Law Faculty. The more populous provinces have more than one law school: Ontario (6), British Columbia (2) and Alberta (2). In addition New Brunswick has two Common Law Faculties; one offering instruction in English and one in French. There are therefore 16 Law Faculties offering Common Law programmes and six Faculties offering Civil Law programmes.

The level of homogeneity among the group of Common Law Faculties and among the group of Civil Law Faculties is sufficient in terms of admission and curriculum, due in part to the requirements of professional accreditation, so that some observations about their roles and responsibilities as one of the levels of gatekeeping for the legal profession can be made. It is apparent and important to note that there are numerous differences among the various law schools. The commonalities are tremendous but one should not conclude that they are identical.

* Professor and Associate Dean, Faculty of Law, University of Windsor. The author wishes to thank Ms Jeanine Watt and Mr Tom Serafimovsky, students at the faculty during the preparation of the paper in 1986–87, for their thorough research assistance and unique insight into the issues of access to legal education and profession. In addition the author is grateful to Professors R Simmonds (McGill), D Purich (Native Law Centre, Saskatchewan), J Berryman (Windsor) and Dean N Gold (Windsor) for their helpful comments on previous drafts.

Similar comments can be made about the governing bodies of the legal profession in each jurisdiction. Each has its own unique requirements for professional qualification. The differences may not be great in some situations while in others they are significant.

This examination of issues of access will focus primarily upon access to legal education at the university level. This was selected because a university law degree is a prerequisite to professional qualification and therefore law school admission is critical to a determination of access, not simply to a legal education, but also the profession.

Canada is an example of a system where access to professional qualification is controlled, at least initially, and to a great extent, by decisions of admission by the Law Faculties. There are few alternative routes to professional quali-fication. Although the history varies among the provinces, since the 1950s a university law degree has been a requirement for admission to the legal profession. Alternative routes of access to the legal profession have existed. Persons with law degrees and/or professional credentials from foreign jur-isdictions have applied for admission to the bars of the various provinces. However admission to the practice of law in the respective provinces will usually require, prior to some period of articles or clerkship and Bar admission course, attendance at an accredited Law Faculty for a period of time usually ranging from one semester to two academic years. An independent admission decision by the respective Law Faculties is necessary, in addition to the determination of advanced standing toward professional qualification. Only on rare occasions will an applicant be permitted to substitute qualifying examinations in place of attendance at a Canadian Law Faculty. Therefore, the admission decisions of the Canadian Law Faculties have a tremendous effect upon entry to and the composition of the legal profession.

The profession, particularly through its control of post-university law degree qualification requirements such as the period of articles or clerkship and the Bar admission course and examinations, also plays a gatekeeper's role with regard to access to the profession. Reference will be made below to some of the issues of access directly related to the profession, such as articling, professional qualification and the number of lawyers.

Law school admission criteria

The initial issue of access to legal education and the profession is the criteria employed in the decisions for admission to law school. Since the Civil Law and Common Law programmes are quite distinct, they will be dealt with separ-ately. It should again be noted that the two Faculties which have both Common Law and Civil Law programmes offer a special programme by which graduates can receive both degrees normally after one extra year of study. However admission decisions are initially made to either the Civil Law or the Common Law programme quite separately.

(a) Civil law

Six Canadian Law Faculties offer programmes of study leading to a Civil Law degree, which will entitle the individual to continue to professional qualification in Québec. With the exception of the Civil Law section of the University of Ottawa, which borders Québec, all the Faculties are located in Québec. The language of instruction in the Civil Law programmes, except the one at McGill University, is primarily French and the vast majority of applicants are from Québec. The size of the first-year classes varies considerably among the Faculties, from about 75 to 375.[1] The number of applications received each year is considerably greater than the number of spaces available.

There are four general categories for admission: Students who come directly from the post-secondary college system; those who have completed one or more university degrees; those who have completed the college system and attended university without completing a degree; and those who have been in the workplace, whether or not they have completed a degree. The majority of first-year Civil Law students are admitted directly from the colleges except at McGill University where the proportion is significantly less. With the exception of McGill, a substantial number, but significantly less than those from the colleges, would have completed some university, and most likely have received a degree. It thus would appear that at only one Faculty would there be more than 50% of the first-year class with a previous university degree.

Each of the law schools admits 'adult' or 'mature' students; those who enter after time in the workplace. One has a fixed percentage of the places available in the first-year class allocated for mature students, while another has a 'ceiling'. The others do not have fixed numbers of spaces, although one Faculty determines the number of places available based upon the proportion of applications received in each of the categories.

The criteria for admission are different for each of the categories. For the majority of first-year admissions, those who come directly from the college system in Québec, the single most important factor is the transcript of grades. Three of the six Faculties use the grades as the sole criterion. One Faculty employs the college grades and score achieved on an aptitude test (not the Law School Admission Test which is used at almost all the Common Law Faculties), applying a mathematical formula, which places greater emphasis upon college grades. Another Faculty, which also places the greatest weight on the college grades, also requires academic reference and information from the candidate about his/her career goals and extracurricular activities. One Faculty appears to place greater weight on other factors than college grades, such as background experiences, a presentation by the candidate and a special law-related questionnaire. Interviews are utilised by the latter two schools.

For the applicants who have attended university, each Faculty places different weight on university and college grades. Only one Faculty appears to have preferences for certain disciplines, assuming comparable grades. It appears that only two Faculties have a preference for applicants who have undertaken university study, which would account for the fact that those Faculties appear to have the highest percentage of entering students with university education.

Finally, the definition and criteria for admission of mature students varies among the schools. Most of the Faculties appear to place a great deal of weight on interviews with the candidates. Factors which are considered include the age (minimum varies from 21 to 23), the length and type of work experience, and educational background.

(b) Common law

Sixteen Law Faculties offer programmes of study leading to a Bachelor of Laws degree, which can qualify the graduate to pursue professional qualification in any province or territory in Canada. One Faculty provides instruction primarily in French, a few offer some instruction in French and for the majority, the language of instruction is English. One Faculty requires its Common Law students to do what amounts to the private law component of the first year of the Civil Law degree. This, as well as other coursework, requires this Faculty to demand at least reading proficiency in French from its incoming common law class, despite the fact its language of instruction is English.

The number of places available in the first year varies considerably, from approximately 35 (at the francophone Common Law Faculty) to 325. There are significantly more applications for admission than places available in the first-year classes.

Generally speaking, there are three categories of admission candidates: applicants with a minimum of two or three years of undergraduate university education ('regular' applicants), applicants who have spent some time in the workforce ('mature' applicants) and applicants who are of native Canadian ancestry (discussed in a separate section below).[2] The vast majority of first year students at Common Law Faculties are admitted in the category of regular applicants. A small proportion of first-year students are mature applicants and an even smaller number of native Canadians attend first-year law school.

Most Common Law Faculties do not have geographic preferences. However, Faculties, which are the only law school in the province, have some sort of preference for their own residents. A couple have quotas based upon residence and some have a preference, in addition to the home province, for residents of the two territories and the two provinces which do not have Law Faculties.

The determinaton of admission for regular applicants is based primarily upon two criteria: grades achieved at university and performance on the Law School Admission Test (LSAT). Most Law Faculties require a minimum of two years undergraduate study at university. Three Faculties require a minimum of three years and one places a condition requiring the promise of future completion of a third year of undergraduate study upon successful applicants who have only two years of pre-law study. The remaining Faculties appear to have an informal preference for applicants with more than two years of undergraduate study.

With the exception of the University of Moncton, which offers its programme in French, all the law schools consider the applicant's performance on the LSAT. This American test, which claims to be a predictor of success in first-year law studies, has been the subject of concern and, at times, criticism.[3] Most Law Faculties factor LSAT scores in with a grade point average to produce a 'ranking' of regular applicants so that offers of acceptance can be made. The value of the LSAT score and grade point average varies but it would appear that grade point average factors in with greater weight.

Some law schools have other criteria which are also considered in evaluating regular applicants. These include non-academic achievement, work experience, linguistic, socio-economic and ethnic backgrounds, community involvement, and physical disability.

One Faculty, this author's own, makes a particular point of basing and being seen to base all its admission decisions, excepting native Canadian applicants, upon an evaluation of the applicant's ability not only to succeed in the study of law, but also upon the applicant's potential to contribute to society, the law school and the profession. This Faculty has no minimum requirements in terms of university education or LSAT scores and makes no admission decision based upon a mathematical calculation of those factors. The selection of first-year students is based upon an evaluation of the applicant's credentials including an autobiographical questionnaire and academic and non-academic references. As described in the admission information and Faculty Calendar, the specific criteria employed are: university or other post-secondary programme, work experience, community involvement, personal accomplishments, career objectives, personal considerations (such as illness, disabilities, unusual family or other responsibilities) and LSAT scores.

With the exception of the University of Windsor, the other Law Faculties have a separate discretionary category of admission for mature candidates. The definition and criteria for evaluation of mature candidates vary. Some Faculties employ a minimum age requirement (between 25 and 30) while others require a minimum number of years of non-academic or work experience (usually five). Most require a minimum amount of university education. Curiously, some require the same minimum of university study as with the regular applicants. Presumably, then, mature applicants would not be as academically competitive or they would have been admitted as regular applicants. All Law Faculties waive or relax the minimum standards which are employed in evaluating regular applicants. However some Faculties do have minimum standards in terms of grades and LSAT scores specific to the mature category.

In various ways all these Faculties, in the evaluation of mature candidates, attempt to assess at least some of the factors such as work experience, maturity, personal or other disadvantages, physical handicaps and potential to contribute to society. It is unclear how many places in each Faculty's first-year class are available to mature students, or how such a determination is made. It would appear that, as with the Civil Law Faculties, some Common Law Faculties have a fixed number or proportion of the class allocated for mature students while others have a ceiling.

This descriptive summary of admission criteria in Canada raises some access questions. It is clear that the vast majority of Canadian law students are admitted primarily, if not solely, based upon their post-secondary academic performance and, in the Common Law Faculties, the Law School Admission Test score. There does not appear to be any systematic delineation of goals for law school admission which would explain the reason for selection of these factors as the sole or major criteria. It might be said that undergraduate education is an important predictor of success at law study. There is intuitive appeal for such an approach. However, unless the goal is to select those who will achieve the highest grades in law study (which would require a major longitudinal study for verification) there appears to be a large number of applicants who would, based on the factors, be 'qualified' to study law, in that they are not likely to fail. Furthermore Law Faculties which employ mandatory, or even suggested, grade distribution schemes appear to be coun-ter-acting an admission policy which seeks to select those who will achieve the highest grades. If the Faculties are successful in the application of such admission criteria for first-year law students, it would be necessary to artificially devalue the students' performances at law school in order to 'fit' a pre-determined grade distribution scheme.

Perhaps the greatest concern with such admission criteria is that admission based solely upon grades or grades and LSAT must accept any imperfections, biases and failures of the pre-law school education system as a whole and fails to consider the educational situation or experience of the individual applicant or particular class of applicants. If the allegation is at all true that the Canadian education system has cultural and other biases, this type of admission practice perpetuates such biases. The result is that ultimately the legal profession itself will reflect those biases for generations to come.

There is an inherent assumption in such a system of admission selection that all applicants are relatively equal so that differences in grades achieved are valid indicators of different potential and accomplishment. Since the Canadian education system is not uniform in terms of content or quality and the individuals in Canada's heterogeneous society are clearly not identical, it is difficult to accept the validity of the premises for such admissions determinations. The academic criterion is certainly a valid and relevant factor in an admissions decision. However the importance of pre-law university education, it is submitted, is not the grade point average but rather the individual's achievements in light of his/her personal situation and the extent to which that achievement can provide an indicator of the potential to succeed in law study.

Finally, the use of such limited criteria fails to consider qualities, characteristics and factors, other than academic accomplishment to date and the LSAT prediction of relative success in first-year law study, which may be relevant and important to competency, and hopefully excellence, in a career as a legal professional.

The major difficulty in departing, in any significant way, from the current practice, is the lack of 'quantifiable' criteria which will allow the admission system to continue to be administratively workable. The experience at the University of Windsor, which does not make any admissions decisions based upon such a mathematical calculation, indicates that a departure from current practice elsewhere will require an increase in labour and a significant commitment on the part of the Faculty, the Admissions Committee and to some degree the University administration in terms of funding. Windsor's is not the only method by which broader based admissions decisions could be made. Some other Canadian Law Faculties are attempting to employ broader based criteria in a more limited way. However any broader based system will require more effort.

Serious consideration of the policy aspects of the determination of admission criteria is essential. It is not sufficient simply to rely upon the discretionary mature category as an adequate compensation for the alleged deficiencies. The mature student category accounts for a limited number of places for first-year students and therefore does not address these concerns in terms of the majority of future legal professionals. Further, it is submitted that younger students should also be evaluated by criteria which each Law Faculty determines to be important to the educational goals of the institution with reference to the profession and the variety of career prospects of their graduates. Choices must be made among the many applicants. While it may be 'administratively defensible' to point to 'objective criteria' in the form of grade point averages and LSAT scores, Canadian Law Faculties can and should confront the issues of access to legal education through a re-examination of the objectives and criteria employed in making the choices of who is in and who is not.

Half-time legal study

Almost all law school legal education in Canada requires full-time study for three academic years. This creates a significant barrier to legal education to those with disabilities, family, financial and other responsibilities. A half-time legal study programme, requiring six years to complete the law degree would appear to provide an important alternative route for legal study. Three Common Law Faculties have established limited half-time programmes and at least three others plan to institute a programme in the near future.

It is important that the programme of study and scheduling of required courses be designed so as to permit a real ability on the part of the student to maintain the work or family commitments and still have an adequate opportunity for study and learning. A half-time programme should also allow the student, at appropriate points in time, to switch to full-time study should his/her circumstances or commitments allow.

There do not appear to be significant educational or administrative concerns which militate strongly against the adoption of half-time study programmes at more Law Faculties in Canada. This would certainly enhance access to legal education to those whose circumstances are such as to render them unable to study full-time.

The gender gap

The proportion of women in the legal profession is directly related to the gender gap in Canadian law schools. This problem will be examined from the perspective of law school admission as well as career opportunities.

Although statistics regarding the number of male and female members of the legal profession in each of the provinces and territories were not forthcoming in response to an inquiry, based upon the information available, it appears safe to conclude that, at present, outside of Québec, the female membership in the legal profession is 15–20%. In Québec slightly more than 24% of the notaries are women. Furthermore since the increase in the proportion of women law students has been a relatively recent phenomenon,[4] one can safely assume that the proportional representation of women in the profession previously was much lower.

The initial point of inquiry must be admission to law schools.[5] The proportion of female law students rose sharply in the late 1960s and 1970s. Although national statistics were not collected at this time, the Ontario experience, it is asserted, is sufficiently indicative of the phenomenon among Common Law schools.[6] In 1977–78 women comprised approximately 31% of the Ontario first-year law school population, compared with the 1986–87 figure of 43.5%.[7] (The Canada-wide English language Common Law Faculty figure for 1986–87 is 42.5%.) It is likely that there will continue to be an increasing number of women entering the legal profession, at least for the foreseeable future.

It is important to attempt to identify reasons for this phenomenon. One plausible explanation can be found by analogy to the proportion of university Master degrees being awarded to women during this time. While the percentge of Bachelor degrees awarded to women increased slightly between 1978 and

1982 (48.5% to 50.9%), there was a marked increase in the percentage of Master degrees being awarded to women (32.8% to 40.6%).[8] One hypothesis is that whatever was previously acting as a barrier to women pursuing graduate work at the Master's level was also inhibiting women from pursuing a legal education. This is not a particularly satisfactory explanation because it does not identify the factors which have increased (or previously inhibited) access to legal education and graduate work. However it does indicate that further study is necessary.

Three other possible explanations are worthy of note. The 1986–87 Canadian English speaking Common Law school statistics indicate that 42.5% of the students are female. Yet only 36.62% of the applications received were from women and approximately 40% of the offers of places in the class were made to women. One might conclude that, on the whole, the women who apply are more qualified than the men, based upon whatever criteria are employed in admissions selection among the various law schools. Since none of the law schools indicates quotas for women students, that conclusion is reinforced. However it must be borne in mind that an unknown, but significant number of candidates apply to more than one Law Faculty. It may be that a greater proportion of the males to whom offers are made, have greater choice as to which law school to attend. The type of data necessary to analyse these hypotheses is difficult to obtain.

While close to 50% of university bachelor degrees and 40% of Master degrees are awarded to women, only 37% of the applications to law school are from women. There may be a number of reasons for this apparent lesser interest in law as an educational goal. Certainly the small proportion of women in the legal profession would lend credence to the theory that there are insufficient career role models. Further, it may be that a greater proportion of women than men pursue careers immediately after receipt of a Bachelor degree. This may include the decision to pursue a career in the home.

Another hypothesis may be that, as yet, the profession as a whole has not made accommodations for the social and biological realities of women in practice. The quality of life currently representative of the profession may dissuade qualified men and women who prefer primary or equal commitment to family and other interests, rather than to the 'firm'. A disproportionate number of women already prefer to become sole practitioners or enter industry in order to control their work hours. If there is to be a serious narrowing of the gender gap, more flexibility may be necessary, including half-time lawyering or job-sharing plans.

Gender would also appear to be a factor in access to the legal profession subsequent to graduation from law school. Studies conducted in British Columbia[9] and Ontario[10] both conclude that women encounter greater difficulty in obtaining articling positions. Furthermore the Ontario study, which was conducted in 1979 with recent graduates of the Bar Admission Course, indicated that a greater percentage of women than men did not have permanent legal employment upon completion of the Bar Admission Course in Ontario, although the gap appears to be narrowing, and it took women longer to secure permanent legal employment.[11] Finally, the study also indicated a gender-related salary differential. Larger percentages of female than male respondents appeared in the lowest salary category and larger percentages of male than female respondents appeared in the highest salary category.[12] Marie Huxter, in the Ontario study, also identified a significant difference in the kinds of questions asked of the male and female respondents when they were interviewed for articling positions or permanent legal employment.[13]

Although the two studies of the relationship between gender and post-law school employment opportunities were conducted in the 1970s, there has been little evidence of any significant change in the situation. Perhaps with the increased number of women in the legal profession since the latest study in 1979 and the progression over time of the status and influence of women lawyers within the law firms, the opportunities for female law graduates may be improving.

Native Canadians

Native people in Canada have never been represented in any significant or proportionate way in the legal profession. The number of native Canadian lawyers has been woefully inadequate. In 1972 there were only five lawyers in all of Canada known to be of native ancestry.[14] In 1981, there were approximately 70 lawyers known to be of native ancestry among a lawyer population of 34,200.[15] The status of native lawyers in terms of influence and input in the governance of the profession has not been significant, to say the least.

Several factors have contributed to this situation.[16] A major barrier to natives attending Canadian law schools was the admission requirement of completion of a minimum of two years of undergraduate university study. Since, until the 1970s, there were few native Canadians pursuing university study, the 'pool' of potential applicants was severely restricted.

Professor R Carter, the first director of the Program of Legal Studies for Native People, also identified two further problems militating against persons of native ancestry gaining admission to law school and ultimately the legal profession.[17] Given the highly competitive nature of the usual Canadian Common Law school admission selection, based primarily upon undergraduate grades and Law School Admission Test scores, native Canadian applicants are disadvantaged. Professor Carter indicates that the undergraduate university performances of native applicants are often lower than that which would otherwise be achieved. He attributes this to inadequate educational facilities at the primary and secondary levels. Furthermore Professor Carter points out that Law School Admission Test scores, as acknowledged by the test designers, may be of questionable predictive value in indicating a candidate's ability when s/he has an educational and cultural background significantly different from the average middle-class person.

For these, and other reasons, the Program of Legal Studies for Native People was established in 1973 at the University of Saskatchewan Native Law Centre. The programme consists of an eight-week summer orientation course open to 'status' and 'non-status' native people. Financial assistance, primarily from the Federal Departments of Indian and Northern Affairs and Justice, is available to cover tuition, books and living expenses. The goal of the programme is to provide the students with the nature and methodology of legal study in order to better prepare the graduates for full-time legal study.

The programme of study includes methodology and content in usual first-year law courses such as Torts, Contracts, Criminal Law, Property as well as Legal Writing and Research and Native Law and a moot court. Class instruction is provided by Faculty from among the Canadian law schools and tutorials are led by graduates from the programme itself. The students are assessed and graded, based upon four criteria: language facility, reasoning and analytical ability, motivation to succeed in law study and work habits.[18] An overall grade indicating the teaching group's prediction of the student's probability of academic success in full-time law study is also made.

The programme's success in preparing its graduates for law school study should be measured, not so much on the student's knowledge of the substantive course material, but rather upon the student's learning of the methodology and discipline of the study of law. While familiarity with material likely to be encountered in the first year of law school is valuable in assisting the native Canadian law student through the adjustment period encountered by all first-year students, the finite nature of the substantive knowledge will eventually be exhausted. Without solid methodological grounding, the native Canadian law student will encounter significant difficulty with new substantive materials and in courses which were not offered in the summer programme.

From the viewpoint of access to legal education, the initial achievement of the Program of Legal Studies for Native Canadians is the placement and success of native Canadians in the Law Faculties. From the inception of the programme in 1973 until October 1985, 202 of a total of 302 registrants completed the eight-week course and were recommended to the law schools. One hundred and eighty-nine of the candidates who were recommended did enrol in a law school and 73 had graduated from law studies while 47 were enrolled at that time in one of the three years of their law school studies.[19] The vast majority of the graduates of the programme who attended law school (at least 182 of 189) gained admission into law school because of the programme and the discretionary admissions policies which have developed at the law schools.[20]

A second and related achievement in terms of access has been the establishment, at all the English language Common Law schools, of a discretionary admission category for native Canadian applicants. The criteria employed in evaluating applications varies. Some Faculties have a separate category for native Canadians while a few consider the applicants in a discretionary category of disadvantaged persons. All Faculties appear to have relaxed minimum standards. As well, all Faculties encourage attendance at, while some require successful completion of, the Program of Legal Studies for Native Canadians. Reference to the various Faculty calendars indicates that only one faculty guarantees automatic admission to all native Canadian applicants who successfully complete and are recommended by the programme. However it appears that the practice of most faculties is to grant admission to successful graduates of the programme.

In light of Professor Carter's comments, referred to above, regarding undergraduate university and Law School Admission Test scores, it is worth noting that it appears that all but one Faculty (the University of Windsor) require that the applicant write the LSAT, although there may be no, or a relaxed, minimum score. Furthermore some Faculties require a minimum of two years of undergraduate university education, although there is a relaxed standard regarding grades achieved. Since the Saskatchewan programme has been successful in its objectives of providing successful graduates with a good methodological and substantive pre-law school education and of predicting the probability of success in law studies, one might legitimately call into question arbitrary minimum requirements such as two years of undergraduate university education, or the writing of the Law School Admission Test.

The two-year university requirement may be justified on grounds other than its value as a predictor of success in the study of law. One such reason may be the value of a general education to the understanding and ultimately the practice of the law. While this may be an important consideration, an examination of the curriculum and teaching at Canadian law schools and Bar Admission Courses does not indicate much congruency with this premise. Traditionally, legal education in Canada has placed little emphasis or value upon the educational or other experiences of the students or on interdisciplinary study of law.

The Law School Admission Test requirement is perhaps more perplexing. If Professor Carter's comments are correct that the scores of native Canadian applicants for the reason he mentions are of questionable predictive value, and further noting that the teaching group provides predictions of success after eight weeks of close teaching/learning contact, the relevance of this requirement can be called into question. Perhaps these scores may be used in some statistical validity study, either internal to the admissions policy of an individual faculty or among all the Faculties with native Canadian law students. However if that were the reason for the requirement, the study should have been undertaken and completed by now so that more solid grounds for the requirement could be proffered.

If Faculties are employing relaxed LSAT score standards, then perhaps they are using the score differentials to select from among the group of native Canadian applicants. However it is suggested that such a practice could only be useful and justified if the scores achieved by native Canadian applicants have validity as a predictor of success in law studies, even among the non-homogeneous group of native Canadians. Finally it must also be borne in mind that the cost of writing the Law School Admission Test is not insignificant.

The ultimate success of the Program of Legal Studies for Native Canadians must be measured by any increased access to admission to Canadian law schools and ultimately the legal profession. Professor Carter reports that by 1979 there were 39 native Canadian lawyers and 35 persons of native ancestry pursuing full-time legal studies.[21] Donald Purich, current Director of the Native Law Centre, at a meeting in February 1987, reported that 90 graduates of the programme had completed a Bachelor of Laws degree, that 60 persons were currently attending law school and that there were approximately 120 native Canadian lawyers.[22] Mr Purich estimated that, based upon proportional population figures, there should be 1200–1400 native Canadians in the legal profession.

Admission of native Canadians to first-year law study appears to be increasing. In the 1986–87 academic year there were 27 native Canadians admitted (1.4% of all first year admissions), compared with 24 in 1985–86 (1.26%) and 14 in 1984–85 (.80%).[23] Canadian Census figures for 1981 indicate that native peoples represent 2.02% of the Canadian population.[24]

The number of native Canadians admitted to first-year law studies in any given year is increasing, but is not significant. However, by the beginning of the next decade, there will have been a sufficient number of native Canadians who have entered into legal education so that an analysis of the impact of the Program of Legal Studies for Native Canadians in enhancing access to not just legal education but also the legal profession can be made. It will be necessary to examine admission to law schools, success rate in legal study, admission to the profession and career selection and progress.

It would appear that the Program of Legal Studies for Native Canadians has been successful in increasing access to legal education for Canadians of native ancestry. However it is also apparent that there is a long way yet to go.

Language

Although Canada is officially a bilingual country, the functional level of bilingualism is in need of improvement. This situation is mirrored particularly in Canadian Common Law Faculties. As mentioned above, one Common Law Faculty offers instruction primarily in French. A few, mostly in central Canada, offer a section or some instruction in French. Therefore francophones, outside Québec, have few opportunities for a legal education. Furthermore francophone lawyers, outside Québec, work primarily in an anglophone legal environment.[25] The situation appears to be improving in a number of provinces.

Anglophones in Québec can, if they wish, complete an English language Common Law degree outside Québec and pursue professional qualification in Québec. However some functional level of bilingualism would be required for professional qualification.

A major language difficulty in access to legal education is encountered by native Canadians, particularly in remote areas of northern Canada where knowledge of English or French is limited. To date, undergraduate university and legal education is unavailable to those native Canadians.

Mobility

A graduate with a Canadian Common Law degree is eligible to pursue professional qualification in any of the provinces (except Québec) or territories. The requirements for articles and/or Bar admission vary depending upon povincial (or territorial) law society regulations and the individual's professional legal qualifications and experience. The reverse is not the same for graduates with Canadian Civil Law degrees. However, some Common Law Faculties will admit a graduate with a Civil Law degree as an advanced standing student. S/he will then receive a Bachelor of Laws degree (or a Certificate of Accreditation from the Joint Committee on Accreditation) after one or two years of study, depending upon the requirements of the particular Faculty. As mentioned previously, two Faculties offer combined degree programmes, through which both a Civil and Common Law degree can be obtained after four years of study.

International mobility into Canada, as described previously, is difficult and is regulated by the law societies of the respective provinces and territories. Applicants who wish to qualify in the Common Law jurisdictions of Canada with law degrees and/or professional qualifications from foreign jurisdictions are referred to the Joint Committee on Accreditation (formerly the Joint Committee on Foreign Accreditation) composed of an Executive Secretary, from the Faculty of Law, University of Ottawa, and representatives of the Federation of Law Societies of Canada and the Committee of Canadian Law Deans. The Joint Committee will evaluate the credentials of the individual taking into account the length of legal training, when and where the training was obtained, academic standing, post-qualification legal experience and the applicability of the applicant's professional background to the Canadian legal system. The Committee will specify the amount, if any, of advanced standing the applicant would receive toward a Certificate of Qualification and what further requirements the applicant must meet for the Certificate of Qualification. In the vast majority of instances where some advanced standing is recommended, the applicant will also be required to complete a specified period of study (including a number of mandatory courses) in an LLB programme at a Canadian Law Faculty, ranging from the equivalent of half a year to two years of full-time study. However it should be recognised that the recommendation of the Joint Committee does not in any way gain admission to a Canadian Law Faculty. Those admission decisions are made by each Law Faculty employing its own admission criteria. Furthermore, not all the law societies of the Common Law jurisdictions in Canada accept the Certificate of Qualification.

Professional qualification

Every Law Society requires some period of articles or clerkship and a Bar admission or professional legal training course before admission to the Bar.[26] The length of time of articles and length and nature of the professional qualification course vary.[27] The longest of the professional qualification processes, after completion of the law degree, is in Ontario, where the period of articles is 12 months and the Bar Admission Course is from September until February after completion of articles. The length of the Ontario requirement can cause a financial hardship for individuals, particularly during the Bar Admission Course when s/he may not have any income. This may force individuals to postpone completion of the Bar Admission Course.

The most important access issue relating to professional qualification is the articling requirement. Law students are expected to secure their own articling positions. While the law societies and law schools provide some assistance, it is essentially the student's responsibility.

There appears to be little information other than the studies carried out in Ontario[28] and British Columbia[29] regarding the difficulties in obtaining articles. As mentioned above, both studies identify difficulties female law students have encountered in obtaining articling positions. The Huxter study in Ontario identified some other factors; such as age, geographic preference, size of law firm preferred, grades achieved and law school attended, which appear to have an impact on the search.[30] In addition Huxter examined personal factors which may have helped or hindered in obtaining articles or permanent legal employment.[31] While the study is not conclusive, the six factors most often referred to (as either a help or hindrance) were: family, social, business or other contacts; work experience; race, colour, national origin and creed; languages spoken; age; and sex.[32] It is difficult to assess the scale of any problems or to extrapolate from the findings other than to say that the respondents perceived these to be factors which were relevant to and significant to securing articles or permanent legal employment. However this does indicate that access to the legal profession may be significantly affected by these factors.

The numbers issue

Canada, with a current population of 25–26 million people, has 16 Law Faculties which grant Common Law degrees, six which grant Civil Law degrees and one Department of Law which grants a Bachelor of Arts degree with a major in law.[33] The issue of the numbers in the legal profession and in law schools is periodically raised, most often but not exclusively by the profession itself.

Most recently the Law Society of Upper Canada (Ontario) in 1981 established a Special Committee on Numbers of Lawyers. The committee reported its findings and recommendations in 1983.[34] In addition, the Canada-US Law Institute, in 1981, sponsored a conference entitled 'Are There Too Many Lawyers?' at the Faculty of Law, University of Western Ontario. This conference examined the issue of numbers in the legal profession from a variety of perspectives and from a multi-disciplinary viewpoint.[35] The conference papers present a thorough examination of this complex question.

There was a marked increase in the number of law students in Canada in the early 1960s[36] and then again in the 1970s, due in part to the establishment of a number of new Common Law Faculties.[37] This, combined with no decrease in enrolment in the other Law Faculties, produced a significant increase in the number of law graduates.[38] However this increase alone is not conclusive of a numbers problem. A number of factors need to be considered in such analysis. Only three of these factors will be raised in this discussion. The literature referred to in the footnotes provides further discussion of these and other concerns.

The first issue relates to the job market for law graduates and the need for the services the graduates are trained to provide. One of the guidelines often referred to in such an analysis is the ratio of lawyers to population. However the value of such a ratio has been questioned and it has been suggested that a more appropriate measure is one which compares the rate of increase in the number of lawyers with the real economic growth rate.[39] Therefore it becomes much more difficult to predict the demand for lawyers in the future. Since there is at least a four-year time frame (three years of law school plus normally at least a year of articles and Bar admission) involved between admission and professional certification, a fairly accurate economic forecast would be essential if there were to be a more stringent limitation on law school admission based upon the need for lawyers.

A second issue is the correlation between the number of law students and the societal need for practising lawyers. Canadian Law Faculties maintain that their graduates, while academically qualified for continuation through the process toward professional qualification, are also academically prepared for the pursuit of careers other than the traditional practice of law, such as public life, government service, industry, commerce and business. In Ontario, for example the percentage of those who study law with the intention of practicing has fallen from a high of about 90% to closer to 70%.[40] There has been a similar decline in Ontario in the number of lawyers who are members of the Law Society and who are in actual private practice.[41] If there are students pursuing a legal education with no intention of practising law, then arguably a limitation on admission should not be based solely on market demand for lawyers.

Other approaches to limitations upon the number of practising lawyers, assuming the appropriate number could be determined, include 'gatekeeping' at the entry to articles, Bar admission or professional certification. The Ontario Special Committee on Numbers of Lawyers considered such alternatives and ultimately rejected them.[42]

The third factor relating to the number of law students and lawyers is the funding of university Faculties of Law. All are funded substantially by government. In addition to the more obvious point that provincial governments determine the number of Law Faculties which will be established and funded, the level of government funding to universities will have an indirect effect upon the number of places available for law students. The most recent experience in Canada of government examination of law school enrolment was the report of the Commission on the Future Development of the Universities of Ontario, which did not recommend a reduction in overall intake or the closure of any of Ontario's six Law Faculties.[43] The Commission noted the difficulties in predicting the demand for the services of lawyers, the relative constancy of the number of law students at Ontario Law Faculties and, based upon the Ontario system of funding universities, that the cost of legal education is very little more than general Arts and Science programmes.

It appears that, for the time being at least, the 'numbers debate' will not have an effect on access to legal education or the profession in Canada. The Report of the Special Committee in Ontario was received by Convocation of the Law Society but no specific measures to limit the number of places in Ontario law schools, the Bar Admission Course or the profession were adopted or implemented. No other province appears likely to address the matter in the foreseeable future.

Conclusion

The Canadian experiences regarding access to legal education and the profession reveal that the issues have existed for many decades, while attempts at solutions has been a much more recent phenomen. It has been since the early 1970s that the admission of women, native Canadians and 'mature' students has become a concern. Steeped in tradition, the Canadian Law Faculties and Law Societies have been slow to move. One assessment of the state of legal education after more than a decade of progress is discouraging:

> ... the law student population in the 1980s probably resembles that of the 1950s in a socioeconomic sense: it remains heavily skewed toward the children of middle class and professional families.[44]

Canada has been fortunate in that it has not experienced significant financial barriers to study. Government funding of the universities and of student loan and bursary programmes has attempted to create relatively equal access. However as the costs of education have increased at a greater rate than the government support, the greater the likelihood that finances become a more significant issue of access. This is an especially pronounced problem for 'mature' students who may have family and other financial responsibilities and who may not be eligible for bursaries. It is argued that, despite the government supported system, legal education and ultimately the profession as well are not available to a large number of qualified but economically disadvantaged individuals.[45]

Canada, which is an example of a system of dual responsibility for legal education and professional qualification, has experienced on occasion strained relations between the Law Faculties and the profession. The profession has been known to observe that the Law Faculties have not been discharging their duties with sufficient vigour because the Faculties employ a curriculum far removed from the realities of practice and do not fail enough students. The Faculties, for their part, note that the articling experience and Bar Admission Course are poorly structured and supervised educational experiences, and that the failure rate at the Bar Admission Course is smaller than at the law schools. To some degree this history calls for greater co-operation between the two parties in identifying and addressing the issues of access. A step in that direction appears to have been taken as a result of a National Conference on Legal Education, sponsored by the Federation of Law Societies of Canada and held in October 1985. In addition to the discussions which took place at the conference among representatives of the Law Faculties, the judiciary, the governing bodies of the various law societies and legal practitioners, a more structured format for dialogue between the law societies and law schools has emerged, in the form of a standing committee of the Federation and the Committee of Canadian Law Deans called the National Committee on Legal Education.

Over the past two decades there have been some important access initiatives. The admission of mature students to legal education has broadened to a degree the experiential backgrounds of law students and new members of the profession. The Program of Legal Studies for Native People and changes in admissions policies of the Law Faculties relating to graduates of the programme have contributed significantly in providing access for native Canadians. As well, the development of half-time legal study will be important in making legal education available to those who are otherwise qualified but who are unable for family, financial or other personal reasons to undertake legal study on a full-time basis.

The most striking difficulty in preparing this paper was the significant lack of information about who are the law students and the members of the legal profession of Canada. The dearth of demographic information is of concern, if one is of the opinion that the legal profession may not be representative, in any significant way, of the Canadian population. Law Faculties maintain statistics about age, gender, grade point averages and, where relevant, LSAT scores. However little, even impressionistic, information about the socio-economic, linguistic, ethnic, cultural or marital and family status, etc backgrounds of law students is known. It is not possible to venture a guess about whether law school admission is, even by serendipity, representative of the Canadian mosaic.

The demographic information available from the Law Societies about membership in the profession was no more helpful. Information even about gender representation in the profession was not complete. Resort to the literature has produced information regarding gender, some of which was referred to above, and one recent study regarding professional opportunity in the Ontario legal profession.[46]

Canada is an example of a single route system with the Law Faculties serving as the main gatekeepers to the profession. The resolution of a number of the issues of access will likely be implemented initially at the Law Faculty level. However it will be necessary to obtain and evaluate more data about the profession in order to assess the scale of the problems. The Canadian legal education system does appear to favour certain individuals to the disadvantage of others without much systematic understanding of the phenomenon.

NOTES

1. The admission information for the Civil Law Faculties is taken primarily from Germain Brière 'Les Conditions d'Admission Dans Les Facultés de Droit du Québec' (1980) 11 revue Générale de Droit 359–364.
2. The admission information for the Common Law Faculties is taken from information shared among the organisation of admissions offices of the Faculties, called CLASSI, and a questionnaire administered in the summer of 1986.
3. Concerns have, over the years, been expressed about, for example, cultural, racial and gender biases. See eg, Allan Nairn and Associates *The Reign of ETS: The Corporation That Makes Up Minds* (1980); The Ralph Nader Report on the Educational Testing Service.
4. David Stager 'The Market for Lawyers in Ontario: 1931 to 1981, and Beyond' (1983) 6 Canada-United States Law Journal 113 at 115.
5. The author has little statistical information regarding the six Civil Law schools. However it appears that there is less of a gender gap in those institutions, which may provide an explanation for the 24% women notary figure.
6. Although this is admittedly unscientific, the current Ontario statistics are similar to the Canadian-wide Common Law Law Faculty statistics. Furthermore the trends, and not the precision of the figures, are important for the discussion.
7. Some other Ontario first-year statistics, for comparison are: 1973–74 there were 18.35% women; 1975–76 there were 27.25% women; 1979–80 – 33.59%; 1981–82 – 37.86%; 1983–84 – 42.02%.
8. Statistics Canada *Canada Yearbook 1985* (1985) at 139.
9. Lynn Smith, Marylee Stephenson and Gina Quijano 'The Legal Profession and Women: Finding Articles in British Columbia' (1973) 8 UBC Law Review 137 at 157.
10. Marie T Huxter 'Survey of Employment Opportunities for Articling Students and Graduates of the Bar Admission Course in Ontario' (1981) XV Gazette 169 at 175.
11. Ibid at 179–80.
12. Ibid at 186.
13. Ibid at 188–95.
14. Roger Carter 'University of Saskatchewan: Program of Legal Studies for Native People' (1980) 4 Can Community LJ 28 at 29.
15. Donald J Purich 'Affirmative Action in Canadian Law Schools: The Native Student in Law School' (1986–87) 51 Sask LR 79.
16. See generally, Ibid at 82–90.
17. Carter, supra n 14 at 29.
18. Ibid at 32. The programme is undergoing some curricular changes which will likely result in an increased focus on skills important to the study of law.
19. Purich, supra n 15 at 102–103.
20. Ibid at 95.
21. Ibid at 29.
22. Minutes of a meeting of the Admissions Committee of the Faculty of Law, University of Windsor, 18 February 1988.
23. These figures are of admission to first year law in all the English language Common Law schools. They are based upon statistical information shared among the admissions personnel from each faculty.
24. Statistics Canada, supra n 8 at 51, 61. The total population of Canada was 24,343,000 and native peoples was 491,460. There is some debate regarding the number of native Canadians; see Purich, supra n 15 at fn 10.
25. See eg, Peter B Annis 'Bilingualism and The Law Society of Upper Canada' (1983) XVII Gazette 175–221.
26. This information is based upon a survey of the governing bodies of the legal profession conducted in the summer of 1986. See Frank Maczko and Elaine S McKenna-Kay 'criteria for Admission to the Bar and Articles' in Mr Justice Roy J Matas and Deborah J McCawley, eds *Legal Education in Canada* (Federation of Law Societies of Canada, Montreal, 1987) 635–676.
27. It should be noted that the Québec Bar requires articles for six months and completion of the Professional Legal Training Program. However the Québec Notaries require only a one-year university course for a Diploma of Notarial Law following a law degree.
28. Huxter, supra n 10 at 169.
29. Smith, Stephenson and Quijano, supra n 9.

30 Huxter, supra n 10 at 173–9.
31 Ibid at 195–202.
32 Ibid at 195.
33 The BA degree with a law major, granted by Carleton University, is not recognised for professional qualification.
34 'The Report of The Special Committee on Numbers of Lawyers' (1983) XVII Gazette 222.
35 See, Bruce Feldthusen 'Are There too Many Lawyers?' (1982) 2 Windsor Yearb Access Justice 224. The conference papers appear in (1983) 6 Canada-United States Law Journal 98–213.
36 Stager, supra n 4 at 115.
37 These include the University of Windsor, which began admitting students in 1968, the University of Victoria (1975), the University of Calgary (1976) and the University of Moncton (1978).
38 There has been relative stability in law school enrolment since the late 1970s.
39 Stager, supra n 4 at 118.
40 Supra n 34 at 233.
41 Stager, supra n 4 at 116.
42 Supra n 34 at 236–8.
43 The Commission on the Future Development of the Universities of Ontario *Ontario Universities: Options and Futures* (December 1984) at 11.
44 Consultative Group on Research and Education in Law *Law and Learning* (Ministry of Supply and Services Canada, Ottawa, 1984) at 19. Commonly referred to as the Arthurs' Report, this was prepared by the Consultative Group, chaired by Harry W Arthurs, for the Social Sciences and Humanities Research Council of Canada.
45 Ibid.
46 Barry D Adam and Kathleen A Lahey 'Professional Opportunities: A Survey of the Ontario Legal Profession' (1981) 59 Can Bar Review 674–86.

7 Access to legal education and the legal professions in England

*Neil Kibble**

Introduction

Black and working-class students are under-represented in legal education. Given the importance of legal education in determining who is able to enter the professions, access to it is fundamental in shaping the kind of profession we have and the kind of society we become.

A socially and ethnically diverse profession is better fitted to understand and serve the legal needs of a socially and ethnically diverse society. Professional and public recognition of this is growing in so far as the provision of legal services to working-class and black populations is concerned. The Lord Chancellor himself has acknowledged the need for more black judges and magistrates.[1] The capacity of the criminal justice system to deliver and to be seen to deliver justice for all, while it remains in predominantly white hands, is increasingly questioned.

Yet the argument for diversity in the legal profession and in the judiciary goes beyond the need for racial justice throughout the criminal process. It rests upon the value to society of opening up participation in the legal and political process to all of its citizens.

This chapter outlines the present gender, race and class composition of the professions, and reviews the process of professional qualification. Legal education is the starting point and focus of this review: current educational provision, the composition of the student body, and law admissions policies are considered. The implications for access to legal education of government higher education and expenditure policies are also examined. Finally, the chapter reviews the vocational stages of professional qualification to see what kind of control they exert over the composition of the professions.

The composition of the professions

Although the class character of the Bar has broadened since the Second World War, and public schools and Oxbridge no longer enjoy the virtual monopoly they once did, the dominance of the professional/managerial classes remains.[2] It appears that the solicitors' profession has a similar class profile, though recent data are sparse and it is not easy to estimate the impact of changes in the qualification process that have taken place in the past twenty years. As of

---

* Senior Lecturer in Law, South Bank Polytechnic.

1988, 90% of entrants to the solicitors' profession and 97% of entrants to the Bar are graduates. The class composition of higher education, and as we shall see, of University legal education in particular, therefore exerts a controlling influence on the class composition of both professions.

Women were excluded from the Bar until 1919 and their numbers in practice remained minimal until the 1960s. In 1985 women accounted for 13% of barristers. Though still very low, the figure represents a significant increase since the 1960s, largely attributable to the growing participation of women in undergraduate legal education. Women now account for about 40% of law students and the same proportion of those being called to the Bar.[3]

Women were also excluded from the solicitors' profession until 1919, and until the mid-1970s the profession contained fewer than 5% women. Women's entry into the profession has increased steadily since then for the same reason as has women's entry to the Bar and women now account for 50% of new articles.[4] As of 1987 the proportion of women on the roll had risen to 19%. Low though this figure is, it probably overstates the proportion of women solicitors actually practising.[5]

The discrimination that women face in both professions has been well-documented.[6] Women barristers experience greater difficulties securing both pupillages and tenancies than men.[7] They face discrimination both from heads of chambers and from barristers' clerks.[8] Consequently, women barristers are concentrated in the less remunerative, non-specialist areas of practice – criminal, general civil, family. A 1977–78 Senate survey established that their presence in these areas of work did not simply reflect the women barristers' choice – over half felt disadvantaged in getting the kind of work they wanted.[9] Discrimination also blocks the progress of women within the profession, ensuring their under-representation in positions of seniority – heads of chambers, benchers, members of Senate, QCs and judges. Thus, earnings differentials between men and women barristers increase with time in practice.[10]

The discrimination against women solicitors has been thoroughly documented by the Women's Careers Working Party, established by the Law Society, whose report was published in January 1988.[11] Of solicitors admitted in 1977, 65% of men are partners, compared to only 34% of women. Only 11% of the men are still assistant solicitors, while 32% of the women are.[12] The Working Party report also confirmed the high drop-out of women from the profession.[13] As with women barristers there is also a tendency for women solicitors to be found in areas considered appropriate for their gender: probate and trust, family and domestic conveyancing.[14] The report concluded that there was a good deal of discrimination, direct and indirect, within the profession.

Perhaps in response to the situation prevailing in private practice, the number of women solicitors entering industry, commerce or local/national government between 1983 and 1986 rose at twice the rate of those becoming assistant solicitors.[15]

Black barristers constitute just over 5% of the practising Bar – a proportion equivalent to the Black British population within England and Wales.[16] This level of representation is a legacy of the role played by the Inns of Court School of Law in the training of barristers from Commonwealth jurisdictions.

The situation in the solicitors' profession is very different. The Law Society's Ethnic Monitoring Survey, whose results were released in July 1988,[17] found a total of 618 minority solicitors. Afro-Caribbean and African solicitors together account for less than 0.2% of all solicitors on the roll. The survey also found that the numbers of minority lawyers are increasing.[18] More than 10% of students currently enrolled with the Law Society classified themselves as not being of white/European origin.

Racial discrimination is a serious problem in both professions. The degree of de facto racial segregation at the Bar has been documented. In 1983 nearly 80% of black barristers practised in a mere 14 sets of chambers: over 80% of chambers did not contain a single black barrister.[19] In its 1984 report, the Race Relations Committee of the Senate under the chairmanship of Lord Justice Browne-Wilkinson indicated the reason for this degree of segregation:[20]

> Everyone starting at the Bar at the present day faces formidable problems in getting a tenancy. In our judgment a black barrister faces one further problem: an unwillingness in chambers to treat him as a serious contender for a vacancy.

Black barristers have consistently maintained that they were unwelcome in white chambers, particularly those specialist chambers doing the more lucrative and prestigious tax, shipping and patent work.[21] The situation is now slowly changing. The monitoring carried out by the Race Relations Committee shows a small movement of black pupils and tenants into specialist chambers. Whereas in October 1983 only one practitioner in specialist chambers was 'other than white', the number had risen to 17 in October 1985.[22] A national Race Relations Survey, carried out on behalf of the Bar Council, is inquiring into the ethnic composition of chambers, and into recruitment practices. The Survey Report is expected in early 1989.

The solicitors' profession was slower to recognise the problem of discrimination. In 1983 a Law Society Working Party reported that it had found no evidence of racial discrimination. This was hardly surprising given the way in which the Working Party carried out its work.[23] The First National Conference on Minority Entry to the Legal Profession in June 1985 was a turning-point. At the conference, some 300 black lawyers and law students voiced their concerns about discrimination and racism in both professions.[24] Subsequently, the present Race Relations Committee of the Law Society was established and agreed to carry out ethnic monitoring, some results of which have been noted above. In 1988, the Law Society appointed an Ethnic Minority Careers Officer to encourage black law students into the profession.

In addition to revealing the negligible numbers of black solicitors, the monitoring survey also indicated that ethnic minority solicitors disproportionately work as sole practitioners (22% compared to 9% of all solicitors), or in firms with fewer than four solicitors (80% as opposed to 56% for all solicitors).

The Survey Report speculates that ethnic minority solicitors are located in small firms with other ethnic minority practitioners.[25] Assuming the speculation to be correct, which seems likely, this pattern of de facto segregation resembles the situation at the Bar and would seem to confirm the fears expressed eight years earlier by the Royal Commission on Legal Services:[26]

> The Commission was particularly concerned that ... firms of solicitors composed exclusively of members of ethnic minorities would set up in practices in areas with a substantial minority population ... there would be a clear division on racial lines in the practice of the law and to some observers in the administration of justice itself.

Some within the professions argue that discrimination is a thing of the past and that increasingly women and black solicitors and barristers will be represented at all levels. To test this claim we must consider whether the qualification process is perpetuating the present pattern of under-representation and stratification.

Access to legal education

Our investigation of the process of professional qualification begins at the academic stage, and with legal education. This is especially appropriate given legal education's influence on entry to both professions. Abel rightly noted the central role of legal education in determining the professions' composition.[27] Seventy-five per cent of solicitors and 84% of barristers entering the professions are law graduates.

This is a particularly interesting and important time to consider access to legal education. Following several years of relative government inattention, the Education Reform Act, and the White Papers, 'Higher Education – Meeting the Challenge' and 'Top-up Loans for Students'[28] have rapidly taken higher education into the centre of political debate and controversy.

The government activity has been prompted in part by major demographic changes. Between 1983 and 1994 the number of 18-year-olds is expected to fall by 35%.[29] This decline in the 18-year-old population carries dramatic implications for the numbers of candidates seeking entry to higher education holding A level qualifications. In the face of these changes the government has recently declared its commitment to wider access.[30]

Underlying the current flurry of debate seems to lie the assumption that, like it or not, the demographic changes will oblige formerly reluctant institutions to become open and responsive and to admit a broader range of students. Regardless of whether this scenario holds as true for legal education as it does for higher education generally, it is clear that the future of access to legal education cannot be understood in isolation from the current debate on higher education.

The growth of legal education: Universities and Polytechnics

There has been a major expansion in legal education in the last fifty years. In 1938/9 only slightly more than 1,300 students were in full-time undergraduate legal education. In the 1980s that figure has risen to about 14,500, producing in 1985/6 over 4,000 law graduates. The rate of growth, substantial throughout the 1970s, has slowed significantly during the 1980s, and the number of law graduates for 1985/6 was in fact down slightly from the previous year.[31]

The expansion in student numbers has been matched by an expansion in the number and range of institutions offering law degrees and in the variety of modes of study available. In the late 1960s fewer than twenty law faculties existed. Now over fifty different institutions offer full-time law degrees, over twenty offer mixed, joint or modular degrees, about twenty offer part-time degrees, and the University of London offers an external degree. Together these various types of provision service over 18,000 students.

A major feature of the expansion in legal education has been its development and growth beyond the Universities and into the Polytechnics since the late 1960s. Twenty-one Polytechnics now offer law degrees, and they accounted in 1981/2 for just over 40% of law students.[32] This share is undoubtedly greater today: Since 1980/1 there has been a 27% increase in full-time students (all subjects), in Polytechnics and Colleges, and only a 1% increase in students at Universities.[33]

Polytechnics were conceived as having a distinctive role from that of the Universities. They had an explicit concern with vocational education and with building closer links to commerce, industry and the professions. They offered a greater range of courses including non-degree and part-time courses, thereby attracting a broader range of students. They also took a larger proportion of those students from the local community – thus their field of operation was local/national, rather than national/international like the Universities. Universities are the more prestigious institutions and enjoy higher status within both the labour market and the wider society.

For many, Polytechnics are simply inferior institutions catering for less able students. However expressed, the stratification within legal education has repercussions which persist throughout the qualification process and into subsequent employment. It also has major consequences for the manner in which 'access problems' are articulated and understood within legal education.

The composition of the student body

The class composition of entrants to higher education, and of legal education in particular, is not unlike that of the legal professions. Hence the limited impact on the latter of the growing dominance of law student entry. A 1978/9 survey of first-year law students at Polytechnics and Universities (excluding Oxbridge) found that 70% were from professional/managerial backgrounds and 13% from working-class backgrounds.[34] Furthermore it is clear now that the class composition of University education actually narrowed during the 1970s.[35] This may partially be attributable to the broadening of entry which occurred during this period in terms of gender.

Accounting for less than 20% of University or Polytechnic law students in the late 1960s, women now account for about 45% of law graduates.[36] Their class position is however even more exalted than that of their male colleagues. The 1978/9 survey referred to above, found that 78% of women were from professional/managerial backgrounds, compared with 65% of the men. Clearly, the barriers confronting the entry of working-class women into higher education remain substantial. Indeed, despite the general increase in the participation of women within higher education, the proportion of women from working-class backgrounds entering Universities has actually fallen.[37]

Turning to the question of the racial composition of legal education, the absence of statistics on Black British participation and the very limited volume of research on the issue, are a serious obstacle to analysis and reform. This is so seven years after the Rampton Report recommended that all Universities, Polytechnics and Colleges of Higher Education should carry out ethnic monitoring. However, both the Polytechnic and University Admissions Systems (PCAS and UCCA) announced in November 1988 that ethnic monitoring would be introduced for 1990 admissions.

Latest estimates suggest a national figure of about 300 to 400 Black British law students,[38] and that the vast majority attend Polytechnics. London is the home of most Black British law graduates. The class profile of Black British law students is also a key to their experience. Compared to white students, a substantially higher proportion of black students come from working-class backgrounds.[39]

Admissions policies

How do current approaches to admissions affect the composition of legal education? Despite the expansion that has occurred, demand for legal education vastly exceeds supply. An admissions survey conducted in 1984 estimated that only approximately 40% of applicants secure places.[40] This level of competition allows law departments to impose highly selective entry requirements in which performance in public examinations – the General Certificate of Education Advanced Levels (GCE A levels) – plays the central role.

The 1984 survey showed that 70% of University law departments demanded at least 3 A level passes and that none surveyed asked for fewer than 10 points (equivalent to a B and 2 Cs) for those taking 3 A levels.[41] Since then, many University law departments have increased their standard offers to between 12 and 14 points. Those Universities prepared to make offers to students taking only 2 A levels usually require very high grades. Polytechnics, while generally accepting lower grades, also centre their requirements around A level achievement. Mature student entry will be considered below.

Fulton observes (speaking of higher education in general) that 'it is not the possession of A levels, but the achievement of a carefully prescribed A level score which is the single crucial element in determining whether a candidate is admitted.'[42] The growing competition for places has led to increases in the A level score required.

It is working-class children who have been disproportionately squeezed out by this growing competition since 1981.[43] The reliance on the A level standard also excludes many of the Black British population who wish to enter legal education. Lyon's survey of the student population of one Inner London Polytechnic which admits an unusually high proportion of ethnic minority and working-class students provides a telling picture of the racially exclusionary impact of current law admissions.[44] While over 70% of Asian and European students at the Polytechnic had gained at least one A level qualification, only 45% of Caribbean students had done so. The majority of the Caribbean students had entered as mature students or via alternative routes. Fourteen per cent of the Caribbean students had entered the Polytechnic via an Access Course.[45] Forty-one per cent were 25-years-old or older.[46] They would not find a place in institutions whose admissions practice is geared towards school-leaving students with high A level scores.

Support for the continued use of the A level standard rests on its administrative efficiency in rationing scarce places on law degrees and on its meritocratic basis. Certainly, admissions procedures which base conditional offers on A level achievement (specifying minimum grades) are bureaucratically efficient. This is not to say that the process is entirely mechanical or that A level performance is the sole criterion. The academic references and the student's personal statement on the application form provide information which the admissions tutor may consider prior to deciding whether or not to make an offer and if so whether it should be conditional or unconditional. Student interviews may also be held. However, approximately 70% of students are made offers conditional on their examination performance and once those are made, the process does become largely mechanical.

Grades are set at a level which it is estimated will produce the required number of new students. But the grade levels are also used to promote the status of the department or institution,[47] signalling its quality and the extent of demand for its courses. The importance of this latter function should not be overlooked.[48]

> ... in the absence of many of the other discriminators found in other national systems (salaries, staff-student ratios and resources, all of which the authorities attempt to equalise across the British system) admissions standards have become perhaps the chief currency of academic prestige for employers and for academics themselves.

Those functions – to allocate places efficiently, and to maintain the course's academic reputation – both serve to discourage the flexibility which could do much to change the exclusionary nature of law admissions.

The legitimacy of the rationing process rests on the view that fairness demands the selection of better qualified candidates, as judged by A level performance, ahead of those who are less qualified. However, as Fulton notes, the educational criticisms of the use of A level performance to determine entry suggest that this legitimacy has a somewhat precarious base.[49]

In particular, A levels are tests of achievement, assessed almost exclusively by examinations which call more for the reproduction of acquired information than for the demonstration of critical, analytical skills. But the fact that A levels are tests of achievement has a further implication for their fairness as a rationing device. For those who enjoyed similar educational opportunities, A level performance may be a useful indicator of current preparedness for higher education. For these whose educational experience was limited in some way, whether by discrimination, inadequacy of resources, interruption to studies or other adverse circumstances, A level performance may be highly misleading.

Though it is true to say that the context within which the educational achievement occurred may be taken into account if volunteered on the application form or elicited at interview, in practice this rarely happens. Few 'non-traditional' entrants have the confidence to insist upon their fitness for study in the face of an apparently indifferent record of achievement. Some believe that whatever the context within which it was accomplished, their indifferent record proves that they are not the 'clever' or 'bright' students. Others may be acutely conscious that institutional racism within the educational system has contributed to an academic record which does not reflect their true ability. In either event, such students may have profound misgivings about whether they belong or are welcome in higher education at all. As a result, personal statements and student references too often merely reflect the quality of assistance and advice offered by a particular school, and underline the apparent superiority of the traditionally qualified school-leaving student.

Admissions policies are determining the composition of the legal profession and judiciary well into the next century. The longer that law departments continue to rely so heavily on A level grades in determining entry to legal education, the longer they will continue to exclude black and working-class students. The argument that this exclusion is essential for the maintenance of standards and in the cause of equity between applicants is not persuasive. It rests on unwarranted, though deeply embedded assumptions about who the 'quality' students really are, about which students are 'fit' to enter legal education.[50] Until these are abandoned they will continue to cast a pall over the positive initiatives that have already been made, and those still to come.

Financial barriers

The barriers to entry into legal education neither start nor end with formal entry requirements. For many students, the cost of full-time legal education (compounded by the costs of the professional qualification process to follow), are a major deterrent. This is so despite the mandatory awards that are currently available for British residents undertaking an approved course of higher education. The award pays the tuition fees in full and provides a means-tested maintenance allowance. The value of mandatory awards has fallen substantially in recent years, and student financial support is set to deteriorate further with the government's introduction of a loans scheme, which is discussed further below.

The growing inadequacy of financial support particularly deters working-class students from proceeding into higher education.[51] The 1988 Report of the Equal Opportunities Group established by the National Advisory Body for Public Sector Higher Education (NAB) indicated that finance was also a 'great barrier to access for many black people and members of other ethnic minority groups'.[52]

Those students who nevertheless proceed into higher education are increasingly dependent upon social security and housing benefit, parental support, bank overdrafts and part-time employment during the academic term as well as during vacations. The 1987 survey into student income and expenditure commissioned by the DES revealed that over 40% of students had overdrafts at the end of the academic year.[53] The NAB Equal Opportunities Report details the major shortcomings of the present system for financial support and the way in which mature students in particular are disadvantaged by it.[54]

The inadequacy of financial support not only has an exclusionary impact in terms of entry, but an inhibiting effect on survival on the course and on examination success. The considerable burden of part-time employment undertaken during the term by many students with family responsibilities and without wealth or family income, inhibits effective participation in the course. For many students, paid employment in the summer vacation is also essential in order to repay outstanding overdrafts. Those law students who most need to establish professional connections through summer placements are therefore often the least able to do so.

Racial/class exclusivity

The exclusive image projected by law and legal education, particularly in terms of race and class, also acts as a deterrent to entry, leading some students to believe that legal education is not for them. The NAB Equal Opportunities Report 'Action For Access' observed[55]:

> We believe that outreach work is part of a positive strategy for recruitment of under represented groups. It is evident that many sections of the population feel that higher education is 'not for them'. It is the institution's responsibility to seek mechanisms to help overcome these attitudes.

The levels of demand uncovered by those institutions actively seeking 'non-traditional' entrants, (especially via new forms of provision such as Access Courses and part-time degrees), underline the changes that become possible once institutions effectively signal that they are open to ethnic minority and working-class populations.

Few institutions seem to be aware of the extent to which they are perceived as 'white' institutions – run by white people for the benefit of white people. Even local Further Education Colleges, many of which contain significant proportions of black students are not generally seen as accessible or open.[56]

But, like the inadequacy of financial support, the exclusive racial and class image of legal education has an impact going beyond entry to the survival and success of students. Very little research has been carried out into the experience of Black British students within higher education. However, many black lawyers and law students acknowledge that isolation, discouragement and lack of support were (are) features of their legal education and training.[57] To many black students, educational establishments appear to reflect the racism experienced in wider society.

Notwithstanding the experiences of black law students and lawyers, higher education institutions are generally reluctant to accept that race and discrimination are real issues inside the institutions as well as outside. According to a survey conducted in 1986,[58] the majority of law departments are not concerned about the under-representation of Black British students. Most of those surveyed did not keep statistics or monitor in any way the ethnic backgrounds of staff and students, nor were they seeking to increase the proportion of black staff.

Institutions are inclined to assert that the long-term presence within them of black overseas students establishes that they are free of discrimination. This response ignores the complexity of contemporary racism in Britain, explored by Gilroy in 'There Ain't No Black in the Union Jack'.[59] In fact, one is struck by how often references to black students are automatically assumed to be references to overseas students resident in the Caribbean or Africa. The existence of a Black British population is simply overlooked.

Yet the appointment of black staff is the most persistent demand of black law students. A 1987 survey of black students at an inner London Polytechnic, designed to canvass support for the creation of an Afro-Caribbean grouping, revealed instead that the appointment of mainstream black academic staff was the priority.

Salman Rushdie described this clash of fundamentally different perceptions:[60]

> Britain is now two entirely different worlds, and the one you inherit is determined by the colour of your skin ... Very few white people ... are willing to believe the descriptions of contemporary reality offered by blacks.

Mature student entry/Part-time degrees/Access courses

Mature entry schemes, for students aged 21 and over, provide opportunities for those who may have missed out on higher education earlier in their lives for a variety of reasons. They are an excellent means of broadening access to legal education because traditional entry qualifications are not required.

Fears that mature students would be unprepared for higher education and unable to bear the burden of intensive study are being met by a growing body of evidence pointing to their success.[61] This evidence applies equally to mature students who enter without academic qualifications and to those who satisfy the traditional entry requirements. Despite this evidence and despite the fact that mature students are generally welcomed by academic staff for their life experience and motivation, their presence on law degrees remains fairly limited.

Lee's 1984 Law Admissions Survey showed that 85% of Universities and 50% of Polytechnics had less than one-tenth mature students intake.[62] It is difficult to estimate whether these proportions have increased since then, though growing competition for places on Polytechnic and University law degrees has probably held down mature entry levels. In higher education generally, the number of mature men students on full-time first degree courses rose only by 2.8% between 1979 and 1986.[63] The increase in the number of mature women was greater – 13% over the same period.

The potential impact of mature entry on the social composition of the student body is limited by a number of factors. First, many institutions require mature entrants to have formal entry qualifications, (half the Universities according to the Law Admissions Survey). Second, the general inadequacy of financial support for students is even worse for mature students. Third, women mature students in particular are excluded by the absence of childcare facilities and by the extent to which domestic responsibilities are rarely taken into account in planning course provision. The problems which confront women mature students are detailed in a 1985 Further Education Unit (FEU) publication.[64]

Part-time degrees are an important alternative source of legal education because they admit students unable to study full-time for financial, family or employment reasons. Established in the Polytechnics during the 1970s, the vast majority of places on part-time law degrees is still offered by Polytechnics. In the seven years leading up to 1988 the growth of part-time courses has greatly exceeded that of the full-time courses. Whereas enrolments on full-time law degrees increased 20% during that time, enrolments on part-time degrees increased 103%.[65] Entry requirements are also more flexible than for full-time degrees. Marsh found that only 32% of law students admitted to part-time degrees had A levels.[66] Thus, part-time degrees provide valuable opportunities for mature working-class and ethnic minority students.

However, this form of provision has its drawbacks. Particularly in the early years of part-time law degrees, attrition rates were very high (approximately 70%).[67] Though these rates have dropped with growing experience, they still stand at between fifty and sixty per cent. This remains considerably higher than those on full-time University law degrees (5–10%) or on full-time Polytechnic law degrees (20%).[68] Because of this attrition rate, the annual figures for part-time law degree conferrals remains relatively small – just less than 300 in 1987/8.[69]

Law Access courses represent a more direct intervention into the recruitment process. Access courses were originally established in the late 1970s by Metropolitan Education Authorities to train more black social workers and teachers. However they now provide an alternative route into many fields of higher education for students who have suffered 'educational disadvantage', and over the last ten years they have compiled an impressive record of achievement.[70]

The first Law Access course started in London in September 1983. The Vauxhall College/South Bank Polytechnic course is a one-year full-time course supported by ILEA discretionary awards that prepares students for entry onto the law degree. The course is not a foundation law course designed to introduce students to basic legal doctrine. Its curriculum is centred around communication and analytical skills. Using a carefully constructed set of oral and written exercises, students are gradually immersed in the range of skills demanded on the law degree:

– accurate reading of complex written materials
– construction of clear, persuasive argument
– critical analysis of argument
– interpretation and application of rules
– case analysis and problem solving.

Four Law Access courses are now operating, and there are several other Access courses which feed into a range of degrees including law. A Certificate in Legal Method course has also been established in the Extra-Mural Department of the University of London, whose explicit aim is to prepare students for law degree study and which targets students from ethnic minorities.

Because Access courses actively intervene in recruitment and prepare students whose existing level of skills would not warrant direct entry onto law degrees, their class and racial composition is very different to that of law students who enter via other routes. Approximately 80% of the Vauxhall College Access students are mature black students. About the same proportion are women, and the majority are from working-class backgrounds. Students from the Vauxhall College course perform on the law degree as well as students with traditional entry qualifications. The results they have obtained over several years demonstrate that a very poor record of academic achievement can be transformed into good performance on law degrees, if appropriate preparation is given.

Unqualified and non-traditionally qualified students, whether having entered via the Access course or as mature students, have established a proven record of good law degree performance. That record exposes the fallacy of longstanding assumptions about the academic superiority of A level students. It also challenges the legitimacy of our dependence on A level performance as the principal rationing device within legal education. In addition, the broadened entry has had a stimulating effect on the academic life of the institutions concerned by virtue of the diversity that has been introduced into a formerly quite homogeneous student population.

Government policy on higher education

We noted above that demographic change had prompted the government to declare its commitment to wider access. The latter months of 1988 have seen a stream of ministerial statements emphasising the government's commitment to increasing the participation of under-represented groups in higher education:[71]

> With the number of 18-year-olds set to fall sharply in the 1990s, higher education faces both a challenge and an opportunity to broaden the range of those who have access to it ...
> I personally have no doubt that a broadening of opportunities to participate in higher education can do much to promote social integration, but I also believe that achieving a more open system is wholly compatible with maintaining high standards.

Nevertheless there are a number of other elements to government policy against which this commitment to access needs to be set: in particular, the removal of Polytechnics from local authority control and their establishment as independent corporate bodies answerable to a new planning and funding body (the Polytechnics and Colleges Funding Council or PCFC); the call for closer and more extensive links between higher education and commerce/industry so that the need for skilled manpower is met more effectively; and, looming over all this the overriding concern to control public expenditure.

This paper can scarcely begin to note all the possible configurations of this increasingly complex set of political and demographic changes. However, a number of points may help to identify some of the critical issues for access as legal education moves into the 1990s.

Whatever else has happened, demographic change and government rhetoric have created the possibility of a widening of opportunities. Some broadening in the racial and social composition of the law student body is already taking place, and demographic changes will ensure the continuation of this trend. Over two-thirds of the ethnic minority population are aged under 15 compared to only one-fifth of the white population. Increasingly, a larger proportion of school-leavers will be of ethnic minority origin.[72] However, we should be very wary of concluding that government policy, aided and abetted by demographic shifts, will lead to a substantial widening of access.

1 The limitations of demography

The full-time degree (particularly the University full-time degree) is the overwhelming source of law graduates, and students with A level qualifications are the overwhelming source of law students. In numerical terms, Access courses, mature entry and part-time degrees have not even begun to challenge this dominance.

The demographic change which has already occurred has not prevented a steady rise in the A level points scores of entrants to University law degrees. In 1987, 72% of such entrants had scores of 12 points or more, compared with 56% in 1982.[73] Nor has the change contributed to a widening of UK domiciled access into University law degrees. The proportion of students entering on the basis of A level qualifications remained steady at 89% between 1982 and 1984. While this proportion dropped to 84% for entrants between 1985 and 1987, the difference was made up by a 5% increase in the proportion of entrants with foreign qualifications.[74]

Nor are the demographic changes still to come likely to extend non-traditional entry within the University sector. The impact of the shortfall in the number of 18-year-olds is unlikely to be felt evenly throughout legal education.[75]

> Access is the word of the moment. Everyone concerned with higher education seems to be talking about it, and with the population of 18-year-olds falling by a third, it seems to be assumed that an expansion of opportunities will occur automatically ...
> But the attitude of individual departments to widening access to full-time places is likely to be influenced by whether they are in a rationing or recruiting situation, and most are still having to ration. Widening access will therefore require not only a policy but a means of implementing it. Demography of itself will not do it for us.

If any law departments are obliged to give up rationing and start recruiting it will be the Polytechnics – unable simply to 'poach' traditionally qualified students from the next rung down on the academic ladder.

In fact, the introduction of the student loan scheme (see below) may prompt many students to opt for more vocationally oriented courses where the prospects of securing subsequent employment are better. If a larger proportion of the 18-year-old students with A level qualifications seek entry to law degree courses, such a shift in the pattern of demand would tend to further diminish the impact of the demographic changes as far as subjects like law are concerned.

It is therefore possible that throughout this period of demographic change, the major movement in legal education may be away from wider access – if by that we mean a broadening of the social and racial composition of UK domiciled entry to law degrees. A number of other factors also point in this direction.

Some Polytechnics have modelled themselves on the Universities and concentrated on A level entry, while others, notably the inner city Polytechnics, have chosen to concentrate on providing a service within the local community. It is generally the latter which have broadened entry in the variety of ways outlined above. If Universities and the like-minded Polytechnics retain their present levels of A level entry, those Polytechnics which have widened access may feel considerable pressure to 'moderate' their admissions policies. Some Polytechnic law departments already fear that if they are seen to broaden entry 'excessively', current assumptions about who the 'quality' students are may lead to their 'ghettoisation'. In particular they fear the consequences for their students of the erosion of the value of their credentials in the labour market.

The extent to which University-led notions of 'excellence' and 'quality' have a chilling effect on access was underlined in a recent study of how Colleges and Polytechnics responded to National Advisory Board (NAB) planning.[76] The study found that Colleges and Polytechnics adopted definitions of 'efficiency' and 'quality' that threatened access to courses and innovation within courses. Quality came to be equated with academic University type courses and research.

2 The PCFC and the shift to independent corporate status

The government decision to remove Polytechnics from local authority control and to establish them as independent bodies with corporate status, also has implications for access. Local authorities were instrumental in encouraging and supporting many of the equal opportunities initiatives which have broadened entry to higher education. It is uncertain to what extent this active commitment to equal opportunities will be taken up by the PCFC. The government brief to the PCFC suggests that, in the future, Polytechnics may be getting a rather different message.

The government stresses the need for greater efficiency within institutions and are determined to achieve lower costs per student. Indeed, it is through achieving 'further gains in value for Money' that institutions, according to the government, will be able to widen access.[77] Yet this is a sector which has seen funding per student drop by over 14% in the last five years.[78]

One very specific aspect of this drive for greater efficiency is that the PCFC will be allocating funding on the basis of output of graduates, not on the number of students enrolled. This may lead law departments to adopt even more restrictive selection procedures in order to reduce wastage rates.[79]

Improving student support would also have this effect, but would impose additional staffing costs.

From the public statements that have been made so far, the dominant ethos of the move to independent corporate status seems to be one of encouraging institutions to seek private funding, and of encouraging competition and the entrepreneurial spirit.[80] Law departments are generally well placed to respond to this. There is likely to be great demand for the provision of full-cost courses including short courses for continuing professional education and for para-legal qualifications.

While there is much that is positive in these trends, it is also likely that innovation will be concentrated on courses which generate income. The Deputy Director of Staffordshire Polytechnic, speaking at the 1988 Association of Law Teachers Conference, foresaw a big expansion in *non-PCFC* work.[81]

> Non-PCFC work (short courses, overseas students, full cost students, consultancy) will move from the periphery to the core of our work. It must be at full cost and should generate surplus income. There is an enormous market for this work for lawyers to exploit.

A considerable further investment in full and part-time degrees and on preparatory courses is unlikely because there will be a direct incentive to release staff resources from them in order to develop and administer courses which attract income. If there is any broadening of the ethnic composition of law degrees it is likely to be the product of increased numbers of overseas students. Where widening of access occurs, it is likely to be concentrated on vocational and para-professional courses.

3 Student financial support

The government's attempt to reconcile its stated commitment to wider access with its overriding aim of reducing public expenditure, has led to the floating of a variety of plans for higher education funding which include top-up loans and voucher systems. The former has been the subject of a White Paper, the latter (as of late 1988) the subject only of civil service leaks.

Recently the argument that any major expansion in participation in higher education will require the introduction of some kind of voucher/loan system has gained wider acceptance in educational circles. Oliver Fulton wrote in 1986:[82]

> Essentially, the idea of loan finance is neutral: it is possible to devise schemes which can range from the highly progressive to the highly restrictive. Fear of the most restrictive versions should not discourage us from trying to develop a combined system ... which would ... reflect reasonably fairly the balance of advantages which accrue both to society and to the individual from participation in higher education.

The government has been able to argue that only a loan system will allow for a substantial expansion of access to higher education. However, as of late 1988, the details which have emerged about their proposals do not encourage one to believe that their purpose is to expand access. Critics of the proposed scheme seem agreed that despite the rhetoric about access, the 'obsessive desire to reduce public spending is the driving force behind the White Paper.'[83]

According to the Top-Up loan scheme, loans will be introduced from 1990. Over the three years the loan will initially be £1,150 (£420 in the first and second years, £310 in the third year). The loan will be at a real interest rate of zero, increased only in line with inflation. The maintenance grant payable to students will be frozen at £2,230, and the loan increased as the value of the grant declines with inflation. The loan will increase until it matches the combined value of the grant and parental contribution (when it accounts for half of the student's total financial support). The loan scheme is therefore not so much a top-up as a slow motion grant replacement scheme.

From 1990, according to the White Paper, students will cease to be eligible for a range of welfare benefits (income support, unemployment and housing benefit) unless they are single parents or disabled. Partners and dependants of students will remain eligible. The denial of these benefits will have a severe impact on many students, leaving them even worse off than before. The National Union of Students has estimated that a student over 25 could expect to claim £1,360 in benefits for the full year.[84]

The scheme does nothing to address the overwhelming inadequacy of *existing* levels of support. This degree of underfunding imposes on many students a massive burden of loans and overdrafts. Many students are obliged to work part-time during the term (often as much as between 18 and 25 hours per week). This takes a heavy toll on academic performance. The evidence shows that *increased* student support is necessary to meet the overwhelming financial burdens borne by many black and working-class students.

There are two other serious problems with the loan proposals that have particular relevance in this context. First, the government has not understood the extent to which many working-class and minority students and their families perceive entry into higher education as a highly uncertain and daunting process. The culture of exclusivity, particularly in terms of race and class, that surrounds higher education means that many students simply have no expectation at all of entering into it. In 1963, the Robbins Committee argued that loans would be an undesirable disincentive at a time when people were just beginning to acquire the 'habit' of education. That argument is just as powerful today with respect to groups of people who are under-represented in higher education.

Second, the accumulation of the debt over a period of years means that loans operate particularly harshly for students on longer courses. Law students will face the prospect of loans not only during their undergraduate degrees but also during their Finals courses.

Access students are therefore doubly threatened by the loans scheme. Full-time Law Access students will face no less than *five years* of loan dependency. Many will simply not feel able to set out on the long path into the profession, especially given their lack of self-confidence about their prospects of success, and their ambivalence about whether they belong in higher education at all.

Of those that enter the process despite their misgivings many will find that the pressure to reduce the burden of the loan by engaging in part-time work is irresistible. The pattern of exclusion, attrition and lowered performance looks set to continue.

The sketchy information now available regarding the voucher system suggests that in the form being envisaged by the present government, it too will not encourage wider access.[85] If the value of the voucher is tied to A level performance, based on the notion that they should vary according to the student's 'academic merit', the scheme will reinforce the narrow social entry and stratification that already exists.

4 'Flexible' provision

The government's intention of reducing public expenditure is also reflected in its call for the development of more flexible and cheaper forms of provision. At first glance, the move towards more flexible provision seems an attractive prospect in the context of widening access. It is, after all, what critics of the narrow range of entry to higher education have been calling for.

Certainly, there is an unanswerable case for greater flexibility in both the duration and intensity of preparatory courses. In some contexts, short intensive courses of three or six weeks may be appropriate (see the report on 20-day courses for the unemployed run by the Workers' Educational Association, which make extensive use of individual tutorials.[86]) In other contexts, part-time day or evening courses offered in modules will be appropriate. Students would either work through all modules or be guided to specific ones, dependent on their level of skills. However, these types of courses are not cheap alternatives to standard full-time provision. They require a high level of individual student support.

For most students returning to study after long absences, after earlier negative experiences of education, or after prolonged periods of unemployment, individual tutorial support, support from fellow students, and personal counselling are vital. The rebuilding of self-confidence and the development of critical/analytical skills necessary for higher education is an intensive and demanding process. Though not all students require a full-time one year course of study, many do, and without that option available, admissions to Access courses will simply become more restrictive. And yet few within the DES or local authorities anticipate discretionary awards for full-time Access students continuing behond 1990.

Threats to the future of Access courses in London as a result of the government's abolition of the Inner London Education Authority, call into question not only government statements on the importance of such courses[87] but also the credibility of the government's commitment to wider access generally. There is therefore reason to fear that the development of more flexible provision may neither be effective nor institutionalised. Underfunded initiatives which leave the central assumptions of the process unchallenged will tend to be marginal and vulnerable to dismantling once the demographic impetus behind wider access has passed. The development of flexible provision may lead to non-traditional entrants increasingly being channelled to alternative, less costly routes by a combination of financial and academic barriers. This would leave the broad educational throughfares – the full-time courses – for A level entrants, and create attrition minefields for the rest.

Those who have worked extensively in access type initiatives know of the large numbers of people desperate to secure academic and professional qualifications as a means of economic survival and personal advancement, and prepared to make incredible sacrifices in order to do so. The potential for exploitation and for the frustration of legitimate expectations is as great as the potential for changing lives.

The future for access to legal education

The last few years have seen the emergence and consolidation of a number of positive initiatives with regard to wider access to legal education. The expansion of part-time law degrees and the growth of Law Access courses have been notable achievements, and they help point the way to further progress. Some Universities and Polytechnics are showing greater flexibility and innovation in admissions procedures, and demographic change may encourage more such developments. From that point of view the prospects for wider access therefore seem very positive.

However, while demographic change may force wider access to higher education generally, its impact in legal education, as we have seen, is likely to be minimal. Without that external pressure, resource constraints within Universities and Polytechnics will discourage the development of more staff-intensive admissions procedures, and greater participation in preparatory or foundation courses. They will therefore tend to allow A levels to continue to play an excessive part in the allocation of Law degree places. Much therefore depends on how actively the University and Polytechnic funding councils encourage institutions to admit non-traditional entrants.

The inadequacy of student support constitutes a major barrier, both to entry and to successful degree completion, for many students. Particularly affected are mature, working-class and black students. The strains imposed by substantial burdens of part-time work and by serious financial worries make the successful academic achievement of students in such circumstances even more creditable. The proposed student loans scheme will act as a further barrier to access, and will operate particularly harshly on students who are confronting an extended and uncertain period of study in an environment which seems alien and unwelcoming.

Accurate prediction of how these contrary tendencies and developments will be resolved is impossible. Nevertheless we can legitimately be sceptical of those who suggest that we are on course for an unprecedented expansion of opportunities within legal education. Progress on access will require action on equal opportunities.

Access to the legal professions

After nearly a century of stability, the structure of the professions is being transformed as long-established restrictive practices begin to crumble. The loss to solicitors of their conveyancing monopoly (which still accounts for 45–50% of solicitors' income) has sent shockwaves reverberating throughout the professions. The work that solicitors do, the training they receive, and the way in which they are organised, are all changing rapidly. The solicitors' search for new markets threatens the barristers' rights of audience and looks set to achieve the 'unthinkable' – the effective fusion of the professions. This period of rapid and fundamental change creates both opportunities and dangers with regard to wider access.

An outline of the qualification process

More than 90% of solicitors entering the profession are graduates, 75% are law graduates.[88] Law graduates are required to attend a one year full-time vocational course prior to sitting the Law Society Final Examination (LSFE). The non-law graduates, who account for approximately 15% of entrants to the profession, are required to attend a one-year full-time vocational course in preparation for the Common Professional Examination (CPE). Having passed their CPE, non-law graduates join the law graduates on the Finals course. On passing the LSFE all intending solicitors then work for two years as articled clerks, or as they are also called, trainee solicitors, prior to qualifying as a solicitor.

The profession retains non-graduate entry and as recently as 1980 14% of entrants came via the diverse routes that account for this entry.[89] However, this proportion has now declined to 3% and non-graduates are no longer a significant source of new solicitors.[90] School-leavers must first take a one-year course to sit for the first part of the Solicitors' First Examination. This is followed by five years in Articles during which part-time study leads to the second part of the First Examination. After this, school-leavers must attend the Finals Course prior to sitting the LSFE.[91] In 1987 there was only one application to take the Solicitors' First Examination and the Law Society is considering its abolition.[92] The route to qualification followed by Fellows of the Institute of Legal Executives (FILEX) is also a lengthy and arduous one.[93] In the circumstances, the decline of these routes of entry is hardly surprising.

Approximately 97% of barristers entering the profession are graduates, 84% are law graduates. All entrants to the profession must join an Inn of Court and keep eight terms (eat twenty-four dinners there over two years, unless they double dine). Law graduates seeking to practise in this country must attend a one year full-time vocational course at the Inns of Court School of Law prior to sitting the Bar Examination.

Non-law graduates are generally required to take the one-year full-time Diploma in Law course prior to entry onto the Bar Examination course. In exceptional circumstances external study for the Diploma is permissible, as is entry via full-time study for the CPE. In very exceptional circumstances part-time study for the CPE is accepted.[94] Non-graduate entry is restricted to a small number of mature students (less than 3% in recent years).[95] If approved by the Joint Admissions Committee, mature entrants are required to attend a two year full-time Diploma in Law course prior to entry onto the Bar Examination Course. In exceptional circumstances, external study for the two-year Diploma is allowed.

Once the intending barristers have passed the Bar examination and been Called to the Bar, all must then spend one year in pupillage. At the end of pupillage barristers who wish to enter private practice must then secure a tenancy in a set of chambers.

Non-law graduate entry

Prior to joining the law graduates on the Finals courses (the Law Society Finals or the Bar Examination), the non-law graduates undertake a one year full-time course: in the case of entrants to the solicitors' profession the Common Professional Examination, in the case of the barristers' profession, the Diploma in Law. Although little has been published concerning the latter, the former has been the subject of excellent surveys by Bryan Read of the Association of Graduate Careers Advisory Services (AGCAS).[96]

The Bar and the Law Society have now both decided to combine the courses to create a genuinely *Common* Professional Examination. Read's surveys therefore point to the barriers encountered at this stage of the qualification process. The two surveys, conducted in 1979 and 1987 reveal that over 90% of CPE students had attended University.[97] Moreover, during those years CPE student intake had become noticeably more selective[98] in terms of their class of degree. CPE students are therefore significantly better qualified than law graduate entrants to the profession.[99]

Demand for places exceeds supply – it is estimated that in 1987 a further 200 places would have been taken had they been made available.[100] The number of places is being increased in 1988/89, but Read's surveys clearly indicate that this expansion will have a limited impact on the profession's social composition.

The surveys show that the inadequacy of financial support is a powerful barrier to students who lack financial resources. Most local authorities choose not to make discretionary awards available to CPE students[101] and it is inevitable that the situation will deteriorate further given present government policy. Over 70% of CPE students surveyed received no grant.[102] The majority were therefore obliged to rely on their own capital or savings, and/or on parents and relatives; a quarter of the students had also taken out bank loans.[103] One survey respondent observed that all the mechanisms were in place for recruiting people from a narrow station into a narrow profession.[104]

Both in 1980 and 1988, Read recommended that central government provide mandatory grants for all CPE students so that the legal profession would be opened 'to all talented graduates regardless of their wealth and background'.[105] Both the professional bodies and the Marre Report on the Future of Legal Education also urged this course of action.[106] However, the option was rejected by the DES in 1987, 'in view of the continuing need to restrain public expenditure'[107] prompting the Law Society in 1988 to reconsider its policy of lobbying for mandatory grants. Thus the problem of inadequate student financial support arises and has an exclusionary impact, not only at the pre-degree and undergraduate stages, but also at the CPE stage.

Finals courses

Inadequate financial support is also a major problem at the Finals stage. Although more local authorities make discretionary awards available to Finals students than they do for the CPE, public spending curbs are keeping the level of awards down.[108] The Inner London Education Authority (ILEA), which has in the past been generous in its provision of discretionary awards, announced in 1988 that it would be reducing the number of grants made available to students studying at the College of Law. Disproportionately affected will be a large number of mature students and black law students in particular.

How is the profession responding to the recruitment crisis and at the same time the inadequacy of financial support, given DES opposition to an extension of mandatory grants? The 'Recruitment Crisis' Report and the Consultative Review of Legal Education reveal that two options are under consideration. First, the expansion of entry onto both CPE and Finals courses by developing alternative forms of provision such as part-time and correspondence study.[109] Second, pressing the government for a centrally funded bursary system or alternatively for a student loan system.[110]

Regarding the latter the 'Recruitment Crisis' Report suggests enthusiasm for the option of targeting bursaries, both for the CPE and the Finals course, on students with first or upper second class degrees, on the grounds that it 'would represent good value for public money'.[111] The argument for this is that had bursaries been targetted in this way in 1987, 83% of students with bursaries would have passed the Finals, compared to the actual overall pass rate of 63%.[112] The Training Committee, concerned at the 'relatively low' pass rate, urge that selection for places on the Finals course be considered, arguing that it would make best use of the limited places.[113]

The development of part-time and correspondence study for the CPE and Finals courses raises much the same dilemma it did in the context of academic legal education. In principle, the benefits of flexible provision for wider access are clear. But in the context of the above statements on selection and 'value for money', there is a danger that less qualified applicants may be restricted to the flexible, cheaper modes of study – with their higher attrition rates – as the full-time courses are closed off by greater academic selectivity and by financial constraints.

To assess the proposal for selection for places on the Finals course, let us consider the Final examination statistics more closely. Statistics for students sitting the Law Society Final Examinations and the Bar Examination show the dominance of University entry, even before examination performance takes effect. Fewer than 30% of the 3,200 students sitting the Law Society Final Examination in 1986 were Polytechnic graduates.[114] Fewer than 20% of the 925 sitting the Bar Examination in 1987 were Polytechnic graduates.[115]

Between 1985 and 1987 the overall pass rates on Law Society Finals improved from 58% to 63%. However, pass rates on the Finals vary considerably depending on the class of degree obtained. In 1987, 83% of Law graduates with first class and upper second-class degrees passed, compared to 46% of those with lower second-class degrees or less.[116] Pass rates are significantly higher for University law graduates than for Polytechnic law graduates. But, a significantly higher proportion of Polytechnic law graduates sitting the Finals exam have lower second-class degrees or less.[117]

The first observation to be made of the proposal, therefore is that it would disproportionately exclude Polytechnic graduates. Given the pattern of student entry to legal education, the proposal would therefore disproportionately exclude black graduates and graduates from working-class backgrounds.

Bar Examination results show that they too constitute a formidable barrier for many students. The overall pass rate in the 1986/7 session stood at 60%.[118] The pass rate for University law graduates was 66% and for Polytechnic law graduates 41%. As with the Law Society Final Examination, pass rates were better for students with upper second-class degrees or higher. Likewise, a higher proportion of University graduates possessed an upper second or better – 49% to the Polytechnics' 28%. Even with the same class of degree, a significant differential between Universities and Polytechnics remains.

In 1989/90 the Bar is introducing a new curriculum into its year of vocational education leading to the Bar Examination. The main feature of the changes is to place much greater emphasis on practical training and skills development. Assessment of the course will no longer be based exclusively on a final written examination. Students will be required to perform satisfactorily in practical work assessments and mid-year tests as well as in the final examination.

These improvements to curriculum, teaching strategy and assessment methods are a very positive development. The move away from knowledge acquisition tested by formal examinations will reduce the advantage currently enjoyed by A level students who have had extensive opportunities to develop excellent examination techniques for such occasions. The changes are therefore a positive contribution to access, especially if early practical assignments are used to give feedback to students and guide them towards improvement.

That is certainly a more positive use for them than having them serve as early 'weeding-out' devices for students who are experiencing difficulties. The achievements of Access courses demonstrate that many students, particularly black and working-class students, are wrongly diagnosed as not being 'up-to-it', not being 'able'.

Increasingly, institutions which have broadened access are introducing writing/study skills support programmes – integrated fully into the course – which emphasise skills development in the areas of problem-solving, argument, logical thinking, examination preparation and work organisation. These programmes improve student survival rates on courses, not only by facilitating skills development but also by building student confidence.

Apprenticeship

Securing an apprenticeship (articles within the solicitors' profession, pupillage at the Bar) presents a very different set of problems as far as access to the professions is concerned.

Abel's survey sets out the barriers to entry imposed by this stage of the qualification process and the changes to these barriers that have taken place during the twentieth century. Especially since the second world war the formidable financial barriers once imposed by articling have been removed – stamp duty and premiums eliminated, length of articles reduced and the introduction of salaries for articled clerks.[119] At the Bar, premiums ceased to be a significant financial burden before they too were abolished. Though salaries have not been introduced, the number of pupillage awards is increasing and some chambers guarantee a minimum income for the second six months.[120] Maintenance during pupillage, particularly because no brief may be accepted during the first six months, remains a barrier.

More recently the availability of apprenticeships has also become a significant barrier as competition has grown. In the late 1970s many applicants for articles were having to write 25/40 letters in order to obtain interviews and an offer of articles.[121] In 1988, the recruitment crisis has profoundly altered this situation. Nevertheless, there is little reason to believe that the factors which affected the ease of obtaining articles in 1980 and 1981 do not still operate:[122] University vs Polytechnic law degree; range and quality of secondary education qualifications; Oxbridge vs non-Oxbridge; better class degree vs lower class of degree.

It is more difficult to establish whether or not there is a shortage of pupillages. In London, where the offering of a pupillage incurs no responsibility on the part of chambers to offer a tenancy subsequently, it would appear that securing a pupillage is not a major problem. However, securing a pupillage in the chambers of one's choice is a different matter: we have already seen the degree of racial segregation that has become established at the Bar. Also, the nature of the work done in chambers where the pupillage is served, places limits on the kind of work that the pupil can subsequently expect to do. Although pupillage still constitutes a financial hurdle to entry to the Bar, obtaining a tenancy is a greater hurdle because of the shortage of space in chambers (though this shortage too has eased).

Recruiting the 'right people', the 'quality' candidates

In 1983, despite the shortage of space that existed at that time, the Senate expressed the view that 'in private practice there is always room for the right person'.[123] As Abel observes, the AGCAS surveys of entry to the Bar reveal just who the right person is: 71% of graduates from Oxford obtained tenancies, 54% from Cambridge, 45% from other Universities and 32% from Polytechnics.[124]

The notion that the 'right people' are always in great demand is one that is heard frequently in both professions. It is also offered as a riposte to the claim that black candidates are experiencing difficulties securing articles, pupillages or tenancies. In its report on the 'Recruitment Crisis' the Law Society's Training Committee stated, on the basis of comments received from firms, that there was no shortage of articles available. 'Starting salaries for articled clerks offered by some City firms reflect the intense competition for the most able people.'[125]

Understanding the use in this context of terms such as the 'able people', 'right person', the 'high-flyer', is essential if we are to appreciate how discrimination takes place. Certainly, discrimination is sometimes overt. There have been numerous instances reported where, for example, the discovery that a candidate for articles or a tenancy is black provokes a horrified reaction.[126] Usually the situation is not so straightforward.

In a paper on black graduates in the labour market, Lyon and Gatley cite research which shows that black graduates tend to take longer than white graduates to find jobs, and tend also to find jobs with lower pay and less status – even when factors like class of degree are taken into account.[127] The Commission for Racial Equality's investigation of ethnic minority recruitment into the accountancy profession showed that black applicants were disproportionately rejected at all stages,[128] despite the absence of any evidence of deliberate discrimination. Lyon and Gatley observed.[129]

> A degree qualification greatly improves the job prospects for black students. But the value of their degrees in the labour market is clearly less for them than it is for their white student compatriots. Complacency about the powers of educational credentials is not in order ...

Lyon and Gatley consider how educational credentials can become less important in occupational success than the more personal qualities and characteristics of employees. The less precise the job description the greater potential there is for personal characteristics to play a significant role. Abel notes that by retaining the hurdles of pupillage, and tenancy the Bar continues 'to control *who* enters private practice ... they are low visibility decisions made by private individuals – pupilmasters, heads of chambers and clerks – who make no secret that they are greatly influenced by personality and background as well as the candidate's technical competence.'[130]

But it is the judgment of technical competence itself which is affected by the candidate's background and other personal characteristics. The skills required of lawyers are vaguely defined – 'You may not be able to define "ability" but you recognise it when you see it.' Their skills are also largely interpersonal – who will fit in and work well as a colleague, who will be accepted as trustworthy and efficient by clients, who will communicate effectively in different contexts. Assumptions about who does or does not possess these skills are socially and culturally determined. That is to say, they are based on the assumed characteristics of people according to their gender or social or racial background. It is within these shared and often unconscious assumptions, which affect the determination of who are the 'able' and the 'right' people, that racism and discrimination lie hidden.[131]

Many within the professions accept that Polytechnic graduates encounter prejudice and discrimination. Both barristers and solicitors acknowledge privately that the Polytechnic degree is widely seen as an inferior qualification for inferior students. This shared assumption is reflected in the selection procedures followed by some firms and chambers. Some automatically reject applications from Polytechnics, others do so unless there is something exceptional about the application. The discriminatory impact of these procedures is self-evident.

Stratification within the professions

In their paper, Lyon and Gatley drew on the work done by Randolph Collins which looked at minorities in the professions in the United States. Collins found that minority candidates tended to be excluded from large, nationally based organisations and therefore obliged to find employment in smaller locally based firms which were more ready to accept them.[132]

A similar pattern seems to have emerged here within both professions. Black solicitors are working disproportionately within smaller firms or as sole practitioners, probably in areas where there are minority communities. Reference has already been made to the better promotion prospects, the higher levels of income and the higher status generally enjoyed in larger firms. Indeed, fears have been expressed within the profession about the viability of sole practitioners. Black barristers are working disproportionately in chambers with a criminal legal aid practice and servicing an increasingly black clientele. Women too are concentrated in less remunerative areas of work and are disproportionately salaried employees within solicitors' firms, not partners. It appears that the professions show an entrenched stratification along both gender and ethnic lines.

There is little doubt that this stratification has its roots early in the educational process.[133]

> It seems likely that in Britain, as in the United States, black minority groups are becoming channelled into the lower end of the educational structure by virtue of a combination of low status, geographical location in inner cities and educational discriminatory practices before they enter a labour market characterised by competition, selection and discrimination.

The depth and persistence of the stratification suggests that we should be careful to ensure that new developments do not unwittingly create opportunities for further stratification. The upsurge of interest in paralegals in late 1988 is a case in point.[134] Though the interest is welcome, the explicit link that has been drawn between the growth of paralegal training and the opening up of the legal profession to ethnic minorities and women is less so.[135]

Women and black students face the prospect of being encouraged to become paralegals where they can use their 'people skills' and carry out tasks that do not require 'the independent exercise of an attorney's judgment'.[136] Black law students attending the Law Society's Recruitment Fair in October 1988 were discouraged and angry to be told more than once that while they would not be taken on as assistant solicitors, they would be welcome as legal executives.[137]

It was not entirely clear whether they were told this because they were black, because they were Polytechnic students or a combination of the two.

The future for entry into the professions

This is a time of ferment within the professions, one that looks set to continue well into the 1990s. As with legal education we are faced with complex and contradictory trends whose impact on entry into the professions is uncertain.

The last few years have seen many positive developments. As a result of the pressure from black barristers and solicitors and from women, both professional bodies have begun to take action against race and sex discrimination. It is important to note that many of the developments in the areas of monitoring and codes of conduct arose out of the work done by the Race Relations Committees in both professions.

Positive steps have also been taken to improve the curriculum, and the teaching and assessment methods employed in the professional examination courses. These will not only improve vocational training for all candidates, but will allow students whose examination skills are not their greatest strength to demonstrate their skills and understanding in other ways.

As of early 1989, the impact on entry of the Lord Chancellor's Green Paper proposals published in February, even if implemented as they stand, is impossible to predict. Speculation is therefore foolhardy. However, it is possible that the proposals will tend to encourage further concentration of the large commercial firms which do the lucrative commercial work. At the other end of the profession, the smaller firms doing publicly funded work may increasingly suffer the disadvantages of the absence of economies of scale when it comes to technology, training and office administration.

Unless positive action is taken to change the present pattern of stratification, women and black solicitors will continue to be located in the smaller, local firms rather than in the large, national organisations. And within the large organisations, women and black solicitors will continue to be concentrated in the lower status, lower earning positions. The market for solicitors' services may be expanding, but that is no guarantee that all will share equally in the expanded market.

As regards entry to the Bar, the ending of exclusive rights of audience will tend to have its greatest impact on barristers doing primarily legally aided work. Black barristers in criminal practices in particular may be inclined to set up in areas where clients are more accessible. The independent Bar after the Lord Chancellor's reforms have been implemented may be a Bar that has lost much of its black membership.

Conclusion

The need for a substantially greater measure of social and racial diversity at all levels within the administration of justice is a pressing one. It will grow rather than diminish and will endure until it is satisfied. We have seen that progress towards that diversity faces many barriers. While some fall outside the immediate bounds of the responsibility of legal education and the professions, others lie at the heart of their traditional practices.

Government policies in higher education do not appear to offer a way forward. They indicate a reluctance to concede that issues of access and equal opportunities issues are inseparable, as well as a naive faith in the power of demographic change to transform institutions. The policies themselves are fraught with contradictions. While the need for wider access is enthusiastically endorsed, and Access courses are recognised as the third major route into higher education, the proposals relating to student finance and the financial constraints within higher education threaten to restrict rather than expand entry.

The present processes of recruitment and admission, both into legal education and the professions, tend to reinforce rather than diminish social and racial divisions. In so doing, they exclude many whose talents and experience neither the professions nor the wider society can afford to neglect.

The costs of obtaining higher education and of becoming professionally qualified inhibit not only entry for many Black British and white working-class students, but also their subsequent survival and success. The relative absence of black academics, administrators, solicitors and judges, means that the support mechanisms, role models and mentors whose existence is taken for granted by white students and lawyers are denied black entrants.

Accordingly, the meritocratic basis of these selection and qualification processes is flawed. It is often argued that 'really able' people will overcome all obstacles and succeed. But black and working-class students should not have to be much better than other students to succeed. That is the essence of discrimination.

The argument that there are no alternatives to these exclusionary and discriminatory processes can no longer be sustained. A substantial body of experience in widening access has been developed. It must be recognised and put to use.

The Lord Chancellor himself has powerfully reinforced the positive steps taken within both professional bodies in recent years in a number of statements addressing the need for more black lawyers and judges. But, whatever progress is made within the professions, its impact will be limited unless similar progress is made within legal education. Access to legal education can and will be substantially widened if government and institutions make deliberate decisions to eliminate the unnecessary barriers which currently restrict access.

First, the financial basis of higher education has to be structured in such a way as to encourage institutions to admit and respond effectively to under-represented groups.[138] Both PCFC and UFC could accomplish this by specifying target numbers of non-traditional entrants. Such a proposal was made (with respect to Polytechnics) by the NAB Equal Opportunities Working Group:[139]

> We believe that when devising the funding methodology for higher education institutions the PCFC should seriously consider the ways in which equal opportunities can be built into it. A sensible, and decisive, method would be to invite institutions to set targets for under-represented groups as part of the PCFC/institution 'contractual' procedure. ... future funding would depend on the institution's performance and endeavours to meet these targets.

Alternatively, PCFC and UFC could provide positive financial incentives for Polytechnics, Colleges and Universities to admit students from under-represented groups and to offer preparatory courses for such groups.

Second, monitoring of the whole range of legal education is as essential as monitoring within the professions. The monitoring should include Universities and Polytechnics, full and part-time courses and all preparatory or Access courses. It should provide for monitoring by gender, ethnic origin, class, age and educational background of applications, withdrawals, class of degree (where relevant), subsequent employment and professional progression.[140]

Responsibility for the monitoring should lie with a national body whose brief should be to promote, support and monitor developments in access and equal opportunities. Such a body should be funded jointly by the government, PCFC and UFC, the Professions and by commercial and industrial sources. The body's composition should be such that it is able to draw on a wider range of experience and knowledge than is currently available within legal education.

The working method of the NAB Equal Opportunities Group and its proposals, contained in 'Action For Access', offer a sound and comprehensive starting point for work on these issues.

Third, many positive initiatives have already been taken which also point the way forward. Among them, the Teaching Fellowships at South Bank Polytechnic for practitioners with an extensive record of work within the black community are an example of a development guided from the outset by black practitioners acting in partnership with the Law School.[141]

Fulton has suggested elsewhere[142] how A level scores could be used not so much as a competitive rationing device, but rather as setting a minimum threshold – leaving other criteria to determine selection or rejection. The papers by Mosston and Cannon in this volume contain descriptions of admissions processes based on such alternative criteria in the US context.[143]

United States law schools have also developed a wide range of preparatory courses during the past twenty years which have produced considerable experience. It would be foolish of us to believe that we cannot learn something from that experience – the successes and failures,[144] in extending the range and improving the quality of our own Access and other preparatory courses.

Finally, US law schools have devised retention programmes, generally aimed at Native American, black, low income students, and which offer financial, tutorial, professional support. Here too we should not ignore the wealth of experience that the programmes have generated.[145] And doubtless there are many other initiatives in this country and throughout the Commonwealth which deserve attention.

Underpinning these initiatives is the recognition that the issue cannot be understood in terms of numbers alone. In the context of ethnic minorities and higher education in the United States, Asa Hilliard, Professor of Urban Education, expressed the point as follows:[146]

> The participation that ethnic minorities should seek in higher education should not be a matter of equity in numbers alone, it should be a matter of equitable participation in the shaping of the institutions in terms of their purposes, priorities and evaluative criteria. Real democracy demands it ... parochial institutions cannot be permitted to wear the mask of universities. They must be transformed.

Both within legal education and within the professions, the issue is not just access but equitable participation at all levels. Entry to legal education and the professions is only the beginning. There is a long way to go.

Acknowledgments

I would like to thank the many colleagues and students whose knowledge and experience helped so much in the writing of this paper. Special thanks to everyone at the Center for Legal Education, City College of New York, and to the many lawyers with whom I have worked here in London. I would also like to thank Michael Hall, Ole Hansen, Ame Harper, William Panton, William Twining and Kay Williams for their comments on an earlier draft of the paper. Finally, I would like to acknowledge my indebtedness to Richard Abel whose work on *The Legal Profession in England and Wales* made my task here so much easier. All errors that remain are mine.

NOTES

¹ *Sunday Times*, 26 February 1989 p A3.
² R L Abel 'The Legal Profession in England and Wales' (1988) p 74/75. See also p 76. Of those called to Gray's Inn in 1984, 12% had working-class fathers.
³ See Abel (1988) p 80.
⁴ P G Marks 'Statistical Report 1987' LSG 2 Sep 1987, p 2446.
⁵ Law Society Report of the Working Party on Women's Careers 'Equal in the Law' (1988) p 10.
⁶ Abel (1988) pp 79–85 and refs.
⁷ H Kennedy 'Women at the Bar' in R Hazell (ed) 'The Bar on Trial' (1978) cited in Abel, p 81.
⁸ Ibid, pp 151–2 and see J Flood 'Barristers' Clerks: The Law's Middlemen' (1983) cited in Abel, p 82.
⁹ Senate of the Inns of Court 'Supplementary Evidence to the Royal Commission on Legal Services' submissions nos 1 and 2 K annex cited in Abel, p 84.
¹⁰ Royal Commission on Legal Services Final Report (1979) volume 2, p 444, cited in Abel, p 84.
¹¹ Report of the Working Party on Women's Careers 'Equal in the Law' (1988). See also P Molyneux 'Association of Women Solicitors – Membership Survey' (1986) 83 LSG 3082.
¹² Working Party on Women's Careers, p 11.
¹³ Ibid, p 12. Of the 1977 admissions only 56% of the women were working full-time, compared to almost 100% of the men.
¹⁴ P Molyneux 'Association of Women Solicitors – Membership Survey' (1986).
¹⁵ P G Marks 'Statistical Report 1987' LSG 2 September 1987, p 2446.
¹⁶ See the Second Report of the NACRO Race Issues Advisory Committee 'Race and Criminal Justice: A Way Forward' (1989) p 10.
¹⁷ 29 LSG 27 July 1988, p 38.
¹⁸ Ibid, p 40.
¹⁹ Abel (1988) p 79.
²⁰ Report to the Senate Race Relations Committee for 1984–5.
²¹ See the comments of Kuttan Menon cited in J Jenkins 'Black Lawyers still fighting for equality' (1987) The Law Magazine 26 June at p 21.
²² Report of the Race Relations Committee 1985/1986 (1986) LSG 27 August at p 2483.
²³ O Hansen 'Black Cloud over Law Society' *Guardian*, 5 June 1985. See also the comments by J Jenkins 'Black Lawyers still fighting for equality' (1987).
²⁴ See J Morton 'Discrimination in the Legal Profession' (A report on the First National Conference on Minority Entry to the Legal Profession) (1985) New LJ 573.
²⁵ 'Ethnic Monitoring Statistics' (The Findings of the Ethnic Monitoring Survey) (1988) 29 LSG 38 27 July.
²⁶ Royal Commission on Legal Services (The Benson Report) (1979) para 35.37.
²⁷ Abel (1988) p 281.
²⁸ 'Higher Education – Meeting the Challenge' Government White Paper (1987) Cmnd 114; 'Top-Up loans for Students' Government White Paper (1988) Cmnd 520; The Education Reform Act (1988).
²⁹ Training Commission Skills Bulletin No 5 (1988) Office for Population Censuses and Surveys.
³⁰ DES Press Release 180/88 14 June 1988 – Robert Jackson calls for a Broader Entry to Higher Education.

[31] 'The Recruitment Crisis' Report of the Law Society Training Committee (May 1988) Appendix 6.

[32] Abel (1988) Table 3.2, p 456.

[33] DES Statistical Bulletin 1/88 'Education Statistics for the United Kingdom' 1987 edition (March 1988) para 9. (HMSO).

[34] P McDonald 'The class of "81" – a glance at the social class composition of recruits in the legal profession' (1982) 9 Journal of Law and Society 267 at pp 268–9.

[35] O Fulton 'Elite Survivals? Entry "Standards" and Procedures for Higher Education Admissions' (1988) 13/1 Studies in Higher Education 15 at p 17.

[36] P J Marks 'Statistical Report 1986' LSG 29 October 1986, p 3259.

[37] B Williamson 'Who Has Access?' at pp 78/9 in 'A Degree of Choice? Higher Education and the Right to Learn' (1986) J Finch and M Rustin (eds) Penguin.

[38] N Saunders 'Ethnic Minorities and Legal Education' unpublished survey conducted 1985/6 (Trent Polytechnic Department of Legal Studies).

[39] E S Lyon 'Unequal Opportunities: Black Minorities and Access to Higher Education' in 'Multi-Ethnic Higher Education in Inner City Areas' Report of the 1986 Joint Conference of South Bank Polytechnic and City College of New York.

[40] R G Lee 'A Survey of Law School Admissions' (1984) 18 Law Teacher 165.

[41] Ibid, pp 167–8. A level grades run from A to E. Points scores are awarded on the basis of these grades (A = 5, B = 4, C = 3, D = 2, E = 1).

[42] O Fulton 'Elite Survivals' p 20.

[43] Ibid, p 22.

[44] E S Lyon 'Unequal Opportunities: Black Minorities and Access to Higher Education' in 'Multi-Ethnic Higher Education in Inner City Areas' Report of the 1986 Joint Conference of South Bank Polytechnic and City College of New York.

[45] Ibid at p 6.

[46] Ibid at p 9.

[47] O Fulton 'Elite Survivals' p 20.

[48] O Fulton 'Principles and Policies' in O Fulton (ed) 'Access to Higher Education' (1981) SRHE.

[49] O Fulton 'Elite Survivals' pp 21/22.

[50] O Fulton 'Elite Survivals' p 16.

[51] O Fulton 'Student Finance' at p 97 in J Finch and M Rustin (eds) 'A Degree of Choice'.

[52] National Advisory Body on Public Sector Higher Education (NAB) Report of the Equal Opportunities Group (1988) 'Action For Access' at p 47.

[53] NUS Briefing on 'Income and Expenditure Survey' (1987).

[54] 'Action For Access' (1988) chapter 6. 'Student Support' pp 47–54.

[55] Ibid, p 42.

[56] FEU 'Black Perspectives on FE Provision: A Summary Document' (1985) FEU.

[57] See also S Tomlinson 'Black Women in Higher Education – Case studies of University Women in Britain' in L Barton and S Walker (eds) 'Race, Class and Education' (1983).

[58] N Saunders 'Ethnic Minorities and Legal Education'.

[59] P Gilroy 'There Ain't No Black In The Union Jack' (1987).

[60] S Rushdie New Society, 9 December 1982.

[61] See A Smithers and A Griffin 'Mature Students at University: Entry Experience and Outcomes' (1986) 11/3 Studies in Higher Education 257 and references on p 268.

[62] R G Lee 'A Survey of Law School Admissions' at p 169.

[63] DES Statistical Bulletin 11/88 August 1988: 'Mature Students in Higher Education – 1975 to 1986' Table 2.

[64] FEU 'Changing the Focus: Women and FE' (1985) FEU.

[65] CNAA Statistics RJH1/52/88.

[66] S B Marsh 'The CNAA Law Degree' (1983) 17 Law Teacher 73, pp 101/2.

[67] S B Marsh 'The CNAA Law Degree' p 103.

[68] CNAA Statistics RJH1/52/88 and R Abel (1988) Table 3.8 p 471.

[69] CNAA Statistics RJH1/52/88.

[70] See P K C Millins 'Access Studies to Higher Education (September 1979–December 1983): A Report' (1984); J Yates and P Davies 'The Progress and Performance of Former Access Students in Higher Education 1984–1986' (1986). See also N Duncan and N W Kibble 'Excellence and Diversity: Admissions Policies in Law Schools' (1986) 10(1) The Law Teacher 36.

[71] See D Gow 'Access, his new flexible friend' *Education Guardian*, 8 November 1988. Also DES Press Release 180/88 'Robert Jackson calls for broader entry to higher education' 14 June 1988.

[72] 'Action For Access' (1988) p 12.
[73] Universities Statistical Record USR/10/2 Undergraduate Analyses Nos 21500, 21501, 21512 and 21513.
[74] Ibid.
[75] A Smithers 'Unlocking the Door' THES September 1988, p 000.
[76] J Pratt and S Silverman 'Responding to Constraint: Policy Management in Higher Education' (1988) OUP. See the commentary by C Weston 'All Tied Up in Central Purse-Strings' *Education Guardian,* 8 November 1988.
[77] 'Higher Education – Meeting the Challenge' Government White Paper (1987). See esp chapter III 'Quality and Efficiency' and p 15.
[78] See the articles setting out the government's instructions to the new funding councils, at p 2 THES, 4 November 1988.
[79] D Murray (Deputy Director of Staffordshire Polytechnic) 'Law Teaching – Facing New Challenges' Paper delivered at Association of Law Teachers (ALT) Conference November 1988.
[80] See p 2 THES, 4 November 1988.
[81] D Murray 'Law Teaching – Facing New Challenges'.
[82] O Fulton 'Student Finance' in 'A Degree of Choice? Higher Education and the Right to Learn' (1986) at pp 103/4. See also J Barnes and N Barr 'Alternative White Paper: Strategies for Higher Education' (1988) Aberdeen University Press.
[83] C Russell 'Baker's fig-leaf fails to hide flaws in loan scheme for students' *Sunday Times,* 13 November 1988, p H2.
[84] O Wotjas ' "Gross deception" as only a tenth of needs covered' THES, 18 November 1988, p 6.
[85] P Wilby 'Battle over Higher Education Becomes Public' *The Independent,* 1 November 1988, p 2.
[86] 'Second Chance to Learn?' (1988) FEU.
[87] 'Higher Education – Meeting the Challenge' at p 10.
[88] 'The Recruitment Crisis' (1988) Appendix 1.
[89] See Abel (1988) Table 2.4 at p 391.
[90] P J Marks 'Statistical Report 1986' LSG 29 October 1986, p 3259; and 'Final Examination Statistics' LSG 19 November 1986, p 3499.
[91] 'The Recruitment Crisis' p 4.
[92] 'Review of Legal Education' Law Society Consultative Paper (August 1988) p 2.
[93] 'The Recruitment Crisis' p 4 and see Abel (1988) p 208.
[94] Letter from D Telling, Sub-Dean of the Inns of Court School of Law, 6 September 1988.
[95] See Abel (1988) p 48.
[96] B Read 'Becoming a Solicitor the Hard Way' (1980) AGCAS; and 'Becoming a Solicitor the Harder Way' (1988) AGCAS.
[97] The Marre Report, ch 13, paras 13.25–13.27.
[98] Read (1980) Table 2, p 11 and Read (1988) Table 2, p 15.
[99] Read (1988) p 2.
[100] 'The Recruitment Crisis' Appendix 10.
[101] Ibid.
[102] Read (1988) p 5.
[103] Ibid, p 5.
[104] Ibid, p 6/7.
[105] Read (1988) p 14.
[106] 'The Recruitment Crisis' p 7 and 'Review of Legal Education' p 3. Marre Report, ch 13, paras 13.28–13.29.
[107] DES letter of 27 July 1987 cited in 'The Recruitment Crisis' p 7.
[108] Abel (1988) p 147.
[109] 'The Recruitment Crisis' Appendix 10 and 'Review of Legal Education' p 1.
[110] 'The Recruitment Crisis' p 7/8 and 'Review of Legal Education' p 3.
[111] 'The Recruitment Crisis' p 8.
[112] Ibid.
[113] Ibid, p 6/7.
[114] 'Final Examination Statistics' LSG 19 November 1986, p 3500.
[115] Inns of Court School of Law: Comparison of Degree and Bar Examination Results for the Academic Session 1986–87.
[116] 'The Recruitment Crisis' p 6.
[117] 'Final Examination Statistics' LSG 19 November 1986, p 3500.
[118] Inns of Court School of Law: Comparison of Degree and Bar Examination Results for the Academic Session 1986–87.

[119] Abel (1988) pp 53–56 and 149–156.

[120] Ibid, p 54.

[121] Ibid, p 153/4.

[122] AGCAS: 'Becoming a Solicitor: A survey of the experiences of law graduates of 1978 seeking to qualify as solicitors in England and Wales' (1980); 'Becoming a Solicitor the new way: A survey of the experiences of law graduates of 1979 seeking to qualify as solicitors in England and Wales' (1981) cited by Abel, p 155.

[123] Cited by Abel (1988) p 59.

[124] AGCAS: 'Becoming a Barrister in the 1980's: A survey of law graduates who took the Bar Final course in the years 1979, 1980 and 1981' (1984) cited by Abel, p 59.

[125] 'The Recruitment Crisis' p 9.

[126] See for example O Hansen 'Black Cloud Over Law Society' *Guardian*, 5 June 1985.

[127] E S Lyon and D A Gatley 'Black Graduates and Labour Market Recruitment' (1988) Higher Education and the Labour Market (HELM) Working Paper No 5. See References on pp 8/9.

[128] CRE 'Chartered Accountancy Training Contracts: Report of a Formal Investigation into Ethnic Minority Recruitment' (1987) cited by E S Lyon and D A Gatley 'Black Graduates and Labour Market Recruitment' at p 9.

[129] E S Lyon and D A Gatley at p 11.

[130] Abel (1988) p 64.

[131] E S Lyon and D A Gatley, pp 11–17.

[132] R Collins 'The Credential Society' (1979) cited by Lyon and Gatley at pp 11–14 and p 23.

[133] E S Lyon and D A Gatley at p 6.

[134] See LSG no 42, 16 November 1988 at p 4; LSG No 39, 26 October 1988, p 3.

[135] LSG No 42, 16 November 1988 at p 4.

[136] Ibid.

[137] For the official report of the Recruitment Fair see LSG No 39, 26 October 1988, p 8.

[138] B Williamson 'Who Has Access?' in Finch J and Rustin M (eds) 'A Degree of Choice? Higher Education and the Right to Learn' (1986) p 89.

[139] 'Action For Access' p 73.

[140] See the 'Action For Access' Monitoring proposals pp 28–32.

[141] For details contact the author.

[142] O Fulton 'Elite Survivals? Entry "Standards" and Procedures for Higher Education Admission' (1988) 13/1 Studies in Higher Education at p 20.

[143] See also S Brown and E Marenco 'Innovative Models for Increasing Minority Access to the Legal Profession' in D White (ed) 'Towards a Diversified Legal Profession' (1981).

[144] The literature is vast but see on the CLEO (Council on Legal Education Opportunity Program) W J Henderson and L Flores 'Implications for Affirmative Admissions After Bakke: Preliminary Analysis of Academic and Bar Performance of Council on Legal Education Opportunity Program Fellows, 1968–1978' from D White (supra). See also the CLEO Symposium (1979) 22 Howard LJ 299. For more general programmes see R O'Neill 'Preferential Admissions: Equalizing Access to Legal Education' (1970) University of Toledo Law Review 281; S J Rosen 'Equalizing Access to Legal Education: Special Programs for Law Students who are not admissible by Traditional Criteria' (1970) University of Toledo Law Review 321.

[145] See 'Rutgers Law School Minority Student Program: Documents from the Faculty Debates' (1979) 31 Rutgers Law Review 857.

[146] A Hilliard 'Ethnic Participation in Higher Education: Philosophical, Economical and Political Perspectives, USA' from 'Multi-Ethnic Higher Education in Inner City Areas' (Report of the 1986 Joint Conference of South Bank Polytechnic and City College of new York at p 3).

8 Access to legal education and the legal profession in India

S P Sathe*

India is a democracy with an elaborately written Constitution, which visualises profound social and economic transformation through the use of law.[1] The legal profession, which includes practising lawyers, judges, law teachers as well as those playing various other legal roles, is bound to play a significant part in monitoring and channelling the social transformation. The Indian legal profession was very prominent in the National Movement for political independence. The lawyers have been in large number in the Constituent Assembly as well as in the Indian Parliament.[2] However, the nature of the roles they played during the National Movement was different from that of the roles they had to play in independent India. During the National Movement, many eminent lawyers had given up their legal professional work in order to devote themselves wholly to the work of the Movement. In the Movement they did not function as lawyers but as mere patriots. There were few occasions when they used their legal talent as lawyers.[3] One author has rightly remarked that after Gandhi's leadership became the most dominant force in Indian politics, practising lawyers no longer led the National Movement. From 1920, lawyers were still in the Movement, but they were no longer there as practising lawyers.[4] Naturally the perspectives of creative and affirmative lawyering, which are required in independent India, were not available to those who visualised the growth of a new society based on justice, social, economic and political.[5] This is obvious from the fact that they did not give much thought to the improvement of legal education after independence.

Legal education: rote learning

Legal education was started by the British in India with the avowed purpose of providing persons capable of rendering legal services of a mundane nature at the lower levels of the system. The higher positions in the Bar were to be occupied by Indians and Englishmen, who had been called to the Bar from one of the Inns in England. Naturally access to higher positions in the profession was restricted to Indians from affluent sections. Law colleges in India have always suffered from neglect by the educational planners. In the report of the Education Commission (known as the *Kothari Commission*) there is unfortunately

---

* Principal, ILS Law College, Pune, India.

no mention of legal education, which was not included within its terms of reference.[6]

Much has been said and written about the neglect of legal education in India. The main defects of this system are (i) it is operated by a large number of part-time teachers, who are practising lawyers, lacking long-term commitment to teaching and research; (ii) students are admitted in large numbers; and (iii) the law schools have poor libraries. Since the law colleges have a large number of part-time teachers, innovations in teaching methods are impossible. The only way to teach is through lectures delivered to 100 or more students with emphasis on the rules rather than on principles. A writer in a Calcutta Review in 1847 had warned that unless legal education stressed principles of law and jurisprudence, Indian lawyers would turn out to be 'pettifoggers ignorant of everything but rules and forms, acts and regulations and reports – stirring up litigation to make their own fortunes out of it'.[7] The emphasis on memory and mere doctrinal understanding of the rules led to rote learning.[8]

A law college is a profitable business as it requires a minimal investment but is sure to earn good revenue through fees. Students rarely attend classes. All they are required to do is to cram some student crammers and pass the examinations. Any graduate can get admission to a law college. The teacher-student ratio is around 1:40. Admission requirements vary according to the place. Where there are private law colleges, practically anybody can get admission. Barring a few law schools, such as that of Delhi University, admissions are easily available. The law colleges do not get financial assistance from the state governments because they are generally considered to be profit-making. They make profit only because of the academically undesirable conditions that prevail in them.[9]

Reforms of professional legal education

Under the Advocates Act 1961, the Bar Council of India (BCI) was given power to make rules for laying down the standards of legal education.[10] In 1966, BCI made rules laying down the standards of legal education and prescribed a three-year degree course for the LLB after a first degree.[11] A holder of such a degree was to be eligible for being enrolled as an advocate under the Advocates Act. This was the first effort by BCI to lend greater seriousness to legal education. BCI desired that legal education should be whole time and that there must be an adequate number of full-time teachers.[12] Various commissions had argued for making legal education more purposeful.[13] Even before the BCI introduced the three-year course, two university law schools, namely Delhi and Banaras, had introduced the three-year model.[14]

The three-year course proposed by BCI was not without opponents. In fact, all arguments which we hear against the controversial five-year course recommended by BCI today were heard in the context of the three-year course in the late sixties. It was said that the three-year course would reduce access of the poorer people to legal education. It would deny opportunities of learning while earning and would be elitist. Ultimately, the Bar Council climbed down on most of the qualitative conditions of the scheme and the law college managements, and others who had vested interests in the perpetuation of the system of part-time and academically deficient system of legal education, were able to survive the new three-year course. The three-year course came, but without the assured qualitative changes.[15] The very people who opposed the three-year course then are today opposing the five-year course drafted by the BCI.

The five-year course contemplates admission of a student after the passing of the XIIth standard public examinations.[16] The other conditions of this course were again so ambitious that its failure was a foregone conclusion. The Bar Council does not have any machinery for effective implementation of the provisions of these rules. Moreover, being an elected body of lawyers, it cannot be expected to stand firm against the vested interests in the present system of legal education. Profit-making managements of private law colleges, degree seeking students who find the present system most convenient, lawyers who find part-time teaching monetarily helpful, have vested interests in opposing any reform of legal education. The stock argument is that any qualitative change would be anti-poor because it would cut down access to legal education and consequently to the legal profession.

Today, there is no qualitative eligibility requirement for admission to a law college. Anyone can get admission if he or she has a degree. The BCI prescribed 40 per cent marks in the degree examination as a minimum requirement for admission to law. The students of the scheduled castes, the scheduled tribes and other backward classes were, however, exempted from this requirement.[17] Under the five-year course, the BCI has prescribed 45 per cent marks at the XIIth examinaton and 50 per cent marks at the graduation examination for admission at the first and the third point of the five-year course respectively. The students of the scheduled castes and scheduled tribes, however, will have to obtain 40 and 45 per cent marks at these examinations for admission respectively. The five-year course is being attacked on the ground that it would be anti-poor. We do not hold any brief for the five-year course because the scheme has many shortcomings. Personally this writer was opposed to it because of various academic deficiencies contained therein. But can it be opposed on the ground that it would cut down access to legal education? To say that the new course would be anti-poor is to assume that today's course is pro-poor. We would like to join issue on this.

It is just not true that the present system of legal education gives equal opportunities to the rich and the poor. Higher education itself is not available to people below the poverty line.[18] From 1975–76 to 1984–85 student enrolment in Law has increased from 141,298 to 195,000. Although this increase is 38 per cent in ten years, actually the ratio of the enrolment in law to total enrolment in higher education has remained constant. In 1975–76, the law students constituted 5.8 per cent of the total enrolment in universities and in 1984–85 they constituted 6 per cent.[19] Any merit-oriented criterion is bound to cut down access to education. But if education is a resource, it should not be wasted and therefore some qualitative/eligibility criterion has to be provided. In an essentially unequal society, equal opportunities for education are bound to be a myth. We can minimise the inequality but we cannot weed it out unless it is weeded out from the social structure itself. Where social inequality prevails, formal equality of opportunities without regard to quali-tative eligibility requirement merely brings down the quality of legal education. When quality of education goes down, again it is the affluent sections which suffer less than the poorer sections, because they can always make up the deficiencies of the education through their better socialisation and wider exposure. Take for example the original side Bar of the Bombay High Court. It is not a mere accident that this Bar has had lawyers like Palkhiwala, H M

Seervai, Ashok Desai, Soli Sorabji and Fali Nariman. Even a casual glance at the class backgrounds of the lawyers of this Bar will reveal that they had benefited from their richer socialisation, wider exposure and better upbringing. Their affluent socio-economic class background doubtless gave them some advantages which enabled them to become better and more successful lawyers, in spite of the sub-standard legal education which they had shared with other members of the society. If the quality of legal education goes up, not they, but those who do not have such affluent background would benefit. The overall societal benefit from such higher quality legal education would doubtless be there. The populist talk of access to the poor indulged in by so-called radicals is really not so much out of concern for the poor as much as for defending the existing system in which they have vested interests.

This does not mean that we would like legal education to be restricted to the well-to-do sections. We can certainly improve the quality of legal education without making it elitist through provision of funds for poor but merited students. Adequate numbers of seats and scholarships could be provided for the backward classes including the scheduled castes, the scheduled tribes and other nomadic tribes etc. The law courses could also be allowed to run on a part-time basis in the mornings, evenings or nights and legal education could also be imparted through distance education etc. This would help ensure access to large numbers of people. But there must be some educational/academic eligibility requirement to ensure that those who come to study law have an aptitude for it and they must be required to put in the prescribed amount of work. Under the present system, employed students are admitted and then in order to accommodate them all the requirements of study and curriculum are practically waived. The governments in India, the central Government as well as the state governments, have to see education as a resource. While it must be available equally to whosoever desires, it should not be wasted. It requires greater investment because investment in education is investment in human resources. Legal education ought not to be seen only from a narrow angle of the training of a court lawyer. Legal education is required for equipping men and women to perform a variety of legal roles requiring a variety of skills, such as problem analysis, oral and written communication, counselling, advocacy and negotiation, the methodologies of legal reasoning and legal research.[20] Legal education is essentially a multi-disciplinary, multi-purpose education which can develop the human resources and idealism needed to strengthen the legal system. The governments must therefore invest more money in legal education for providing more and better trained full-time teachers, better equipped libraries, imaginative methods of teaching and thought-provoking as well as intellectually stimulating teaching materials. This would cut down the physical access of the people to legal education from a short-term perspective, but in the long run would promote a far more equitable access to the professional higher levels and also far more competent legal services to the people. A lawyer, a product of such education, would be able to contribute to national development and social change in a much more constructive manner. It is to be noted that at present there is no legal aid programme in the LLB curriculum of most of the universities. The practising lawyers have been rather hostile to its introduction on the ground that the students, who were not lawyers, could not be entrusted with the work, lest they might harm the clients.[21] This shows how legal education is under-valued. Legal aid clinics in law colleges, besides helping the assimilation of forensic skills, also provide exposure to the social obligations of a lawyer and have a great educative value. This writer introduced legal aid in the ILS Law College, Pune, facing derisive remarks and non-cooperation from leading lawyer members of the faculty. Their hostility was due to their lack of appreciation of the creative aspects of legal education and also the vested interests of the part-time faculty in the rote learning practices that were current in legal education.

We may now have to separate the professional course from the purely academic course. Although standards of passing in both have to be high, the academic course could be taken externally. The professional course, however, will have to be done in a law school because it will involve a good deal of exposure to the processual aspects of the law. Since it should require going through class discussions, seminars, moot courts and attendance at legal aid clinics, law school attendance cannot be dispensed with. The separation of the professional course from the academic courses would also ensure better motivation for the professional course. It is observed that only a small number of those who study law at present intend to join and actually join the Bar.[22] A good many read law just to get an additional degree. Some working students join law in order to improve their qualifications which might earn them a promotion. It was observed by us that the number of those intending to join the profession was higher among those students who joined the new five-year course after passing the XIIth.[23]

Qualitative improvement of legal education may seemingly reduce the access to legal education but in terms of improvement in the quality of lawyering and consequent availabity of the legal services to the poor and the community in general, it would in real terms enhance access to the profession and ultimately to justice.

A just society would require that competent legal services should be available to those who cannot afford to pay for them through a subsidised system of legal aid. Such competent legal services would be available only if there are competent lawyers. A competent lawyer does not merely mean one who is possessed of the legal acumen and skills 'but one who also possesses the right perspectives of the societal obligations of a lawyer. Sensitivity to social urges and aspirations, appreciation of the social dynamics of law and insights into doctrinal and functional aspects of the legal process are essential requisites of a creative lawyer. These ought to be provided through sound legal education. Access to legal education will therefore determine the quality of the lawyers and such quality will ultimately determine access to legal services.[24]

Legal profession: a profile

It is often said that the Indian legal profession is over-crowded.[25] But often there has been a complaint that if one goes out to find a good, trustworthy and competent lawyer, not many are really available.[26] Since touting is prohibited and exploitative and the lawyers cannot advertise their availability,[27] many people do not know whom to consult. In the legal aid centre run by the law college, we often come across complaints of exploitation and neglect of work by lawyers. Touting is rampant in courts and lawyers make free use of touts. The lawyers seldom tell the client that he has no case. Even a hopeless case is accepted and high fees are charged. Receipts for the moneys received are seldom given. There is nothing like scheduled fees that a lawyer charges.

His fees vary with the capacity of the client. In this process both things happen – lawyers take money and do not work and lawyers work and are not paid. Many lawyers told me in private conversation that a good part of their fees had to be waived.[28]

Although there has been a good deal of talk about legal aid in recent years, very little legal aid is really given. The government-sponsored legal aid programme has unfortunately not made much headway. We have heard stories of the legal aid lawyers asking for extra remuneration from the parties.[29] Legal aid is still sporadic and depends upon the benevolence of the lawyers. The senior lawyers have no time for it and the junior ones being engaged in the struggle for existence cannot afford it.[30] True, there has been a good deal of public interest litigation (PIL) and some of it was fought by lawyers with a social commitment. The number of such socially minded lawyers is, however, very small. PIL has given rise to hopes but unless steps are taken to make basic changes in the delivery of justice, these hopes might be belied and might give rise to frustration among people. As things stand, people have begun to feel that law and legal methods are of no use to them. They are turning towards self-help or becoming more and more fatalist. The PIL culture and thrust cannot and ought not to remain confined to the Supreme Court and the High Courts. It must percolate to districts and talukas.[31] The Indian lawyer, by and large, and barring exceptions which are doubtless there, is too much obsessed with litigation. He does not think that his services would be necessary in other situations. He, therefore indulges in negative, legalistic and manipulative lawyering.[32] The ILC Report rightly says:[33]

> Lawyers trained by rote methods may tend to follow rote methods in their practice. Lawyers who received little training in the very range of skills which may make them valuable as professionals may tend to be less useful as professionals ... The profession becomes saturated with lawyers who tend to bring a formal, rule oriented, rigid perspective to their work.

In the moffusil courts, the written statements filed on behalf of the respondents often contain nothing but a total denial of what the plaint has said. Even where facts are to be denied, irrelevant details and irresponsible charges are hurled at the opposite side. In criminal cases, the defence lawyer rarely wins entirely due to his forensic skills. His success is due to inefficient police investigation and/or because the witnesses either tell lies or retract what they have said earlier. The lawyer is unfortunately engaged in tutoring the witnesses to speak lies before the courts. There are complaints that some criminal lawyers are in collusion with the lower police personnel. Sometimes, the police act as touts of the criminal lawyers.

A young lawyer who joins the Bar has to encounter a number of difficulties. There is no guarantee that he will start earning soon. There is a long and uncertain waiting period. A person whose father or near relation is a lawyer or a person who is affluent enough to wait can afford to join the Bar. Therefore Sunshine and Berney had observed in their report that 'only the law student with a substantial financial family backing or with relatives established in practice at the court can even contemplate making a career at the Bar without extreme trepidation.'[34] A young lawyer has to spend long years in the chambers of the senior lawyer. He is often exploited. He is used for doing unskilled jobs, clerical work or at the most for getting affidavits or obtaining adjournments. If you visit Bombay's Esplanade Court or any collector's office in a district, you are likely to come across lawyers soliciting work most shamelessly. There is a cut-throat competition and a large number of them indulge in very unethical practices.[35]

Access to the profession

As contact and influence count a lot in providing opportunities for upward vertical mobility, persons from higher social and economic classes have far better access to higher positions of dominance in the legal profession than the persons from lower strata.[36] Persons from lower socio-economic backgrounds such as scheduled castes, scheduled tribes and women have therefore rarely made headway in this profession. Their survival rate is low and their upward mobility is also less. Women, barring exceptions, have mostly been drop-outs after a few years of practice. Either they get married or take up some other job. Even while they stay in the profession they are very often treated as either show pieces or unwanted lots.[37] A lady lawyer of Delhi told this writer that women have to undergo many more hardships, including expectation of sexual 'favours' from male seniors or other influential persons.

Where contacts and influence count more than merit, dynastic and other ascriptive factors are bound to weigh more for professional ascendancy.[38] In the medical profession, where skills and competence ultimately have to prevail, though there is also good deal of dominance of the higher class, the upward vertical mobility is greater as compared to the legal profession. Women occupy much higher positions in that profession not necessarily as gynaecologists but also in other fields like ophthalmology, general surgery or general medicine. However, we are not suggesting that the medical profession offers equitable opportunities of access. The medical profession, unlike the legal profession, requires large financial investments for access to medical education (in the form of capitation fees or for books and equipment) and later to the medical profession which may require expenses for a place for a clinic and costly equipment required by a consultant. It is a profession the access to which is restricted to the richer sections. Through the facility of bank loans (since there are nationalised banks) this disadvantage could be partially mitigated. However, skill and expertise do matter in that profession more than they matter in the legal profession. In the legal profession the chance element plays a much greater role. In proportion as merit and skills become more important, contact, influence and consequently corruption are bound to become less important. When this happens, access to the profession is facilitated for those who are less favoured by class and kinship backgrounds. How do we make merit and skill count more in the legal profession than contact, influence and manipulation? We know that the importance of these will not totally disappear from any society. We can only reduce it but in proportion as we reduce the factor of ascriptive status, we will make access to the legal profession more equally available.

One way in which access to the legal profession can be increased is by providing for a comprehensive programme of legal aid. The Supreme Court of India has now held that right to legal aid is part of the 'procedure established by law'[39] in accordance with which alone a person's personal liberty or life can be taken away.[40] The court set aside a conviction in a criminal case which was secured without affording the assistance of a lawyer to the accused.[41] It is now really necessary for the government to install a comprehensive legal aid programme. This will doubtless minimise the existing inequalities in the availability of legal services. Through the legal aid programme, merit could supersede influence and high social standing. Simultaneously if we can improve the quality of legal education and expose the lawyer to the possibility of a variety of legal services, their attitude will change. Although higher castes were in large numbers among students of law as well as law practitioners, the caste position is changing and is bound to change as social change becomes articulate.[42]

The recent experiments with the Lok Adalats (people's courts) should also be taken more seriously for finding alternatives to the existing system of justice.[43] Traditionally a lawyer is supposed to prolong and complicate the litigation. This image of the lawyer is so deep-rooted that he is often excluded from many proceedings. The Family Courts Act 1985 which was enacted for providing specialised tribunals to deal with matrimonial and property matters of family law provides that no lawyer shall appear before the family court except as *amicus curiae*.[44] Such provisions are found in various statutes and they show how a lawyer is considered as a nuisance by the legislatures. This view is shared by a large number of people. It prevails because of the negative and manipulative lawyering that has been in practice in this country for a long time. Such provisions prohibit lawyers' access to such proceedings and consequently deny legal expertise to the parties.[45] More positive, affirmative and creative lawyering will not be such a nuisance, on the contrary it will help achieve the objective of conciliation, settlement etc. A lawyer who sees himself relevant not only in litigation will discover diverse uses of his skills which will earn him opportunities for a successful career without having to sacrifice his scruples. However, this does not mean that a legal aid programme and sound legal education are a panacea for all evils. We do not claim that lawyers would overnight turn into a virtuous, socially oriented lot. This is a process which will have to evolve. Further, the legal profession cannot be an island of excellence in an ocean of corruption and selfishness. Unless the overall environment improves, change will not be visible. But the changes in the lawyering methods, which we have foreseen, would doubtless help bring about change in the environment.

Concluding remarks

In India, access to legal education is open to anyone who has obtained a university degree. The examinations held by the universities for law are not demanding and therefore one can pass those examinations easily. The content of legal education is poor. A student is taught rules and doctrines without any insights into their functional application. The emphasis is on memory and rule-mindedness. A student hardly ever bothers to know the interaction between law and society. As a holder of the LLB degree can join the profession, access to the legal profession is also easy and available to persons irrespective of academic excellence. Legal education is not expensive. The annual tuition fees payable by a student are around Rs400 to Rs500. He does not have to buy costly books and there is no other expenditure. For students of the scheduled castes and scheduled tribes there is total exemption from tuition fees and in addition they are given a stipend. Tuition fees exemption is also given to students who are economically backward. Their fees are paid by the government. Thus there are enough provisions for poor and backward class students.

However, although access to the legal profession is open to anybody who gets a LLB degree, survival in the profession as well as ascendancy in the Bar is difficult unless one belongs to the higher socio-economic class. Its composition being such, it is bound to be more pro-rich and pro-status quo. It is unlikely to contribute much to social change. Legal services are not easily available. One reason for such inaccessibility of legal services is the nature of the lawyering practised by lawyers in India. It is negative, legalistic and manipulative. The lawyers are excessively obsessed with litigation. Five per cent of the lawyers monopolise almost 90 per cent of the litigational work. Since these lawyers cannot attend to so many cases at a time, they ask for adjournments and thus cause delays. The lawyers have not shown much interest in providing free legal aid to the poor. Although some lawyers have taken up public interest cases, their number is small. In order that legal services should become easily and widely available, the government must provide for a comprehensive legal aid programme. Through such a programme it should be possible to bring about attitudinal changes among lawyers. If the present negative, legalistic and manipulative lawyering is replaced by affirmative, sensitive and creative lawyering, the quality of legal services will go up. This will also promote greater respect for merit ie skills and hard work of the lawyer. In proportion as merit becomes more important, contact, influence and corruption will become less. In a merit oriented profession, access will get equitably distributed. For achieving this, fundamental changes in the policy of legal education would be necessary.

NOTES

[1] See Part III of the Constitution which contains guarantees of fundamental rights and Part IV which enumerates the directive of state policy. These two parts have to be read as an integrated code. See *Minerva Mills v Union of India* AIR 1980 SC 1789.
[2] In the Constitutent Assembly/Provisional Parliament of 1947–52, 32 per cent of the members were lawyers. See Morris Jones *Parliament in India* 120 (1957); Marc Galanter 'The Study of the Indian Legal Profession' (1968) 3 Law and Society Rev 201, 211; in the first *Lok Sabha* (1952) 35.6 per cent of members were lawyers. The percentage came down to 30.5 in the Second, 24.5 in the Third, 17.5 in the Fourth, 20.5 in the Fifth, 23.4 in the Sixth, 22.2 in the Seventh and 19.0 in the present. See 32 Journal of Parliamentary Information 608–609 (1986); (The Lok Sabha means the lower House of the Indian Parliament); also see *Members of Lok Sabha 1952–84: A Study in Their Socio-Economic Background* p 10, Lok Sabha Secretariat, New Delhi (1985).
[3] Tilak's arguments while defending himself against the charge of sedition were examples of creative lawyering. See S P Sathe 'Tilak's Philosophy of Law' in N R Inamdar (ed) *Political Thought and Leadership of Lokmanya Tilak* (1983) p 119. Similar creative lawyering in support of the freedom struggle was made in the trials of the INA officers held at Red Fort on the eve of Independence. The Indian National Army had been set up by Subhash Bose to fight against the British for Indian independence. The army had been located in Japan. After Japan's surrender in the Second World War, three INA officers were tried for waging war against the King. Mr Bhulabhai Desai, an eminent lawyer and Congress member appeared on behalf of the accused and pleaded that as subjects of a captive nation they had a right to fight for the freedom of their country. See B R Agarwala 'INA Trial' (1984) Popular Jurist, vol I, No 2, p 37. See also *The Transfer of Power 1942–47* Documents Nos 143, 233, 425.
[4] Samuel Schmitthener 'A Sketch of the Development of the Legal Profession in India' (1968–69) 3 L&S Rev 337, 381.
[5] Article 38 of the Constitution of India.
[6] *Education and National Development* report of the Education Commission, 1964–66 (govt of India 1964).

[7] Schmitthener, supra note 4 at 362–363.

[8] Marc Galanter *Competing Equalities* (1984) 514; also see Arthur T von Mehren 'Law and Legal Education in India: Some Observations' (1965) 78 Harvard Law Review 1180–1189.

[9] S P Sathe 'Legal Education in Maharashtra' (1983) 10 Indian Bar Rev 188; T G Bastedo 'Law Colleges and Law Students in Bihar' (1968) 3 L&S Rev 269.

[10] See section 7(h) read with s 49(1), sub-clauses (a–f) and (d) of the Advocates Act 1961.

[11] Bar Council of India Resolution 2/1966 'Standards of Legal Education and Recognition of Degrees in Law for Admission as Advocate' AIR 1966 Journal 3–36.

[12] The Bar Council in 1966 said that at least 25 per cent of the faculty must be of full-time teachers. Under the new rules, which laid down the five-year course, the BCI laid down that not more than 50 per cent of the Faculty shall be of part-time teachers.

[13] *Report of the University Education Commission* (Radhakrishnan Commission) vol I, p 257 (1948); Law Commission of India, Fourteenth Report, pp 520–550 (Ministry of Law, Government of India, 1958); Report of the Legal Education Committee, Bombay (Chagla Committee) 1949; Report of the Committee on the Reorganisation of Legal Education in the University of Delhi (Gajendragadkar Committee) 1964; See generally S K Agrawala (ed) *Legal Education in India* (1973).

[14] P K Tripathi 'In the Quest For Better Legal Education' (1968) 10 JILI 469; Anandji 'Dean's Report: Response to the Banaras Scheme' (1965) 1 Banaras Law Journal p 1.

[15] Russell B Sunshine and Arthur L Berney 'Basic Legal Education in India: An Empirical Study of the Student Perspective at Three Law Colleges' (1970) 12 JILI 39, 41; Bastedo, supra n 9 at 287, n 20.

[16] The XIIth Examination is the final examination conducted by the Higher Secondary School Certificate Examination Board, which is a statutory body, for the students who have completed their school education. After passing this examination, students join the colleges for courses in Arts, Science, Commerce, Medicine or Engineering. It is equivalent to the A level examination in the UK. Until recently, admission to law school was open only to graduates of any of the above faculties (Arts, Science, Commerce etc) but in the five-year course offered by the Bar Council of India (BCI) a student can enter after the XIIth ie without a first degree. This course has not been started by many universities. The BCI has now climbed down to allow the old three-year course after graduation to continue. This has made the prospects of the five-year course bleaker still. The National Law School which is now being started at Bangalore by the BCI however offers the five-year course.

[17] The scheduled castes are castes, races or tribes or parts of or groups within such castes, races or tribes as are declared under article 341 of the Constitution by the President to be scheduled castes for the purpose of the Constitution. The scheduled caste category is intended to comprise those groups isolated and disadvantaged by their untouchability, ie their low status in the traditional Hindu caste system which exposed them to invidious treatment, severe disabilities, and deprivation of economic, social, cultural and political opportunities (Galanter *Competing Equalities* (1984) p 122. The scheduled tribes are tribes or tribal communities or parts or groups within such tribes or tribal communities as are declared to be such tribes by the President under article 342 of the Constitution. This category includes those groups distinguished by tribal characteristics and by their spatial and cultural isolation from the bulk of the population. (Galanter, supra at p 147).

[18] The literacy rate during the independence era rose from 16.67 per cent in 1951 to 36.23 per cent in 1981. That means 63.77 per cent of India's population is illiterate. See *Challenge to Education, a Policy Perspective* (1985) p 22 (Ministry of Education, Govt of India, New Delhi). Illiteracy and poverty almost overlap.

[19] *University Grants Commission – Report for the Year 1984–5* p XIII–Appendix; *UGC – Report for the Year 1979–80* p 119–Appendix VII. Reports submitted to the Government of India in compliance with section 18 of the UGC Act 1956.

[20] See *Legal Education in a Changing World* – Report of the Committee on Legal Education in the Developing Countries p 62 (International Legal Center, New York 1975) hereinafter cited as ILC Report; also see S K Agrawala 'Legal Education and its Relevance to Contemporary Indian Society' (1978) Cochin University Law Review 34; Upendra Baxi 'Towards a Socially Relevant Legal Education' (UGC 1979); William Twining 'Pericles and the Plumber' (1967) 82 LQR 396.

[21] See Sathya Narayan 'Impediments to Implementing Legal Aid' in N L Abhyankar (ed) *Legal Aid* (1982) pp 47, 49. The author says 'But these clinics (run by the law colleges) are chiefly and regularly manned by academicians and students, social workers, who have not (sic) knowledge about the court procedures, and its working ... To establish a sound client-lawyer relationship ... it requires years of practical experience which the students, the law teachers and the social workers do not possess.' The writer is a part-time lecturer in a Poona college.

The views are typical of the practising lawyers' low esteem of the full-time teachers who are here referred to as 'academicians'.

22 Sunshine and Berney found that 33 per cent of the students from Delhi, 25 per cent from Ernaculam and 26 per cent from Bombay intended to practise as lawyers. See supra n 15. In another recently held survey, it was found that 93 per cent of the students who were asked replied that they had chosen law on their own and 208 out of 372 wanted to practise law. See Sathe, Kunchur, Kashikar 'Legal Profession: Its Contribution to Social Change – A Survey of the Pune City Bar' (1984) 13 ICSSR Research Abstracts pp. 111–123 (Jan–June). This survey has also been published in (1983) 10 Indian Bar Review p 47; (1982–1983) 18 & 19 Banaras Law Journal p 40.

23 In a survey of the students studying in the second and third year of the new five-year course at the ILS Law College, Pune, we found a very large percentage of the students (100 per cent in the third year and 85.59 per cent of those in the second year) intending to join the profession. The author gratefully acknowledges the assistance of Ms Suniti Rao, Librarian and Ms Sita Bhatia, Lecturer of the ILS Law College, for conducting such a survey on his behalf. As this sample was too small and of a single college, its findings, however, could not be of any statistical value.

24 See ILC Report, supra n 20 at p 13. The Report says 'A sound system of legal education, properly perceived and utilised, has an important, positive contribution to make to national development.'

25 According to one estimate, there were 183 lawyers per one million of the population in India as against 507 lawyers in the United Kingdom, 1595 in the USA, 947 in New Zealand, 683 in Australia and 769 in Canada. There were wide disparities in state-wise distribution, the undivided Bombay State having 263 lawyers per million people, Orissa having only 75 and Assam 76 per million of the population. This was the state of affairs in 1958. See Upendra Baxi *Sociological Research in India: A Programschrift* (1975) p 25 (ICSSR). Recent information, however, is that there were 336 lawyers approximately for each million people in India in 1982. See Marc Galanter *Competing Equalities* (1984) p 514. Thus the lawyers have increased by almost 80 per cent in 24 years.

26 The Supreme Court rejected petitions for bad drafting in *Sukh Deo Narain v Rajasthan* (1984) 4 SCC 235; *Shantilal Mangaldas v Chunilal Ranchoddas* (1984) 4 SCC 236.

27 Soliciting is forbidden under the rules of professional behaviour. Advertising amounts to soliciting and therefore it is also forbidden. Rule No 36, chapter II of the Standards of Professional Conduct and Etiquette of the Bar Council of India Rules, 1975, framed under s 49(1)(c) of the Advocates Act 1961, read with the proviso. See Devesh Chandra Mukherjee 'India's Stand on Lawyer Advertising and Specialisation' AIR 1981 (Jour) 25.

28 See Sathe et al, supra n 22; also see J S Gandhi *Lawyers and Touts* (1982); J S Gandhi *Sociology of the Legal Profession – Law and Legal System: The Indian Setting* (1987); Marc Galanter 'The Study of the Indian Legal Profession' (1968–69) 3 L&S Rev 201; Peter Rowe 'Indian Lawyers and Political Modernisation: Observations in Four District Towns' (1968–69) 3 L&S Rev 219.

29 See J S Gandhi *Sociology of the Legal Profession* – Ibid at p 46.

30 G Oliver Koppell 'Abstract of the Indian Lawyer as Social Innovator: Legal Aid in India' (1968–69) 3 L&S Rev 299.

31 A most notable public interest litigation which originated in a magistrate's court was a complaint under section 133 of the Criminal Procedure Code which culminated in the Supreme Court decision in *Ratlam Municipality v Vardhichand* AIR 1980 SC 1622. See Sathe *Administrative Law* (1984) p 354.

32 Marc Galanter 'Legal Torpor: Why So Little Has Happened in India After the Bhopal Tragedy' (1985) 20 Texas International Law Journal 273–94; Marc Galanter 'When Legal Worlds Collide: Reflections on Bhopal – The Good Lawyer and the American Law Schools' (1986) 36 Journal of Legal Education 292; See Upendra Baxi 'Towards the Revictimization of the Bhopal Victims'; Introduction to *Inconvenient Forum and Convenient Catastrophe: The Bhopal Case* (1986) (Indian Law Institute).

33 ILC Report, p 49 supra n 20.

34 Sunshine and Berney, supra n 15 at p 75.

35 By unethical practices, we do not mean merely tipping or bribing the clerks to get work done speedily. Speed money is no longer considered corruption. Even in advanced countries this practice prevails. See Ted Finman *Civil Litigation and Professional Responsibility* (1966) p 58 (American Bar Center).

   For an authentic view of what is unethical, see *P D Khandekar v Bar Council of Maharashtra* AIR 1984 SC 110. The court observed that it was professionally improper to prepare fake documents or to draw pleadings knowing that the allegations made were untrue. Also see *M Veerabhadro Rao v Tek Chand* AIR 1985 SC 28; *Vijay Singh v Murarilal* (1979) 4 SCC 758; *Phiroze Shah Gandhi v H.M. Seervai*, AIR 1971 SC 385.

36 See Charles Morrison 'Social Organisation at the District Courts – Colleague Relationships Among Indian Lawyers' (1968–69) 3 L&S Rev pp 251, 253; Peter Rowe 'Indian Lawyers and Political Modernization: Observations in Four District Towns' (1968–69) 3 L&S Rev pp 219, 223.

37 See for experience in England, Rose Pearson and Albie Sachs 'Barristers and Gentlemen: A Critical Look at Sexism in the Legal Profession' (1980) 43 Mod LR 400.

38 Dynastic tendencies are predominant in the Indian Bar. Thus, Samuel Schmitthener says: 'One fourth of the Indian barristers who passed through Lincoln's Inn in the 19th Century were sons of lawyers and judges.' See supra n 4 at 375. Also see George Gadbois 'Indian Supreme Court Judges: A Portrait' (1968) 3 L&S Rev p 317. An empirical study of the Bars at various levels will show that dynastic tendencies have been reinforced in recent years. This is so particularly at the levels of the Supreme Court and the High Courts. Some of the prominent names which can be given as examples are as follows: Senior Advocates whose descendants are in the profession – Mr Ashok Sen, Former Law Minister, Messrs Soli Sorabji, Fali Nariman, Parasaran (at present Attorney General), HM Seervai, Y S Chitaley, Shanti Bhushan, Ram Jethmalani, Milan Bannerji, V M Tarkunde etc. Son/daughter/son-in-law/nephew of the following judges are in the profession: Justice M Hidayatullah, Justice Y V Chandrachud, Justice P N Bhagwati (all former Chief Justices of India), Justice V D Tulzapurkar and Justice Venkataramiah. In the Supreme Court we have had second generation judges such as Fazl Ali and Bhagwati; the son-in-law of Justice P B Gajendragadkar, Former Chief Justice of India (Justice R A Jahagirdar of the Bombay High Court) is a Judge. These examples have been selected at random and on personal knowledge. The persons named here and their descendants have been known for their outstanding legal talent. The dynastic character does not in any way cast aspersions on any of them.

39 Article 21 of the Constitution of India.

40 *M H Hoskot v Maharashtra* AIR 1978 SC 1548; See *Sheela Barse v Maharashtra* AIR 1983 SC 378; *Hussainara Khatoon v Bihar* AIR 1979 SC 1360.

41 *Suk Das v Union Territory of Arunachal Pradesh* AIR 1986 SC 999.

42 Sathe et al, supra n 22, Bastedo, supra n 9.

43 Justice D A Desai says 'Is there any doubt that our justice delivery system, namely adversary system ... is archaic, non-functional and not result-oriented.' He observes that 'the legal profession should be put in the forefront and it must provide leadership.' See D A Desai 'Role and Structure of Legal Profession' 8 Journal of the Bar Council of India (1981) pp 112, 114.

44 Section 13 of the Family Courts Act 1984. See similar provisions in s.28(3) of the Children Act 1960; section 38(2)(f) of the Industrial Disputes Act 1947, etc.

45 See generally Dr N R Madhava Menon 'Lawyer in the Adjudicative Process: An Appraisal of Section 30 of Advocates Act 1961' (1981) 8 Journal of the Bar Council of India p 105.

9 Access to legal education and the legal profession in Jamaica

*Selina Goulbourne**

Introduction

There are broad similarities in the issues relating to access to legal education and the legal profession in Jamaica and England. This is not surprising because the systems of education and law in Jamaica derive from traditions in England from which Jamaica gained independence in 1962. The social and economic conditions of Jamaica, however, had a profound impact on the nature and composition of the profession including entry to it. Expectedly, it has undergone some changes in the post-World War Two period as a result of significant overall improvement in the region. In Jamaica, like the rest of the Commonwealth Caribbean, however, the traditions of the profession and its exclusiveness have continued to be barriers to the kind of access we have come to expect in democratic societies as those which have developed in the region. Moreover, the well-known Anglophone West Indian tradition of maintaining internationally competitive educational standards, coupled with the comparatively rigid class/colour structure have proved to be tenacious barriers to access for ambitious and able members of the black majority. In view of the complexity of the class/colour correlation in Jamaica the problems of access cannot be resolved by positive discrimination in favour of scheduled caste or an oppressed racial majority as is the case in India or Malaysia, respectively.

Unfortunately, whilst the problems of legal education and training have been the subjects of much debate throughout the region during the last two decades, very little attention has been paid to the problem of access to the profession. The principal aim of this paper, therefore, is to invite discussion over the problem of access to the legal profession in the Anglophone Caribbean utilising the specific example of Jamaica which is fairly typical of the region. The discussion is informed by the conviction that informed debate is likely to at least suggest possible solutions to a persistent problem which has been too long ignored. A discussion of this kind, however, must necessarily commence with an appreciation of the historical development of the legal profession and the racial *minority's* exclusion of the black *majority* from participation in the profession.

* Council of Legal Education, London.

174

The development of the legal profession

Following conquest and settlement of the island in the late seventeenth century by the British, the legal profession in Jamaica was very much a free for all, provided, of course, that you were white. There was very little professional control over entry and professional standards. By the late nineteenth century, however, control over entry was being exercised by the local Law Society. The decline of the sugar plantations in the late nineteenth century necessitated the rapid sale of unviable estates. In these circumstances conveyancers were well placed not only to make a comfortable living from land transactions but also to purchase land which was being sold below its market value. The profession also became more attractive as an outlet for the sons of the plantation owners and overseers as well as the emergent wealthy merchants many of whom were Jews. By the late nineteenth century the profession was dominated by a few large solicitors' firms which were exclusively white or Jewish.

The monopoly of the large firms over the most lucrative conveyancing and commercial work was assured by the fact that, unlike their English counterparts, solicitors in Jamaica engaged freely in estate and insurance agency. Although earlier in 1720, the separation of the two branches of the profession was reinforced by legislation, the monopoly of the Bar was restricted to advocacy in the superior courts and solicitors dominated the work of the profession. Solicitors largely controlled entry to the profession since most entrants qualified by obtaining articles with a local firm and taking the English Law Society's examinations externally. Articles were generally obtained through a complex network of family and business contacts and since the offer of articles was considered to be a favour there was no remuneration. As in England, those who did not have financial and/or family support were therefore generally barred from entry.

Training for the Bar was likely to be more expensive for the Jamaican than training for the solicitors' profession because the candidate for the Bar had to join one of the Inns of Court in London and keep terms in England prior to taking the final examinations. This was not a deterrent for the sons of the rich and well-to-do. Traditionally, they were sent abroad, particularly to England, to study and quite often acquired professional training after graduating from university. Generally, these young men returned to join the family business or an established firm of solicitors in Kingston, the commercial, political and social capital city.

Given the class and colour divisions which characterised Jamaican society (Smith, 1974; Gordon, 1987) these sons of the rich were nearly always from white or Jewish families. For example, in 1922 when Norman Washington Manley was called to the Jamaican Bar there were only 11 barristers in practice in the country. Apart from the young Manley, who later not only distinguished himself as the foremost Jamaican barrister of his time but also as one of Jamaica's foremost political leaders following the widespread labour rebellion of 1938 to 1939 (see, for example, Reid, 1985; Nettleford, 1971; Sherlock, 1980), there was only one other black member of the Bar. This was the renowned J A G Smith who from his entry into the legislature just after World War One, was greatly respected for his firm stance in support of civil liberties and democratic causes (Carnegie, 1973).

Ironically, before merger, the specialist branch of the profession, the Bar, became the outlet for the few blacks who were able to gain entry into the profession. There are several factors which may help to explain this extraordinary situation. First, there was the fact that although the Bar involved a tremendous personal or family financial commitment, entry in Jamaica was not dependent on acquisition of a place in chambers. Unlike the situation in England, there was no requirement of pupillage for practice. Secondly, in the early years of practice, black barristers unable to depend on solicitors for work, inevitably became involved with prosecution work or made their names, after 1938, working for the emergent unions, co-operatives etc. The success of many of these early entrants led to the gradual erosion of the resistance of solicitors who were sufficiently aware of their own self-interest to set their colour prejudices aside.

The growth in the strength of the Bar, set in motion by the labour rebellion of 1938 and carried forward by the process of decolonising from the 1940s, was reflected in at least three important developments during the post-World War Two years. The first of these was the passing of the Bar Regulation law in 1960. This greatly increased the scope of the work of the Bar. The legislation permitted barristers to appear in any criminal case uninstructed by a solicitor; they could negotiate out-of-court settlements, apply for probate in non-contentious matters and file matrimonial proceedings. In addition a barrister could, three years after call to the Jamaican Bar, transfer to the solicitor's branch by obtaining an order from the Supreme Court.

Secondly, the development of the local Bar led to a gradual change in the composition of the judiciary. For example, in 1936 there was only one non-white Supreme Court judge in the country and he was a Bahamian. The only Jamaican High Court judge was white, but one Senior Magistrate – a 'brown man' – had acted in the High Court. Most judges came from the United Kingdom. In contrast, in 1987, although all the High Court judges qualified at the English Bar, they were, apart from the Chief Justice, all from the majority non-white/Jewish Jamaican population.

Thirdly, the return of the Peoples' National Party (PNP) to office under the radical leadership of Manley the Younger from 1972 to 1980, witnessed an exodus of middle-class professionals and businessmen from the island. This migration occurred when the Manley government sought to broaden democratic practices so that the resources of the country would be better distributed. The middle-classes, however, felt threatened by the banner of 'democratic socialism' under which the government sought to justify its policies of rapid economic and social change. Clearly, what was involved was middle-class resistance, despite its strong democratic traditions, to any change which would appear to threaten its economic and social position. One reason for the defeat of the PNP in 1980 was the large-scale disillusionment of many of its middle-class supporters, and the return of the Jamaica Labour Party (JLP) to office signalled a resurgence in middle-class confidence (Stone, 1983). Nonetheless, the period of the PNP ministry in the 1970s created opportunities for black men and women to enter the profession on an unprecedented scale. The migration of many lawyers to the USA, Canada and even the United Kingdom during this period provided space for a new generation of young men and women who had benefited from what changes there had been in the educational system since the 1950s.

Despite the development of a strong black Bar, however, the traditions and practices of the profession remain profoundly conservative. There are at least two main explanations of this. First, the process of decolonisation had, before the 1970's, little impact on the national control of the economy (Beckford & Witter, 1982; also Girvan, 1971). Secondly, nationalism in the Commonwealth

Caribbean (H Goulbourne, forthcoming) has not been of a militant kind and perhaps there is nowhere in the region where this is more true than in Jamaica. Consequently, there has been comparatively little determination to change the structures received from the colonial past. Before turning to the problem of access to the profession, it is pertinent to comment briefly on the problem of access to legal education because, as we shall see, access to formal and legal education has been an essential aspect of the overall problem of access to the profession.

Access to legal education

Prior to 1972 the requirements for entry to legal education were the same as pertained in England. Although the University of the West Indies had been established in 1948 and offered training of an international standard in most of the professions, there was no provision for legal education locally or within the English-speaking Caribbean. Nonetheless, improved opportunities in a booming economy (Jefferson, 1972; Girvan, 1971) led to a dramatic increase in the number of barristers qualified in the normal way in London for practice in Jamaica. This increase in numbers soon became a cause for concern to the Law Society of Jamaica. In general, the Society was alarmed by the low academic qualifications required for taking the Bar Examinations, the lack of practical professional training for the Bar, and the state of semi-fusion of the occupation which made it impossible to control professional standards which the Society felt were regrettably low. These questions of standards, rather than access by any disadvantaged group, determined the debate over legal education.

General concern over legal education had, however, been expressed earlier but largely in terms of the manpower needs of the region. In 1963, prior to merger and following a long debate within both branches of the profession, a committee was nominated by the Council of the University of the West Indies with the following terms of reference:

> To consider and make recommendations to the Council on the assistance which the University of the West Indies as part of its service to the West Indian community and in the light of its responsibility for satisfying the intellectual and professional needs in the West Indies should provide for training in the West Indies of legal practitioners with a view to ensuring their admission to practice and the right of audience before the courts of the West Indies; therein to consider all cognate matters relating to the qualifications of practitioners including whether there should continue to be any distinction between barristers and solicitors or whether the two branches of the profession should merge as obtains in most parts of the Commonwealth (The Wooding Committee, 1967).

The Committee, chaired by Sir Hugh Wooding, the Chief Justice of Trinidad and Tobago, firmly endorsed the arguments in favour of a West Indian system of legal education. In his view the following points were of particular importance: the need to foster an understanding of legal developments in the region as distinguished from the common law; an appreciation by lawyers of the economic and political environment in which they are to operate; and the training of personnel who could take up positions being created in the private and public sectors. The main concern in the early 1960's was, therefore, understandably, with the manpower needs of the region following full political independence which had commenced in Jamaica and Trinidad and Tobago in 1962 and by the end of the decade was followed by several others such as Barbados and Guyana.

Anticipating the Jamaica Law Society's anxieties of a decade later, the Wooding Committee felt that a five-year period of training was the minimum that would ensure adequate skills for practice. This would include three years of undergraduate study at the University of the West Indies leading to an LLB degree. This would then be followed by two years of professional training at one of the two law schools to be established and controlled by a Council of Legal Education (CLE), rather than the University of the West Indies. It should be noted that although Wooding was concerned to ensure that all entrants to the profession were adequately trained for practice in the region, it was equally sensitive to the interests of those who had already qualified abroad or embarked on a course prior to the provision of facilities for training locally. It was recognised also that any restriction of entry to locally qualified applicants would create barriers for those of West Indian origin who were born or brought up abroad and who may wish to return to the region to practise. It was envisaged that such a system would provide a more relevant as well as a more rigorous legal training to meet the growing needs of the region.

Following these recommendations, there were long drawn out negotiations between the University and the representatives of the seven participating states – Barbados, the Bahamas, Grenada, Guyana, Dominica, Jamaica and Trinidad and Tobago. The latter had two major concerns. First, they wanted firm control to be exercised in order to ensure that the developmental goals of each contributing territory would be given consideration in the planning of the curriculum, teaching, etc. The representatives of the countries, the attorney-generals, who are generally active politicians, were naturally concerned about justifying the use of public funds in a regional enterprise. They were, secondly, worried about the degree of control to be vested in the CLE. Expectedly, the University was concerned to ensure that the governments did not exercise control over entry, content and method of teaching. Its main worries were over academic freedom and standards. It was finally agreed that the CLE would be vested with sole responsibility for professional training and the overall regulation of entry to the profession. Transitional provisions were made for those who were already or would be qualified abroad before the new system came into operation. Moreover, after the cut off point, nationals of the contributing territories who were legally qualified abroad were given an opportunity to be admitted via transitional professional training. The University's role was formally restricted to its right to have control over the admission of students, the academic stage. In reality, however, since the University is represented on the CLE, the two institutions have more or less equal control over access to legal education and therefore over formal access to the profession.

Given the pivotal role legal education plays in gaining access to the profession it is necessary to look at the regulations which govern access to the University and the law schools. The formal requirements for entry to the Faculty of Law are a minimum of two A levels and 3 O levels. Due to high demand and keen competition, however, candidates normally need to have a minimum of three good A level passes (for example, A or B grades) in order to gain entry. Admissions from each territory are on a quota basis which is determined by the contribution of each territory to the financing of the Faculty. Jamaica has a quota of 35%, but since the smaller territories often do not exhaust their quotas the places are taken up by Jamaica, Trinidad and Barbados, the three largest of the participating territories.

The intake of Jamaicans has fluctuated tremendously though the quota has remained constant over the years, as Table 1 illustrates. The Table shows both the annual total numbers as well as law students admitted to and graduated from the University for the ten year period from 1975 to 1985.

Table 1   UWI Students Admissions and Graduation, 1975–85

Year	Admissions Law		Total Law		Registered University		Degrees Law		Awarded University	
	M	F	M	F	M	F	M	F	M	F
1975	21	8	96	44	1150	1103	28	18	229	288
1976	16	13	86	49	1173	1152	39	12	264	266
1977	13	29	51	61	1169	1266	27	15	256	353
1980	9	10	107*		2635*		17	22	288	396
1981	17	9	54	50	1245	1364	14	17	284	404
1982	11	21	54	57	1346	1466	17	12	303	402
1984	11	13	53	61	1472	1600	17	26	355	404
1985	16	25	49	58	1477	1729	16	11	308	513

Source: Adapted from, University of the West Indies, Official Statistics 1975 to 1985 passim.
* The totals for this year are not disaggregated according to sex.

The fall in the numbers in the period from 1979 to 1981 may be due to the exodus of middle-class professionals from Jamaica following the election of the PNP to a second term in office under the leadership of Michael Manley in 1976. It would not be related to any particular problems of access but may give some indication of the class background of those who had hitherto joined the Faculty. The figures also indicate a significant increase in the number of female students particularly in law. However, the numbers of females graduating in disciplines other than law are proportionately much larger.

Provision is made for the non-typical applicant without the expected GCE O and A Levels. The Faculty has a quota of from 10% to 12% for mature entrants from all the territories. Most entrants of this category have been police officers, clerks of court and legal executives. In addition, there is a Faculty quota for non-law graduates and this category of entrants is exempt from the first year of the law degree programme. Those who have been able to take advantage of this facility have been candidates with outstanding degrees in other disciplines.

The requirements for entry to the law schools were incorporated in a Treaty signed in 1971 by 13, expanded from the original 8, contributing territories. Most entrants are persons who hold a University of the West Indies LLB degree. In addition, individuals who hold a degree of an institution which is recognised by the Council as equivalent to the University of West Indies LLB are eligible for entry subject to the availability of places and to such conditions as the Council may impose. A further exemption from the University of West Indies or equivalent degree applied to any national who commenced a degree programme before the 1 October 1971 and completed the programme before the 1 of October 1974. Entry under these provisions was subject to any conditions imposed at the discretion of the Council after consultation with the

Faculty of Law (Agreement establishing the Council of Legal Education 1972, Art 3). The conditions for eligibility under these provisions were that the candidate undertakes a course of study in the development of constitutions and constitutional law in the West Indies and in the law and legal systems of the West Indies. The course may be taken concurrently with the first six months of the law school programme.

It is interesting to consider briefly the numbers of Jamaicans who graduated from the Norman Manley Law School in the period from 1975 to 1986. Table 2 shows the registration figures for students at the Norman Manley Law School. The table shows again a steady rise in the number of female graduates.

Table 2   Jamaican Graduates from the Norman Manley Law School, 1975–86

Year	Male	Female	Total
1975	13	10	23
1976	18	14	32
1977	22	19	41
1978	37	12	49
1979	28	15	43
1980	14	19	33
1981	16	24	40
1982	17	22	39
1983	17	15	32
1984	17	15	32
1985	15	18	33
1986	19	21	40
Total	233	204	437

Source: Adapted from the Annual Reports 1975–86, Norman Manley Law School.

Under the provisions of the Treaty (Art 5), the governments of the participating states undertook to recognise the Legal Education Certificate as the sole qualification for practice apart from the transitional provisions incorporated in the Treaty (Art 6). These provisions included any national who was on 1 October 1971 qualified for practice as a barrister or solicitor in the territory, and any national who prior to that date was undergoing or had been accepted for a course of legal training leading to any present qualification to practise and who satisfied the requirements of such courses on or before 31 December 1979. A national was widely construed to include a citizen or a person regarded as belonging to any participating territory.

These provisions have posed a threat to the survival of regional professional education since some of the territories – Trinidad and Tobago in particular – were not fully committed to their implementation. The resistance came mainly from those for whom the availability of foreign exchange was not a problem and who preferred to keep their options open and therefore continued to send their children abroad to study. The profession in Jamaica generally applied the regulations rigorously but like others in the region was anxious to ensure the survival of the regional arrangements. A compromise was reached in 1985 when the treaty was amended both as regards admission to practice and the transitional provisions.

The Legal Education Certificate may now be awarded to two additional categories of candidates on completion of a six-month period of training organised by the Council. First, any individual who has obtained a degree from an institution which is recognised by the Council as equivalent to the University of the West Indies law degree and who prior to 1972 had obtained a qualification which would have been recognised by the participating states as a qualification to be admitted to practice. Secondly, any applicant who is the holder of a qualification obtained in a common law jurisdiction for admission to practice in that jurisdiction and which is approved by the Council.

The transitional provisions contained in Article 6 have been substituted and now include any national who was on 1 October 1972 qualified to be admitted to practice as a solicitor or barrister in the territory and any national who, prior to 1 January 1985, had undergone or is undergoing or has been accepted for a course of legal training leading to a qualification which prior to 1972 would have been accepted as a qualification for practice.

These changes are not in keeping with the spirit of the Treaty and the emphasis that was placed on the Caribbean content of the courses to be taught. Not surprisingly, they have caused great resentment amongst those who qualified for entry in the previous ten years. Unfortunately, the long drawn out negotiations over the issue have left little time for consideration of more fundamental problems of access. It is difficult to estimate the numbers who will enjoy the benefits of these changes in the regulations but the danger is that the increase in the number of entrants trained abroad will serve to reinforce the division between them and those trained locally. This division arises from the high regard in which 'foreign' qualifications are held despite the greater relevance and quality of the training that is offered locally.

The impact of the 1971 reforms

The changes introduced in 1972 in the formal requirements for entry to the profession had a positive impact on access although the concern of the reformers was not with the issue of access. Two developments resulted from this salutary departure.

The first of these was that entry to the profession was largely taken out of the control of the profession. This remarkable feat was achieved by the introduction of clinical training for aspirants to the profession. Rather than rely on the profession to provide practical training through articles or pupillage a decision was taken to ensure that every candidate would be exposed to practical training as an integral part of the law schools' curriculum. This includes a ten-week period of in-service training in the summer vacation at the end of the first year of the course at the law schools. In addition in the second year students are required to attend at least one afternoon per week at a legal aid clinic run by the law schools with financial assistance of the host governments and to conduct all matters on behalf of clients allocated to them under the supervision of the Director of the legal aid clinic and the teaching staff of the law school. The work includes client interviewing, giving advice, contacting individuals, insurance companies, government agencies etc on behalf of clients, drafting of pleadings, wills and so forth. Although the scope of the work of the clinic is determined by the limited range of matters which are brought to it, students who are willing to take advantage of the facilities are exposed to a wide range of criminal and civil matters in the category of work which would normally be handled by legal aid clinics in the UK.

The practical training programme has had additional positive effects on access. Two examples should suffice here. First, since students are given a wide selection of firms, government departments etc, to choose from for their in-service training, it gives them an opportunity to make contact with a wide cross-section of the profession. This provides candidates who do not have family or other connections with members of the profession with opportunities to make useful contacts. It is not unusual also for firms to offer employment to graduates who have done their in-service training with them since they have had an opportunity to assess their work. Secondly, with the emphasis on practical training much of the teaching at the law schools is done by practitioners and judges on a part-time basis. The more far-sighted students are thereby given an ideal opportunity to establish contacts within the profession regardless of their class backgrounds.

Secondly, once a candidate has obtained a legal certificate provided he/she has attained the age of 21 years, is not an alien and satisfies the General Legal Council that he/she is of good character, he/she is qualified for enrolment to the legal profession (Legal Profession Act 1971, Art 61). Consequently a graduate of one of the two law schools – Norman Manley in Jamaica and Hugh Wooding in Trinidad – can start a practice independently if he/she fails to get a place in an established firm. This provision removes for the aspirant Jamaican lawyer the main obstacle for his counterpart in England, namely, the right/freedom capacity/ability to set up chambers independently of the well-heeled and well-established in the profession.

The provision of legal education locally and at public expense has resulted in a dramatic increase in the numbers entering the legal profession since 1975. Generally it has given individuals from non-middle class backgrounds an opportunity to compete through the education system for entry to the profession. Prior to 1972 such individuals would not have been able to afford the cost of education abroad and were quite unlikely to have the contacts to be able to arrange to be articled locally. The emphasis, however, on academic criteria for entry to the Faculty does not take account of the inequality created by the education system itself. This consideration together with the length of the period of training continues to impose severe constraints on access to the profession. A word, therefore, about the nature of the general educational system may be relevant at this point.

Compared to most Third World societies, the Commonwealth Caribbean has been well-endowed educationally. Some countries, such as Barbados, compare favourably with developed societies and the school system in the region has produced some of the major intellectual figures of the post-World War Two years. In Jamaica elementary education has been free since 1892 and since the 1950s secondary education has become increasingly available to those with ability. Unfortunately, however, the system has been long characterised by a sharp dualism between elementary and secondary education. The elementary schools were established by the churches to provide basic education for the children of the freedmen. They catered for children between the ages of five and fifteen. These schools were not intended to prepare the pupils for work but rather to instil a sense of morality and discipline. A few of the brighter pupils could stay on as pupil teachers and after a series of examinations enter teachers' training colleges to train as elementary school teachers. The system was devised to ensure the supply of teachers for the elementary schools but provided a route of entry to the civil service and the professions for the few who did not have the benefit of academic training in secondary schools. Many non-white Jamaican lawyers who qualified for entry to the profession by taking the Bar Exams in the 1940s were from this background.

Secondary school education was largely fee paying and privately owned. Pupils would generally qualify for entry to secondary education from private preparatory or secondary schools. The dualism of the system was modified in 1958 by the introduction of the common entrance examinations by which all children could compete for places in the secondary schools at the age of ten. Although most secondary schools (renamed high schools) continued to be privately owned, they received substantial government grants and 70% of places in the schools are reserved for candidates from primary or all age schools (formerly elementary).

Despite these provisions the vast majority of children from state schools do not qualify for entry to the high schools. The level of competition is very high since there are only 10,000 places available at 46 high schools for over 50,000 candidates. The standard of training at state schools is very low in view of the scarcity of resources and the pupil-teacher ratio which is often in excess of 1 to 60. In contrast, those who have the benefit of private education are rarely in classes of more than 30. Most middle-class children start the race at the age of three when they enter private preparatory schools. In addition, most children from these backgrounds, besides being pressured at home are sent to private tuition to supplement the rigorous training they receive at school. In contrast, state school children usually start school at the age of seven. Although some of the more ambitious parents pay for their children to receive private tuition for examinations, the majority are unable to meet with the very high standards required for passing the examinations. Once a candidate fails to qualify for entry to a high school the chances of an academic training are minimal. Pupils at all age schools can take qualifying examinations for transfer to high school at the age of 14+. Only a handful of exceptionally bright students enter higher education through this route.

In 1973, the non-fee paying system was extended to education at all levels in the public sector. Although this move was generally progressive, no attempt was made to ensure that all pupils had an opportunity to compete for high school places by increasing the resources available for primary education. Since there was no means testing, the provision of education at state expense benefited middle class children who were in a better position to obtain places than the more needy pupils. As a result, in the period following the return of the JLP to government in 1980 many more middle-class parents opted to send their children to local institutions for training rather than undertake the cost of training abroad, thus increasing the competition for places.

Another major social constraint on access has been the length of the period of training. The non-typical student, particularly mature students with financial and family commitments, finds this hurdle hard to overcome. No doubt the difficulties are increased by the location of two years of the degree programme in Barbados. This involves dislocation from family and imposes further financial burdens on those who have to make arrangements for children to be looked after in their absence. In most cases where candidates have been able to make the break it has been with the assistance of employers. Until 1985, the government paid the fees, provided a boarding grant and met the cost of the air fares. Students would have to maintain themselves during the vacations and meet the cost of books and any out of pocket expenses. In 1985 the

Jamaican government introduced a system whereby students have to pay a levy called 'cess' to the government to cover one-third of the fees and the boarding grant. The effect of the levy has been to dissuade many mature entrants and those without family or other financial backing from applying for places.

The cess does not apply to the CLE and the administrative authorities of the Norman Manley Law School have, fortunately, been generally sympathetic to the difficulties faced by students and have been willing to permit them to take up employment during their two-year period of training provided it does not conflict with their attendance. Many mature students have taken advantage of this concession but have been severely taxed because of the heavy demands of the course.

In 1981, a team of consultants under the chairmanship of Sir Roy Marshall, the then vice-chancellor of Hull University and himself a Barbadian, was appointed to advise a joint committee of the law schools and the Faculty of Law of steps which could be taken to resolve the problems which were encountered in giving effect to the 1971 Agreement. The committee was made up of prominent academics from the UK, West Indian lawyers and Dr Arthur Brown an economist and former governor of the Bank of Jamaica who was then Deputy Administrator of the United Nations Development Programme. The terms of reference included consideration of issues which would have some impact on access: the possibility of devising a programme of training for para-legal personnel; assessment of the need for legal services in the light of the social and economic developments in the region. As regards legal education, the terms included consideration of the greater use of clinical training, whether examination by continuous assessment assured the adequate preparation of candidates for practice and the feasibility of reducing the length of the course.

The team took evidence from practitioners, members of the judiciary and academic lawyers in Jamaica, Trinidad and Tobago, Barbados and Guyana. Concern was expressed generally as to the need to improve professional standards by raising the requirements for entry to the profession. The profession felt that the minimum pass requirements should be increased and that examination by continuous assessment only in some of the courses taught at the law schools did not ensure that candidates had adequate knowledge. In view of these concerns the consultants recommended that all courses at the law schools be examined by written unseen examinations.

Unfortunately, throughout the discussions very little consideration was given to the relevance of this form of examination to the practical orientation of the training, and the impact it may have on candidates who are unable to perform under the pressure of examinations. Professional training at the law schools had hitherto been designed to prepare students for practice by requiring them to produce written work based on their own research throughout the course rather than to require the accumulation of a defined amount of knowledge based on text books and lectures. It was considered that the student would have acquired a sufficient knowledge of the substantive law at undergraduate level. The course at the law schools was therefore designed to provide a training facility for those who had already demonstrated their ability to grasp the substantive law rather than to impose an additional hurdle to entry to the profession. This intention was put into effect by the practice of not failing students at the end of the second year of training but rather to provide remedial measures throughout the course. Unseen examinations, which, to a large extent, test the ability of the candidate to regurgitate received knowledge will inevitably produce some failures unless the pass mark is flexible. The consultants do not appear to have given consideration to the positive aspects of the system of continuous assessment. The reduction in numbers accords with the wishes of the profession, but creates problems for individuals seeking access and defeats the aims of the governments who have been willing to channel scarce resources into legal education in order to increase the availability of legal services particularly in the public sector.

As regards the length of the course, the consultants did not feel that the absolute length of the course should be reduced despite the obvious difficulties being faced by students. They concluded that the profession was not in a position to provide an apprenticeship system and indeed had shown no interest in doing so. Therefore the period of in service training and the requirement of attendance at the legal aid clinic would have to continue. It was felt, however, that the total period of training could be reduced to 19 months by commencing the course in August and completing in the May of the second year.

The consultants also recommended changes in the syllabuses of the Faculty and the law schools to ensure that the emphasis at the latter would be on practical training. The effect of these changes was that all courses involving substantive law would be taught in the Faculty and the courses at the law schools would be reduced from 15 to 10. Every applicant for a place at the law schools would be required to have done, as part of the law degree, in addition to the compulsory courses, Equity I, Commercial law, Family law, Labour law, Law of Associations and Revenue law. As a result of the reduction of courses at the law schools more time could be spent on training in advocacy and weekly court visits were made compulsory.

The effect of these changes has been to make it more difficult for students to work and attend the course. The consultants recommended that consideration should be given to allowing students during their practical training to have a limited right of audience to alleviate the financial hardship experienced by many. But, unfortunately, the Bar Council which is responsible for the smooth working of the profession has not yet responded favourably to this recommendation.

Whilst the resistance of the profession to greater access has been defended on the grounds that there is a need to improve professional standards and reduce overcrowding no evidence has been forthcoming regarding either. The initiators of the 1971 reforms were informed by the more progressive trends in legal education in several Commonwealth jurisdictions as well as the United States. The limitations of the 1971 reforms were that very little attention appears to have been paid to the response of the profession and to the impact of the education system on the prospects of the majority for entry to the profession in the context of Jamaica.

Access to the legal profession

The legal profession has, formally, lost direct control over entry. It has, however, not only a voice in decisions regarding legal education but also controls entry indirectly through the recruitment policies of the firms. This, therefore, is where the most severe difficulty regarding access in Jamaica shows itself.

Although many graduates set up in practice on their own, this may not always be from choice but rather a result of failure to secure a place with an established firm. Many of the traditional firms will not recruit applicants who do not come from middle-class backgrounds which often also implies a particular race/colour combination. Others, who consider themselves to be progressive, select candidates on their predetermined notion of suitability. The candidate who almost invariably fits the image of the firm is from a middle-class background and is identified from his name, speech, mannerisms and dress. There is no statistical evidence of the class/colour composition of the profession, but recent studies have shown that despite the changes in the class composition of the society in the post-war years, coloured and Indian wage-earners are twice as likely to be middle-class as the blacks, and the whites and other minorities are twice as likely as the coloured wage-earners to be middle-class (Gordon, 1987). In view of the criteria for recruitment it is very unlikely that the number of non-middle-class recruits to established firms will increase.

A few firms recruit on the basis of academic merit, but the pressure on the new recruit to conform to the traditional image of the profession tends to restrict entry into some of the more well-established firms. It is not unusual for such firms to offer their recruits a dress allowance to encourage them to conform to the acceptable dress style. Sometimes mortgages are also offered to enable the young recruit to reside in the more prestigious areas of the city. The emphasis on status symbols, like dress and residence, reflects something of the planter tradition of public display and this is reinforced by exposure to the US media and market.

Generally the profession refuses to take account of the culture and mores of the majority of the population and therefore discriminates against graduates who have not been groomed to a foreign standard. Although the wig and gown have gone, established firms and the judiciary disapprove of the dress and speech which may be described as indigenous and refer disparagingly to graduates of the law school as 'calypso lawyers'. Their criticisms are based not so much on the lack of any professional standards but the new unwillingness of locally trained graduates, some of whom may not be from the 'right' background, to preserve the mystique of the profession.

This conservatism of the profession also has an adverse effect on the careers of female graduates. Women have traditionally excelled in the education system in Jamaica. Traditionally the number of women who have taken degree courses at the University of the West Indies has, except in a few disciplines like education, been significantly less than men as Table 1 shows. However, in the last few years women have made up 50% or more of the undergraduate population at the UWI and at the law schools. Indeed at the Norman Manley Law School in recent years women have almost invariably received the award for the most outstanding student. The achievements of female law graduates are not, however, reflected in their entry to the profession. The well-established firms sometimes recruit female graduates on the basis of their academic performance or because of their social background. Very few of these are offered partnerships. In the three largest firms for example, out of a total of 42 partners, only 5 are female. Despite the Jamaican female's reputation for independence and toughness, very few female attorneys have had outstanding success in advocacy. This appears to be a result of the hostile reception they receive from their male colleagues. The hostility is often reflected in openly abusive remarks in court which makes it difficult for any but the most determined to survive. The scarcity of successful female advocates is reflected in the almost total absence of women in the upper ranks of the judiciary. The impact of discrimination against women is that the majority of female graduates take up employment with banks, insurance companies and public corporations rather than enter private practice. Women, like black men earlier, therefore, need to break out of the restrictions imposed on their upward professional mobility.

Conclusions and recommendations

Although the post-1972 provisions for legal education and training were generally progressive, it has proved very difficult to give effect to the spirit of the reforms because of the instinctive resistance of the profession. Since the barriers to access are not always overt, it is very difficult to recommend reforms which would have any significant impact on the processes of indirect discrimination. The main barriers to access spring from class locations and preferences. Access to general education is a major determinant factor in gaining access to legal education and thence to the profession. The problem of access, therefore, is significantly different from the problem of access in the developed countries of the Commonwealth. The initiatives undertaken through access courses in England, for example, may be quite irrelevant in countries such as Jamaica and, indeed, in the vast majority of the Anglophone Caribbean countries. Whereas in England the problem arises from the majority white population discriminating against non-white minorities through the processes of colonisation the reverse has been the case in the Caribbean. The erosion through democratic processes of this inequitable system in Jamaica is still, of course, incomplete. But in view of the scarcity of resources there is very little sympathy with the view that access to legal education should not be based solely on academic criteria. This is laudable. But it may also, unwittingly, be used to maintain an unjust system of access to a profession which is still considered, alongside medicine, to be of major importance (Stone, 1982).

These remarks suggest a number of pertinent recommendations with respect to improving access to the profession in Jamaica. First, it may be possible, with changes in recruitment policies, to improve access for those who have been able to qualify for entry despite the imbalances of the educational system. The main obstacle to change in this regard is the fact that, in all areas of employment, recruitment is almost entirely by word of mouth. There is no equal opportunities legislation and firms are free to discriminate. Even the most progressive employers argue that since the society is so small everybody knows the candidates for a post and therefore it is unnecessary to advertise posts. The process of recruitment to the profession would be greatly improved if the profession was required to advertise all vacancies. Graduates of the law school generally have to discover through a long and often gruelling process their prospects of successful entry. At present, very little information is available and those who do not have the contacts in the profession waste a lot of time trying to be in 'the know'.

The first step would be for private firms, government departments, public and private corporations etc, to advertise their vacancies through the law school and the Bar Council or the newspapers in the same manner as, say, the University advertises its vacant academic and other posts.

Another positive step would be for all employers to set out their criteria for recruitment. This together with advertisements would ensure that candidates would spend less time looking around and that employers would be in a position to recruit candidates who are most suited to the post. Finally it would be a great step forward if the Bar Council could ensure that all employers adopt standard practices for recruitment. This would resolve many of the problems of professional standards and alleviate the disillusionment experienced by many graduates who are unable to 'pull the right strings' in order to gain entry to the established firms and secure employment.

Secondly, with regard to the perceived overcrowding of the profession, it must be noted that if it is a reality at all, it applies only to Kingston, the traditional location of legal firms. Since the 1970s, some firms have been established in locations away from Duke Street – the equivalent of the chambers in the Inns of Court in London – but these have been in the flourishing environs of New Kingston. In most cases this was done in order to escape the violence which has come to be associated with the older and traditionally commercial area of the city. There has always been a great need for legal services in the rural areas and this problem has not been significantly tackled by the profession. Only very few of the large firms have branches outside Kingston, and where any individual has set up in practice in his home there is a tendency for the local population to believe that his services cannot be as good as those offered by the 'Kingston lawyer'. It would make a great difference to the provision of legal services if more of the prestigious firms set up branches in the rural areas and employed graduates who may have an affinity with the area to run their offices.

The process of change in the legal profession in Jamaica will be slow because the problems raise fundamental social issues in the society. The reforms of 1971 have, significantly, increased the scope of entry to the profession and hopefully, with time, the changes will have greater impact on the profession. The cleavage between the older members of the profession and the locally trained graduate will hopefully be eroded as the generally high calibre and commitment of the new entrants will assert itself.

REFERENCES AND BIBLIOGRAPHY

Barnett, Lloyd *The Constitutional Law of Jamaica* (1977) London: Oxford University Press.
Beckford, George and Witter, Michael *Small Garden ... Bitter Weed: Struggle and Change in Jamaica* (1982) London: Zed Press.
Collymore, George 'The Trinidad Dilemma – To fuse or not to fuse' (October, 1978) West Indian Law Journal.
Council of Legal Education *Legal Education in the West Indies 1963–1972* (1972).
Foner, Nancy *Status and Power in Rural Jamaica* (1973) Teachers' College Press, Columbia University.
Girvan, Norman (ed) *Foreign Capital and Economic Underdevelopment in Jamaica* (1971) Mona: Institute of Social and Economic Research, University of the West Indies.
Gordon, Derek *Class and Social Mobility in Jamaica* (1987) Mona: Institute of Social and Economic Research, University of the West Indies.
Goulbourne, H D 'Teachers and Pressure Group Activity in Jamaica, 1894–1967' (1975) D Phil Thesis, University of Sussex.
Goulbourne, H D *Teachers, Education and Politics in Jamaica, 1892–1972* (1988) London: Macmillan/Warwick University Centre for Caribbean Studies.
Goulbourne, H D (forthcoming) *The Communal Option: Nationalism and Ethnicity on Post-Imperial Britain*.
Jefferson, Owen *The Post-War Economic Development of Jamaica* (1972) Kingston, Institute of Social and Economic Research, University of the West Indies.
Liverpool, N J O and Patchett, Keith 'The Legal Professions in the West Indies' in *Law in the West Indies: Some Recent Trends* (1966) British Institute of International and Comparative Law, Commonwealth Law Series, 6, 1.
Marshall, O R 'Legal Education in the West Indies', ibid.

Norman Manley Law School Handbook, 1987, No 1.

Post, Ken *Arise Ye Starvellings: The Jamaica Labour Rebellion of 1938 and its aftermath* (1938) The Hague: Martinus Nijoff.

Post, Ken *Strike the Iron: A colony at war, Jamaica 1935–45* (1981) New Jersey: Humanities Press.

Reid, Victor *The Horses Of the Morning* (1985) Kingston: Caribbean Authors' Publishing Company Limited.

Smith, M G *Culture, Race and Class in the Commonwealth Caribbean* (1984) Mona: Department of Extra-Mural Studies. University of the West Indies.

Stephens, Evelyn Huber and John D *Democratic Socialism in Jamaica* (1986) London: Macmillan.

Stone, Carl 'Public Opinion, Lawyers and the Legal System in Jamaica' (May, 1982) West Indian Law Journal.

Stone, Carl 'Public Opinion and the 1980 Elections in Jamaica' unpublished manuscript, Department of Government, University of the West Indies, Mona.

Stone, Carl *Class, State and Democracy in Jamaica* (1983) Kingston: Blacknett Publishers.

Watkins, E 'The history of the Jamaican Legal System to 1900' (1969) University of Sheffield, PhD Thesis.

West Indian Law Journal April 1973. Editorial, 'Legal Education in the West Indies'.

West Indian Law Journal October 1979. Editorial, 'Legal Education in the 1970s and 1980s'.

Wooding Committee Report on Legal Education in the West Indies, University of the West Indies, 1967.

10 Access to legal education and the legal profession in Northern Ireland

*Desmond Greer**

Introduction

Northern Ireland remained part of the United Kingdom when the rest of the island of Ireland obtained its independence in the early 1920s.[1] By the Government of Ireland Act 1920, a system of devolved government was introduced, and the Parliament of Northern Ireland was given extensive powers to legislate for 'the peace, order and good government' of the province. The Act of 1920 also established a separate legal system derived from that operative in Ireland before 1920 and closely modelled on the legal system of England and Wales – though with some notable local characteristics.[2] The new jurisdiction extended over an area of some 5,000 square miles and served a population of 1.5 millions.[3] That population has remained stable and homogeneous; a traditionally high birth rate is offset by an equally traditional stream of emigration. There has been no significant immigration over the past 60 years. The 1981 census shows that 59% of the population lives in 'urban' areas, and mostly in the greater Belfast area, which has always been the industrial, commercial, administrative and legal centre of the province.

In broad political terms Northern Ireland was, and remains, divided – in the ratio of 2:1 – between 'unionists' (those, mainly Protestant, who wish to remain within the United Kingdom) and 'nationalists' (those, mainly Roman Catholic, who wish to become part of a single Irish nation). From 1920 to 1972 Northern Ireland was ruled by a government which was exclusively unionist, and by a Parliament in which unionists always had a clear majority. Nationalist discontent with these constitutional arrangements and with the way in which Northern Ireland was administered came to a head in the 1960s in the form of a 'civil rights' campaign over alleged discrimination in the allocation of public housing, voting rights, employment opportunities, etc. The Northern Ireland government and Parliament attempted in various ways to cope with this campaign, but the British government also became increasingly involved. Ultimately, in 1972, the Northern Ireland Parliament was prorogued and 'direct rule' from London introduced, in the form of a Secretary of State for Northern Ireland. With the exception of a short period in 1974, governmental and legislative responsibility for Northern Ireland has since remained with the United Kingdom government and Parliament.

During the early and mid-1970s various measures were enacted, first by the Northern Ireland Parliament and later by the United Kingdom Parliament, to remove the sources of nationalist grievances, and in particular to prevent

* Purpose of Law, the Queen's University, Belfast.

190

religious discrimination and to promote equality of opportunity in employment. But the civil unrest had by 1970 been superseded by an 'armed struggle' designed, on the one hand (republican) to unite Ireland by force of arms and on the other (loyalist) to maintain the union with Great Britain at all costs. The campaign of violence, or 'Troubles' as it is referred to locally, led to the introduction of emergency legislation and this in turn fuelled further allegations of discriminatory and oppressive treatment, primarily by nationalists but sometimes also by unionists.

The use of violence by republicans is not supported by the government of the Republic of Ireland, which has enacted its own emergency legislation to deal with the 'Troubles'. Like the British government – and 'constitutional' politicians in Northern Ireland and elsewhere – they have sought a political solution to the problem. But all attempts from whatever source, including the latest initiative in the form of an Anglo-Irish agreement, have failed either to reach an agreed political settlement or to halt the violence.

The Troubles of the past twenty years have contributed to the other major issue affecting the social fabric of Northern Ireland – a declining economy.[4] Historically the most industrialised part of an essentially agricultural island, the province during the 1960s saw the decline of its traditional industries – shipbuilding, engineering and linen. To a substantial extent this decline was offset by the arrival of multi-national corporations and other new industrial activities. And with the entry of the United Kingdom (and of the Republic of Ireland) into the Common Market in 1972, the agriculture industry received a significant boost. By 1974, unemployment in Northern Ireland had – at 5.7% – reached its lowest post-war average. During the mid-to-late 1970s, however, the multi-national companies began to close their local factories; over-production afflicted the Common Market, and the continuing Troubles inhibited new investment from outside the province. Unemployment began to rise, slowly and then more dramatically. By 1978, the overall rate was 8.3%; six years later it had reached 16.8%. A further source of concern was the decline of manufacturing industry and an ever-increasing reliance on the public sector and on service industries as major sources of employment. By 1986 unemployment had reached 18.7%; paradoxically, for those in employment, the standard of living continued to rise, and the last ten years have seen a substantial increase in commercial activity and individual prosperity.

It is within this social, economic and political context that we have to consider access to legal education and the legal profession in Northern Ireland.

The legal profession in Northern Ireland

The creation of a small jurisdiction by the partition of Ireland in 1920 did not give rise to any suggestion that the legal professions in Northern Ireland might be fused. Instead, separate organisations were quickly established for the solicitors and barristers who practised in the new jurisdiction. The Incorporated Law Society of Northern Ireland was established by Royal Charter in 1922 and its powers were later enshrined in statute – now the Solicitors' (NI) Order 1976.[5] The new Society followed the traditional pattern, but in its activities was circumscribed by a lack of accumulated funds to subsidise current membership subscriptions and (as a result) by dint of a small and largely part-time secretariat. Membership of the Society was not compulsory, but most

solicitors did become members. Nonetheless, for fifty years or so the organisation, like the profession, remained small in size and traditional in outlook.
Most solicitors practised in small firms and were general practitioners; there
simply was no opportunity to specialise. The profession was overwhelmingly
male and mainly middle-aged.

The past fifteen years or so have, however, seen substantial changes in the
solicitors' branch of the profession. The most obvious feature, as in other
jurisdictions, has been the increase in the size of the profession, accompanied
by a significant lowering of the average age.[6] Part of the increase has resulted
from the admission of a significant – though still far from representative –
number of women solicitors.[7] This increased participation has been acknowledged by the Equal Opportunities Commission for Northern Ireland, but a
recent report has concluded that there is still a lack of equality of opportunity
in law as in other professions:

> It might ... be expected that within the professions [women] should be treated
> equally with respect to promotion, positions of professional power, and more
> generally have patterns of career development similar to those of men ... This
> report reveals that this is not the case, that women in fact do have quite different
> career paths from their male colleagues, as well as different promotional pros-
> pects.[8]

The Report considers various reasons why this might be so, and attaches
considerable importance to passive attitudes in careers guidance at school, to
adverse professional attitudes (especially as regards the need for continuity in
employment and in accumulating experience) and to the conflict for many
women between career and family needs.

The religious composition of the profession is obviously a potential issue in
Northern Ireland. Accurate up-to-date information is not available, due to
relevant information having been withheld from the 1981 Census.[9] But the
available evidence tends to suggest that the Roman Catholic minority in the
province is adequately, if not disproportionately, represented in the membership of the legal profession.[10] As we shall see, inequality of opportunity on
grounds of religion has not been a major issue as regards admission to either
branch of the profession.

Similarly, detailed information on the social composition of the profession
is not available. The most that can be said is that the majority of solicitors are
now university graduates and there is evidence to suggest that most university
students come from middle-class backgrounds.[11] It remains possible for a
person to qualify as a solicitor in Northern Ireland without a university degree,
but this avenue to admission is rarely taken. The cost of qualifying as a solicitor
is considerably subsidised from public funds, but the earnings of newly qualified
solicitors are not reliably known. There is obviously some 'wastage' of newly
qualified solicitors who cannot establish themselves financially,[12] but precise
information is not available. A sound financial background may not, therefore,
be strictly necessary for a person thinking of becoming a solicitor – but is
clearly a useful asset.

The earnings of solicitors as a whole are not, however, known. An attempt
to conduct a survey was made by the Royal Commission on Legal Services,
'but, regrettably, the number [of questionnaires] returned was insufficient for
the purposes of statistical analysis'.[13] In spite of the province's economic
difficulties, the amount of legal work has increased substantially in recent
years, but it is not known if it has done so proportionately to the increase in the

number of solicitors. Evidence from 1983 suggested, however, that Northern Ireland has fewer solicitors per head of population than any other part of the British Isles.[14] It remains the case that most solicitors practise in small firms; in 1986, there were 1028 solicitors in private practice, in 520 firms.[15] Although there is some concentration – and a small number of larger firms – in Belfast, almost one-third of the firms are located in towns with a population of less than 20,000.[16] This distribution tends to suggest that the available work is not evenly divided, and that access to the profession is not necessarily access to successful practice. But the high incidence of small firms may also have important consequences in relation to initial admission into the profession.

A separate Inn of Court for Northern Ireland was established in 1926, following a general meeting of the judges and of all barristers practising in the courts of Northern Ireland. The Inn had – and still has – no physical existence, and, following the Irish tradition, barristers practised not from chambers but from a single Bar Library, established in the new Royal Courts of Justice in Belfast. A Bar Council was also established, but effective control of the profession remained with the Benchers of the Inn of Court until 1983, when, following (but not necessarily because of) a recommendation contained in the Report of the Royal Commission on Legal Services, a new 'Constitution' was adopted by agreement between the Benchers and the Bar Council.[17] This reduced considerably the Benchers' powers, and gave them instead to a new 'Executive Council of the Bar' composed mainly of practising barristers. The powers exercised by the Benchers, and now by the Executive Council, are customary, not statutory. Membership of the Inn is compulsory, but confers no practical benefits. While the profession remained small, the traditions of the Bar Library, however, conferred substantial benefits informally on the newly called barrister, particularly in relation to obtaining work – and valuable advice – from more experienced colleagues. But as with the solicitors' branch of the profession the 1970s saw a substantial growth in the size of the profession, and this has brought with it a number of problems. The most obvious is a physical one – the Bar Library is capable only of limited expansion and it is now suggested that it is physically impossible to house more than 300 practitioners. The increased size resulted also in a much younger profession and this change in the age balance may have contributed to the adoption of the new constitution. Finally, as we shall see below, increased numbers – and increased competition – gave rise to calls for a 'numbers' limitation for new admissions to the Bar, with the result that in 1986 the Bar announced that a maximum of 20 new barristers would be admitted in 1987.

The Bar of Northern Ireland is even more predominantly male than the solicitors' profession.[18] Evidence to the Equal Opportunities Commission study suggested that women admitted to the Bar tend to leave it when they get married or have children, and that the effect of this 'career break' is so substantial as to make it impossible for them later to return to practice. In addition, in the Bar as in other professions 'women feel they continually have to "prove" themselves ... before they are accepted as full members of the profession.' In spite of these difficulties more women are now practising as barristers in Northern Ireland, and prospects are, apparently, improving. The overall conclusion of the EOC study, as regards the professions generally, reflects this slow progress:

> The general picture is that, to adapt to the challenges of equal opportunities, some changes have taken place. These are mainly of a formal kind and relate to

equalisation of salaries, conditions of work and formal criteria in respect of such matters as access to the profession, opportunities for promotion and career development. Values and attitudes, however, change much more slowly. Consequently the decision to pursue a professional career demands from women extra commitment, determination and willingness to take on [additional] responsibility.[19]

Although the matters in which progress is acknowledged are surely more substantial than merely 'formal', the thrust of the Report is that much remains to be done to secure genuine equality of opportunity for women in both sides of the legal profession, as in the other professions included in the study.

Again, as with the solicitors' branch of the profession, the religious composition of the Bar could be, but has not become, a contentious issue, except occasionally in relation to judicial appointments.[20] Prior to 1972 it was the case that most of those appointed to judicial office were Protestant – but it was always maintained that religion was *not* taken into account and that any imbalance was due at least in part to a reluctance by Roman Catholic barristers to accept appointment. Since 1972, however, the religious composition of the Bench has tended more closely to represent the proportions in the general population. There has been no similar controversy as regards the elevation of junior barristers to Queen's Counsel, nor has there been any adverse comment on the religious composition of the Bar generally.

Information is not available on the social composition of the Bar; by tradition it is, of course, open to all and it may be that this is more the case than in England. That, at any rate, is what leading members of the Bar of Northern Ireland like to think. As we shall see below, the cost of qualifying as a barrister has dropped substantially since the early 1970s, and this should in theory have eased access to the profession. In addition, for much of the past ten years, it was generally accepted that newly-called barristers could expect to earn enough to live on within one year of call. In recent years, however, the position has changed somewhat, and the general belief now is that some newly-called barristers are finding it extremely difficult to make ends meet. All this is hearsay or rumour; detailed information is not available. The Bar Council conducted a survey of barristers' earnings in Northern Ireland for the Royal Commission on Legal Services,[21] but the results were of limited value even in 1979 and must be of even less relevance in 1987. As with solicitors, it seems likely that the available work is not evenly distributed and that access to the Bar likewise does not guarantee a substantial practice or remuneration.

Professional training and admission to the professions[22]

Prior to 1977, admission to the solicitors' branch of the profession was by way of a three-year apprenticeship, attendance at Law Society lectures and successful completion of Law Society examinations. Any university graduate could be indentured to a solicitor; *honours* law graduates received some minor concessions. Non-graduate law clerks could also be admitted as apprentices provided they had completed at least seven years of appropriate service in a solicitor's office. There was no formal limit on the number entering the profession. In practice, of course, an apprentice had to find a qualified solicitor willing to take him into articles, but there was no apparent difficulty – at least for graduates – in this respect.

Admission to the Bar was for many years restricted to those with Arts degrees – a requirement interpreted with such formal logic that BA degrees which were in effect law degrees were held to suffice. In practice those who obtained 'genuine' Arts degrees usually also obtained a law degree, although practice varied. During the 1960s, the Inn of Court decided that *any* degree would suffice, and thereafter most intending barristers were law graduates. The absence of an Inn of Court as such, and shortage of funds, prompted the Benchers in 1928 to revive an old Irish requirement that those seeking call to the Bar must attend an English Inn – and further, in the case of Northern Ireland students, take the English Bar Finals Examination in London. This expensive requirement had to be ended in 1972 when 'new-style' Bar Finals were introduced in London and the Benchers in Northern Ireland, in con-junction with the Faculty of Law at Queen's University, organised their own Bar Final course and examination.

The Northern Ireland Bar Final course and examination was seen as purely a stop-gap measure. Interest in professional legal education had been stimu-lated by the Report of the Ormrod Committee[23] and, locally, a Report had been published expressing dissatisfaction with the 'apprentice' system of train-ing for intending solicitors.[24] The overall result was that in February 1972 the Minister for Education for Northern Ireland appointed a committee under the chairmanship of Professor Arthur Armitage (who had been a member of the Ormrod Committee)

> to consider and make recommendations upon –
> (a) education and training for professional qualifications in the two branches of the legal profession in Northern Ireland; and
> (b) what additional resources would be needed to implement those rec-ommendations.

In its Report published in 1973 the Armitage Committee adopted the three-stage analysis recommended by the Ormrod Committee and proposed that the institutional part of the professional stage be provided through a one-year full-time vocational course at an Institute of Professional Legal Studies. The Institute, which would provide courses for both intending solicitors and bar-risters, would be situated within the Queen's University and thus 'be seen as an extension of the existing provision and the building on to it of a system of professional legal education which ... provides for the close co-operation of University and the Professions ...' The Report went on to explain that

> Essentially this Institute would have responsibility revocably delegated to it by the Professional Bodies for providing the courses, examinations and assessments which are required to be satisfied before admission.[25]

Although constitutionally – and physically – part of the university the interests of the professions were to be fully represented in the governing body – to be called 'the Council of Legal Education (Northern Ireland)' – which would be presided over by the Lord Chief Justice or his nominee being a person holding high judicial office. In addition, the professional bodies were to retain their existing powers to decide whether or not a particular applicant was a fit and proper person to be admitted into the profession. The Institute would have a full-time Director and three other full-time posts established at Senior Lecturer level. The cost of the Institute – both capital and recurrent – was to be met by way of an earmarked grant by the Department of Education for Northern Ireland to the university. It was expected that applications by Institute students for discretionary awards (of study grants) would be considered 'sym-pathetically'.

The Report dealt briefly with the remaining stages of professional training. The 'in-training' aspect of the professional stage would follow the vocational course at the Institute. It was envisaged that the Benchers would make more formal arrangements for a one-year pupillage, and that in the case of solicitors in-training would be by way of limited practice for three years as an assistant solicitor in an existing firm. As regards continuing education the Committee 'envisage this to be an important function of the Institute and ... should be provided under self-financing arrangements made with the Professions.'

The recommendations in the Armitage Report were in due course accepted by both professional bodies, by the Queen's University and (most importantly) by the Department of Education for Northern Ireland. The Council of Legal Education (NI) and the Institute of Professional Legal Studies were set up by University statute in 1976, and the first Director appointed. Working with a temporary, part-time Adviser, the Director and the other members of staff of the Institute set up the new vocational course, and the first students were admitted in October 1977. Before considering the work of the Institute in detail, and its effect on access to the professions, we may briefly trace its history during the past ten years. In 1978–9 the Institute came under the scrutiny of the Royal Commission on Legal Services which reported as follows:

> A number of us visited the Institute and were impressed by the work it is doing and particularly the close working relationship that has developed between the Institute, the university and the profession itself. All concerned recognise that it is too early to reach hard and fast conclusions about the success of the scheme, but the indications are that the new educational system will in the main achieve its objectives.[26]

The Royal Commission then drew attention to a number of particular points and recommended 'a comprehensive review' in three years' time. That review was conducted by a further Committee appointed by the Minister of State of the Department of Education for Northern Ireland in 1983

> to review the work of the Institute of Professional Legal Studies; to consider the future of the Institute in the light of public and professional requirements; to consider the most appropriate arrangements for the funding of the Institute and how the students admitted to it should be supported financially; to consider the matters referred to in ... the Report of the Royal Commission on Legal Services, and to make all necessary recommendations.

The Committee, which was chaired by Professor Bromley, published its report in May 1985. Its principal recommendation was that the Institute should be retained in much the same form; but in other recommendations the Committee suggested that a number of changes were required, in particular to improve the 'vocational' nature of the Institute course and to involve the profession more actively in the development of the Institute and in the running of its courses. The Bromley Report was accepted in principle by the Inn of Court, the Queen's University and the Department of Education. But its principal recommendation was not immediately acceptable to the Law Society, many of whose members saw the Institute as being too little under the control of the Law Society, whose responsibility it was to determine entry into the profession.[27] Various discussions took place and eventually, in late 1986 the Society decided to put the matter to its members in the form of a referendum. In February 1987, the Society voted by a majority (roughly) of two to one to accept the Bromley Report.[28] The position as of the time of writing is, therefore, that the Institute remains part of the Queen's University, funded by earmarked grant from DENI as before, and the particular recommendations of the Bromley Report will be implemented as soon as may be practicable.

This short summary of the development of the Institute over the past ten years or so conceals a number of difficulties and tensions in legal education in Northern Ireland which have been present for some time but which have become particularly evident in recent years.

The requirement of a recognised law degree

Entry to the legal profession in Northern Ireland, and particularly to the solicitors' branch of the profession, became a predominantly graduate entry rather earlier than in England and Wales.[29] This was probably due to the practical and economic difficulty for professional bodies with scarce resources of arranging education and training for the small number of those seeking to enter the profession before 1960. During the 1950s and 1960s the graduates became predominantly law graduates, so that by the early 1970s, when the matter fell to be resolved in England and Wales by the Ormrod Committee, a law degree had already become in practice the normal method of entry into the profession in Northern Ireland. Thus it was that the Armitage Committee apparently had no difficulty in recommending that the Ormrod principle be accepted, and in turn this principle was endorsed without discussion in the Bromley Report.[30] At the same time, both Armitage and Bromley readily accepted the Ormrod decision (later approved by the Royal Commission on Legal Services) that a law degree should not become the *sole* method of entry. The real problem for the Bromley Committee was that by the 1980s the number of applications for admission to the profession, particularly from law graduates, far exceeded the number of places available. In this situation, as we shall see, the focus of attention became the importance of having a *good* law degree.

While a law degree remained per se a qualification for entry to the profession, the Law Society and Inn of Court adopted a generous approach to the recognition of 'acceptable' degree courses. As with the professional bodies in England and Wales, the degree had to contain six 'core' courses; but no other requirements were imposed. Thus, almost all university and polytechnic (CNAA) law degrees in Great Britain[31] and the Republic of Ireland were 'recognised', in addition to the LLB course in the Queen's University of Belfast. But as the number of law graduates increased beyond the capacity of the profession to absorb them, the attention turned to the question of selection as between one law graduate and another. In so far as this might turn on the class of degree obtained, the professional bodies appear to have become concerned that performance in the 'core' courses, traditionally taught in the early stages of a law degree, played little or no part in that process. In 1983, therefore, they decided to add Evidence and Company Law to the list of required courses[32] – in effect, it would seem, to inject a 'core' element into the classification of the degree. That at any rate appears the most likely rationale behind a decision which was never satisfactorily explained, particularly since few solicitors in Northern Ireland, and even fewer barristers, undertake much company law work, and few solicitors appear as advocates, even in the county courts.

In spite of this development, a person wishing to qualify for admission to the legal profession in Northern Ireland by obtaining a law degree still has a wide choice. He may apply to five university law schools in the United Kingdom through UCCA, to four polytechnic law schools through PCAS, and to four university law schools in the Republic of Ireland.[33] The total number of such applications from persons normally resident in Northern Ireland is not known. There are normally about 450 applicants to Queen's University, approximately one-half of whom put that university first in their list of applications.[34] Ultimately about 160 applicants are accepted by some university, with 95–100 (or 60%) going to Queen's University. Analysis of applications from law graduates for admission to the ILPS[35] suggests that most applicants – and certainly most successful applicants – come from QUB or from university law schools in England and Wales. The comparatively small number of applications from England and Wales, however, suggests that many persons from Northern Ireland who go 'across the water' to study law do not return at the end of the course. This is indeed part of a more general phenomenon which has given rise to considerable concern – the suggestion of a 'brain drain' from a province which badly needs the impetus which its most able children could provide. Recent studies[36] have suggested that about one-third of Northern Ireland school leavers would prefer to attend a university or polytechnic in Great Britain. This percentage has remained fairly constant in recent years, but cause for concern nonetheless remains for at least four reasons. First, the quality (at least in terms of A level results) of those who enter universities in Great Britain tends to be higher than those who enter universities in Northern Ireland. However this general concern may not apply to law students; even though law is a popular subject for students leaving Northern Ireland, such students tend to have much the same A levels as those entering the Faculty of Law in Belfast.[37] A second cause for concern is the religious and gender composition of the 'leavers' – in particular, Protestant males (47%) are much more likely to go to British universities than Roman Catholic males (20%). Thirdly, there is evidence that the Northern Ireland graduates of British universities who do return to the province tend to be less well qualified than those who do not. Finally, there is no compensating flow of students from Great Britain to Northern Ireland. In theory, this need not affect admission to the legal profession, since most law degrees in Great Britain are 'recognised' by the Law Society and Inn of Court in Northern Ireland, and prior residence in Northern Ireland is not a prerequisite for admission. In practice, however, few non-Northern Ireland residents apply for admission to the profession.[38]

It is not clear to what extent the general pattern of emigration is true also of law graduates, and thus difficult to assess the effect it may have on the composition of the legal profession. But admission to the legal profession does seem in practice to be confined to those born and bred in Northern Ireland, and the pattern of leaving to study in Great Britain may affect the overall quality of the profession, as well as its religious and gender composition.

Admission to law degree courses

Admission to law degree courses in Great Britain, Northern Ireland and the Republic of Ireland is highly competitive. Although provision is made for those with other qualifications, admission to these courses depends principally on a good performance in A level examinations.[39] Some law faculties interview applicants; A level performance may also be supplemented by referees' reports (usually from the school principal) or occasionally by 'aptitude' or other tests. But A level performance is normally conclusive – a policy open to criticism on at least three grounds.

First, it is widely conceded that the level of correlation between A level results and degree performance is limited – both generally, and also specifically as regards law.[40] Combined with this criticism is the opinion that this reliance on A levels may not be in the best interests of the legal profession:

> Universities should use wider criteria than academic attainment at school when selecting law students for admission. In particular, we wish to see more account taken of the following considerations: firstly, each applicant's aptitude for, and interest in, the study of law; secondly, the need for a student population more varied in age and socio-economic background so as to create a better educational environment; and, thirdly, the need to ensure that all pupils of ability and potential, from whatever school background, have a real opportunity to study law at university if they so wish.[41]

This approach may be attractive in principle, but it is difficult to implement in practice. A partial answer, of course, is that entry to the legal profession (or at least to the solicitors' branch) is not restricted to graduates, let alone law graduates, and that these other methods of entry may provide the profession with a broader mixture of entrants. But this is too sanguine an expectation, given the acceptance, in theory and in practice, of the Ormrod principle that a law degree should be the normal method of entry. The problem for the universities has been to devise alternative criteria for admission which can be seen to be valid, fair and objective. The Scottish Royal Commission on Legal Services commended Glasgow University's experiment with the 'Princeton Aptitude Test',[42] but although other such experiments have been tried, no acceptable test has yet been produced.[43] In this respect Northern Ireland simply awaits developments elsewhere – the introduction in the province of new or 'non-academic' criteria for admission to university is fraught with difficulty in a divided and suspicious community.

If access to law degree courses depends in practice on A level performance, then what about access to A levels? In an interesting contrast with their Scottish counterparts, the Royal Commission on Legal Services in England and Wales and Northern Ireland dismissed this as none of their concern:

> This [A level] requirement ... operates as a bar to children who have not had an adequate education or who left school at the earliest permitted age to earn a living. The effect is that most of those who enter the professions come from the middle and upper income groups. The professions cannot redress this by assuming the functions of schools and sixth form colleges. Only the educational system can redress social imbalance in the numbers of those reaching the required academic standard ...[44]

In fact, access to A levels has generated considerable controversy in Northern Ireland, with reference to gender and social class, as well as religion.[45] Broadly speaking, secondary education in the province takes one of two forms –

grammar school or intermediate school. Entry to grammar schools is largely determined by a selection process applied at age 11, although some schools (particularly in rural areas) now operate on a non-selective ('comprehensive') basis and a small number of pupils obtain grammar school places on a non-selective private (fee-paying) basis. The result of this system is that about 35% of 11–18 year olds in Northern Ireland attend grammar schools – and it is they who normally take A level examinations. Thus, in 1984, 87% of those who obtained at least one A level pass were grammar school pupils.[46] This system of selective education has been severely criticised as suffering from 'obvious faults' in practice and as putting 'sponsorship' before 'contest mobility' in the educational process.[47] It also tends to produce the phenomenon referred to in the RCLS report – that most Northern Ireland A level pupils are middle-class. This factor has led commentators to conclude that 'social class remains a significant disadvantaging factor in the education of children and young adults.'[48] At the same time it has to be noted that the age participation ratio in higher education in Northern Ireland (at 19.5 in 1985) tends to be higher than in Great Britain (at 14.2 in 1986). But it is also the case that there is in the province a longer 'tail' of very poorly qualified school-leavers.

The selection system at age 11 tends to operate to the disadvantage of girls[49] – but in fact more girls than boys now obtain 3 or more A level passes. As a result, the representation of women in higher education in Northern Ireland has increased dramatically over the past twenty years – from 27% of those enrolled in universities in 1966–67, to 47% in 1984–85.[50] This general pattern has been reflected in the law schools; thus the number of women graduating from the Faculty of Law in Belfast has increased from an annual average of 3 (or 15% of the total) in the years 1960–1963 to 44 (49% of the total) in the years 1983–1986.

The most potentially divisive issue as regards access to A levels in Northern Ireland is again religious background. However, although a higher proportion of Protestant children attend grammar schools (in 1983–4, 20%, as compared with 17% of Roman Catholic children) there is no longer any significant distinction in levels of achievement either as regards A level results or entry to higher education.[51] Thus in 1986–87 the proportion of Roman Catholics entering higher education was in proportion to their representation at that age in the general population. As regards entry into law degree courses, the evidence suggests that the proportion is actually higher than in the population at large.[52]

Non-law graduates and non-graduates

As already explained, acceptance of the Ormrod principle does not prevent – though it may discourage – the admission to the legal profession of those who do not possess a law degree. Special provision has, in fact, been made for two separate categories of such applicants – graduates in a discipline other than law, and non-graduates with experience of legal practice.

Prior to 1977 graduates of any discipline were freely eligible to become solicitors' apprentices, although some benefits accrued to those with honours law degrees. The Armitage Report[53] recommended that provision should continue to be made for non-law graduates and proposed the creation of a two-year 'academic' course, essentially in the 'core' law subjects in the Faculty of Law in Belfast, but under the control of the Council of Legal Education. Into this course each year would be accepted 10 non-law graduates who, on passing examinations at the prescribed level,[54] would automatically qualify for a place in the 'vocational' course for solicitors or barristers at the Institute of Professional Legal Studies. Since the vocational course was limited to 70 students, provision was therefore made for one-seventh of the places to be taken by non-law graduates. This recommendation was implemented in 1977, admission to the 'Certificate in Academic Legal Studies' course being determined primarily by 'academic' achievement, ie the class of degree obtained. However, the continuation of the 'alternative' methods of qualifying for admission to the profession meant that, for some time thereafter, non-law graduates who failed to gain admittance to the CALS course could still become apprenticed and qualify as solicitors in that way. No such alternative was available to would-be Bar students. In 1985 the Bromley Report[55] recommended that the Institute course should become the sole method of entry to the profession, and that the provision for non-law graduates should be continued, albeit in amended form. The intake quota for the CALS course was to be increased to 15, to allow for the 4–5 non-law graduates who had hitherto qualified each year by the alternative route. But the Report also recommended that those passing the 'academic' course should no longer qualify automatically for admission to the Institute; instead, they should compete for the available places with law graduates. Finally, to assist those in employment or without adequate financial support,[56] the CALS course should be available on a full- or part-time basis. Save as regards the increase from 10–15 students each year, these recommendations were implemented in 1986. Acceptance of the second proposal (to end the automatic qualification for admission to the Institute) has reduced demand for admission to the 'academic' course – but this has been offset to some extent by the availability of part-time study.

The principal category of non-graduate entry to the profession is the 'seven-year-man' – the person who has served for at least seven years as a (managing) clerk in a solicitor's office.[57] It also appears open to the Bar to admit a person as a student who, through his employment, has, in the opinion of the Inn of Court, gained sufficient legal experience.[58] Prior to 1987, such persons qualified for admission as a solicitor or barrister through the alternatives to the Institute. From 1987, however, it appears that, as recommended by the Bromley Committee, they will qualify (if at all) through taking the 'vocational' course at the Institute on a part-time basis. If recent years are anything to go by, the number qualifying in this way will be very small.

The Institute of Professional Legal Studies

It will by now have become obvious that admission to the legal profession in Northern Ireland has in recent years been bedevilled by a 'numbers' problem – the demand for admission has exceeded the supply of available places – and that this has increasingly required the development of criteria for admission which enable a proper selection to be made from those who already possess the minimum qualifications for entry. Furthermore, the success of the Institute has been such that it was for many years the normal channel of entry and now has become so exclusively. Thus the question of admission to the profession is inextricably intertwined with the question of admission to the Institute, and this has given rise to a number of difficult and interrelated problems.

(a) Numbers seeking admission to the profession

On the basis of the then rate of application for admission to the profession, the Armitage Committee estimated that a total of 50 places at the Institute for bar and solicitor students would be adequate.[59] From its inauguration in 1977 the Institute in fact catered for some 70 students (usually 20 Bar and 50 solicitor students), but this was insufficient to satisfy the demand. An immediate consequence was the decision by both professional bodies to retain the pre-1977 methods of entry into the professions as 'alternative courses' to the Institute.[60] In both cases applicants had to be graduates but the only other requirement (other than being a 'fit and proper' person) was application to, and rejection by, the Institute. Although technically 'temporary', these alternative courses continued for many years to provide a wider entry into the profession, despite the limit on the number of places at the Institute. The continuation of these alternative courses was contrary to the spirit of the Armitage Report and gave rise to three particular problems, viz:

(i)   Intending solicitors taking the alternative course gained an advantage over Institute students through immediate entry into the profession. As apprentices they gained immediate practical office experience and may therefore have obtained a tactical advantage from a career point of view over Institute students who sought admission to an office one year later. No equivalent advantage was obtained by Bar students, but the Bar Final course did enable a person to qualify for the Bar on a part-time basis.

(ii) From an educational point of view the continued existence of alternative courses to some extent kept alive the issue of the most appropriate form of training, particularly for intending solicitors. The Institute course was clearly preferable to the ad hoc course provided for the Bar Final Examination, and indeed, after a few years that course was discontinued. But the continued availability of qualification as a solicitor by articles was accompanied by assertions of their superiority over the Institute course as a form of training.[61] This in turn led to criticisms of the Institute course as insufficiently 'practical', to reservations about the quality of Institute students, and may also have contributed to the decision by the Law Society in 1979 to require Institute 'graduates' to serve a one-year apprenticeship before being admitted as solicitors, even as solicitors with limited practice certificates.

(iii) The continued availability of the alternative courses threatened to undermine the somewhat precarious case for public funding of the Institute.[62] The Armitage Committee had emphasised that the two professional bodies in Northern Ireland had been set up with no financial assistance from the parent bodies in Dublin and had, therefore, required support from public funds for professional activities. Thus, there was an historical case for government support for professional training, particularly if this was provided by an educational institution already financed predominantly from public funds. The alternative courses, on the other hand, had been largely self-financing. The case for public funding of the Institute required, therefore, an unequivocal assurance by the professional bodies that the new method of training was preferable to the old, so that it could be clearly seen to be in the public interest to provide government support for it. It was difficult to give such an assurance when the alternative courses were still evidently regarded by the professional bodies as an equally acceptable method of entry.

The driving force behind the decision to continue the alternative courses was that they alone could enable the professions to maintain the principle of 'open' entry so long a tradition of both the Bar and the Law Society. Historically, anyone who met the necessary minimum qualifications could enter the profession; market forces would prevent excessive numbers from continuing in practice. But this theory came under intense pressure in the late 1970s as the numbers seeking admission to, and the numbers already in, the profession continued to grow. In addition the Department of Education was starting to insist that public support for professional training must be linked to an assessment of employment needs.[63] The Inn of Court was the first to acknowledge the need for control, and in 1984 it closed the alternative method of qualifying for the Bar by ending the Bar Final Examination.[64] In the same year the Law Society announced that it was restricting admission to its 'alternative' course to 15. That limitation was temporarily lifted in 1986 for reasons which will be explained below. But in 1987, as recommended in the Bromley Report, the number of places at the Institute for intending solicitors was increased by a maximum of 20, and the Law Society announced that its alternative course would no longer be available. The number of places at the Institute in future will, presumably, be determined as proposed in the Bromley Report, viz 'an agreed maximum number of students ... [which] should be agreed by the Council of Legal Education, on a triennial basis, after consultation with the Executive Council of the Inn of Court and the Council of the Law Society, on the understanding that the Department of Education would have to be satisfied that the number was realistic having regard to the number of people which the profession could absorb.'[65] It remains to be seen how this recommendation will operate in practice.

(b) Control over admission to the profession

Both professions have the right to control entry to their branch of the profession; but the Institute, as envisaged by Armitage, would be formally a part of the University and thus subject to its admissions' policies and requirements. The Armitage Report sought to reconcile this potential difficulty by two recommendations:

(i) Essentially the Institute would have responsibility 'revocably delegated' to it by the professions to provide the educational courses, examinations and assessments required by the professions to be satisfied before admission.
(ii) The professions were to retain unfettered their existing powers to decide whether or not a particular student was a fit and proper person to be admitted into the profession. On this account, students would first have to be admitted as students of the Inn of Court or the Law Society *before* they could obtain a place for the vocational course at the Institute.

These recommendations were, in effect, written into the University statute which formally created the Institute. The Armitage solution was, however, an uneasy one. It might have worked had there been less pressure for places at the Institute; equally, it gave rise to little difficulty as long as 'alternative' courses remained available for those not admitted to the Institute. But as the number of applicants increased, and the availability of alternative courses diminished, attention came to be focused on the decision to admit to the Institute. From the outset, the Council of Legal Education had regarded this as a matter not for the Institute alone, but for an Admissions Committee of the Council. This included the Director of the Institute; but it also included two representatives from the Law Society, one representative of the Inn of Court and a member of the Faculty of Law (representing not the Faculty as such, but the general interest of the University). It appears that this procedure had generally remained acceptable to the Bar – but, latterly (and particularly arising out of proposals to end the alternative course) had not remained acceptable to many members of the Law Society. Their concern stemmed from the continuation of the Institute as part of the university; as stated in the Bromley Report, their fear was that 'control over admission will pass from the profession to the University or a body responsible to it.' The Bromley Committee considered that such a fear was 'ill-founded' because 'delegation is and will remain revocable.'[66] The Bromley Committee might also have pointed out that Article 6(2) of the Solicitors' (NI) Order 1976 explicitly provides for such delegation:

> The [education] regulations may make the opinion, consent or approval ... of any examining or other body or authority named in the regulations ... material for the purposes of any provision of the regulations.

In any case the Law Society is a constituent member of the Institute, and, in practice, its representatives on the Admissions Committee played a major role in admissions decisions. These explanations failed to satisfy the Law Society. From the University's point of view, its Charter and statutes were said to prevent the delegation of responsibility for the admission of students to a body not in any way, even formally, responsible to it. If the Institute was to remain a part of the University, the Law Society could not, as such, be given the power to decide who were to be admitted as University students. Although the Bromley Committee at times considered that these differing responsibilities were 'irreconcilable', it eventually recommended a new compromise:

> The Council of Legal Education should set up two selection committees, one for each branch of the profession, consisting of:
> three members of the side of the profession concerned (of whom at least one must be a member of the Council of Legal Education);
> the Director of the Institute ...
> one other member of the Council of Legal Education.[67]

If the 'other member' was a University member of the Council (as Bromley considered 'might be desirable'), the Admissions Committee could be viewed by the University as having a University majority, and by the Law Society (and the Bar) as having a majority of its representatives.

This recommendation failed to satisfy many members of the Law Society, who, as a result, urged the Society to reject the Bromley Report and to establish its own Institute under its full direction and control.[68] Such was the appeal of this proposal that the feasibility of such an Institute was carefully considered. The Law Society accepted (as Bromley had emphasised) that an 'independent' Institute could not receive any public funding. However, it was estimated that a Law Society Institute could be financed by a combination of student fees (paid indirectly by their masters through the introduction of an agreed minimum wage for apprentices) and a direct levy (of approximately £60 per annum) on all practising solicitors.[69] In the event, this proposal was rejected early in 1987, and the Law Society formally accepted 'the Bromley Report'.[70] This acceptance included the particular recommendation as to the composition of the Admissions Committee. But the method of selection of Institute students already adopted by the Council of Legal Education meant that the new Admissions Committees would have comparatively little say in determining admissions to the Institute.

(c) Method of selection of Institute students

From 1977 to 1985, the principal basis of selection for admission to the Institute was academic achievement in the form of degree classification. Though never a formal qualification, it came to be accepted that any law graduate with second-class upper division honours (or a first) could normally expect to be admitted, and that anyone with a low 2.2 or worse would be rejected. The good-to-better 2.2s were interviewed by the Admissions Committee of the Institute and allocated to the available places by reference to referees' reports and performance at the interview. One effect of this method of selection was to stimulate undergraduate law students, particularly at Queen's University, to gear their work (and allegedly select optional courses) for finals in order to obtain a 2.1. In practice the percentage of 2.1 degrees awarded by the Faculty of Law at Queen's became somewhat higher than in law faculties in England and Wales. This led to allegations from some members of the legal profession that Queen's was awarding its students that class of honours so that a higher percentage would gain admission to the Institute.[71] This allegation was strenuously denied by the Faculty; in any case, final degree examinations at Queen's are monitored by six external examiners (normally from universities in England and Wales). The profession nonetheless remained suspicious and this suspicion, coupled with unease over the selection of optional courses by final year students at Queen's and other law faculties, played some part in the decision, made jointly by the Inn of Court and Law Society in 1983, to add Company Law and Evidence to the list of 'core' courses necessary to make a law degree 'acceptable'.

At the same time there was continuing concern from the professional bodies that selection for admission to the Institute should be determined wholly or substantially by *academic* achievement. This concern intensified as admission to the Institute steadily became more equivalent to admission to the profession. The professions contended that there is no necessary correlation between academic achievement and ability to be an effective practitioner. Given that different skills may well be involved this contention has at least some superficial validity. Since, however, there is no agreement on the attributes of 'an effective practitioner' and a fair amount of disagreement on the assessment of 'academic achievement', the contention may be difficult to prove, even on the balance of probabilities. The profession's view was, nonetheless, accepted by the Bromley Committee which, as a result, concluded that:

> There is considerable merit in requiring all applicants [for admission to the Institute] to undergo a common written test of practical competence which must be capable of being objectively evaluated.

Rather more realistically the Committee added:

> When it is necessary to reject applicants who meet minimum standards which have
> hitherto been acceptable to the profession, a written test is the most acceptable and
> defensible method of selection.[72]

A precedent was available from Dublin, where the Incorporated Law Society
of Ireland have operated a restricted entry for several years. This is effected
by means of an 'entrance' examination which must be taken by all applicants.
The examination consists of a number of papers broadly in the form of
university law examination papers. It does not, therefore, purport to test
anything other than 'academic' skills; there is no attempt to assess eg aptitude
for practice, as such.[73] The form of the examination has been criticised for
duplicating university degree examinations and for tending to make the law
degree a qualifying course for admission to the profession. Representatives of
the Irish Law Society gave evidence to the Bromley Committee, but the
Committee, without giving reasons, rejected this approach.

The Committee also considered the use of 'Aptitude and Character/
Personality Tests'. However, this approach had in 1979 been investigated by
the Law Society of England and Wales, which had concluded that 'it was not
possible to identify with sufficient accuracy qualities needed by a prospective
solicitor so as to create an aptitude or personality test for admission to the
profession.'[74]

The Bromley Committee therefore came to its 'Practical test' by a process
of elimination:

> We recommend that the questions set should be such as to test a student's ability
> to apply his knowledge of law in a practical way. This should reveal:
>
> (a) his capacity to elicit relevant facts from a mass of information;
> (b) his ability to handle available material;
> (c) his ability to express himself clearly;
> (d) his common sense;
> (e) his numeracy.
>
> Our view is that these written tests should be long enough to be discriminatory
> but not so long as to create an unreasonable load for examinees or examiners.
> We therefore recommend that the test should take place on a date to be decided
> by the Council of Legal Education and that each candidate should sit two three-
> hour papers (with most questions compulsory), one of which would be common
> for all candidates and one geared to the branch of the profession to which he is
> seeking admission.

The setting of such a test was to be undertaken by a working party set up by
the Council of Legal Education and including members of the education
committees of the two professional bodies. The Bromley Committee recognised
that the task would not be an easy one – 'no similar jurisdiction employs such
a test and ... lack of experience elsewhere will make the task more difficult.'
The Committee therefore accepted that the Council of Legal Education 'may
need additional advice on the preparation of such tests so that they may
achieve in a fair and objective manner the [stated] aims ...'[75]

Not surprisingly this proposal proved to be one of the most controversial
recommendations of the Bromley Committee. In September 1985, however,
the Council of Legal Education decided to implement the Bromley Report by:

> (a) setting the proposed test, placing the applicants in an order of merit with
>   regard to their performance in the test, comparing their test result with their
>   degree result, offering places to those who performed well in both, excluding

those who performed poorly in both, and interviewing those whose cases presented an anomaly . . .[76]

A working party set up by the Council drew up two three-hour tests each consisting of two compulsory sets of questions arising out of long and complex factual situations. Neither the working party nor the Council apparently sought 'additional advice' on the composition of these tests and also, contrary to the proposal in the Bromley Report, it was decided that both papers should be sat by all applicants, whether intending solicitors or barristers.

Persons applying for admission to the Institute in 1986–87 were at the end of February 1986 notified in writing by the Director of the Institute that the tests would be held in April 1986, and that 'The results of the test will be taken into account with other available information such as quality of degree, references, etc. Following such consideration it may still be necessary to interview a small proportion of the applicants.' In the event, some 150 applicants sat the test on 2 April. At this stage no decision had been made as to the weight to be given to performance in the test (as compared eg with degree performance), but in June 1986 the Institute Admissions Committee agreed:

(a) to offer places without interview to all applicants within the first 50 places in the Admissions Test who held at least a 2.2 degree, and to those placed in the 51–60 range who held 2.1 degrees;
(b) to interview all other applicants who held 2.1 degrees;
(c) to interview those placed in the 51–70 range who held 2.2 degrees;
(d) to interview the applicant in the 16th place who held a third class degree, and
(e) to reject those placed below 71 who held 2.2 degrees.[77]

The application of this weighting led in August 1986 to 19 graduates with 2.1 degrees being refused admission to the Institute, and to 24 graduates with 2.2 degrees being accepted. Vociferous protests were made by and on behalf of the rejected applicants with 2.1 degrees, and one lodged a 'test' case with the University Visitor, claiming that the practical test had been introduced without adequate notice or explanation.[78] While this case was being considered by Lord Scarman, the Law Society announced that it would, for one year only, remove its restriction on entry to the alternative course.[79] This restriction had itself resulted in difficulty and was in 1986 held by the High Court to have been introduced in circumstances which made it ultra vires.[80] As a result of the decision to allow open access to the alternative course, most, if not all, the disappointed 19 became apprentices and qualified as solicitors under this alternative route.

Notwithstanding these events, the Council of Legal Education announced that a similar test would be held on 21 December 1986 for persons wishing to enter the Institute in 1987–1988. At much the same time the Inn of Court announced that it would thereafter require graduate applicants for admission to the Bar to have obtained at least lower second-class honours in their degrees. Further consideration was, however, given by the Council to the question of weighting as between class of degree and test result, and shortly before the test was due to be taken, all candidates were advised in writing as follows:

(1) The test papers will be marked by the internal and external examiners of the Institute.
(2) The test papers will be marked out of a total of 200. This mark will be known as the TM (test mark).

(3) An additional mark will be added to each student's TM according to their degree result:

First-class honours degree	TM + 60
Upper second-class honours degree	TM + 45
Lower second-class honours degree	TM + 30
Third-class honours degree	TM + 15
Pass degree	TM

(4) The resulting final marks (FM) will be placed in an order of merit.

(5) If there are 60 places available to law graduates, places will normally be offered without interview to the first 50 applicants judged by FM. Similarly, if there are 80 places available to law graduates, places will be offered automatically to the first 70 applicants.

(6) The next 20 applicants (61–80 or 71–90) will be interviewed for the remaining 10 places. The Admissions Committee in cases judged by them to require special consideration may interview other applicants.

(7) All remaining applicants will be rejected without interview.

In March 1987, Lord Scarman reported that he had rejected the test case. In the summer of 1987 the application of the new weighting system gave rise to little or no controversy and the Council of Legal Education subsequently decided to apply the same system for admissions in 1988.

Nonetheless, this Bromley recommendation and its implementation raise many important and difficult issues which range beyond the scope of this paper. In broad terms, the 'practical test' is open to criticism on at least four grounds:

(a) The purported distinction between 'academic' and 'practical' skills is a false dichotomy – all the skills stated to be revealed by the practical test are equally tested in 'academic' examinations.

(b) Assuming the distinction is valid, the basis on which some 'practical' skills, rather than others, have been selected as particularly relevant, is not stated.

(c) No attempt has been made to ensure that performance in the test as set from time to time validly reflects the student's ability in the stipulated skills.

(d) Proper consideration has not been given to the weight to be attached to performance in the test, as compared eg to performance in university degree examinations.

Points (a) and (b) can be met by confession and avoidance. The stipulated 'practical' skills may also be tested in 'academic' examinations, but so are other skills which are, perhaps, not so relevant to professional practice. Equally, successful solicitors and barristers possess skills other than those listed; but it can hardly be denied that the stipulated skills are important for any practitioner. It would thus appear that points (c) and (d) create the greatest difficulty. As regards (c), the Institute had previously conducted at least one experimental test on the lines suggested by the Bromley Committee, and compared the students' performance in that test both with degree performance and with performance in the Institute's own examinations. This analysis (unfortunately not referred to in the Bromley Report) apparently provided some evidence in support of the practical test, but was far from conclusive. Surprisingly, Miss Napier did not in her appeal seek to challenge the validity of the test, and Lord Scarman therefore considered that this was not a matter for him to decide. But he did comment rather pointedly:

I confess I find it hard to understand how at this stage of a law graduate's career any evaluation of practical competence could be other than a matter of opinion of the examiners.[81]

When it had decided to introduce the practical test, the Council of Legal Education also decided to review each year 'the accuracy of the test by comparison with students' performance at the Institute and, in time, if possible, performance in practice . . .'[82] Some analysis of the 1987 results will, therefore, have been undertaken, although no information has been released by the Council. Since, however, the Council in November 1987 decided to continue unaltered both the form of the test and the 'new' weighting system introduced in December 1986, it seems reasonable to conclude that the evidence to date suggests that the test (at least when combined with degree results) does provide some indication at least of likely performance in the Institute examinations.

This brings us to (d) above – the weighting as between practical test and degree results. On the face of it, the outcome of the first practical test appeared to give it undue weight, in that 24 candidates with lower second-class honours were admitted in preference to candidates with a better class of degree. But on further analysis it appears that 60% of all applicants with 2.1 honours succeeded in obtaining admission to the Institute as opposed to 37% of those with 2.2 honours. There was, therefore, some correlation between class of degree and practical test performance. It has also to be said that it was reasonable to suppose that those obtaining higher degrees would normally tend to do better in the test than those with weaker degrees. In other words the results of the practical test may indeed raise doubts about the weight to be given to it; but they may also raise the question why so many students awarded 2.1 degrees obviously did badly in it.

The new formula adopted at the end of 1987 formally recognises the importance attached to class of degree while still enabling precedence to be given to an applicant who obtains a good test mark. It remains to be seen how valid this weighting is, in terms of performance in the Institute examinations.

(d) Admission of Institute students into the profession

It was consistently reiterated in both the Armitage and Bromley Reports that the creation of the Institute did not represent any derogation from the principle that the power to admit to the profession remained solely and exclusively with the respective professional bodies. Rather, the professional bodies, by accepting the Institute course, were thereby revocably delegating to it the responsibility for part of the training of their students. Other admission requirements remained under the direct control of the profession. To date, three such requirements have been stipulated, viz:

 (i) An intending solicitor or barrister must satisfy the relevant professional body that he or she is a fit person (a) to be registered as a student of the Law Society or of the Inn of Court, and later (b) to be admitted as a solicitor or as a barrister.
 (ii) An intending barrister must, since 1987, have obtained at least lower second-class honours in his or her degree.
(iii) An intending solicitor or barrister must complete a specified period as an apprentice or pupil, subject to such conditions as the Law Society or Inn of Court may require.

These requirements are expressly laid down by regulations, which may, of course, be amended from time to time. But it now appears, at least in the case of the Law Society, that other requirements may be added even if not stipulated in these regulations. In *Re Haughey*[83] H applied to the Law Society in 1985 to be registered as an 'alternative course' apprentice. The application was refused on the grounds that he had not been placed among the first 15 applicants. He applied again in 1986 and was refused admission on the grounds that he had not satisfied the Law Society as to his suitability to be accepted as a registered student. This requirement did not appear in the 1985 regulations, and when these regulations were held to be invalid as having been made in an ultra vires manner,[84] H applied for an order of mandamus directing the Law Society to register him as a student. Gibson LJ refused to make such an order; although H had apparently satisfied the requirements of the 1985 regulations (other than the numbers limitation) the Law Society were not precluded from applying considerations other than those stipulated in the regulations. The learned Lord Justice drew attention to the fact that the Law Society derived its powers from a royal charter and, in the words of Lord Denning:

> ... in the case of a society incorporated by royal charter, the doctrine of ultra vires has no place ...[85]

Thus, although the 1985 provisions made no reference to 'suitability', the Law Society were entitled to take this into account, and, if so minded, to reject H's 1986 application on that basis. To grant mandamus would therefore deprive the Law Society of a power with which it had been invested by its charter.

This decision appears to confer wide discretionary powers on the Law Society which are inconsistent with its statutory obligations in relation to the making of regulations. It may, however, be that the decision can best be understood as limited to the particular – and most unusual – circumstances of the case.

Little is known concerning the application of the 'fit person' requirement. The Law Society's regulations do, however, give two particular examples of an 'unfit' person, viz (i) an undischarged bankrupt, and (ii) a person convicted of a criminal offence of such a nature as in the opinion of the Society's Education Committee makes his registration undesirable. The Inn of Court regulations contain similar provisions. It is not known how many applicants have been rejected as 'unfit' under these specific provisions or under the more general requirement.

As regards other training requirements, both Ormrod and Armitage recommended that the period of institutional training for law graduates should be complemented by a period of 'in-office training' – three years as a solicitor with a limited practice certificate or one year as a pupil barrister.[86] Although this recommendation was accepted by the professional bodies in Northern Ireland, it has since been modified in ways which may affect access either to the Institute or to the profession in general.

Following its initial decision, the Law Society became concerned that a person, on leaving the Institute with little or no practical experience of actual office practice, should immediately qualify as a solicitor (even if only with a limited practice certificate). In 1979, therefore, the 'in-office' requirement was changed to one year's articles, followed by two years as a limited-practice solicitor. This was more a change of status than substance; no additional training courses or examinations were introduced. This change did little to satisfy those solicitors who felt that the Institute course itself was not sufficiently 'practical' and in March 1983 two-thirds of solicitors responding to a Law Society questionnaire voted in favour of a new system of training which more closely combined the Institute and articles.[87] Although the Law Society could have taken up this matter with the Council of Legal Education at any time, it was not until the Bromley Committee was set up that proposals for change were made. That Committee accepted that it was 'of the utmost importance that training at an institute and training in practice should be more closely integrated' and it went on to accept the Law Society's proposals for a two-year apprenticeship (which would include one year at the Institute), followed by a two-year period as a limited-practice solicitor.[88] In particular the Committee accepted the proposal that intending solicitors should spend three months in an office as an apprentice before commencing the Institute course. It seems fairly clear from the Bromley Report as a whole that the Committee envisaged that obtaining such an apprenticeship would take place *after* the operation of the Institute selection process. Otherwise that process could be undermined by an applicant's failure to obtain articles – in effect, giving to individual firms of solicitors the power to decide admission to the profession. It was indeed contended by some that the Institute selection process should be available only to those who had already obtained masters, but this view did not prevail. As it is, however, the system envisaged by the Bromley Committee will only operate satisfactorily if all those successful in the Institute selection process are able to obtain articles.[89] The Law Society's Education Committee is therefore considering a register of eligible[90] masters, but it has emphasised that 'there would be no question of compulsion.'[91] In short, the choice of apprentice will remain with the master.

As recommended in the Armitage Report, the Inn of Court required intending barristers to serve a one-year pupillage (now with a barrister of not less than seven years' standing from an approved list) on completion of the Institute course. No additional courses or examinations were involved, but the pupil barrister was required to complete the first six months of the pupillage without receiving any remuneration and 'to the satisfaction of the Benchers'. The RCLS considered that guidelines for the proper conduct of pupillage should be laid down, and that topping-up courses and practical instruction should be provided to supplement the Institute course.[92] This was not done, and the Bromley Report concluded that 'in most cases only six months' effective pupillage takes place and ... once a pupil has completed the six-month non-practising period, little or no effective supervision takes place.'[93] The Committee recommended a two-year pupillage which would include one year at the Institute, and additional supervision and assessment during the period of practising pupillage. These recommendations have not been accepted.

(e) Financial support

If we leave aside the general debate over the adequacy or otherwise of local education authority grants to undergraduate students, the first financial hurdle for law graduates may come immediately after graduation. Intending solicitors must enter articles and negotiate a salary with an eligible solicitor. The Law Society has, as yet, rejected the suggestion that there should be a 'minimum wage' for apprentices, and thus the matter is left to individual negotiation. As regards the vocational course at the Institute, both solicitor and Bar students are eligible for 'mandatory' means-tested bursaries provided by the Depart-

ment of Education for Northern Ireland. The negotiations following acceptance of the Bromley Report had resulted in the generous decision by the
Department to provide 50 such bursaries directly, as opposed to encouraging
local authorities to take a 'sympathetic' approach to discretionary awards (as
recommended in the Armitage Report). For several years the additional 20
places at the Institute were taken by those who could afford to pay the relevant
fees privately. However, further negotiations in 1979–80 led to the number of
bursaries being increased to 70.[94] The Bromley Report argued in favour of the
continuation of this arrangement, on the grounds:

> (a) There is a strong public interest in securing the most suitable training of
>   members of the legal profession which should extend to providing financial
>   support for those in training.
> (b) The University and the Institute can plan sensibly for this course only if they
>   are assured of continuing financial resources ...
> (e) We believe it necessary to ensure that students, qualified to do so, should
>   have the opportunity to enter the profession irrespective of their financial
>   position and we consider that this would not be possible in all cases if students
>   were dependent on loans or private finance ... Even if a loan were possible,
>   a student would need to raise about £3,300 which would have to be repaid
>   with interest ... That would be an unduly heavy commitment for young
>   barristers and solicitors many of whom would probably not be in a position
>   to make any substantial repayment of the loan for some years ...
> (f) The profession is not in a position to provide financial support for the students
>   during their year at the Institute.
> (g) The present system is comparable with that in Scotland which, like Northern
>   Ireland, is a small jurisdiction.[95]

These arguments apparently carried the day, and the Department of Education agreed to continue to provide 70 bursaries. However, implementation
of the Bromley Report meant that the intake to the Institute increased to 90,
so that (as indeed recognised in the Report) 20 places would be available only
to those who could afford to pay for them privately. This system will operate
for the first time in 1988–89, and it has recently been announced that the
bursaries will be given to those placed 1–70 in the selection process,[96] 10 of the
fee-paying places will normally be offered to those applicants who are placed
71–80 in the selection process, the next 20 applicants (ie those placed 81–100)
will normally be interviewed by the appropriate selection committee for the
remaining 10 fee-paying places. In short, both bursaries and fee-paying places
will normally be awarded on the basis of merit, as opposed to financial need.

Non-law graduates who are selected for admission to the Institute qualify
for the same financial support as law graduates. But their access to this stage
may be hampered by the lack of financial support for the 'conversion' course
in the 'core' law subjects. In theory, graduates admitted to the CALS course
in the Faculty of Law may be awarded 'discretionary' grants by local education
authorities; in practice, no such grants are awarded for this course. As a result,
a number of these students did experience financial difficulties and to mitigate
this problem the Bromley Report recommended that the course be made
available on a part-time basis. This recommendation was implemented in
1986.[97]

On completion of the Institute apprenticeship stage of his training, a graduate, whether law or non-law, must practise for two years as a solicitor with a
limited practice certificate – ie as an assistant solicitor in an existing firm. This
may or may not be the firm in which he served his apprenticeship – and again

his financial support during this period is a matter of individual negotiation. There is some evidence that solicitors, finding themselves in something of a buyer's market, accept persons only for the apprenticeship period, and at a low rate of remuneration. It is not, however, known how widespread this practice is – but it could obviously create difficulties for the would-be solicitor both during the apprenticeship itself and in finding another office to accept him as an assistant solicitor.

Bar students may also experience financial difficulties during pupillage. Prior to 1979 the Inn of Court allowed pupil-barristers to earn fees throughout the whole six-month pupillage period. In 1979 that period was increased to one year and it was stipulated that fee-earning work could not be undertaken during the first six months. This restriction gave rise to concern:

> It will ... be necessary for the governing body of the profession to find a way of dealing with the problem of finance for pupils during the first six months of pupillage ... It is unacceptable that entry to the Bar should be limited to those who have the financial resources to tide them over this period.[98]

Nothing, however, was done until 1984 when it was decided that a pupil, after three months' non-practising pupillage, could appear before a Master of the Supreme Court in a case in which his pupil-master or another practising barrister had already been briefed. Any fees so earned would obviously help a pupil him over until the six months had elapsed.

Provision has now been made for non-graduates to qualify as solicitors or barristers on a part-time basis, concurrent with their employment.[99] The main obstacle for them is not, therefore, likely to be financial, but the lengthy qualifying period.

NOTES

[1] For a general introduction to 'the Northern Ireland problem' see eg Buckland *A History of Northern Ireland* (1981); Watt (ed) *The Constitution of Northern Ireland: Problems and Prospects* (1981). The constitutional arrangements are discussed from a legal perspective in Calvert *Constitutional Law in Northern Ireland* (1968); Palley 'The Evolution, Disintegration and Possible Reconstruction of the Northern Ireland Constitution' (1972) 1 Anglo-Am L Rev 368; Hadfield 'Committees of the House of Commons and Northern Ireland Affairs' (1981) 32 NILQ 199.

[2] See generally, Dickson *The Legal System of Northern Ireland* (1984); Greer and Boyle *The Legal Systems North and South* (New Ireland Forum, 1984).

[3] See generally *Ulster Year Book* (1986); Northern Ireland Census Reports (1981) and Northern Ireland Annual Abstract of Statistics (No 5, 1986). Recent developments are analysed in Compton *Demographic Trends in Northern Ireland* (1986).

[4] See eg Harvey and Rea *The Northern Ireland Economy* (1983).

[5] See generally, Final Report of the Royal Commission on Legal Services (Cmnd 7648, 1979) (hereafter referred to as 'RCLS Report') vol I, Part V. Although the Commission accepted that there still were differences between the two jurisdictions, they considered that their analysis of, and recommendations relating to, the provision of legal services in England and Wales were, in general, applicable also in Northern Ireland.

[6] The 1961 Census showed that 25.5% of all lawyers (ie barristers, solicitors and judges) were under the age of 35; by 1981, this figure had grown to 51.9%.

[7] In 1971 women represented 34.5% of those in employment, but only 3.6% of lawyers; in 1981 the figures were 38.6% and 11.6% respectively. By 1984, 27 (5%) of principal solicitors, and 139 (18%) of assistant solicitors were women.

[8] Agnew et al *Women in the Professions* (1987) p 7. A woman lawyer was quoted (p 52) as saying: 'I don't think that I will be judged on the same standards ... because I am a woman. I will have to prove my reliability in addition to the standard of my work.' It was also suggested (pp 39–41) that 'there were some implicit restrictions on the range of work for women in law ... Very few women were "on the criminal side" and ... "few women are trusted [by the

public] with large amounts of money" ... [but] women are expected to deal with family and matrimonial law.'

9   In the 1971 Census 15.6% of lawyers did not give their religion; of those who did, 27.9% were Roman Catholic. In 1981, the figures were 19.7% and 37.8% respectively.
10   See eg Osborne and Cormack *Religion, Occupation and Employment 1971–1981* (1987) pp 53, 69.
11   See eg Cormack et al *Higher Education Demand Survey* (Interim Report, 1986).
12   In 1987, 41 solicitors (3.4% of the total) were said by the Law Society to be 'unemployed'.
13   RCLS Report, vol 1, pp 673, 705.
14   Northern Ireland, 1:1583; England and Wales, 1:1150; Scotland, 1:916; Republic of Ireland, 1:1245.
15   *The Writ* (Journal of the Law Society of Northern Ireland) (August 1986), p 8.
16   An analysis of the telephone directory for 1985 showed that there were 186 firms (37.5%) in Belfast, 113 firms (23%) in other cities and towns with a population of 20,000 +, and 196 firms (39.5%) in other parts of the province. The Belfast firms employed 658 (56.5%) of the 1165 solicitors in the province in 1986 (*The Writ* (August 1986), p 8).
17   RCLS Report, vol 1, pp 702–3; Constitution of the Honourable Society of the Inn of Court of Northern Ireland (1984) regs 5, 8, 10.
18   In 1988, there were no women QCs (out of 33), but 58 (out of 301) junior barristers were women. It should be noted that few, if any, women barristers have yet been in continuous practice for the length of time normally required for appointment as a QC.
19   Agnew et al, op cit, chapters V and VI, esp pp 81, 83.
20   See eg *Doyle v Economist Newspaper Ltd* [1980] NI 171.
21   RCLS Report, vol II, p 759, showing average gross income in 1974–5 as being £19,964 for QCs, and £7,327 for juniors.
22   See generally, Report of the Committee on Legal Education in Northern Ireland (Cmnd 579, 1973) (hereafter 'the Armitage Report'), RCLS Report, vol 1, pp 709–715 and Report of the Committee on Professional Legal Education in Northern Ireland (1985) (hereafter 'the Bromley Report').
23   Report of the Committee on Legal Education (Cmnd 4595, 1971).
24   Report of the Committee appointed by the Solicitors' Apprentices Society to consider Current Conditions of Apprenticeship (1969) 20 NILQ 393.
25   Armitage Report, p 29.
26   RCLS Report, p 712.
27   See eg Law Society of Northern Ireland *Annual Report of the Council 1984–85* p 18.
28   *The Writ* (April 1987), p 3.
29   Cp Armitage Report, pp 25–6, RCLS Report, vol 1, p 630.
30   Armitage Report, p 25; Bromley Report, p 24.
31   Difficulties arise in respect of graduates of law schools in Scotland which do not offer 'English law' degrees.
32   See Solicitors Admission and Training Regulations 1983; Education Regulations of the Inn of Court of Northern Ireland (1983), reg 8A.
33   The regulations governing grants for university students make no general distinction between any of these choices from a financial point of view, although obviously the higher cost of living away from home and the cost of travel may lead to increased costs for a Northern Ireland student (or his family) who chooses to study in Great Britain or the Republic of Ireland.
34   Information provided by the Queen's University, Belfast. The Armitage Report (p 27) had recommended a 'topping-up' course in Northern Ireland law for non-Queen's University law graduates, but this recommendation was never implemented.
35   Information provided by the Institute of Professional Legal Studies.
36   See eg Osborne et al *Education and Policy in Northern Ireland* (1987) chapters 1, 16.
37   Compton *Demographic Trends in Northern Ireland* (1986) p 140, referring to 1984 statistics, when the UCCA 'target' set by the Faculty of Law in Queen's University was BBB. That target was raised in 1987 to ABB.
38   Between 1977 and 1984 there were on average 11 'foreign' applications per year for admission to the Institute; none was accepted. From the outset, the Council of Legal Education stipulated that so long as the pressure for places persists, intention to practise in Northern Ireland should be taken into account by the Admissions Committee.
39   Other educational qualifications are also accepted, and there is normally special provision for 'mature' students. Thus, in Queen's University, a person over 23 may be admitted as an undergraduate student 'without fulfilling the ordinary entrance requirements'. A small number of LLB students are accepted each year on this basis. For other provisions for 'mature' applicants, see below, p 201.
40   An internal survey carried out in the Faculty of Law of Queen's University in 1987 produced 'a very weak correlation' between A level and LLB examination results.

41 Report of the Royal Commission on Legal Services in Scotland (Cmnd 7846, 1980) p 245.
42 Ibid.
43 See eg Choppin and Orr *Aptitude Testing at Eighteen Plus* (1976).
44 RCLS Report, vol 1, p 629.
45 See eg Cormack and Osborne (eds) *Religion, Education and Employment: Aspects of Equal Opportunity in Northern Ireland* (1983); Osborne et al, 'Class, Sex, Religion and Destination: Participation and Higher Education in Northern Ireland' (1984) 9 Stud Higher Ed 123; Osborne and Cormack *Religion, Occupations and Employment* (1987); Osborne et al *Education and Policy in Northern Ireland* (1987).
46 Dept of Education for Northern Ireland *Statistical Bulletin* No 1/1986 (Table 1).
47 See eg Osborne et al *Education and Policy in Northern Ireland* (1987) chapter 1, citing Turner 'Modes of Social Ascent through Education' in Halsey et al (eds) *Education, Economy and Society* (1961) pp 121–139: 'Contest mobility tends to delay the final award as long as practicable, to permit a fair race; sponsored mobility tends to place the selection point as early in life as practicable, to ensure control over selection and training.'
48 Ibid, p 11. See also Compton *Demographic Trends in Northern Ireland* (1986) pp 132–4 (higher social class pupils more likely to seek entry, and be admitted, to higher education).
49 Girls tend to perform better in the selection process, but are awarded only the same percentage of passes as boys – see eg Johnston and Rooney 'Gender Differences in Education' in Osborne et al *Education and Policy in Northern Ireland* (1987) p 124. In 1988 this practice was held to constitute unlawful discrimination contrary to the Sex Discrimination (NI) Order 1976, art 3(1)–(a) see *Re the Equal Opportunities Commission Application* [1989] 3 BNIL 25.
50 Ibid, p 132. Cf Compton, op cit, n 48 (91% of male school leavers with A levels intended to enter higher education, as compared with 88% of females).
51 Livingstone 'Equality of Opportunity in Education in Northern Ireland' in Osborne et al *Education and Policy in Northern Ireland* (1987) pp 52–3. 55% of Roman Catholic children attending grammar schools obtained 2 or more A levels in 1984, as compared with 53% of Protestant children. See also Murray and Osborne 'Educational Qualifications and Religious Affiliation' in Cormack and Osborne (eds) *Religion, Education and Employment; Aspects of Equal Opportunity in Northern Ireland* (1983) chapter 7, and Compton, op cit, n 48, p 134.
52 Osborne and Cormack *Religion, Occupations and Employment 1971–1981* (1987) p 53; Osborne et al 'Political Arithmetic, Higher Education and Religion in Northern Ireland' in Cormack and Osborne (eds) *Religion, Education and Employment: Aspects of Equal Opportunity in Northern Ireland* (1983) chapter 9 (esp pp 184, 197).
53 Pp 27–28.
54 The 'pass' mark for such students was set at 45%, as opposed to 40% for LLB students. This was considered appropriate since law graduates in effect required a good 2.2 to obtain a place in the Institute.
55 Pp 25, 27.
56 Graduates enrolling for the 'pre-Institute' course are eligible only for discretionary awards and these are now rarely granted.
57 Strictly, 'a person not less than 29 years of age who has served as a law clerk to a solicitor for a period of seven years'. There is also special provision for mature applicants not less than 30 years of age who have acquired some special qualification or experience.
58 Bromley Report, p 12.
59 P 18.
60 However, changes were made to provide some assimilation, in that those qualifying by apprenticeship now also had to serve a two-year period with a limited practice certificate. In addition, the apprenticeship period for law graduates was reduced to 2 years, and that for non-law graduates increased to 4 years.
61 In 1983, for example, 18% of solicitors responding to a Law Society questionnaire expressed a preference for a return to the apprenticeship system: Law Society of Northern Ireland *Annual Report of the Council 1982–83* p 13.
62 The annual cost of the Institute, and of bursaries for Institute students, is approximately £250,000 in 1987 terms.
63 Bromley Report, p 22.
64 Between 1978 and 1983 an average of 7 students per year had qualified for admission to the Bar in this way (as opposed to an annual average of 15 through the Institute).
65 Bromley Report, p 24.
66 P 25.
67 Ibid, pp 27–8.
68 A compromise proposal that 20 additional Institute places, which would not attract bursaries, should be filled by the Law Society rather than by the Admissions Committee, was reported

to have been considered unacceptable by the Queen's University: Law Society of Northern Ireland *Annual Report of the Council 1985–86* p 17.

69 The Inn of Court had already indicated that it had no assets to contribute to the costs of the Institute – and, indeed, it was not at all clear what would happen to Bar students if the Law Society went ahead with its own private arrangements.
70 *The Writ* (April 1987) p 3.
71 In fact the number of Institute applications from QUB law graduates increased from an annual average of 76 in 1978–80, to 97 in 1984–86; but the average number *accepted* each year (47) remained almost constant. However, the average number of successful applications from other law graduates declined from 18 per year during 1978–80, to 14 per year during 1984–86.
72 Bromley Report, p 26.
73 See eg Incorporated Law Society of Ireland *How to become a Solicitor* (1983) p 7. A summary of the examination results for 1986 is given in 80 Gaz Inc Law Soc Ir 99.
74 Bromley Report, p 26.
75 Ibid, pp 26–27.
76 See *Re Napier,* Report and Decision of the Board of Visitors of the Queen's University of Belfast (Lord Scarman), February 1987 (hereafter referred to as '*Napier Decision*') p 10.
77 *Napier Decision,* p 24.
78 See n 76 above. The appeal was dismissed on the grounds that sufficient notice had been given both (i) as to what was required of an applicant in the written test, and (ii) as to what were the relevant matters for consideration in determining who should be selected to fill the limited places available. In short, Lord Scarman was satisfied that Miss Napier had been given sufficient notice to do herself justice in the test. It was further held that in the absence of any suggestion of bias, unfair discrimination or prejudice against her, the University had no duty to disclose to Miss Napier the precise grounds on which the decision to reject her application was actually taken. *Napier Decision* pp 19–21.
79 *The Writ* (August 1986) p 1.
80 *Re Maher* [1986] 16 NIJB 1 (the numbers limitation had been imposed by a transitional scheme which had not been made by the Council of the Law Society in the proper form of a Regulation made with the concurrence of the Lord Chief Justice, as required by the Solicitors' (NI) Order 1976).
81 *Napier Decision,* p 12.
82 Ibid, p 11.
83 [1986] 16 NIJB 17.
84 *Re Maher* (above, n 80).
85 *Institution of Mechanical Engineers v Cane* [1961] AC 696, 724–5. See also *Attorney-General v Manchester Corp* [1906] 1 Ch 643 and *Baroness of Wenlock v River Dee Co* (0000) 36 ChD 675n.
86 Ormrod Report, para 185; Armitage Report, p 37.
87 Law Society of Northern Ireland *Annual Report of the Council 1982–83* p 13.
88 Bromley Report, p 12.
89 'There is no doubt that the Society will be subject to unfavourable criticism if otherwise acceptable ... students are prevented from entering professional education through lack of masters.' *The Writ* (Autumn 1987) p 8.
90 At present a master must have been a principal solicitor for a period in excess of three years, and each such principal is entitled to have only one apprentice.
91 *The Writ* (Autumn 1987) p 8.
92 RCLS Report, p 714.
93 Bromley Report, pp 12–13.
94 Ibid, pp 22, 34.
95 Ibid, pp 35–6.
96 Subject to the requirement that intending barristers must, irrespective of their 'final marks', have at least lower second class honours in their degree. It is also subject to 'the overriding discretion of the Selection Committee in cases judged by them to require special consideration'.
97 Bromley Report, p 25. The part-time course extends over 3 years; the full-time course remains a 2-year course.
98 RCLS Report, p 714.
99 Bromley Report, pp 11–12.

11 Access to legal education and the legal profession in Scotland

*Alan Paterson**

Introduction

Compared with most of the countries which feature in this book, Scotland has a relatively homogeneous population. It is doubtful if it could meaningfully be described as a multicultural society and the overwhelming majority speak one language – English. In sharp contrast to the picture in England and Wales, ethnic minorities make up only 1% of the Scottish population. (The approximate breakdown is 30,000 Asian, 14,000 Chinese, 2,000 Afro-Caribbean and 4,000 others.)[1] According to the most recent census – in 1981 – the Scots population of 5,035,315 (about one eleventh of the total population of the United Kingdom) is almost evenly distributed on gender lines.[2] Its class divisions are equally marked. In terms of the socio-economic status of the household head the class breakdown of the population in 1981 was 5% Professional, 21% Managerial, 12% Skilled Non-Manual, 32% Skilled Manual, 18% Semi-Skilled, 7% Unskilled and 5% Unclassifiable (including students and the armed forces). Perhaps because of these demographic features, the access barriers to legal education and the profession for ethnic minorities Scotland have hitherto attracted little attention. Casual empiricism suggests that there may be a problem, but not of the magnitude of the barriers imposed by class and gender.

The legal profession in Scotland (as in England) is a divided one. By far the larger sector consists of solicitors (formerly known also as 'writers' or 'law agents'). Of the 6,544 practising solicitors in 1988 82% (5,349) worked in private practice (either on their own or in partnerships), 16% (1,020) in local and central government and 2% in industry and commerce. Traditionally solicitors in private practice in Scotland have been seen as, and have seen themselves as, general men of business. As such, they have offered professional services in a wide variety of areas ranging from the purchase, sale and lease of land and other property to the making of wills and the administration of trusts and estates, from advice on commercial, company, tax and family matters to advice and (in the lower courts) advocacy in civil and criminal litigation.

The smaller sector of the profession consists of the Bar or Faculty of Advocates. About 250 advocates practise privately and a further 30 or so are employed in industry, commerce and central government or are instructed on a full-time basis by central government. With one or two minor exceptions, advocates cannot receive instructions direct from clients, but only through practising solicitors. The hundred or so 'professional' judges in Scotland are

* Professor of Law, Strathclyde University.

not normally regarded as members of the legal profession (though curiously, judges who are appointed from the Bar – ie all superior court judges and the majority of the inferior court judges – continue to be members of the Faculty of Advocates).

Historical background

Members of the Bar in Scotland in the seventeenth century were largely drawn from the higher social strata. The majority of them had had a university education – usually from a continental university – which was followed by written and oral examinations in Latin. During the latter part of the eighteenth century there was a partial erosion of the financial barriers to entry to the Bar which led to an influx of sons of professionals or non-landed families. With the emergence of private colleges of Scots law and the establishment of Chairs in Law at Edinburgh[3] and Glasgow Universities in the first part of the century, a cheaper, if second best alternative to an expensive continental education was at hand. Following this, in 1750 the rules of admission to the Faculty were altered requiring intrants to have a knowledge of both Scots and civil law.

Solicitors in the seventeenth and eighteenth centuries came from more humble backgrounds and qualified by apprenticeship followed by an oral examination. There was no central body of solicitors and admission was controlled by the local Faculties attached to the more important inferior courts and by a prestigious Society, the Writers to the Signet, with a near monopoly in instructing advocates before the supreme courts in Scotland – the Court of Session and the High Court of Justiciary. Until the nineteenth century the Society generally drew its members from less exalted ranks than the Faculty. Being a 'WS' (as Writers were colloquially known) carried some social status and the potential for substantial financial rewards, but it lacked the cachet of being an advocate. Yet the Society was not without its social pretensions. Thus apprentice Writers seem to have had a choice whether they wore a wig of their own hair but dancing and fencing lessons were deemed 'absolutely necessary' (Shaw, 1983: 26). These pretensions were probably exacerbated by the establishment of a rival prestigious Society – the Solicitors of the Supreme Court (the SSC Society) – which began to make considerable inroads into the WS Society's share of the agency work in the supreme courts.

It was in the nineteenth century that attendance at Scottish university law courses became a common feature in the education of Scottish lawyers. An 1825 statute laid down that all procurators, writers and law agents should serve an apprenticeship of at least three years and in addition satisfy the examination requirements of their Society or Faculty. For many apprentices (particularly in Edinburgh and Glasgow) attendance at the university classes (in the early mornings and evenings) was the preferred method of acquiring the requisite knowledge in order to pass their examinations. For advocates attendance at university classes were strongly recommended and for Writers to the Signet and SSCs it was compulsory. But attendance at classes meant no more than that. The great majority of students did not sit university examinations, taking instead those set by the Societies or Faculties. Even though the fees for attending university classes were low, apprentices did not receive a salary and often had to pay for the privilege of being trained. For those taking the prestige apprenticeships of the WS and SSC Societies a longer apprenticeship period, very substantial fees[4] and the additional cost of acquiring the social graces were the norm. Similarly, advocates had to fund themselves through university and college classes, pay an entrance fee and support themselves throughout the early, lean, years of practice. In short, access to the legal profession in Scotland from the seventeenth century to the start of the twentieth century was controlled by three factors: gender,[5] social class background and wealth.

Education and recruitment in modern times

Entry to the solicitor's branch of the profession changed significantly in the first half of the twentieth century. Compulsory passes in certain university law classes became a requirement for every intrant in 1926 and graduates with the appropriate subjects in their law degrees were once more exempted from all the professional examinations. As a result law degrees followed by an apprenticeship became (by the late 1940s) the most common route for new intrants to the profession. A decade later, three-quarters of the intrants took law degrees, a trend which was reinforced by the abolition of the part-time law degrees and the introduction of the full time LLB degree as a first degree. in 1961. Thus, by 1979 96% of intrants to the solicitor's profession were graduates with a Scottish law degree.

Looking at admissions in more detail, it can be seen that the great majority of intending solicitors in the late 1970s took a three or four-year LLB degree. Depending on the subjects taken at university, this would usually confer exemption from the examinations set by the professional body for solicitors – the Law Society of Scotland – which was established in 1949. This was normally followed by a two-year apprenticeship and a further year of practical training with a limited practising certificate (making a total of 6–7 years). However, for reasons unrelated to the requirements of vocational training, students with at least an upper second class honours LLB degree or a previous MA degree were exempted the year of practical training. Barristers and solicitors from England, Wales, Northern Ireland and Ireland as well as non-LLB graduates and persons who had served five years as a clerk in a Scottish law office could qualify with a three-year apprenticeship and passes in (or exemptions from) the professional examinations. Finally, school-leavers and mature intrants (the former requiring a higher level of academic attainment) could qualify by passing the professional examinations and taking a five-year apprenticeship.

In the Faculty of Advocates the position was somewhat similar. Of the intrants to the Bar in the period 1975–78 some 95% had taken a Scots LLB degree and half of them had another degree besides (Hughes Commission, 1980: 242). Most of them were therefore exempt from the professional exam-inations,[6] although non-law graduates or non-graduates were not. Thereafter intrants were required to spend between 12 and 27 months as an apprentice in a solicitor's office (depending on the quality of their law degrees), followed by 8 to 11 months of 'devilling' (without pay) to a junior counsel of at least five-years standing. It can be seen, therefore, that at least de jure mature students and non-graduates could enter both branches of the profession even if de facto it might be hard for them to find an apprenticeship or to support themselves during a sustained period of low pay.

The academic stage

As Table 1 shows there are five law schools in Scotland. They are all attached to universities. There are no private law schools, no part-time schools, no non-university (eg polytechnic) schools and there is no provision for distance learning. Although the schools vary in size and antiquity the main differentiating feature between the intake of each school is not social class but geographical location. Each school tends to draw at least half of its admissions from its own part of the country. In its own eyes, at least, the largest and oldest law school (Edinburgh) is also the most prestigious. But the similarity of admissions criteria amongst all five schools and the absence of a consensus amongst firms recruiting trainees or the Faculty of Advocates as to the relative merits of the schools has meant that informal career tracks from prestige law schools to the elite firms of the profession are less evident in Scotland than in America or England.

Many more applications are made to the Scottish law schools than can be admitted. The Scottish figures over the past fifteen years show a steady increase in the demand for places. In 1972 2,301 applications were received for 463 places (a ratio of 4.9:1). In 1976, 3,110 applications were chasing 598 places (a ratio of 5.2:1) but in 1983 following government-imposed cuts there were only 500 places but 3,410 applications (a ratio of 6.8:1). Finally, in 1986 there were 540 places and 3,505 applications (a ratio of 6.5:1). These figures suggest that demand in Scotland is running at half the level of demand in England and Wales but when multiple applications are taken into account it is likely that the real level of demand in both countries is nearer to about 2.2 applicants for each law school place. Even this is a misleading figure, however, since the law schools, faced with an excess of demand over supply have responded by insisting that most intrants be at least 17-years-old at entry and achieve a high level of academic attainment at school. This is sufficient to deter many potential applicants. Selection is almost solely based on secondary school performance in the Scottish Certificate of Education 'Higher' examinations – although a minority of students are admitted on the basis of performance in English A level examinations. There is no equivalent of the United States Law School Admissions Test, and few applicants are interviewed.

This apparently meritocratic admissions procedure has undoubted but unintended effects on the social composition of student population in the law schools. In Scotland there is a strong correlation between social class background and academic achievement in the SCE Higher examinations (Mcpherson and Willms, 1987). Not surprisingly, therefore, such evidence as we have suggests that law students in Scotland form a relatively homogeneous population. The social background of the students (judged by parental occupation) does not vary greatly between the law schools. In each, students from the professional and managerial classes are heavily over-represented. Thus in Glasgow 77% of law students admitted from 1971–79 and in Edinburgh 68% of law students admitted from 1976–80 were from the professional and managerial classes. A survey of students carried out in 1978–79 on behalf of the Royal Commission on Legal Services in Scotland (The Hughes Commission, 1980) revealed that 61% of the student body at law schools was drawn from 22% of the population. There is a well-established tradition of legal families in Scotland (particularly at the Bar) so it was not surprising that the Hughes research also found that 15% of law students had close relatives who were or had been lawyers in Scotland. Surveys of intrants carried out by the Law Society of Scotland (the latest in 1980) produced similar results (as did a recent survey in England, Podmore, 1980: 31). However there is some evidence that these figures are lower than once was the case. Certainly preliminary research on the records of the law schools suggests that the largest single parental occupational group from which Scottish law students are now drawn is the teaching profession.

There are even fewer statistics as to the ethnic background of law students in Scotland. Such evidence as there is suggests that Asian students are gaining admission to a lesser extent than their proportion of the total population (about half a per cent) might warrant and that Chinese students are even less common. However, the available evidence also suggests that this is as much the product of choice and the attitude of ethnic minority groups to the law as under-achievement in Highers or the admissions policy of the law schools. Scottish law schools receive few applications from foreign students seeking an under-graduate law degree, irrespective of ethnic origin.

Unquestionably the most striking feature of the current law student population is the proportion of females. In 1970 less than 20% of law students in Scotland were female. By 1980 the figure had risen to 40% and in 1984 there were as many female intrants to the five law schools as males. (By 1986 numbers of female intrants had marginally declined – to 49% of admissions). The rise in the number of female students, however, has resulted in the student body becoming ever more elitest in its social origins. It might have been thought that the availability of a government grant to all full-time first degree law students from 1961 onwards (covering all fees, and maintenance where parental means were limited) would have boosted student numbers from the lower income sector. But the correlation of social background and academic achievement worked against them. True, there was an 80% rise in the number of law students between the early 1960s and 1977 as Table 1 below reveals, which was directly due to the growth in higher education and in government funding during the period. But much of the growth was attributable to an influx of middle-class female students who gradually squeezed out the working-class male students.

Table 1   Total Number of Undergraduate Students in Law in Scotland

	1965/6	1970/1	1975/6	1977/8	1980/1
Aberdeen	124	212	352	414	380
Dundee	123	192	243	274	287
Edinburgh	430	443	508	511	512
Glasgow	357	299	391	435	447
Strathclyde	–	114	206	230	224
Total	1034	1260	1700	1864	1850

Source: Hughes Commission, 1980

Admissions to the Scottish law schools reached their peak in 1976 when a total of 587 students embarked on a course of legal study. Since then government cuts in higher education have reduced admissions but as Table 2 below suggests the downward trend in admissions of the early 1980s seems now to have been halted if not reversed. Table 2 also shows that, despite rising fees, the proportion of students with a prior degree (who do not qualify for a grant and for whom bursaries are in short supply) entering law schools has only slightly declined. Thirdly, the Table shows that the proportion of mature students (ie aged 23 or over) being admitted has remained relatively static in the last six years.

Table 2 Admissions to Scottish Law Schools 1981–86

Year	Total Admissions	Admissions with prior Degree	% Total	Mature Admissions	% Total
1981	567	47	8	34	6
1982	511	51	10	39	8
1983	500	40	8	42	8
1984	543	38	7	27	5
1985	539	37	7	33	6
1986	540	34	6	37	7

Source: The Law Schools

The almost total reliance on academic achievement as the determining factor for admission to law school obviously has disquieting features. First, because many critics allege that success in Scottish school examinations reflects more on a candidate's ability to regurgitate material rather than his or her intellectual prowess. Secondly, because of the disturbing correlation between social background and achievement in school examinations. The Hughes Commission (1980: 245) came out against a quota for socially disadvantaged applicants or positive discrimination on their behalf. They suggested, instead, the reduction of the present high entry requirements in examination grades to a 'realistic minimum level' coupled with the introduction of an aptitude test. These proposals fell on deaf ears. The law schools probably considered that they catered for 'late developing' working-class applicants by the existence in each law school of informal quotas for mature intrants. However, the Higher grades required of mature entrants for legal study are well in excess of the minimum entry requirements set by the universities.

Recently there have been a few more hopeful developments. Mature students can offer passes in Open University examinations (distance learning) to meet entry standards. Aberdeen University runs an Access course for mature students and a very meritorious performance in the course can lead to admission to the law school. Thirdly, in three of the other law schools (Edinburgh, Glasgow and Strathclyde) in partial recognition of the correlation between social class background and grades in the SCE Higher examinations, affirmative action programmes have been established to assist applicants from disadvantaged backgrounds to gain entry to law school. Most recently of all, Glasgow and Strathclyde Universities together with Glasgow College of Technology began (in 1987) to participate in a College/University Entrance Scheme (CUES) promoted by the Strathclyde Regional Authority to encourage pupils from designated schools in deprived areas in Glasgow to enter higher education. As part of CUES the academic selectors have been urged to grant conditional places to applicants with borderline grades in their school examinations, with admission dependent on an adequate performance in a ten-week summer school mounted at Glasgow University. The course is designed to assist potential intrants in the fields of Chemistry, Physics, Mathematics and 'Communication Skills'.

However, to date these schemes have had little impact on admission to Scottish law schools. Mainly this is because none of the law schools are prepared to reduce their entry requirements by much more than a grade in the Higher examinations – so candidates who have been made conditional offers under the schemes usually fail to obtain the necessary examination grades required for the 'reduced' entry standard. Nor are there any plans to include legal studies in the list of subjects offered in the CUES summer school. Moreover, even if disadvantaged students were beginning to be admitted under these schemes the quota of places for them is less than five places per law school and there is no provision for additional support and coaching in the first year of study for such intrants.

Vocational training

Before 1980, although the curriculum of the typical LLB student contained 'professional' subjects to gain exemption from the professional examinations, it would have been very misleading to describe the LLB degree as providing vocational training in professional skills. With the expansion of the law schools in the 1960s and 1970s a substantial academic legal profession emerged. Practitioners who taught part-time gradually were replaced by full-time academics, many of whom had never qualified as practitioners. They did not see the LLB degree as necessarily being a vocational one and had no interest in teaching professional skills. Indeed, the introduction of more and more academic law subjects in the curriculum began to produce severe problems of space, if students were also to take the 'professional' subjects. Academic awareness of this problem coincided with an increasingly awareness in practitioners and graduates of problems with apprenticeships, caused partly by the unprecedented demand for apprenticeships during the 1970s (see Table 4).

By the late 1960s law graduates expected a higher standard of training than the profession was providing. A report by the Law Apprentices' Association in 1973/74 commented on the rudimentary arrangements for practical training in many firms, the lack of a training syllabus, and the absence of assessment during or after training. Following lengthy discussions between the universities and the Law Society, a one-year, full-time, post-graduate Diploma in Legal Practice was introduced in 1980. It is taught at the universities but the tutors are all practitioners (a curious reversal of the trend toward full-time academics which began in the 1960s). The Diploma was designed not merely to free space in the undergraduate curriculum but also to remedy perceived deficiencies in apprenticeships. In consequence the admission regulations for both branches of the profession were amended to require all intrants to the profession (except former advocates, barristers or solicitors from England, Wales, Northern Ireland and the Republic of Ireland) to take the Diploma. In one respect this does not represent a major new access hurdle either for graduate or non-graduate intrants since, like their counterparts in Northern Ireland (but unlike those in England) almost all of the students taking this vocational course are entitled to a full government grant. However, government cuts in higher education spending have meant that in 1987–88 and 1988–89 only 390 grants for the Diploma have been available. As Table 3 shows this figure is well below the number of law graduates produced in recent years and also below the number of Diploma graduates in each of the past five years. Even if every applicant (graduate and non-graduate) can find a Diploma place because some of the universties are willing (as they have been to date) to create

Table 3   University Graduates

Year	Law Graduates	Diploma Graduates
1970	312	
1971	352	
1972	329	
1973	350	
1974	371	
1975	406	
1976	443	
1977	487	
1978	503	
1979	545	
1980	529	
1981	542	230
1982	483	407
1983	486	425
1984	529	454
1985	468	464
1986	464	415
1987	468	400

Source: Law Society, the Law Schools

sufficient 'non-funded' places to accommodate them, an access barrier has been created for certain intrants. At present the government grants are allocated to each of the universities in proportions agreed between the universities. However the criteria for the award of a grant is achievement in degree or professional examinations. Even were these regarded as reasonable tests of 'merit', since it is the universities which actually award the grants the risk must arise of law graduates being favoured over the non-graduate applicants. Yet, it might well be argued that success in examinations is of little relevance as a predictor of professional competence. The bulk of lawyering involves administration, information broking, negotiating, interviewing, counselling, communicating and cultivating clients – activities which require skills which are not measured in academic achievement. A review body consisting of representatives from the profession and the universities recently admitted the weakness of the existing criteria, but did not recommend their replacement since it was unable to identify a more suitable alternative.

Following the introduction of the Diploma, apprenticeships were abolished. But they were replaced by 'contracts of training' or 'traineeships' which closely resembled them except that it was no longer necessary for an employer to provide a balanced training ie one that covered conveyancing, litigation and trusts and executries. This change, together with a new rule that solicitors cannot accept 'near-relatives' as trainees have made traineeships marginally more accessible than apprenticeships. For LLB graduates who have completed the Diploma, the post-Diploma traineeship lasts for two years, during the second of which the trainee holds a limited practising certificate. For school leavers, mature intrants or non-law graduates a three-year pre-Diploma training contract is required, then the Diploma, followed by a two-year post-Diploma traineeship. Advocates and barristers from the rest of the British Isles now have to enter non-Diploma training contracts but solicitors from the rest of the British Isles are exempt from this requirement.

Table 4 shows that following a decline in apprenticeships during the early 1960s the demand for apprenticeships (fueled by the ever increasing stream of

Table 4   Apprenticeships 1935–1979 – Traineeships 1982–8

Year	Apprentices/ Trainees	Year	Apprentices/ Trainees
1935	170	1969	215
1950	174	1970	248
1951	173	1971	245
1952	155	1972	278
1953	145	1973	315
1954	108	1974	314
1955	83	1975	328
1956	85	1976	354
1957	83	1977	385
1958	93	1978	390
1959	105	1979	430
1960	78	1982	392
1961	75	1983	399
1962	35	1984	393
1963	47	1985	420
1964	113	1986	360
1969	215	1987	365
1970	248	1988	384

Source: Law Society

LLB graduates) grew steadily from 1964 to 1979. Tables 3 and 4 suggest that approximately 80% of law graduates in the late seventies were going on to the profession. One unexpected consequence of the introduction of the Diploma and traineeships has been that the perennial student desire 'to keep one's options open' has led to 90% of graduates since 1980 wanting to take the Diploma. It is for this reason that although law graduates peaked in 1979 the number of graduates seeking entry to the profession has not yet begun to drop.

Admission to the profession

Entry to the Faculty of Advocates is regulated by the Faculty, not by legislation. Candidates must (a) pass, or gain exemption from, the relevant professional examinations (b) pass special examinations in evidence, procedure and professional ethics (c) complete the Diploma and traineeship period and (d) complete nine months pupillage or 'devilling' to a practising member of the Faculty. The public defence (in Latin) of a civil law thesis was only abolished in 1966 but long before then it had become a formality. So too had the vote by Faculty on admissions but this is still retained. The real barrier to entry, however, remains what it has always been – money. As in England 'devils' receive no remuneration during pupillage and substantial fees (even in these days of legal aid) do not start to come in for a further nine months or more. In addition to finding living expenses for two years, intrants must pay entry fees which, together with the cost of wig, gown and formal attire totals in excess of £1,000. Table 5 shows that admissions over the last decade have been running at an average of fifteen intrants a year. This is high, but not as high as in the early eighteenth and nineteenth centuries. However, the rate of female admissions (27 in the decade) is unprecedented.

Table 5   Admissions to the Faculty of Advocates

Year	Male	Female	All
1975	15	2	17
1976	11	2	15
1977	8	3	11
1978	15	–	15
1979	17	–	17
1980	13	2	15
1981	9	4	13
1982	10	2	12
1983	9	4	13
1984	9	–	9
1985	14	1	15
1986	13	4	17
1987	18	10	28

Under the latest statutory provisions[7] no person can be admitted as a Scottish solicitor unless they are 21 years of age, have completed a course of training approved by the Law Society Council, passed the necessary professional examinations (or gained exemption therefrom), been awarded the Diploma in Legal Practice, satisfied the Law Society Council that he or she is a fit and proper person to be a solicitor and paid the necessary admission dues (approximately £70.00 at present). Tables 4 and 6 demonstrate dramatically the cyclical variations in admissions to the profession which have been integral to its history. Thus it can be seen that during the late 1950s and early 1960s entry to the profession was declining rapidly.[8] Since 1970, however, the numbers of intrants have been steadily rising (between 1970 and 1984 the annual rate of admissions increased from 112 to 427, a rise of 280%). While the overall increase in numbers reached its peak five years ago, a third trend, the rapid growth in the number of women entering the profession has assuredly not come to an end. The increase in female students has led to a similar increase in the numbers of female intrants to the profession. (Forty-six per cent of those admitted to practice as solicitors in 1988 as compared with 22% of those in 1975, were female. See Table 8, below.)

Control of entry to the profession

According to the market control theorists (Abel, 1982; Larson, 1977) whose ideas seem to have achieved a very wide currency in recent times, the foregoing account of developments in legal education and recruitment to the profession can best be summed up as the profession struggling to attain, and ultimately losing, control over the supply of legal services. In reality, it is far from clear that the profession has ever been so organised that it could easily determine its own size. The ascriptive barriers to entry to the Bar in England identified by Abel (1982, 1986) have long applied in Scotland also (with the important exception that the lack of a chambers system has always made pupillage and entry to the Faculty rather easier than in England). The need to be self-

Table 6 Solicitors Admitted to the Profession between 1949 and 1988

Year	Male	Female	All
1949	182	9	191
1950	160	10	170
1951	137	12	149
1952	113	12	125
1954	93	16	109
1955	118	16	134
1956	97	12	109
1957	80	7	87
1958	74	7	81
1959	73	9	82
1960	77	6	83
1961	86	8	94
1962	82	11	93
1963	63	13	76
1964	65	4	69
1965	46	7	53
1966	73	16	89
1967	117	24	141
1968	97	13	110
1969	126	22	148
1970	102	10	112
1971	183	29	212
1972	189	35	224
1973	206	35	241
1974	202	41	243
1975	230	67	297
1976	224	59	283
1977	225	82	307
1978	239	69	308
1979	244	106	350
1980	265	132	397
1981	261	135	396
1982	242	139	381
1983	264	154	418
1984	256	171	427
1985	233	182	415
1986	233	186	419
1987	197	190	387
1988	207	175	382

Source: Law Society

supporting for two years (or to have a working wife or an understanding bank manager, or both) has not changed with the recent increase in law graduates. The Faculty could have introduced a loans scheme, or bursaries or paid those in pupillage from the proceeds of a levy. Having chosen to do none of these things it is difficult to see in what way the Faculty has lost what measure of supply control it once possessed.

Again, the ascriptive barriers for would-be solicitors have been similar on both sides of the border. But it is far from clear that the solicitor's profession exercised substantial control over these barriers. The stamp duty payable on entry (abolished in 1947) and the usefulness of contacts in the profession for those seeking an apprenticeship were not subject to professional control. Even the supply of apprenticeships has never been directly controlled by the Law Society Council or its predecessors though it was influenced, from time to time, by the prestigious Societies and the local Faculties of Procurators (some of whom restricted apprenticeships to relatives of existing practitioners). In the main, the supply of apprenticeships (and now traineeships) has been left to individual legal firms working on an ad hoc basis. In practice, only about one-third of the legal firms in Scotland take trainees. Together they are responsible for about 90% of the traineeships, the remainder being located in local and central government departments. Today the Law Society recommended salary rates for post-Diploma trainees are £5,700 in the first year rising to £7,150 in the second (there are no recommended rates for pre-Diploma trainees who may receive considerably less). However, as we saw earlier, before 1960 it was not uncommon for apprentices to have to pay a premium to their firms for agreeing to take them and to receive little or nothing by way of remuneration. While this state of affairs may have been the outcome of market forces it is not clear that these were matters that 'the profession' ever controlled. If so, it cannot be said to have lost that which it never possessed.

Although concerned by the decline in admissions in the early 1960s, the substantial increase in admissions in the 1970s and 1980s and a potential shortfall in the 1990s, the Society's main response so far to these fluctuations has been to issue exhortations to the law schools and to commission manpower surveys. The Council has not endeavoured to reduce the numbers of intrants by raising the standard of the professional examinations (which are currently easier than their university counterparts) or that of the Diploma (which is taught and marked by members of the profession). It has not pressed for Diploma places to be limited and it is very unusual for anyone to be banned from entry to the profession on the grounds of 'moral unfitness'. The leaders of the profession did try in 1984 and 1985 to emulate their English counterparts by introducing a ban on solicitors with less than three years post-qualifying experience from setting up in practice on their own (allegedly on quality control grounds). However, this was rejected by the younger members of the profession because of its supply control implications and the proposal has been shelved for the time being. Nor has mandatory continuing education been introduced for new intrants (as in England and Wales).

The advent of almost universal graduate entry also does not represent a loss of supply control by the profession, for the latter still can stipulate the university courses (and their content) that confer exemption from the professional examinations, as well as the contents of the Diploma course. One can argue instead that the profession has retained control of legal education in these crucial respects but successfully passed most of the burden of training intrants to the universities (as occurred in the United States), the state (which foots the bill) and the small minority of the profession who teach the Diploma for very meagre financial rewards. Abel (1982) claims that graduate entry caused the major increases in women entering the profession in the twentieth century, which significantly eroded the profession's supply control. Even if the prejudice against women in the professions can be viewed largely as a supply control issue, this argument is difficult to sustain. Women have been able to graduate from law school and enter the profession since 1920, yet it was only in the 1970s that their numbers began to rise. Perhaps the fairest conclusion to draw is that the profession's powers to regulate its size have not changed greatly in the past century and that the profession has rarely tried to exercise such powers as it does possess (Slater, 1982).

Access to the profession

The principal sectors within the solicitor's profession in Scotland and the respective changes in these sectors since 1954 are set out in Table 7. Thus it can be seen that in 1954 some 13% of the practising profession worked out-with the private sector, a figure which had risen to 20% by 1975 dropping to 18% in 1988 (the comparative figures in England in 1975 and 1986 being

Table 7 Breakdown of Practising Solicitors

	1954	*1975*	*1988*
Private Practice Principals	2420	2608 (8)	3578 (48)
Qualified Assistants	445	336 (− 25)	1771 (298)
Local Government	253	400 (70)	561 (123)
Central Government & Public Bodies	106	283 (167)	456 (330)
Industry/Commerce	48	36 (− 25)	175 (265)
Miscellaneous	34	3	99
Total	3306	3666 (11)	6643 (100)

Source: Law Society
Note: Figures in round brackets refer to the % change since 1954.

13%). Clearly the central government sector (with a rise of 330% in thirty years) has been the major growth area during this period with the local government sector also showing a steady increase. But in both cases the major growth occurred before 1975 and not in the last decade. In-house lawyers in the commercial world on the other hand, while remaining a comparatively rare animal in Scotland have also been increasing – but all the increases came in the last decade. In fact, during the last decade the private sector has grown faster than the public sector (the respective percentages being 63% and 49%) despite the fact that this has been the period of the major increase in admissions and female admissions in particular. The Table clearly shows, however, that the private profession has so far absorbed these increases by greatly expanding the qualified assistants' sector rather than the number of partners or sole practitioners. It seems, therefore, that the substantial subordinate sector within legal offices which existed in the nineteenth and early twentieth centuries has been cyclically recreated.

The major impact of the changing patterns of education and recruitment, outlined above, has been the growth in women practitioners. After a long battle through the courts and Parliament women won the right to graduate from Scottish universities in 1889. The first female students did not enrol in Scottish law schools until 1907 and it was only after the Sex Disqualification (Removal) Act 1919 that women were permitted to enter the profession. Yet despite the increase in graduate entry in Scotland from this period the numbers of women entering the profession do not show any signs of increasing sub-stantially for many years. The first female advocate was admitted in 1923 but the next did not arrive until 1949. By 1987 a mere 45 women had ever been admitted to the Faculty of Advocates (most of them after 1980) and in 1989 only 35 of the 250 practising advocates (14 per cent) were female. Work done by Paxton (1984) shows that female advocates now encounter little prejudice from their male colleagues and that prejudice amongst instructing solicitors (once a considerable problem) has now markedly declined. Moreover the flexibility of work at the Bar makes it a profession eminently suited for married women with domestic ties. Despite this (and contrary to the English position) women have always formed a smaller proportion of the Bar than of the solicitors' profession.

On the solicitors' side a survey conducted in 1972 indicated that at that date only 4% of the practising profession were women. Tables 6 and 8 show us that the substantial rise in female admissions to the solicitors' profession began in the early 1970s a few years before the increase in female advocates. This is long after graduate entry had become the norm in Scotland and ten years after the introduction of the full time LLB degree with government grants for all students. It appears that the cause of the rise in female solicitors (from 13% to 25.5% of all solicitors on the roll in the last decade) must lie not so much in graduate entry as the changes in intellectual climate during the sixties (and the rise of the feminist movement in particular).

Table 8   Enrolled Female Solicitors

Year	Female Admissions to Profession	% of all Admissions	Women on the Roll	% of all Solicitors on the Roll
1975	31	11	–	9
1976	59	21	514	10.5
1977	82	27	583	11
1978	69	22	654	12
1979	106	30	749	13
1980	132	33	864	15
1981	135	34	980	16
1982	139	36	1102	17
1983	154	37	1212	18
1984	171	40	1370	20
1985	182	44	1520	21
1986	186	44	1709	23
1987	190	49	1864	24
1988	175	46	2047	25.5

Source: Law Society

Nevertheless, the fact that 46% of intrants to the profession are now female does not necessarily entail that discrimination against women in the profession has been eliminated. An attitude study of women solicitors in Scotland conducted in 1984 (Millar, 1985) revealed that many women in the profession consider that they have encountered discrimination in their careers and that male attitudes in the profession have not changed to meet modern conditions. Strong support was elicited for changes in working practices including the introduction of part-time partnerships, home-based legal practice and leave of absence provisions.

The available statistics afford some empirical support for the survey results. Women have yet to become principals in any significant numbers. In 1961 of the 1,209 principals (partners or sole practitioners) in Edinburgh and Glasgow a mere 5 were women. By 1985 there were 1,530 principals in Scotland's two main cities of whom only 86 (6%) were women despite the fact that 19% of all practising solicitors in the two cities were now women. (The low figure can partly be attributed to the fact that the increases of the 1970s have not yet worked through the system. Yet it is an ominous sign that of the 148 principals in Scotland's six largest firms in 1984, only two were women.) Nor is it clear whether female assistant solicitors are being offered profit-sharing as opposed to salaried partnerships as often as their male counterparts. Nevertheless, whatever difficulties women have experienced, the available data (including the 1984 survey) does not suggest that Scottish women (unlike their American sisters) have turned disproportionately to employment in the non-private sector of the profession.

The influx of women into the legal profession in the last decade is unlikely to have greatly altered the class composition of the profession, although no accurate figures are available. The social background of advocates and solicitors in previous centuries has already been discussed. The absence of university grants and the dearth of scholarships or bursaries, the premiums required of law apprentices until the mid-twentieth century, the meagre salaries of apprentices and assistants, the stamp duty payable by new intrants until 1947, the 'goodwill' payments required of many new partners until the sixties, the importance of family connections and the class consciousness of certain firms, must have ensured that practising solicitors in Scotland in the first sixty years of the twentieth century were predominantly middle class in origin – as in England and in the United States. As we have already seen the introduction of university grants and the increase in salaries since that time – developments which might have broadened the social base of the profession have been offset, in part or in whole, by the substantial increase in middle-class women entering the profession through the law schools, which has diminished the potential for lower income males to enter the profession. The ethnic base of the profession is equally homogeneous since few of the minority students who do enter law school appear to seek admission to either branch of the profession.

Conclusion

In terms of the ideal model set forth in William Twining's paper the Scottish experience in relation to access to legal education and the legal profession is something of a curate's egg. There is no evidence that the best possible selection criteria are used for admission to legal study and considerable evidence that social class background influences the outcome of SCE Higher examinations. That said, recently published research suggests that comprehensive schooling has begun to reduce the gap in examination achievement between the lower and upper ends of the social spectrum in Scotland, without a general levelling down in attainment (McPherson and Willms, 1987).

The evidence also suggests that the reforms of the last decade have not made it any easier for para-legals and other non-law graduates to gain admission to the profession. This despite the creation of Higher National Certificate and

Higher National Diploma courses in Legal Studies in Scottish Technical Colleges. In part this is because neither the Law Society nor the universities wish to encourage what they see as 'back door routes' to the profession. As a result they are reluctant to treat either the HNC or the HND courses as equivalent to SCE Higher examinations for admissions purposes. Although 75 non-law graduates have commenced three-year pre-Diploma traineeships since 1981 (with 14 in 1987 alone) comparatively few have taken the Diploma since it was introduced. While the present grant allocation procedures contain the possibility of discrimination against such candidates there is no evidence that they have actually been discriminated against by Diploma Admissions Officers and some evidence to the contrary. Moreover the Law Society possesses the discretion to exempt applicants from the Diploma in special circumstances. It is understood that the fact that a candidate could not obtain a Diploma place or support themselves without a grant might be sufficient cause for the exemption to be granted. Thus in one case an applicant from the Western Isles who had a family and lived outwith easy travelling distance to a university law school was granted exemption from the Diploma. Such applicants are, however, required to take a three-year non-Diploma traineeship.

Again it is not clear that the replacement of apprenticeships by traineeships has had much impact on the problem of access. While the removal of the requirement to give a balanced training and the ban on providing traineeships to close relatives has marginally improved access, the rise in the recommended salary rates for post-Diploma trainees (as compared with apprentices) has made some firms less willing to take trainees.

If this represented the whole picture, the outlook for those concerned with problem of access to legal education and the profession in Scotland would be a gloomy one. However, there are some more optimistic features about the Scottish experience. The creation of three affirmative action programmes in law schools was a positive step forward and could represent a foundation on which to build if the antipathy of certain academic lawyers and the suspicion of most school headmasters can be overcome. There are multiple entry routes to both branches of the profession and there is sufficient flexibility for late developers to gain entry to the profession. The common training for solicitors and advocates avoids premature specialisation and there is considerable scope for lateral mobility between the various branches of the profession throughout the British Isles. Moreover, the absence of the three-year rule in Scotland reduces the total qualifying period to a minimum of five or six years. In sum then, the Scottish system has certain redeeming features, but the vedict for now must be: could do better.

NOTES

1 See Annual Report of the Scottish Council for Racial Equality 1983/4 p 25.
2 The exact figures are 2,428,472 males and 2,606,843 females.
3 The Chairs of Civil and of Scots law in Edinburgh being funded by the novel expedient of a tax of 2 pence Scots on every pint of ale or beer sold in the City of Edinburgh, Black, 1982: 33.
4 In 1851 WS apprentices had to pay a fee of £500.
5 Women were not permitted to join the profession in Scotland before the twentieth century.
6 A law degree containing the appropriate subjects had guaranteed exemption from the Faculty's professional examinations since 1919.
7 The Solicitors (Scotland) Act 1980, s 6.
8 Between 1949 and 1965 the annual rate of admissions fell from 191 to 53 – a sufficient decline to alarm even the Law Society (Law Society, 1956).

REFERENCES

Abel, Richard L 'The Politics of the Market for Legal Services' in Philip A Thomas (ed) *Law in the Balance* (1982) Oxford: Martin Robertson.

Abel, Richard L 'The Decline of Professionalism?' (1986) 49 Modern Law Review 1.

Black, Robert, 'Practice and Precept in Scots Law' (1982) 27 Juridical Review 31.

Hughes Commission *The Royal Commission on Legal Services in Scotland, Report* (1980) (2 vols) (Cmnd 7846/1) Edinburgh: HMSO.

Larson, Magali Sarfatti *The Rise of Professionalism* (1977) Berkeley: University of California Press.

Law Society 'Editorial' (1956) 1 Journal of the Law Society of Scotland 12.

McPherson and Willms 'Equalisation and improvement: Some effects of comprehensive reorganisation in Scotland' (1987) 21 Sociology 509.

Millar, William M 'The Role of Women in the Profession' (1985) 30 Journal of the Law Society of Scotland 86.

Paxton, Adele 'Getting Even?' (1984) *Scots Law Times* (*News*) 53.

Podmore, David *Solicitors and the Wider Community* (1980) London: Heinemann.

Shaw, John Stuart *The Management of Scottish Society, 1707–1764* (1983) Edinburgh: John Donald Publishers.

Slater, Caroline 'Manpower Planning' (1982) 27 Journal of the Law Society of Scotland 51.

Twining, William 'Access to Legal Education and the Legal Profession: A Commonwealth Perspective' (1986) Access to Justice Lecture, Windsor, Ontario (April, 1986): Chapter 1 of this volume is a revised version of this lecture.

12 Access to legal education and the legal profession in Zambia

Chuma Himonga* and Chaloka Beyani†

1 Introduction

As a developing country, Zambia has placed much emphasis on the use of law in the development process to promote the welfare of its people. In these circumstances, accessibility to legal education and the legal profession is of great importance. It enhances capacity for effective use of law as a tool for development. Enlightenment of the community in respect of individual rights and freedoms and resort to the process of justice is also in large measure dependent on access to legal education and the legal profession.

This chapter explores issues pertaining to the situation in Zambia. It is divided into six parts. Part two examines the institutional structure for access to legal education and the legal profession. Part three focuses on the means of recruitment into mainstream legal education and the legal profession. In this respect, the criteria for admission to the University of Zambia School of Law and legal practice are discussed, along with their effect on access to legal education and the legal profession. Part four deals with the various routes of entry into the legal profession in Zambia. Part five discusses the factors affecting access to legal education and the legal profession in Zambia. And part six provides the conclusion to the chapter.

2 Institutional structure for access to legal education and the legal profession

In Zambia, the School of Law at the University of Zambia, and the Law Practice Institute provide legal education and determine entry into the legal profession. The School of Law provides mainstream legal education.

The Bachelor of Laws degree programme is the School's base in legal education. It is of three years' duration, consisting of both full-time and part-time classes. The latter are intended to give access to legal education to those who cannot, for certain reasons, afford to attend full-time classes.

The Law Practice institute conducts professional legal education on behalf of the Council of Legal Education. The latter is a government created corporate body under whose auspices professional legal education is provided and overseen. Its functions include approval of courses of study offered by any Uni-

* Lecturer, School of Law, University of Zambia.
† Lecturer, School of Law, University of Zambia.

versity or institution, in order to determine the reference of such courses to the programme set by the Council for the purposes of admission of legal practitioners to the Bar.[1] The programme of the Council, as conducted by the Law Practice Institute, is of one academic year's duration,[2] and is oriented towards professional legal practice. It is evident that both the School of Law and the Law Practice Institute play complementary roles in determining access to legal education and the legal profession in Zambia. Students graduate from the basic legal education programme in the School of Law. They then proceed to enrol at the Law Practice Institute to obtain their professional legal training.

Table 1 School of Law Enrolment by Programme, 1983 and 1984

PROGRAMME	1983			1984		
	M	F	TOTAL	M	F	TOTAL
Part-time	11	2	13	21	1	22
Full-time	16	13	29	17	15	32
	27	15	42	38	16	54

The School of Law is thus an entry route into legal education. The Law Practice Institute is an exit route into the legal profession. But an insight on how these institutions influence and determine accessibility to legal education and the legal profession may be given by examining their mode of recruiting students.

3 Recruitment to legal education and the legal profession

Entry into mainstream legal education in Zambia is provided entirely by the School of Law. It is appropriate therefore to examine its procedure and criteria for admission of students. Such procedures and criteria bear directly upon the issue of access to legal education, and of course, to the legal profession itself.

Admission to the School of Law may be by direct or indirect entry. As regards the former, persons who hold a degree of a recognised University or other institution of any country may be admitted to the School directly for the LLB degree as part- or full-time students. This group, however, constitutes a very small part of the School's intake. In the past two years, for example, this group has constituted only about 10% of the total intake. The number is restricted largely by unavailability of places as existing places have to be shared with students currently studying in the University and enrolled in the School in their second year of study at the University, as well as students who are taken on for non-degree programmes (ie Certificate in Law). Emphasis is, in practice, also placed upon enrolment of a larger number of students currently studying in the University who do not already hold any degree qualifications.

As regards indirect entry, students who obtain admission into the School of Law are initially enrolled as students in the School of Humanities and Social Sciences in their first year at the University. Those who wish to study law apply for admission to the Law School towards the end of their first year in Humanities and Social Sciences.

In this arrangement, the Law School is given a quota allocation of 13% of the total students enrolled in the School of Humanities and Social Sciences. In turn, this entails that the admission criterion used by the School is high and competitive. The School of Law has a fixed cut-off point above which students who will be admitted to the School must score in their examinations in Humanities and Social Sciences. At present, the cut-off point is an average of B grade. Given this procedure, students are admitted to law studies on the basis of their performance in Humanities and Social Sciences.

This procedure has a limiting effect on access to legal education in Zambia. For example, the number of students who gain admission to full-time studies in the School of Law is severely limited. Consequently, in recent years, the intake of students by the School of Law has ranged between 40 and 50 students.[3] This represents only 4% of the total average enrolment of slightly over one thousand for the University as a whole. For example, in 1983 the University had a total intake of 1,351 first entrants to the University. Only 54 of these subsequently enrolled into the School of Law in their second year of study of the University.[4]

The drop out rate of law students minimally affects access to legal education. Once students are admitted to law studies, they must work quite hard in order to remain in the School. Of the 42 students who were admitted to the School of Law in 1983, 33 (78.6%) graduated in 1986. Such a low drop out rate is mainly attributable to the School's flexible approach towards satisfactory performance by students. A student who fails in one course may proceed but repeat the course failed. A student who fails in two courses may repeat the whole year, and only a student who fails in three courses may be excluded from the School altogether. In fact, not all students who drop out do so because of having failed the course; some of them withdraw with permission with a view to resuming their studies in future.

Table 2   Higher Education Enrolment by Institution and Sex 1983–1984

	1983			1984		
INSTITUTION	M	F	TOTAL	M	F	TOTAL
University of Zambia	962	389	1351	1135	211	1346
Law Practice Institute	36	12	48	26	5	31
Higher Education Total Enrolment	6153	2508	8661	6224	2228	8452

Source: Annual Reports of Ministry of Higher Education and Department of Technical Education and Vocational Training, 1982–84; Computer Lists, University of Zambia Computer Centre and Records at Ministry of Agriculture and Water Development, Lusaka, 1984; Annual Report, Ministry of Higher Education (forthcoming); Records at Ministry of Agriculture and Water Development, Training Sector, Mulungushi House, Lusaka.

After students have graduated in law from the University of Zambia they are, upon application, admitted to the Law Practice Institute to undergo professional legal training essential to their admission to the Bar. Criteria for admission to the Law Practice Institute are set by the Legal Practitioners' Act.[5] The basic requirement for admission to the Institute is possession of a law degree from the University of Zambia or any other University. Provided that in the latter case, the University in question must be approved by the Council of Legal Education and have its law degree recognised as being academically equivalent to that of the University of Zambia.[6]

Under this procedure, all law graduates from the University of Zambia are virtually assured of admission to professional legal training. However, not all of them opt for professional legal training. At the same time, there are a few law graduates from other Universities. This means that in all cases, the intake of students for professional legal education is not a total reflection of the number of students who graduate from law studies at the University of Zambia, although the majority of them are. In 1985, there were thirty-four (34) students who enrolled at the Law Practice Institute. In 1986 forty-four (44) students enrolled. An average of about thirty-nine (39) students enrol for Legal practitioners' Qualifying Examinations course at the Law Practice Institute each year.

Nevertheless, the admission criteria and procedures of the School of Law have a severe controlling impact on access to legal education and the legal profession in Zambia. Enrolment of students to professional legal training is directly dependent on the number of law graduates from the University of Zambia. As the Law Practice Institute provides the bridging link between basic legal education and the entry into the legal profession, it could be said that the School of Law has an overall embracing, determining influence on access to the legal profession in Zambia.

It is true that the Law Practice Institute has a significantly high failure rate. But it does not have a set drop-out procedure. Students who fail at any level are allowed two other attempts to resit examinations in the courses in which they failed. If a student has failed to pass in all of three attempts, she or he is barred from attempting any Legal Practitioners' Examinations for a period of five years. While this procedure delays entry into the legal profession, it cannot be conceived of as a hindrance to access to the legal profession in the same way as the procedures and admission criteria of the School of Law are.

4 The legal profession

There are several ways by which access to the legal profession may be gained in Zambia. Firstly, a person in possession of a Bachelor's degree in law from the University of Zambia or a University approved by the Council of Legal Education may qualify for admission to the legal profession upon passing the Legal Practitioners' Qualifying Examination at the Law Practice Institute.[7] The proportion of students who qualify for admission to the legal profession, as indicated by the number of people who enrol for and pass the Practitioners Qualifying Examination, is about 43%.[8]

However, a law graduate may do two years' service in the Republic as an articled clerk under articles of clerkship to a practitioner as an alternative to attending the course of study at the Law Practice Institute. But such an articled clerk must proceed to sit and pass the Legal Practitioners' Qualifying Examination in order to be admitted to the legal profession.[9]

Secondly, a person may qualify to be admitted as a legal practitioner if she or he is a qualified lawyer of any Commonwealth country which applies as its predominant basic system of law the common law or has a legal system founded upon the common law.[10] Such a person must have practised law for at least three years in his or her country and served at least six months in Zambia in Offices such as the Legal Practitioners' Office, or the Judicial or the Legal Secretary's Department. His or her work must be certified as satisfactory by the officer under whom he or she has served. As an alternative to the six months' service, the lawyer in question may attend the one-year post-graduate course at the Law Practice Institute.[11] In any case, a Commonwealth lawyer qualifying under the foregoing conditions must also pass the Legal Practitioners' Qualifying Examination.

Thirdly, a person may be admitted to the legal profession through articles of clerkship under a prescribed practitioner in Zambia after a specified period determined by the Council of Legal Education.[12] Different periods of articled clerkship may be prescribed for different people depending on the actual experience of the individual clerk in the Office of the Practitioner and on any other matters deemed relevant by the Council of Legal Education.[13]

To qualify for articles of clerkship, a person must possess a University of Zambia Law Degree. Alternatively, such a person must have passed an examination prescribed by the Council of Legal Education.[14] After completion of the articles of clerkship, the articled clerk is further required to sit and pass the Legal Practitioners' Qualifying Examination.[15]

The final stage in gaining admission to the legal profession involves the Chief Justice. At this stage, persons seeking admission must produce to the Chief Justice a Certificate issued by the Council of Legal Education, certifying that all requirements pertaining to academic and professional qualifications of such persons have been satisfied. In addition, an application for admission must also be submitted to the Chief Justice. The Chief Justice must then satisfy himself that the applicant is of good character before admitting him to the profession.[16]

5 Factors affecting access to legal education and the legal profession

Access to legal education in Zambia cannot, in itself, be conceived of as an issue. It is not affected by factors peculiar to it, other than those which relate to higher education in general. Education in Zambia is mainly provided by government-run institutions. Every Zambian student at an institution of higher learning receives sponsorship by government through a bursary, regardless of tribe, sex, religion or any other considerations.

However, given the fact that Zambia's institutional structure of education is pyramidical, fewer students gain access to institutions of higher learning as compared to many that gain access in the early stages but drop out of the system in the later stages. In these circumstances, one's ability to perform well in examinations at junior and secondary school basically determines one's access to higher education, and subsequently to legal education.

Factors which affect access to legal education and the legal profession are discernible in the entry route into legal education. In this regard, a factor worthy of emphasis is the selection process to the School of Law and limitations on existing facilities in the School. As stated earlier, the School of Law's main intake of students is taken from students who are originally admitted into the School of Humanities and Social Sciences.

As the intake of students into the School of Law is limited by a quota set by the Senate of the University of Zambia, the School of Law and the School of Humanities and Social Sciences have to 'share' the students between them. Entry into the School is thus limited. Admission of more students into the Law

School than is normally the case would mean that fewer students would remain in the School of Humanities and Social Sciences.

To forestall this state of affairs, the Law School could, as a short term measure, have its own original intake of students admitted in their first year into the School of Humanities, if only to learn basic and elementary aspects of Social Sciences. These students would not be part of the intake of students into the School of Humanities. Perhaps such an arrangement could eliminate the competition for students between Law and Humanities, and would thereby increase the intake of students in law, by removing the Law School's dependency on a quota allocation of students from Humanities.

As a long-term measure though, the Law School should only admit those students who have already obtained a basic degree in some field other than law. There would then not be any other limitations on the numbers of students to be admitted to the School, other than those set by the School itself to suit its facilities. Both measures would go a long way in widening the present scope of access to legal education and the legal profession in Zambia.

It is also obvious that the School's existing facilities, in terms both of accommodation and staff, can only handle the small number of students presently admitted in the School (ie 40–50 students). An expansion of these facilities is, therefore, imperative in order to widen the scope of access to legal education and the legal profession in the country.

At present, the main route of entry to the legal profession is the University of Zambia Law degree. Other alternative routes are the foreign, Commonwealth qualified lawyers and the Articles of Clerkship. Few lawyers, however, qualify through these routes. For example, between 1974 and 1980, only 12 people registered for the Legal Qualifying Examination through Articles of clerkship.[17] This represents an average of two students per year.

There are proposals to abolish the Articles of Clerkship as a route of entry into the profession.[18] This will leave the University degree and the foreign route as the only routes of entry into the legal profession. The main reason advanced for abolishing the Articles of Clerkship as a route of entry into the profession is that the route is rarely taken by University graduates. So the academic quality of other students who qualify for Articles of Clerkship is very poor, thus contributing to lowering of standards of the profession.[19]

Access to the legal profession may also be perceived in terms of the small size of the profession and the distribution of lawyers, geographically and in different sectors of the Zambian economy. In this respect, a few factors, both historical and geographical, have in one way or another affected the character of the legal profession in Zambia. Historically, the legal profession in Zambia has been organised and run by a professional body. Between 1962 and 1973 the Law Society of Zambia was the body around which the legal profession was organised. It was considered that this Society militated against the growth of the legal profession in Zambia. Membership of the society was open only to persons who had obtained their legal training or qualification in England or from certain acceptable Universities. On this ground, most Zambians were excluded from the legal profession.[20]

As a result, in 1973, the Law Association of Zambia Act was enacted to replace the Law Society. The Association was geared towards expansion of the legal profession in Zambia. It liberalised its entry requirements for membership by providing for ordinary and associate membership.[21] Ordinary membership is open to legal practitioners, within Zambia or outside Zambia, and to law graduates of the University of Zambia. Associate membership is

Table 3   Students Registered for the Postgraduate Course at the Law Practice Institute, 1976–87

Year of Registration	No of Students			Pass
	Total	M	F	
1976–77	28	25	3	11
1977–78	41	41	–	16
1978–79	48	40	8	27
1979–80	34	29	5	4
1980–81	36	27	9	14
1981–82	33	21	12	19
1982–83	49	38	11	13
1983–84	48	36	12	30
1984–85	31	26	5	21
1985–86	34	–	–	27
1986–87	44	25	19	–
TOTAL	426	308	84	182

Source: Figures extracted from the Registrar of Students at the LPI by the Secretary, Mrs Mukelabai.

available to students of law, articled clerks and managing clerks of legal practitioners.

In offering broad membership, the Law Association aimed at providing a forum for all members of the legal profession to associate closely and articulate their activities for the development of the law in Zambia.

The geographical factor has hindered the expansion of services by the profession to rural and remote areas. Legal practice is concentrated largely in urban and peri-urban areas in Zambia. Associated with this imbalance is the availability of the market, infrastructure and better facilities in urban and peri-urban areas. Therefore, as long as rural areas remain unattractive in terms of business and facilities, the legal profession will for long remain a monopoly of the urban and peri-urban areas.

In approximate terms, there are about six hundred lawyers in Zambia.[22] This figure is far too small in comparison to the size of the country's population. The largest concentration of these lawyers is in the private sector, with the public sector absorbing only a small number of lawyers each year.[23]

The argument that the legal profession is saturated is quite common in some quarters of the society. This may be relatively true on two accounts, urban and peri-urban areas, where the market, and conditions are good. First, rural areas, and many growing townships, are virtually without lawyers or legal services. Second, many lawyers in Zambia are concerned mainly with the most traditional function of a lawyer, litigation. Fierce competition for the market in this respect cannot but lead to the alluring assumption that there are too many lawyers in the country.

By contrast, there are many areas of growing demand for legal services and lawyers in Zambia. As Ndulo has pointed out,[24] there is a dearth of lawyers in such areas as intellectual property law, taxation, investments, and international trade and business law, to mention only a few.

Clearly, there is need in Zambia to increase the legal profession to reflect the size of the country's population as well as to meet the demand in the new, emerging areas of law. Moreover, the legal profession itself must take measures to ensure that the geographical location of lawyers in Zambia is well-balanced between urban and rural areas.

Coupled with the need to expand the capacity of legal education to produce more lawyers is, of course, the need for the School of Law to re-examine its entire curriculum and design it in such a way as to gear itself to producing lawyers in fields where they are demanded most, and lawyers who are well versed with the country's developmental requirements.

Recently, the legal profession has instituted some measures in addition to existing ones such as the Legal Aid Scheme in order to meet the ever growing demand for legal services by the public. In this respect, the Law Association of Zambia has inaugurated a Citizen's Advisory Bureau and also conducts a weekly law programme on television. These measures may be seen as attempts to improve the public's accessibility to legal services and the legal profession.

The Citizen's Advisory Bureau has been established with the objective of rendering free legal services to a specified sector of the community. Its target group are persons in need of legal assistance but who are unable to afford fees charged by private legal practitioners. Eligibility of applicants for legal service will be determined by a 'means test' which still has to be worked out. The 'means test' would, however, take into account an applicant's income in such a way that a ceiling would be set beyond which an applicant would not be eligible for legal service by the bureau. Cases that will be dealt with by the Bureau will obviously vary. But priority will be given to cases involving criminal, public interest or community related class actions, wrongful dismissals and deprivation of social services and amenities.

A Citizen's Advisory Board is being established to oversee the running and operations of the Bureau. The Board will comprise a member of the faculty of the School of Law; a student at the Law Practice Institute; members of the Legal Aid Committee of the Law Association of Zambia; one representative from each of the Social Welfare, Police and Prisons departments; and any other person whom the Board may co-opt. In rendering legal services, the Bureau will utilise practising lawyers, academic staff of the Law School, law students and students at the Law Practice Institute.

The weekly law programme consists of a series of discussions by lawyers on significant legal issues that are of interest to the community eg fundamental rights and freedoms of the individual, distribution of property between spouses after divorce or following death of one of the spouses, discrimination against women, and business law. The law programme is thus aimed at enlightening the public on certain fundamental legal problems.

Although both the Citizen's Advisory Bureau and the law programme are welcome initiatives towards overcoming the problem of access to legal services, nevertheless they do bear inherent limitations. The Citizen's Advisory Bureau, when fully operational, will only be available in major urban areas where lawyers are concentrated. The majority of the poor people for whom it is

Table 4   Legal Practitioners in Zambia 1965–1985

Year Enrolled to Bar	M	F
1965	20	–
1966	13	–
1967	30	–
1968	21	–
1969	6	–
1970	8	–
1971	34	1
1972	27	1
1973	36	3
1974	17	1
1975	20	2
1976	35	1
1977	20	2
1978	36	2
1979	47	3
1980	28	5
1981	36	5
1982	42	12
1983	31	5
1984	36	16
1985	27	3
	570	62

Source: High Court of Zambia Roll of Barristers, Solicitors and Notaries Public.

meant are in the rural areas still without legal service. Similarly, the law programme can only be viewed by those who own television sets. Most of these are relatively well-to-do. Many people in rural, and even urban areas, have no access to the programme. It may be worthwhile to introduce the law programme on radio as well and in all the major indigenous spoken languages. At least many people, including some in rural areas do have access to radio.

Table 5   Employment Distribution of Lawyers 1983 and 1984

YEAR	Parastatal and Private Commercial Sector	Government – Central and Local – Sector	Private Legal Practice	Unclassified	Total
1983	22	112	128	8	270
1984	19	112	134	7	272

Source: The Law list of Zambia in the 1983 and 1984 Law Directory and Legal Calendars, The Government Printer, Lusaka 1983 and 1984 respectively; 1983 Annual Report of the Judiciary and the Magistracy, the Government Printer, Lusaka, 1984 and figures supplied by the Permanent Secretary of Legal Affairs, Dr J Kanganja.

Conclusion

This chapter has modestly discussed the issue of access to legal education and the legal profession in Zambia. The main route of entry into legal education and the legal profession is the School of Law at the University of Zambia via the Law Practice Institute. By and large, access to legal education is an issue only in the context of access to higher education as a whole in Zambia, determined by the pyramidical structure of the system of education in the country.

Entry into legal education in the School of Law is largely determined by the Senate of the University of Zambia through a quota restricting students admitted into the School. This quota is set at 13% of the students enrolled in the School of Humanities.

The basic entry requirement to the legal profession is possession of the LLB degree either from the University of Zambia, or from a recognised University. Other routes of entry into the legal profession include articled clerkship and admission of foreign qualified lawyers of three years' standing from Commonwealth countries.

So far the main factor determining entry into the legal education and, subsequently, into the legal profession is the pyramidical structure of the system of education in the country. This is the context in which access to legal education is an issue. In this respect, the problem of access to legal education and the legal profession is compounded by the quota ceiling on the number of students admitted into Law School, along with the School's limited facilities in terms of staff and accommodation for students.

Consequently, the size of the legal profession in Zambia is quite small and is concentrated in urban areas. Many people, especially in rural areas are without access to legal services. The latter are also lacking in such important fields as intellectual property law, taxation, investments, international trade law and business law.

The Law Association has taken limited measures to improve accessibility to legal services by introduction of the Citizen's Advisory Bureau to give free legal assistance to the needy, and a weekly television programme which focuses on various aspects of the law in Zambia.

In order to expand the scope of access to legal education and the legal profession in Zambia, it is suggested that: firstly, the School of Law ought to have its own original intake of students as a short term measure to circumvent the quota limitation on the number of students admitted into the School. Secondly, the School of Law should directly admit students who have a basic degree in some other field, as a long-term measure, to overcome limitation on access to legal education by virtue of entry restriction as a result of students being 'shared' between the Law School and the School of Humanities and Social Sciences. Thirdly, there must be a corresponding expansion of the School of Law's lecture room facilities as well as employment of more teaching staff to cope with increased intake of students; and, fourthly, the Law School's curriculum must be redesigned to introduce courses in the fields of intellectual property law, taxation, investments, and international trade law in which there is an increasing demand for legal services and the current state of the legal profession cannot adequately cope. It is the authors' considered view that the implementation of the foregoing suggestions would go a long way in widening the scope of access to legal education in Zambia.

NOTES

[1] Legal Practitioners Act, Cap 48 of the Laws of Zambia.
[2] There are attempts, as from next year, to lengthen the duration of the programme at the Law Practice Institute in order to improve the quality of legal practice.
[3] See Table 1.
[4] See Table 2 and Table 1.
[5] Cap 48 of The Laws of Zambia.
[6] Legal Practitioners Act, s11 A(a).
[7] Ibid, s11A(a) (b) (i) (c).
[8] See Table 3.
[9] Legal Practitioners Act, s11 A(b) (ii) (c).
[10] Ibid, s11 B(a) (i) (I).
[11] Ibid, s11 B(b) (i) (II).
[12] Ibid, s12.
[13] Ibid, s12(2)(a).
[14] Ibid, s12(2)(b). The courses for the prescribed examination are in two parts. Part I consists of Law of Contract, Torts, Criminal Law, Evidence and Constitutional Law. Part II consists of Commercial Law, Land Law, Administrative Law and Jurisprudence.
[15] Ibid, s12(1)(c).
[16] Ibid, s13(1)(a)(b).
[17] See Articles of Clerkship register, Council of Legal Education.
[18] See the proposed Legal Practitioners (Amendment) Act 1985 (Bill).
[19] Interviews with the Chief Justice, November, 1986.
[20] Zambia, Parliamentary Debates, 1973, Col 1319.
[21] Law Association of Zambia Act, s5.
[22] See Table 4.
[23] See Table 5, on Employment Distribution of Lawyers, 1983 and 1984.
[24] See Muna Ndulo 'Legal Education in Zambia: Pedagogical Issues' (1986) 2 Lesotho Law Journal 75. See also, C Himonga and C Beyani 'Access to Legal Education and the Legal Profession in Zambia', *Commonwealth Legal Education Newsletter* (1988) April and July, Annex II; M Mbao 'Some Reflections on Legal Education in Zambia' (1986) 12 Law Association Journal (June).

13 Access to legal education and the legal profession in Zimbabwe

*Reg Austin**

Post-independence transition to non-racial access

Consistent with the discrimination against black citizens which characterised Rhodesian settler rule, access to legal education and the legal profession was deliberately and almost totally denied to blacks until Zimbabwe's independence in 1980. This fact, combined with the exodus, particularly of whites in the legal branches of the civil service, resulted in the democratically elected government having to take radical measures to deal with the situation. One aspect of this was the establishment of crash courses, initially taught largely by academics in the Law Department of the University of Zimbabwe to specially recruited students who would not have qualified for normal entry to the University. These were destined to fill posts as prosecutors and magistrates in the Magistrates' Courts and as presiding officers in the newly created Community and Primary Courts.

The training of prosecutors and magistrates, who are full-time civil servants, continued as a part-time, special programme at the University until the end of 1986. These students were examined in a slimmed-down core of subjects in first criminal and then civil law, but received no degree. Their training was recognised only to a limited extent, by the government alone. This measure did not effectively change the pattern of access to legal education or to the legal profession, but was a temporary measure to fill a gap in certain government legal services with persons who were not offered a full legal education.

Another dimension of government action to deal with the situation was more fundamental and radical. While the government, the University and the legal profession of Rhodesia were assiduously excluding blacks from the law, the process of liberation and preparation for a majority ruled Zimbabwe included a vigorous element of legal education and practice. Thus, at independence in April 1980, there was a significant black 'diaspora' of Zimbabwean lawyers, educated in a wide range of Law Schools from Kiev to California, including a good number who had qualified as Barristers at the Inns of Court.

Under the existing regulations for admission to the legal profession most of these 'foreign' qualified lawyers would have had to submit themselves to a period of further, local, legal education and to seek admission before the Court. The argument for maintaining that control was the historically familiar 'maintenance of standards', combined with the more specific point that the common law of Zimbabwe (Roman-Dutch Law) would not have been that in

---

* Dean, Faculty of Law, University of Zimbabwe.

which these lawyers of the 'diaspora' had been educated. The new government of Zimbabwe, as its policy of Reconciliation demonstrated, was sensitive to the need for continuity. On balance, however, the combination of the demand for change, the absurdity of the racial discrimination in the Rhodesian legal establishment and the need for qualified and politically reliable lawyers to serve the new State, decided the government to take radical steps in relation to both access to the profession and access to legal education.

This decision was concretised in the Legal Practitioners' Act of 1981. The Act opened the profession to Zimbabweans who had qualified abroad and had neither practical experience nor academic training in Zimbabwe. Even this provision demonstrated a caution and readiness to compromise with the establishment, on the part of the new government. The lawyers entitled to be registered under this law were restricted to those with degrees from designated foreign countries where the common law was English or Roman-Dutch, and English was an official language. In addition, the Minister was empowered to declare that qualifications from other countries where English was an official language would be a basis for registration. The effect was that those who had qualified in most Commonwealth countries (and South Africa where many whites obtained their legal education) were able to practise immediately in Zimbabwe. To show the restrictiveness of the law, it was only after February 1985, when it was added by Ministerial declaration, that Scots qualifications were recognised as such a basis. A notable result of this formulation was the fact that Zimbabwean lawyers with a legal education in Socialist States were not able to become Legal Practitioners under this law.

After transition

The McNally Committee Report

Apart from the restrictions on the scope of the dispensation on access to the profession, there was also a time-limit built into the law. This opening up of access to the profession was an interim arrangement which expired at the end of 1985, having commenced at the end of May 1981. In June 1985 the Minister of Justice, Legal and Parliamentary Affairs set up a *Committee to Enquire into the Qualifications for Registration as a Legal Practitioner* under the Chairmanship of Mr Justice N J McNally.[1] The Committee concluded that the 'political purpose' of the interim period – 'to make allowance for all those who for essentially political reasons were obliged to study abroad' had been achieved. It recommended a short extension, to 31 July, 1986, essentially to enable a number of white Zimbabweans studying law in South Africa, where final results might be delayed until the following June, to benefit from the interim arrangement. This was accepted by government.

The mandate of the McNally Committee was not to undertake a fundamental re-examination of the basic issues posed in the outline of this project. Rather than the questions raised regarding Xanadu and other far-reaching possibilities of change, it was restricted to a rather narrow consideration of two basic propositions: whether entry to the profession (especially the private sector) be made more restrictive and determined ultimately by the profession, or that entry be based in essence upon the legal education and training offered at the University of Zimbabwe, as determined by government and provided for in legislation. The former position was supported in the main by the Law Society of Zimbabwe, representing the private profession, and the latter by a variety of individuals and organisations, including some members of the University and black lawyers in practice but outside the Law Society. Law students at the time also supported the latter approach. The restrictive approach was seen by democratic lawyers (see below) as a means of potential control or even exclusion of a new generation of more radical 'law in context' educated graduates of the University of Zimbabwe from the private profession.

The Committee's Final Report sought to steer a course between the two positions. It stated on the one hand that 'provided a graduate (of the University of Zimbabwe) has passed satisfactorily in (required) subjects ... we would expect him to be entitled to the Law Practice Diploma without further study.'[2] In the same vein it stated that 'the university should remain the primary source of public legal education in Zimbabwe. It provides such education to every qualified Zimbabwean, at the expense of the State. This education has been and must continue to be designed to ensure both the academic excellence and professional competence required by all sectors of the legal profession. In order to do this, the requirements of each sector, including private legal practice, should be available in clearly laid down and published criteria, so that the University can offer a programme to its publicly funded students, which will ensure their competence for admission to any sector of the profession. In relation to the private sector this will mean that the Council of Legal Education (which the Report proposed be set up) *will grant exemptions* (emphasis added) from the examinations for the Law Practice Diploma on the basis of such criteria to law graduates with appropriate passes.'[3] But on the other hand, it stated that 'it is (not) right to expect the Law Department (of the University) to be the sole arbiter of what training is needed by a legal practitioner.'[4]

Ultimately it recommended that government should set up a new supervisory body, (the Council of Legal Education – CLE) which in the final analysis should have (through its power of exemption) the right to judge all University legal education, and if it so decided, to require additional training of graduates (including those from the University of Zimbabwe) before their admission as *private* legal practitioners.[5]

The Final Report of the McNally Committee was submitted to the Minister in March 1986 with the recommendation that new regulations for entry to the profession be brought into force in January 1987. It is an indication of the controversy generated by the Report that the government of Zimbabwe has yet to act upon the issue. In the interim a new Minister (Cde Emmerson Mnangagwa) has replaced the Minister (Cde Eddison Zvogbo), who appointed the Committee and received the Report. One interesting development arising from the concern generated by this public discussion of a matter often regarded as the preserve of the legal elite, was the emergence of a radical organisation of lawyers (in public and private practice as well as in academe) articulating a strong argument in favour of a more explicitly democratic dispensation in the law, legal education and access to the law in Zimbabwe. This organisation is the Zimbabwe Association of Democratic Jurists (ZADJ). The debate generated a combination of radical and nationalist sentiment which has required government to consider carefully the implications of unqualified acceptance of the McNally Report.

This background is necessary to understand the fact that the question of access to legal education and to the profession in Zimbabwe is at this time (May, 1988) still in the process of development, with the possibility of access to the profession being resolved in very different ways. Currently it is still governed by the 1981 Legal Practitioners' Act.

Access to legal education

Until 1965 Attorneys and Advocates, the two branches of the Southern Rhodesian legal profession, were educated in Universities in South Africa or the United Kingdom, and subject to a local examination (Advocates) or a period of articles (Attorneys) before admission. Attorneys could qualify for practice without a degree, after serving a longer period of Articles and passing a series of approved examinations. Most public lawyers serving as magistrates and prosecutors qualified by way of public examinations, but law graduates were also employed. In 1965, the first formal teaching for a law degree was offered at the University (opened in 1953). The degree was the LLB in Roman-Dutch law of the University of London. Local graduates were in the same position as graduates from outside the country, required to do either Articles or the Advocates' qualifying examination. In 1977 the Department of Law at the University offered a one-year course leading to a degree entitled LLB which was recognised as an alternative qualification for admission as an advocate. Earlier, in 1972, the London LLB had been replaced by an entirely local law degree – the Bachelor of Law, abbreviated as the BL. The curriculum for the BL followed exactly the subjects offered for the London LLB, with students consuming the rather heavier diet of five courses in each of the three years, and examinations at the end of each year. The examinations were moderated and supervised by a single external examiner. Until 1982 this examiner had always been from a Faculty in the United Kingdom. Since then the external examiner has been from Kenya (Professor Okoth'Ogendo), Mozambique (Professor Albie Sachs), and Dar es Salaam (Professor Joe Kanyiwanyi).

Legal education at the 'non-racial' University College of Rhodesia

Admission to the University College of Rhodesia was formally open to all races. Until 1980, however, the number of black law students was small and always less than the number of whites. The staff included no blacks until after independence. The formal basis of admission was performance in the A level examinations of one or another of the Examinations Boards in the United Kingdom. During the pre-independence years the Law Department, in common with other parts of the University, experienced political tensions between students (especially black students) and the authorities. A number of black students were forced to discontinue their studies during the 1970s, several of them leaving to join the National Liberation Army.

The reality of 'Non-racialism' at the University is poignantly illustrated in an editorial by the Head of the Department of Law in Volume 2 (1969) of the Rhodesian Law Journal.

In a plea to the profession and government to employ more black graduates, the editor (disarmingly describing himself as a 'disillusioned reactionary') expressed the following views:

(L)ack of flexibility and originality of mind ... is almost the only cause of failure amongst (black law students).
Africans as a class (sic) find it more difficult than non-Africans as a class to make the transition from school work to a university law course, and
(T)he tradition of forming and expressing an independent judgment seems markedly less strong among Africans than among Europeans.

The plea, not surprisingly, had little effect.

Access since 1980

Independence brought an explosion in admissions to the University, including the Law Department. In 1980, 90 students were admitted to the BL programme. The criterion for admission remained, as it does today, a minimum of points based upon A level results. When University policy demanded that larger numbers be taken in it was found that it was not necessary to go below 7 points (on a E = 1 to A = 5 scale) to fill the year. Policy in the University set academic merit, based strictly upon the A level mechanism, as the basis for admission. No special compensatory or reverse discrimination was allowed. Thus no special quota was set for women students or other groups. In fact the result of simply enlarging the intake and removing other barriers was a dramatic change in the racial ratio. Since 1980 well over 90% of the student intake has been of black Zimbabwean students. In spite of all the distortions of the colonial education system the secondary schools, government, private and mission, produced an A level output which filled the rapidly expanded capacity of the single national University. In 1988 this output has reached a point where the number of qualified school leavers is greater than the intake of the University. The sexual bias, abolished in law but dominant in the social practice of a still transforming society is discernible in the intake of Law, but the percentage of women has in general risen since 1980 and stands at 25% for the class of 1988.

Class and colour were generally identical in the colonial period. There emerged, during the 1970s, a growing black middle class, though it was still physically 'lumped-in' with the black working class and peasantry by the Rhodesian system. This situation has altered quite dramatically since 1980, and a significant black bourgeoisie now exists, especially in the main cities of Zimbabwe. One educational dimension of this, combined with a determined government policy to spread and egalitarianise public education, has been a significant rise in the number of places available in private schools in Zimbabwe. The private schools appear to be as popular with the new elite as they are with wealthier whites who have always considered education to be the critical guarantee of success, if not supremacy. There is, as yet, no overall survey available of the working of the admission policy of the University in the context of the evolving class structures in Zimbabwe. Governmental support for students is generous and open to more or less all candidates admitted. In addition, the reality of the extended family makes such research more complex. An uncle, or an elder brother or sister with a decent job has as clear an obligation to finance a younger relative's education as a parent in other societies. On the face of it a high proportion of law students are still from homes where the father is a worker or peasant farmer. The point may soon be reached where the proportion of students from a bourgeois background will be disproportionate to the population. At present no policy to deal with such a situation has been evolved, but given the breadth of secondary education available and the motivation of pupils it may be reasonable to hope that high academic entry qualifications will not result in a flood of admissions from petty bourgeois backgrounds. The case of white students, essentially from such backgrounds, gives some credence to this assumption. It is worth noting that part of the dramatic change since 1980 in ratio of students admitted, in terms of race, may be attributed to the fact that many white Zimbabweans study in South African Universities. The Zimbabwean government has been generous with the foreign currency allowances needed for such study, provided the student could show there was no place available for her at the local University. The fact is that admission to South African Law Schools is based upon the five years' secondary schooling, South African Matric examination, rather than the six-year A level qualification. Thus, several white students who are not qualified for admission to the Law School and whose parents could afford it, have followed this avenue for their legal education.

Current admission practice

In 1988 the newly established Faculty of Law replaced the former Department of Law in the Faculty of Commerce and Law. The intake of students for the current session is between 87 and 90 students. This is a predetermined number based upon the library space, staffing and practical workshop space available. The places offered will have gone to students whose first choice of subject was law, and who achieved a minimum of 9 points at A level. Some, about 10%, are mature entry students. They are largely from public service (Police and Zimbabwe National Army in particular), supported by their Ministry, and have passed a Mature Entry examination set by the University. It is a matter of policy that the Faculty offers a quota of places to mature students. The record of such students in law is good, and their contribution to the quality of the student body is positive. In addition the Faculty seeks, as a matter of policy, to offer about 5% of its places to students who are refugees from South Africa and Namibia. The admission of non-Zimbabweans is governed by a clear governmental policy which emphasises the primacy of places for local nationals, and requires authority for the admission of any foreign student. In practice the foreign students admitted are those supported by the relevant Liberation Movements of South Africa or Namibia.

This year (1988) the Faculty introduces a new four year degree – the LLB (Hons). Thus until the end of 1989 there will be three undergraduate programmes running in the Faculty: the BL the LLB (Hons) and the one-year LLB professional qualification. The last of these will be phased out as the final step for qualification for registration as a legal practitioner, but a final date for this has yet to be determined.

Access to professional training

Admissions to the LLB professional course in 1988 is expected to be about 70 students. This is largely determined by the BL graduating class, which has a right to admission (59 in 1988), and the space and staff available for a programme involving 10 taught courses and a compulsory and assessed participation in a Legal Aid Clinic. As will be seen below, this degree is the normal means for young Zimbabweans to enter the profession. For two years after independence the programme remained very small and racially unrepresentative. For some reason it was categorised by the University as a postgraduate programme. Under Ministry of Education regulations financial support for a postgraduate degree requires a minimum 2(i) first degree, and a specific application for a government scholarship. The result of this was that between 1980 and 1983 many black BL graduates did not proceed to the LLB. When it was pointed out to the Ministry of Education that the LLB was an essential qualification for a BL graduate to become a practising lawyer, it was immediately agreed that all BL graduates be given support as of right. One result of the 'oversight' in 1981 and 1982 is that the graduates of those three years, together with those who failed and have to repeat the programme, and graduates of other Law Schools who wish to obtain the professional qualification, must still seek places on the LLB degree course.

Failure rates

The failure rate on the BL programme since 1983 has been about 3% overall. Given the increasingly high level of entry qualification this is expected to remain low or be reduced. Students must pass all subjects to be able to proceed to the following year. The same policy will apply to the new LLB (Hons) degree. Students who have failed have in most cases been allowed to repeat the year, reducing the actual casualty rate to virtually nil. The same has not been true of the LLB programme, which has suffered from the fact that it was introduced with too little thought and advance planning. An overall failure rate, after supplementary examinations, of about 8% has beset it since its extension in 1981. A particular feature has been a particularly high rate of failure in the Book-keeping and Accounts course. To deal with this, the policy was adopted that a student would be entitled to repeat this particular examination as often as necessary until she passed it. More comprehensive failures may require the student to repeat the programme or the examinations only, or to re-apply after a two-year period for re-admission. This last option can be difficult since there is a finite limit on places, and pressure since 1983 has been intense. To deal with this it has been the policy to give preference to students who have not previously attempted the degree, and as regards those who are repeating, to prefer those who are in government service. The LLB has also been the means for students seeking lateral mobility to qualify for practice in Zimbabwe. For those who have no practical experience elsewhere but a foreign degree, it is the only means of qualifying for registration. Given the fact that non-citizens are not entitled to be registered and the fact that few Zimbabweans now study for undergraduate law degrees abroad, except in South Africa, there have been very few, if any, such students in the past three years.

The need for part-time and extra-mural legal education

One problem which needs to be mentioned is the widespread demand in Zimbabwe for part-time and extra-mural study for a law degree. At one stage in the late 1970s students were admitted to an extra-mural course provided by the Department of Law. Candidates were mainly legal civil servants wishing to obtain the BL degree. Tuition consisted of recordings of lecturers' live lectures, taped tutorials and marking of students' essays by the full-time faculty at the Department. A high percentage of failures occurred, and the teaching was not seen as an effective use of time by the academics. The programme was stopped at independence. Had it been continued it would have been overwhelmed by would-be students. At present a good number of Zimbabweans undertake legal studies extra-murally with UNISA in Pretoria (despite a requirement for Afrikaans as a subject) or with the University of London. One problem they face is foreign currency which is needed to pay for these courses and is short in Zimbabwe. Some of those demanding a local extra-mural programme are the prosecutors, magistrates and presiding officers who went through the special courses in the early 1980s and who now face severe obstacles to promotion without a degree. The University has given consideration to the idea of an extra-mural degree, but has made no recommendations. The view of the Faculty of Law is that this is an urgent national need, which should be met. It is determined, however, that proper facilities in terms of library and tuition must be provided and that this should not be a 'second-hand' course provided by tired tutors after hours.

The only para-legal system in Zimbabwe at present is the very limited experiment being conducted in Harare and Bulawayo by the Zimbabwe Legal Resources Foundation. No consideration has yet been given to providing any further training for such persons outside of the present experiment.

The curriculum

Law in context

Since 1982 there has been a policy in the University to teach law in a critical perspective, and in the economic and social context of Zimbabwean realities. This contrasts sharply with the explicitly commercial and black-letter approach before that time, well represented by the fact that law was taught in the Faculty of Commerce and Law. The isolation of Rhodesia from world developments and the strongly anti-intellectual traditions of the colonial era have combined to give this new approach the appearance, in the eyes of many in the profession and graduates of the earlier era, that what is being taught is politics rather than law. This tension, seems to have been common in jurisdictions where 'law in context' has been introduced during the past twenty years. However, it has been further emphasised in Zimbabwe by the coexistence and juxtapositioning of a governing party which describes itself as Marxist Leninist, a policy of Reconciliation, and an economic structure dominated by foreign capital and controlled largely by the same community which held sway under the Rhodesian Front. The legal system, with important changes in the area of family law and certain constitutional rights, is a perfect microcosm of the contradictions, and remains largely unamended. This is particularly true in the field of economic law. The University is committed to making itself the University *of* Zimbabwe rather than the University merely *in* Zimbabwe. Transformation has been a major theme since 1980.

In these circumstances the Faculty faces a considerable challenge. Does it teach the law as it is, or does it approach the law and its teaching in a way which looks forward? Since 1982, it has chosen the latter course. The process, however, has had built-in problems, particularly the qualifications and perspectives of the existing teachers. In 1982 expatriate lecturers were still necessary, and a majority of the teachers were not only white but many were inherited from the colonial past. Thus a thorough-going curriculum change was not possible. Those who could, and would, taught their subjects in an economic and social context. A few adopted an explicitly Marxist approach. But until 1988, the subjects in the curriculum remained in broad terms, the same as they had been in 1980. The essential prerequisites to fundamental development were staff development and careful recruitment. By 1987 the balance of academics had been changed and a strategic element of the staff consisted of post-independence Zimbabwean graduates who had gone on to complete a minimum of post-graduate studies up to Masters level. A variety of resources had been used, including an invaluable and imaginative contribution from the University of Oslo's Faculty of Laws. With this new manpower base it is now possible for the Faculty to move, as it is doing, to a new degree structure and further curriculum development.

LLB (Hons) degree

The objective of this new degree is to produce a better and more useful law graduate in Zimbabwe. The degree is described as 'integrated' to contrast with the former dichotomy between the 'academic' (substantive) BL and the 'practical' (procedural) LLB. The Faculty was convinced that in a developing country such as ours we could not afford to have allegedly trained lawyers who knew nothing of how the law can be made 'to work'. It was also the view that a knowledge of the substantive law would be improved by an awareness of the remedies within the system. Apart from these considerations there was a real need to change the very unsatisfactory structure within which the Faculty has had to teach procedural law – namely the old LLB.

Unplanned skills training

It is appropriate at this point to further explain the origin and nature of this old LLB degree. It was originally introduced to replace the Advocates admission examinations. In 1981, the Legal Practitioners Act abolished the distinction between Advocates and Attorneys and created a single profession, all to be called Legal Practitioners. One result (largely unplanned for and in no sense – of either staffing or resources – provided for) was that the Department of Law was expected to provide – at the drop of a hat – a single and comprehensive training system for this new professional. This would be done by grafting any additional training needed for the formation of the skills of the attorney, notary and conveyancer onto the courses designed for the advocate. The advocates' simple book-keeping needs would be supplemented by training for the more critical skills needed by the Legal Practitioner to maintain Trust Accounts. All this was done at a few months' notice. A heavily over-burdened course was to be taken, in an effective eight months by the BL graduate, and this would (subject to one year of 'supervised' practice after registration) produce a practitioner as skilled as a graduate who had spent two years in Articles in an attorney's office. The remarkable fact is that in many cases this objective was achieved. Indeed between 1982 and 1987 a significant group of black lawyers from working-class or peasant backgrounds and with an exposure to critical legal education, have entered the profession, both public and private. But it was at a price in terms of dissatisfaction and frustration for the LLB students and teachers, as well as a distorted conception of the law and its different dimensions.

Thus in 1983 the Department began seriously to seek a new structure for its teaching and a new curriculum. In the same context it pressed for the establishment of a separate Faculty of Law within which to achieve its purpose. The outcome, in 1988, is a new Faculty, with three Departments – Private, Procedural and Public Law – and a Legal Aid Clinic under the Faculty. In addition the new LLB (Hons), was introduced.

There are some indications of change in the programme: the integration of substantive with procedural subjects, the concentration in the fourth year upon clinical work on the one hand and a considerable dissertation on the other, new subjects such as Women's Law and the (still being negotiated) plan for attaching students during their second and third long vacations, to work situations of first, public and then, private law. But the success, or otherwise, of the new degree will only be clear as graduates emerge into the real world. Will they be the better lawyers they are planned to be? Will they be prepared as lawyers to press for the changes their critical education has exposed them to? Or will their values be adjusted from concern for non-discrimination, service to the underprivileged, defence of national resources and the fundamental need for structural change, to concern for their first Mercedes Benz as the hallmark of their being a real lawyer? Whatever they become, the Faculty is determined to show that critical law graduates can also be credible and efficient lawyers. At the end of the day that is one important method of ensuring their access to the profession, and thus the access of the population to persons trained to be good, concerned lawyers.

Access to the legal profession

As outlined above access to the profession is currently regulated by the 1981 Legal Practitioners Act. The interim period has expired and no special access to the profession is now available. Access involves two stages: registration and independent practice, in partnership or on her own account. To qualify for registration as a Legal Practitioner the applicant must show that she is a citizen of Zimbabwe and has one or other of the following:

 (i) the BL and the LLB degree of the University of Zimbabwe (or its predecessors);
 (ii) a foreign law degree from a designated country, *plus* either the LLB of the University of Zimbabwe or passes in (or exemption from) the Zimbabwe Local Examinations set and marked by the Board of Examiners established under the regulations;
 (iii) the BL or a foreign law degree *plus* admission in a designated foreign country *plus* passes or exemptions in the Zimbabwe Local Examinations;
 (iv) the equivalent of a foreign law degree, *plus* entitlement to admission in a designated foreign country, but for lack of residence and/or the lack of a pass in a language other than English, *plus* passes or exemptions in the

Zimbabwe Local Examinations. (This is designed for and is generally used by Zimbabweans who have graduated in South Africa);

(v) admission as a lawyer in a designated foreign country *plus* either the University of Zimbabwe LLB or passes or exemptions in the Zimbabwe Local Examinations;

(vi) has been a Judge, Attorney General or Senior Counsel in Zimbabwe or a designated country.

Following registration, the Legal Practitioner must spend twelve months under 'practical training'. The recognised forms of such practical training are:

(i) employment as a legal clerk or assistant by a legal practitioner of at least two years' standing in Zimbabwe who has been approved by the Minister after consultation with the Board of Examiners and the President of the Law Society;

(ii) employment as a public prosecutor or law officer in the Attorney General's office or in the Ministry of Justice, Legal and Parliamentary Affairs;

(iii) employment involving responsibility for the examination of Deeds in the Deeds Registry Office in Zimbabwe;

(iv) employment in such other legal occupation as is, in the opinion of the Board of Examiners, equivalent to any of the three categories above.

Open access to the profession under the Legal Practitioners Act 1981

Thus, the current reality of access to the profession in Zimbabwe is that every Zimbabwean who is qualified to enter the Faculty of Law and who graduates first with the BL and then the LLB degree, is able to become a legal practitioner with relative ease. The major breach in the wall of exclusivity, preserved so carefully by the private profession before 1980, has been the right of all graduates of the Law School to register as legal practitioners. During the 1970s one of the techniques employed to keep the number of black students down to a minimum, was to advise them (not incorrectly) that the prospects of employment in private practice were virtually nil. Today the majority of graduates find posts in government which enable them to complete the year of practical training and then, if they wish, to become independent practitioners. In fact most of the post-independence graduates who have gone into private practice have entered existing firms. Those who have then 'gone it alone' have been through the mill of private practice, rather than launch themselves from an exclusively public law base. Despite this fact, the overwhelming feeling among the new generation of black Zimbabwean lawyers is that they cherish and wish to preserve the 'open door' to the profession which Cde Simbi Mubako (the first Minister of Justice and Constitutional Affairs of Zimbabwe) created with the Legal Practitioners Act 1981. At present the daughters and sons of peasants and workers who can achieve the necessary A level results will gain admission, with full governmental financial support, to the Faculty of Law Degree. Provided there is a government post for them when they graduate (and to date there always has been) their access to the profession is only a matter of time, and a reasonable one year at that.

Legal services – an urban privilege

The number of practitioners in private practice in Zimbabwe is still very small and very urban based. Figures given in Annexure B to the McNally Report show that as at 10 March, 1986 there were a total of 261 private practitioners in the country, to be found in 65 separate firms. More than two-thirds of these were partners and only 86 qualified assistants. Of the 261 lawyers 210 were centered in the two main cities, Harare and Bulawayo, two-thirds of them being based in the capital – Harare. There are seven other towns in the country with a total of 22 lawyers practising in them. Again 14 of these are in the two large centres of Gweru and Mutare. Given the fact that the vast majority of the people of Zimbabwe live in the rural areas, it is clear that there is a severe distortion in the distribution of legal services. To date, however, no great concern or outcry exists as to this state of affairs. The only attempt at an outreach or even an essaying of needs among those who are neither geographically nor financially within reach of existing services, is the experimental para-legal project undertaken by the Legal Resources Foundation. Legal Aid is extremely limited and restricted again to the urban centres, the largest organised operation being the Legal Aid Clinic in the Faculty of Law in Harare. In addition a very restricted *Pro Deo* and *In forma Pauperis* service is demanded of private practice. In this sense it is clear that a great need probably exists for 'appropriate' legal services in the country. It is equally clear that as presently structured and financed, the private practitioners cannot and will not meet this need. At present there is no research or planning being actively undertaken to analyse or solve the situation. If it is accepted as a problem and is to be solved, one thing is clear, it will require many more lawyers than now exist to deal with it. Even more clearly it will require a different breed of lawyers and a much improved system of legal education to meet the need.

In this context brief mention needs to be made again of the, as yet, unimplemented recommendations of the McNally Committee on qualification for registration. These excited critical comment among many black Zimbabwean lawyers, most of whom do not yet enjoy a place in the highest financial echelons of the legal elite. On the one hand the Committee took note of the plans of the University to integrate its legal education in the new LLB (Hons) degree and to improve its 'product'. It expressed the view that 'the University should remain the primary source of public legal education in Zimbabwe.' It noted that such education was available 'to every qualified Zimbabwean, at the expense of the State'. But while it expected each sector of the profession – including private practice – to make clear its needs, so that the University education could provide for them, it concluded that the existing law, which automatically bestowed the right of registration upon the LLB graduate of the University of Zimbabwe, should be changed. In place of legislative endorsement it proposes that endorsement, and in this sense control, on an on-going basis, be placed in the hands of the Council of Legal Education, which 'in relation to private practice' would be empowered to grant exemptions from further training and examinations (and thus effectively access to the private sector of the profession) to graduates from any University. Where exemptions are denied, the graduate would need to undergo further training and testing for the Law Practice Diploma and entry into the private profession. It recommended that such training be made more easily available to those who are able to gain employment in the private sector, through a system of subsidy to the employers.[6]

Criticism of the recommendations concentrated first upon the attempt to retreat from the established 'open door' (after five years of education and training) to the profession, both public and private; on the selection of the private sector for this restriction, and upon the power to be placed in the hands of a non-governmental (though government established) Council. It is interesting to note the critics' preference for control to remain in the hands of the broader democratic and politically responsible Parliament rather than the specialist and expert hands of a Council made up of the Chief Justice, the Secretary for Justice, the President of the Law Society, the Vice-Chancellor of the University, the Attorney-General and the Secretary of the Law Society.

The debate surrounding this issue may be seen as an interesting microcosm of political and ideological developments in Zimbabwe since 1980. What is perhaps unusual is that the issues have been sharply raised in the context of access to the legal profession. This may be explained by the fact that discriminatory restriction upon entry to the legal profession, normally managed by more subtle class processes in developed capitalist societies, was crudely racial in Rhodesia. At independence in Zimbabwe this clearly had to be changed. The articulate and dominant ideology of the Liberation Movement-based government in 1980 was more than merely nationalist and anti-racist, it was explicitly democratic and proclaimed itself to be responsive to the interests of the working class and peasants. Thus, instead of an ad hoc, once and for all time opening up of the white legal professional monopoly to qualified black Zimbabwean lawyers, there was introduced an unusually structured system providing for legal education and access to the profession for all Zimbabweans, immediately and in the future. The fact that the discrimination struck directly at important members of the new elite was also, no doubt, a significant factor. By 1985 the demands for a return to 'the good old days' had reasserted themselves. The State was somewhat distanced from the democratic demands of the liberation era, and felt it needed to listen to the establishment. Yet the events of the past two years relating to legal education and access to law in Zimbabwe also show, that, even in this most unlikely corner of society, the struggle (for justice) continues.

NOTES

[1] The Committee had eight members, five including the Chairman, originating from private practice, one from the Attorney General's office, and two (including the author) from the University of Zimbabwe.

[2] Para 5.5 p 8.

[3] Para 5.6 p 9.

[4] Para 5.6 p 9.

[5] The CLE would be in the classic mould of an 'independent' body, consisting of a Board of Trustees – to decide policy – and a Board of Management to implement it. The Trustees would be: the Chief Justice, the Secretary for Justice, the President of the Law Society, the Vice-Chancellor of the University of Zimbabwe, the Attorney General and the Secretary of the Law Society. The Board of Management would consist of a chairman appointed by the Chief Justice, being a Judge or former Judge, and four others appointed by the Trustees: one nominated by the Minister of Justice, Legal and Parliamentary Affairs, one by the Law Faculty of the University of Zimbabwe and two by the Council of the Law Society of Zimbabwe (paragraph 8.1.1 to 8.1.3).

14 Legal practitioner mobility in the Commonwealth

*Campbell McLachlan**

1 Legal practitioner mobility and the Rule of Law

Of all the legal ties which bind the Commonwealth, perhaps the most significant are those of personal interchange within the community of legal practitioners. Yet this human dimension of Commonwealth legal cooperation has never received sustained examination at the pan-Commonwealth level.[1]

The burden of this paper is to examine the nature of, and reasons for, legal practitioner mobility in the Commonwealth. It is argued that the case for mobility in the Commonwealth is based on a significantly different set of fundamental premises to those informing approaches to transnational legal practice at the regional or international level. The justification for freedom of movement within the Commonwealth stems not from a concept of the transnational lawyer servicing the needs of international business and the free flow of capital, but rather, and in contrast, from the special nature of the Commonwealth as a cooperative community and from a shared basis of law and principle, which not only gives reality to the concept of a Commonwealth legal profession, but also provides, in the idea of the Rule of Law, the underpinning of a Commonwealth approach to mobility.

It is emphatically not suggested that freedom of movement is an absolute good. Rules restricting the admission of overseas lawyers exist as an extension of the same purpose which motivates domestic admission rules, namely, the maintenance of educational and ethical standards for the protection of the public. As such, admission rules are a vital function of Bar Associations and Law Societies. What is argued here is that restrictions of mobility should bear a necessary and rational connection to the objective of public protection. They must be justified as restrictions on otherwise important human rights and libertarian objectives. These rights include the right of the individual to counsel of their choice[2] and the freedom from discrimination on grounds of nationality.[3] The objective at the pan-Commonwealth level is the development of a network of regulations which are consistent with each other, thus ensuring fairness in the treatment accorded to overseas practitioners in Commonwealth countries. This objective will also support and enhance other important objectives in Commonwealth legal cooperation.

An approach based on the Rule of Law is to be distinguished from

* PhD (London); LLB (Hons) (Victoria University of Wellington, New Zealand); Diploma *cum laude* (Hague Academy of International Law); Barrister and Solicitor (New Zealand); Herbert Smith (Solicitor) London. The writer was consultant to the Legal Division of the Commonwealth Secretariat on Legal Practitioner Mobility.

approaches to transnational legal practice commonly taken at international and regional levels. The typical context taken for transnational practice is intimately linked with international commerce and the consequent development of multi-national law firms. This economic basis is reflected in the work of the European Economic Community towards free movement of lawyers within member states. While the phenomena of transnational law and legal practice are extremely significant, and have placed novel stresses on existing systems of regulation, they are largely irrelevant to the Commonwealth scene. The Commonwealth is not a trading association. The assumptions of free trade, of the free movement of goods, capital, services and persons which were part of the ideology of the Empire are now eroded beyond all recognition. Commonwealth citizenship is (almost) an empty shell. Trade, with its concomitant demand for legal services, now finds new centres and markets outside the confines of the Commonwealth circle. But this is not to underrate the continuing significance of the Commonwealth as a cooperative community. Indeed, the modern Commonwealth is in many ways unique within the international polity in its potential for cooperation, and the practical forms which such cooperation takes. Nowhere is this more meaningful than in the legal area, where a common legal heritage facilitates, indeed requires, cooperation.

Thus the ensuing sections of this paper will explore firstly the wider contours of transnational legal practice. It will then locate the existing Commonwealth approaches within this framework. Then, in Part 4, the case for and against freedom of movement will be examined and, finally, some proposed reforms, and their fate in Commonwealth fora, will be discussed.

2 Transnational legal practice

(a) The emergence of transnational law

The practice of law as a profession is peculiarly rooted within the borders of the nation state. The lawyer, whether barrister, solicitor, advocate or attorney, is admitted to, and practises as, an officer of the court. Moreover, as such, the lawyer owes a duty to the court which transcends his duty to the client, and which engages ethical, and ultimately, disciplinary, responsibilities. Moreover, most law is domestic in its origin and scope. Thus the content of the legal system in which a lawyer is trained is likely to be radically different to that encountered by a counterpart in a neighbouring jurisdiction. In this respect the lawyer as a professional is in a markedly different position to the doctor, the architect, the accountant. Much of legal practice is concerned almost solely with domestic affairs, and most lawyers have only intermittent contact with foreign or international legal issues.

However, for all that, there is an increasing development of transnational law, and of a consequent need for transnational legal practice. Transnational law is a by-product of the increasing interdependence of the world, reflected in trading patterns as much as in cooperation between states. As their clients have become more mobile, and as technology has released new possibilities in trade, exchange and communication, so too have lawyers increased their mobility, and extended their frames of reference beyond national boundaries. Much of this new work has gone undetected by the traditional regulatory framework for the simple reason that the mere provision of services to clients without the establishment of an overseas office does not engage any administrative attention. More significantly, especially in the Commonwealth/ Common Law context, the range of activities restricted to an admitted member of the local legal profession is relatively small (and shrinking all the time). Apart from the right to appear before domestic courts, only the drawing of documents of a notarial nature, such as transfers of title to land and grants of probate, are vouchsafed to admitted lawyers.[4] Although it is an offence to hold oneself out falsely as an admitted practitioner, there is no monopoly in common law countries on the giving of advice on domestic law. Thus the huge, and lucrative, areas of contractual negotiation and drafting, tax and estate planning, company law and arbitration are open to anyone, admitted or not. Only convention has left these fields largely in the hands of the local profession.

(b) The European Community experience

The subtleties and difficulties which the expansion of transnational legal practice can pose for the law are nicely reflected in the experience of the EEC.[5] The EEC, as an economic community, has, as one of its fundamental objectives, the creation within the borders of the community of a free market in services.[6] That such a free market was intended to include the legal profession is beyond question. Indeed the new legal framework of European law, created as a result of the Treaty of Rome, made legal professional mobility even more imperative than other forms of professional mobility. However, the practical obstacles in the way of this community objective proved considerable. The uncertainties and difficulties stemmed from the very nature of law and legal practice within Europe. The continent is deeply divided in its legal systems. Indeed, there is no real agreement on which people fall within a common definition of the legal profession. Moreover there are very different attitudes to reserved activities, and thus to the scope for the practice of law by foreign lawyers. In Germany, for example, advice on domestic law is reserved to the local Bar. In France, the branch offices of English solicitors' firms have been dubbed *installations sauvages*. Language, too, poses a real practical hurdle to appearing before foreign courts and drafting documents. Few of these difficulties and divergencies exist in the Commonwealth context.

The geographical and economic unity of Europe has created the opportunity for many different degrees of interpenetration by Community nationals in each other's countries. The provision of services on an occasional basis proved a relatively easy hurdle, and was facilitated by a Community Directive in 1977[7] which allowed Community lawyers to practise as foreign lawyers in other Community countries, and to appear before foreign courts, subject to certain conditions. More difficult to resolve has been the issue of establishment. It has been unclear whether this involves establishment simply as a foreign lawyer, in which case there is the problem of which Bar Association is to exercise ethical and disciplinary control, that of the home State or that of the host State. If, on the other hand, establishment involves full admission to practise as a local lawyer, the problems of equivalence of educational standards, substantive differences in domestic laws and language must be confronted. Although a number of European Court decisions have gone some way forwards clarifying the position,[8] it has proved necessary to promulgate a Council Directive to achieve freedom of establishment in this latter sense by means of recognition of educational qualifications. Despite the intensive lobbying of the Consultative Committee of the Bars and Law Societies of the European Community (CCBE)[9] the Directive[10] applies across the board to the professions. A separate directive for the legal profession has not been thought appropriate. The Directive lays down a general system for the recognition of all professional qualifications gained after at least three years study. It provides that member states may require applicants from other member states to undergo either an adaptation period or, at the option of the applicant or, in the case of the legal profession, the option of the member state an aptitude test. The express purpose of this system is to adapt professionals to local conditions and not to required extensive retraining.

These aspects of transnational legal practice have not figured large within the Commonwealth. Of course the Commonwealth is not immune from the development of transnational law. Trade and investment, arbitration and litigation involve Commonwealth countries in cross-border flows of legal services, as well as goods and capital. The Bhopal disaster in India, and subsequent efforts by American attorneys to attract the litigation to the United States are only a graphic reminder of this. But, with the exception of a handful of major trading centres, such as London and Hong Kong, large-scale interpenetration of legal practice has not proved necessary or desirable. Thus there have been few attempts at the regulation of foreign lawyers, who do not seek full admission to the local Bar. In England, where there has been an extensive development of overseas lawyers practising as such, the Law Society, the Senate of the Bar and the Home Office have developed special rules, including an undertaking not to hold oneself out as a local lawyer and to abide by ethical standards, which is a precondition of immigration.[11] The Isle of Man has recently enacted legislation controlling overseas lawyers practising on the island because of its status as a tax haven.[12] The Caribbean operates more freely as a regional grouping within the Commonwealth.[13]

Otherwise, the Commonwealth framework is based on the paradigm of an individual lawyer seeking either general admission to practise law full-time in another Commonwealth jurisdiction, or special ad hoc admission for the purpose of representing a client before the courts of another Commonwealth jurisdiction. In the next section, the maze of national rules developed to regulate this process is surveyed to display the range of possible approaches.

3 Existing Commonwealth approaches

The legislation on the admission of overseas lawyers in a Commonwealth jurisdiction, although bewilderingly diverse and obscure, displays a common concern with the two narrowly focused types of admission, characterised as general admission and special admission.[14] In all cases the applicant will be a practitioner fully qualified, admitted and able to practise in his home jurisdiction. The concern is thus with the mobility of practitioners, and not with student mobility, a related and equally important, but separate area of Commonwealth cooperation, which receives attention in other fora.[15]

(a) Threshold requirements for general admission

Three basic types of approach have been taken to the recognition of overseas qualifications for the purposes of general admission. Firstly, a 'fixed list' scheme involves nominating a catalogue of countries whose practitioners will be recognised for admission. The list is typically constructed on the basis of bilateral negotiations to ensure reciprocity and equivalence. This position prevails for admission to the solicitor's profession in England and in Scotland. It has also been adopted in, for example, many of the Australian States, Brunei, Cyprus, Malawi, Papua New Guinea, Western Samoa, Hong Kong, Gibraltar, Uganda, Tuvalu, Singapore and Sierra Leone. An examination of the jurisdictions recognised under these lists still reveals a heavy bias toward the United Kingdom professional qualifications. This may have its historical roots in the role which United Kingdom legal education formerly played (and still does to a greatly reduced extent) in training practitioners from other Commonwealth countries. The fixed list scheme can operate unfairly by drawing distinctions between overseas lawyers on the basis of the provenance of their qualifications rather than their fitness to practise. This can amount to unjustifiable discrimination. Moreover, it is increasingly difficult to keep such lists up-to-date with the growing membership of the Commonwealth and the development of new courses of legal education.

A second approach is the discretionary scheme. This leaves the assessment of all overseas practitioners in the hands of a qualifications committee. This 'system' prevails now in New Zealand[16] and in Mauritius.[17] It has also recently developed in Canada with the advent of the Joint Committee on Foreign Accreditation. That Committee is a national body appointed by the Federation of Law Societies of Canada and the Committee of Canadian Law Deans. It reviews applicants' qualifications and experience and makes recommendations on further education in Canada. The Committee has declined to state the criteria on which it makes these assessments, and does not give reasons in individual cases. Successful completion of such courses or examinations as are prescribed by the Committee leads to the grant of a certificate of qualification. Five Canadian provinces now recognise such a certificate, typically as a threshold requirement for entry as a student-at-law into a further course of study and practical training in the particular province. The certificate may be in addition to other qualification required by the province.

Discretionary schemes have the advantage that no applicant is automatically precluded from admission, but they do in practice substantially impede freedom of movement. Applicants cannot be sure in advance of their acceptability. The principle of certainty in the law is eroded. Applicants may find themselves subject to onerous further education requirements, amounting to a substantial retraining. It is difficult for qualifications committees to establish adequate criteria for the assessment of overseas legal education, and tempting to err in favour of re-training. There is no guarantee of equal treatment as between individual applicants.

A third option, and the preferred model adopted in this paper, is a general description scheme, whereby either practitioners from Common Law or Commonwealth jurisdictions are generally recognised by the host state, subject to such additional educational requirements as are necessary to enable the overseas lawyer to adapt to the special characteristics of the host legal system. A good example of such a scheme is to be found in the Caribbean.

In 1971 a number of Commonwealth Caribbean countries signed an Agreement Establishing a Council of Legal Education. This agreement was designed to establish a unified system of legal education and admission to the states party to the Agreement. It made the primary qualification for admission the Legal Education Certificate, granted by the Council of Legal Education after a period of study at the University of the West Indies and at the Council's law schools. Recognition of other qualifications was to be phased out unless agreements were specifically concluded by individual states on a reciprocal basis. In fact the legislation of a number of member states continued to recognise other qualifications and there were subsequent derogations from the unified approach. Then in 1983, a Supplemental Agreement provided a new means for practitioners from other countries to gain the Legal Education Certificate, and thus qualify to practise in member countries. If the applicant holds a degree equivalent to the University of the West Indies LLB degree and possesses either a United Kingdom professional qualification or a qualification obtained in a Common Law jurisdiction and approved by the Council, then he may obtain a Legal Education Certificate on completion of a six-month training course organised by the Council. The exact status of this new method of qualification varies according to the particular participating country. However, the outline of the scheme is clear enough: a duly qualified Common Law practitioner may practise on completion of a six-month course, designed to orientate them to Caribbean legal needs.

General Description also forms the basis for the newly revised regulations on admission to the English Bar. There the applicant must be a 'practitioner in the common law', defined as one who has been in practice for three years in a jurisdiction which is the applicant's home and where the law is substantially equivalent to the common law of England and Wales. In Zimbabwe the applicant must have obtained a law degree and have been admitted to practise in a 'designated foreign country' – a country in which the common law is Roman-Dutch or English, and English is the official language. In Zambia the applicant must be a qualified lawyer 'in a State which is or was a member of the Commonwealth and which applies as its predominant basic system of law the Common Law or a legal system founded upon the Common Law'. Other variations on this approach are to be found in The Gambia, Ghana, Kiribati, Tonga, Vanuatu, Turks and Caicos Islands, Cayman Islands, Bermuda, Tanzania, Kenya and Seychelles.

(b) Ancillary provisions

(i) Retraining

As a practical matter, it will be equally important to the overseas applicant, once having crossed the initial threshold, that the additional educational requirements are not unduly onerous. Further education imposed by the host state may be an important element in the protection of the public, but it may equally operate as an unnecessarily restrictive practice, especially if it attempts to ensure exact educational equivalence, as the Canadian scheme does. It is however important to orientate the overseas practitioner to the special characteristics of the host legal system. For this purpose, some countries simply specify elements of existing legal education courses, or require a period of pupillage or articles of clerkship. The alternative, and it is submitted preferable, approach is to develop a special adaptation course.

(ii) Citizenship

A requirement that the applicant first acquire citizenship of the host state can operate as an unjustifiable bar on overseas lawyers. In *Reyners*,[18] the European Court held that a citizenship requirement had no necessary connection with fitness to practise law and was thus an unjustifiable infringement of the applicant's rights. A similar approach was taken by the United States Court in *Griffiths*.[19] In Canada, two cases have now considered the citizenship requirements for entry to the legal profession in the light of the Canadian Charter of Rights and Freedoms, which is part of the Canadian Constitution. In the first case, *Law Society of Upper Canada v Skapinker*,[20] an American applicant failed before the Supreme Court, but his case was pleaded under the mobility rights section 6(2). It was held that this section did not apply to qualifications for a profession, nor did it extend outside free movement between the Canadian provinces. However, on 17 April 1985, section 15 of the Charter dealing with non-discrimination came into force. In *Andrews v Law Society of British Columbia*[21] an English applicant challenged successfully the citizenship requirement on appeal to the British Columbia Court of Appeal. McLachlin JA, delivering the judgment of the court, found that none of the reasons offered for the citizenship requirement, that is, the role of lawyers in government and the commitment to and knowledge of Canadian society which citizenship implies, offered convincing justification for the requirement, which was thus prejudicial discrimination.

Despite this, citizenship is still a requirement in many Commonwealth countries. Permanent residence is a useful alternative means of ensuring the necessary level of commitment by the overseas applicant to the host society. This can be done with a simple requirement of ordinary or permanent residence, or, as in The Gambia, Lesotho and Nauru, with a more specific definition including maintaining an office or chambers or residing for a certain length of time each year.

(iii) Special admission

Finally, a number of Commonwealth countries, but not all of them, make special provision in their legislation for ad hoc admission in order to conduct a particular case. Special considerations apply in this situation, which are not present in the arguments for general admission. One may consider the following factors:

– the client's right to choose their legal representative, especially where the client is not a national of the host country;
– the need in some cases for specialist legal advice which no-one in the host Bar can provide;
– the interests of justice where the case involves political elements which call for disinterested outside counsel;
– the right of legal practitioners to be free to provide their services to their clients.

Adequate safeguards for the public and a degree of local accountability can be ensured by requiring outside counsel to act on the instructions of a local solicitor or to appear with local counsel.

Research into the approaches taken in Commonwealth countries to the admission of overseas practitioners does not, then, disclose any consistency, whether between jurisdictions, or indeed in the provisions of a single jurisdiction. Often the legislation is the result of ad hoc reactions to particular problems, or was constructed in the light of historical circumstances which no longer apply. Greater recognition is often accorded to lawyers who have qualified in countries, such as the United Kingdom, where legal education has long been provided. Lawyers who have qualified in countries which are geographically much closer, but where the system of legal education is newer may find there is no recognition of their professional qualification. Thus, lawyers from one part of Africa wishing to practise in another often find it easier to requalify in England first, there being no recognition of their home qualification. Similarly, difficulties have been experienced in the Pacific, because of the limited recognition accorded to the University of Papua New Guinea LLB.

All of this is understandable under the present situation, where each country, acting alone, must attempt to assure itself of equivalence and reciprocity in relation to other Commonwealth countries. However, the inevitable discrimination and unfairness could be avoided by a coordinated Commonwealth approach. Before such an approach is proposed, however, it is first necessary to examine the arguments which may be made against mobility and those for it. This will involve a working through of the principles and objectives stated at the outset.

4 The case for and against freedom of movement

Freedom of movement is an emotional subject, on which passions are easily aroused. Judging by the volume of recent amendments to the legislation in Commonwealth countries, and the continuing frequency of amendment, the topic is one of perennial fascination (and perhaps frustration) to Law Societies and Bar Associations. Indeed, a number of societies, including those of England, Australia and Hong Kong, are currently considering reform. Nevertheless, perhaps because the subject is an emotional one, it has rarely been subjected to a balanced analysis. It is submitted that detailed research into the existing position (now provided by the author's technical survey) and an analysis of the pros and cons are pre-conditions to a balanced reform.

(a) The arguments contra

The basic reason for admission requirements generally is, of course, to protect the public by ensuring adequate educational and ethical standards. Three considerations have, however, been advanced in the past, for imposing further restrictions on overseas practitioners seeking local admission.

(i) Protection of local legal education

The development of vital and self-reliant local legal education has been a major Commonwealth achievement in the last quarter of a century. Such a development would only have been possible if local law students, who had habitually gone abroad for their legal education, were encouraged to undertake their training at home. This necessitated a restriction on the recognition of overseas qualifications. This policy was influential in the initial establishment of the Caribbean Council of Legal Education in 1971, and also influenced Mauritius in its new Law Practitioners Act 1984, which was revised to inaugurate their first law school in the University of Mauritius. However, the period of initial development is now beginning to stabilise. There are few countries in the modern Commonwealth which are still dependent on overseas legal education. Most countries have well-established systems and faculties which are not susceptible to erosion by increased mobility. The 1983 Caribbean Supplemental Agreement is, perhaps, a reflection of this. Indeed it is the newer qualifications which have the most to gain from wider recognition.

(ii) Protection of the host legal profession

An equally valid objection has been made on the basis that enhanced practitioner mobility undermines the strength of the host Bar. Local lawyers can be denied the opportunity to develop specialised skills if the most complex and lucrative work is taken by overseas lawyers. The need for a strong and independent local Bar was recently stressed by the Chief Justice of Hong Kong, Sir Denys Roberts, in laying down guidelines for the ad hoc admission of English Queen's Counsel for particular cases in the colony.[22] Strength and independence also have a human rights aspect. Thus, a 1978 amendment in Malaysia,[23] sanctioned the waiver by the Attorney General of the normal admission requirements in particular cases. This was inserted cynically by the Malaysian government to defeat a resolution of the Malaysian Bar Council, calling on its members to protest against the Emergency (Security Trials) (Amendment) Regulations 1975, issued under the Internal Security Act 1961, by boycotting all proceedings taken under the Regulations. Further, the local profession can fail to develop as the responsive servant of society if lawyers simply commute from abroad with no commitment to the host society, as is currently the case in some small southern African jurisdictions which are dominated by South African practitioners.[25] Nevertheless, these objections relate more to the way practitioner mobility is approached rather than to the idea itself.

(iii) The interests of the host society

While the Commonwealth shares a common legal heritage, it is important to take account of the divergences between legal systems. These are not confined to the level of detail. Major differences of approach occur where legal systems take account of indigenous customary laws or religious laws or where they draw upon legal traditions quite distinct from the Common Law. Weisbrot, for instance, has cited the domination of the Papua New Guinea legal profession by expatriates, as a result of a liberal recognition regime, as one of the contributing factors to the failure of the development of an indigenous jurisprudence in PNG.[26] Moreover, Commonwealth courts and legislatures are continuously adapting the law to local needs. These developments have the important consequence that a qualification in the knowledge of the law of one jurisdiction does not necessarily equip the lawyer with sufficient knowledge in the law of other Commonwealth jurisdictions. Cultural diversity is also an important factor: language, religion, different social environments, all these place new demands on the overseas lawyer. Although the picture of Commonwealth law is still overwhelmingly one of unity these factors do need to be recognised, and suggest the inclusion, in any rational scheme for practitioner mobility, of a specially designed adaptation course, which would introduce overseas lawyers, within a short time frame, to the special features of the host country's legal system. This is the approach newly adopted in the Caribbean, and in Europe.

(b) The arguments pro

It is not suggested that freedom of movement in the Commonwealth legal profession is an absolute good. Nor is it suggested that there should be absolute freedom of movement. A rational Commonwealth system of practitioner mobility must strike a balance between the significant policies outlined above for restriction, and the principles now advanced for greater freedom of movement. These principles share a common concern with the enhancement of the Rule of Law within the Commonwealth.

(i) The right to choose counsel

Increasingly lawyers, along with other professional groups, are having their rules and practices examined to ensure that the client receives the best possible service. This policy may be seen at work in the many reports of national Monopolies and Restrictive Trade Practices Commissions in Commonwealth countries, which have touched on advertising restrictions, fee scales, the conveyancing monopoly, the 'two counsel' rule, and many other restrictions typically found in the legal profession.[27] Conditions of entry to the profession have also come under the spotlight. At an international level, the OECD (Organisation for Economic Cooperation and Development) has issued a Report on Competition Policy and the Professions,[28] in which it recommends, inter alia, that member governments reconsider provisions for the entry of foreign nationals to ensure that they are really in the best interests of the public. While this principle can be interpreted as an aspect of the economic policies of the free market and increased competition, and this is very much the context of the EEC debate, it also serves important Rule of Law functions. The legal profession does not exist solely for its own enrichment, nor, indeed, simply to advise its clients. It also exercises a public duty in the administration of justice. To this end, it is necessary that society as a whole is provided with the widest possible choice of counsel. This principle enjoys particular cogency in relation to representation before the courts, although it is not limited to that arena. Representation by outside counsel may on occasion be required in the interests of fairness to the party, who may, for instance, be a foreign national himself. Further, in human rights cases or those challenging governmental action, outside counsel may be able to provide valuable support to the local Bar. The right to choose does not, of course, involve sweeping away all restrictions on practice. What it does involve is a presumption of freedom: that restrictions on freedom should only exist for the benefit of the public, and not for the benefit of the local profession. They should not operate to the detriment of the public.

(ii) The principle of non-discrimination

Enhancement of the client's freedom is complemented by enhancement of the lawyer's freedom. As discussed above, a number of key appellate decisions have now established that the principle of non-discrimination applies to requirements of nationality imposed for the admission of lawyers. However the principle has a wider application than just citizenship, it involves a further aspect of the presumption of freedom: that restrictions on admission should have a necessary and rational connection with the applicant's fitness to practise law, and not operate unfairly or unduly restrictively.

(iii) Development of a common legal heritage

Despite many domestic divergences, and the existence of some distinct legal traditions, the Commonwealth shares a common legal heritage. Shared rules and values are to be found in every aspect of Commonwealth legal systems from the content of the basic law, to Constitutions, judicial decisions (even shared courts), identical statutes, exchanged law reform proposals and, most importantly here, a common understanding of the role and functions of the legal profession. Commonwealth lawyers tend to take these features for granted, but comparison with the European scene shows the unique advantages which the Commonwealth possesses. If the Commonwealth is a reality in any field, it is in the law. This has three consequences for practitioner mobility. First, there is reality in the claim of a transferable professional skill, because the content of the law taught and practised in Commonwealth countries is very similar. Second, there is a single 'Commonwealth legal profession', because the forms and patterns of practice are substantially similar. Third, enhanced mobility would foster the exchange of ideas, which is the life-blood of the development of a common legal heritage. This would in turn enhance the Rule of Law, by enhancing the awareness of and development of the law.

(iv) Development of Commonwealth legal cooperation

The Commonwealth does operate in a unique way as a cooperative community on legal matters.[29] This involves many technical matters of both civil and criminal law, such as the recognition and enforcement of judgments, service of process and taking of evidence, administration of estates, and extradition. At the 1986 Meeting of Law Ministers in Harare, two further Commonwealth schemes for legal cooperation were adopted relating to mutual assistance in criminal matters and the transfer of convicted offenders.[30] These new instruments lead the world in cooperation to combat crime, and are likely to receive widespread enactment in Commonwealth countries. This process of closer legal cooperation is continuing, and can only lead to the need for greater practitioner mobility. For instance, paragraph 16(3) of the Scheme relating to Mutual Assistance in Criminal Matters, provides, in relation to the examination of witnesses, that:

The request may ask that, so far as the law of the requested country permits, the accused person or his legal representative may attend the examination of the witness and ask questions of the witness.

When drafting the Scheme, Senior Law Officials noted the utility of having the accused's own legal representative present during the examination of witnesses in other Commonwealth countries.[31]

5 A balanced reform

Consideration of the inequities inherent in the present 'system' of practitioner mobility within the Commonwealth, and of the Rule of Law objectives which a more rational approach would further, led to a proposal that practitioner mobility itself become the subject of Commonwealth cooperation. Thus far, this paper has attempted to demonstrate that the Commonwealth has both a unique basis for such cooperation, and a unique imperative to do so. The proposal, which was submitted in 1986 for consideration by Law Ministers and by the Commonwealth Lawyers' Association was essentially just a refinement of the best features of existing systems, balancing the conflicting policies and principles in the light of a presumption of freedom.

In outline, the scheme proposed involved a basis of the general recognition of Commonwealth legal professional qualifications coupled with an orientation course, of no more than six months' duration, in the host state to introduce the overseas lawyer to the distinctive aspects of the host legal system. Citizenship requirements were to be abolished, although a permanent residence undertaking could be stipulated. Special ad hoc admission was to receive separate recognition in all Commonwealth countries.

Law Ministers were invited to consider the following issues:

(i) whether there is value in approaching legal practitioner mobility on the basis of pan-Commonwealth discussion and cooperation;

(ii) whether the advantages to Commonwealth societies and the principles of freedom of movement justify a reconsideration of existing legislation on the admission of overseas practitioners, especially in the light of the changing nature of legal education in the Commonwealth and of the need to develop tangible links to give effect to the common legal heritage of the Commonwealth;

(iii) whether any discussions on the review of existing provisions should proceed on the basis of the underlying unity of the Commonwealth legal profession and a presumption of common legal educational standards;

(iv) whether, in cases of general admission, the connection with the host country should take the form of a residence commitment to the host society without unduly discriminating against the overseas applicant on grounds of nationality;

(v) whether further education requirements should be designed for the special purpose of orientating the overseas applicant to the particular characteristics of the host legal system, without amounting to an onerous period of retraining;

(vi) whether the interests of fairness require more widespread provision in the Commonwealth for the special admission of overseas practitioners in order to conduct particular cases.

In their Communiqué, they included the following passage on legal education and practitioner mobility:

> Ministers recorded their appreciation for the report on legal practitioner mobility within the Commonwealth presented to the Meeting, and expressed the view that the movement of Commonwealth lawyers between jurisdictions played a useful role in enhancing the flow of professional experience between the countries concerned. They also invited the Commonwealth Secretary-General to explore ways and means of promoting cooperation among the Commonwealth countries in respect of admission of students of other Commonwealth countries in their respective Law Schools, on reasonable terms, and also the mobility of advocates within the Commonwealth.

At the professional level, the Law Ministers discussion paper formed the basis for a meeting to discuss reform of the Overseas Solicitors (Admission) Orders and the Colonial Solicitors Act 1900 held by the Law Societies of England and Wales, Scotland and Northern Ireland. It was also discussed, though not very constructively or fruitfully, at the Eighth Commonwealth Law Conference, Ocho Rios, Jamaica, September 1986. As to that meeting, one recalls the prophetic words of Thomas Colchester, former Secretary of the Commonwealth Legal Education Association:[32]

> Interrecognition of qualifications and degrees has been up before Commonwealth Education Conferences without getting far and, within my knowledge, before Commonwealth conferences of doctors and architects. Everyone approves the idea (like religion and marriage), India and Sri Lanka with enthusiasm, but some governments stalk round the difficulties with some suspicion. Canadians bring up inter-provincial troubles. All this you must know better than us from EEC experiences.

Professor Harvey reported the Jamaica meeting in the Solicitors' Journal:[33]

> Particularly interesting, too, was the discussion under the aegis of the Commonwealth Lawyers Association of solicitors' advertising, and the problems of the lack of mobility between Commonwealth states, which was treated to a clear and detailed survey by Campbell McLachlan. The rather negative view of many of those present, including the open admission in some quarters that restriction of mobility was a justifiable restrictive practice, was rather depressing. Nevertheless many interesting points were raised.

Mobility within Europe is now becoming a reality. Law Ministers have given a mandate to the Commonwealth Secretary-General to explore ways and means of promoting cooperation among Commonwealth countries in respect of the mobility of lawyers. Commonwealth legal cooperation is growing apace, but this area, where there is a cogent case for reform in concert, where so many domestic bodies are striving to do alone what could more effectively be done together, has not so far seen the implementation of a cooperative effort. Let us hope that the modern Commonwealth can turn the tide on practitioner mobility in its furtherance of the Rule of Law.

NOTES

1 The research for this paper was conducted for the Commonwealth Secretariat and the Commonwealth Lawyers' Association, and published as: McLachlan, CA *Admission of Commonwealth Lawyers: A Technical Survey for Commonwealth Law Ministers and the Commonwealth Lawyers' Association* (London, 1985). A discussion paper 'Legal Practitioner Mobility in the Commonwealth' was prepared for the Meeting of Commonwealth Law Ministers, Zimbabwe, 26 July–1 August

1986, and is published in the collected conference papers. Additionally (April 1986) Volume 2 number 1 *The Commonwealth Lawyer* was devoted to Freedom of Movement in the Commonwealth Legal Profession. For comparative approaches see: Spedding, LS *Transnational Legal Practice in the EEC and United States* (Transnational Publishers, 1987) and Campbell, D *Transnational Legal Practice: A Survey of Selected Countries* (Kluwer, Deventer, 1982). The writer is grateful to Dr Spedding and Transnational Publishers for allowing him to refer to Dr Spedding's book before publication.

[2] International Covenant on Civil and Political Rights 1966, Article 14(3)(b) and (d).

[3] Ibid, Article 2 and the International Convention on the Elimination of all Forms of Racial Discrimination.

[4] See, for example, Solicitors Act 1974 (England and Wales), sections 20–27. The restrictions on conveyanciging have now been modified by the creation of licensed conveyancers, and proposals for conveyancing by banks and building societies, see Administration of Justice Act 1985 and Building Societies Bill 1986.

[5] See Spedding, supra n 1, and also her article 'European Perspectives' in (April 1986) 2 no 1 The Commonwealth Lawyer 8.

[6] The Treaty of Rome, Article 3(c). Article 7(1) establishes a principle of non-discrimination on the basis of nationality; Articles 52 to 58 confer a right of establishment on self-employed persons, including members of the professions, and Articles 59–66 confer a freedom to supply services.

[7] Directive 77/249 (22 March 1977).

[8] See notably *Reyners v Belgian State* [1974] ECR 631, 2 CLR 305; *Van Binsbergen v Bestuur van de Bediijfsveieniging voor de Metaalvijverheid* [1974] ECR 299, [1975] 1 CMLR 298; *Thieffrey v Paris Bar Council* [1977] ECR 765, 2 CMLR 373; *Patrick v Minister of Cultural Affairs* [1977] ECR 1199, 2 CMLR 523; *L'Ordre des Avocats au Barreau de Paris v Ono Klopp* [1985] 1 CMLR 99.

[9] The CCBE drafts have included Zurich 10/80 (1980) and Athens 5/82 (1982), as well as a 1986 draft.

[10] Council Directive of 21 December 1988 on a general system for the recognition of higher education diplomas awarded on completion of professional education and training of at least three years duration.

[11] See: 'Notes for Guidance' published by the International Relations Department of the Law Society; the report by T J B Costello on England and Wales in Campbell (ed), supra n 1, 87; and Vaughan, O and Sheldon, M 'An English Viewpoint' (Program on Practising Law Abroad, ABA, London, 1984).

[12] Legal Practitioners Registration Act 1986 (Isle of Man).

[13] See Newton, V *Information Needs and Research Practices of the Commonwealth Caribbean Legal Profession* (GPO, Barbados, 1981) chapter 2.

[14] For details of national legislation referred to in this part see the author's technical survey, supra n 1.

[15] See: 'Report of the Working Party on the Problems of Commonwealth Law Students Studying Overseas' (Meeting of Commonwealth Law Teachers, Cumberland Lodge, 24–26 April 1987, Commonwealth Legal Education Association, London, 1987).

[16] Law Practitioners Act 1982. A previous reciprocal arrangement with the Australian State of Victoria recognised under the Law Practitioners (Victoria Reciprocity) Order 1937 SR 1937/242, has just been abolished: (12 March 1986) 234 *Lawtalk* 2.

[17] Law Practitioners Act 1984; for comment see Pillay, A G 'Overall Control of the Legal Profession in Mauritius' (1986) 2 no 2 The Commonwealth Lawyer 26.

[18] [1974] ECR 631, 2 CMLR 305.

[19] 413 US 717, 93 S C 2851, 37 L Ed 2d 910 (1973).

[20] (1984) 9 DLR (4d) 161.

[21] [1986] 4 WWR 242.

[22] *Re Coles* (Miscellaneous Proceedings 1984 No 2762, 18 October 1984). The guidelines are summarised in the technical survey supra n 1, 154.

[23] Legal Profession Act 1976, Part IIA, as added by Act 419/1978.

[24] See Skrine, J S H 'Malaysia' in Campbell (ed) supra n 1, 245, 249–250.

[25] See Somolekae, R 'Overall Control of the Legal Profession in Botswana' (December 1986) 2 No 2 The Commonwealth Lawyer 20.

[26] Weisbrot, D 'Papua New Guinea's Indigenous Jurisprudence and the Legacy of Colonialism' (1987) 26–7.

[27] See generally the various issues of *The Commonwealth Lawyer*, and also: McLachlan, C A 'The Legal Profession in the Marketplace' [1985] NZLJ 105.

[28] (Paris, November 1984). For comment see McLachlan, C A 'Meeting the Consumers' Demands' (April 1985) 1 no 4 The Commonwealth Lawyer 7, 9.

272 Legal practitioner mobility in the Commonwealth

[29] See Dale, W *The Modern Commonwealth* (Commonwealth Law Series, Butterworths, London, 1982); McClean, D *Recognition of Family Judgments in the Commonwealth* (Commonwealth Law Series, Butterworths, London, 1983); Patchett, K *Recognition of Commercial Judgments and Awards in the Commonwealth* (Commonwealth Law Series, Butterworths, London, 1984); Aust, A 'The Theory and Practice of Informal International Instruments' (1986) 35 ICLQ 787.

[30] Refer to the Communiqué and Minutes of the Meeting of Commonwealth Ministers.

[31] Mutual Assistance in the Administration of Justice. Meeting of Senior Officials to Consider Draft Schemes. 27 January–7 February 1986, Marlborough House, London, UK (Commonwealth Secretariat, London, 1986) 44–48.

[32] Letter to Babette Brown, International Affairs Division, The Law Society, 15 July 1982.

[33] (1986) 130 Solicitors' Journal 743.

15 Legal education as restrictive practice: a sceptical view

*Rajeev Dhavan**

I

There must be times when legal academics feel a deep cynicism about their function and role. Apart from those whose extra-curricular lives stretch to private practice or involvement in public affairs and those not quite blessed with the disquieting truth that much of their research is part of an awful game to determine their caste status in the academic hierarchy, most law teachers are aware that their otherwise ambivalent intimations of social importance are sharpened greatly because of the enormous power they possess as 'gate keepers' to select those who should cross the first threshold towards a professional career and increased upward social mobility.[1] This cynicism often infects students who view legal education less as a guide to understanding and more as a passport – more likely a visa – to the ultimate goal of joining the profession. And, as this 'gate keeper' role becomes more central – even obsessive – two questions begin to haunt at the deliberations of the legal academy. At the time of entrance to the law school, the gate keepers ask: 'What kind of candidates do *we* really want?' Once in, the entrant is taken through an ever intensifying marathon of seminars, papers, take-home assessments, compulsory attendance requirements and examinations in order to determine the answer to the second crop of questions: 'Is this student good enough to be a lawyer? What further indication of the candidate's ability can we give to the professional market? Would we be lowering our standards in allowing this candidate to proceed to become a professional?' There is a peculiar savagery that attends this process even though it is justified in the name of public responsibility and fairness. The market does not really want to know about the student. In the symbolism of degree classification, an accurate estimate of his labour power is reified into an immutable category of market classification.

Although this is hardly a reason for reposing any additional faith in them, the 'gate keepers' have done well. Unlike their counterparts of the guild system of the Middle Ages who relied solely on personal selection and commendation (a method which continues to be used for most PhD programmes), our contemporary faculty 'gate keepers' have to discipline their decision making within the ideological constraints of egalitarianism and rationalism. Expectations of equal treatment have to be satisfied by providing rational criteria for selection. Examinations and assessments – otherwise notorious for inconsistency and profoundly skewed for testing only certain abilities under stress conditions – and other selection and classificatory techniques acquire an *ex cathedra* status as objective determinative techniques. The 'gate keepers' have not just done

* Advocate, Supreme Court; Hon. Professor, Indian Law Institute, India.

their jobs but crowned their efforts with legitimacy along with respect and sympathy for their unparalleled predicament. Certain imperatives remain crucial to the management of the law school: the overriding necessity to 'thin' down the number of applicants in order to make the institution more manageable within the resources available to it, the need to portray the selection incumbent on this 'thinning' process as non-discriminatory and otherwise fair, and developing a system of signification to communicate a student's worth to the professional market. These imperatives also assert the continuing relevance of the law school to the 'real' world of law, lawyering and legal practice as well as the political economy as a whole.

As this cynical re-assessment of the law school obtrudes into our consciousness, something of the quality of education as an end-in-itself is lost, for education is itself also a complex social process enmeshed in wider considerations about structuring power relations, preserving or amending the status quo, and providing social mobility to influence the reconstitution of the mosaic of social life. If, after all this, students begin to develop canny insights into their university legal education as an inevitable but unnecessary interlude in their progress to the professional life, who can blame them for the popular adaptation of a Fitzgerald translation of a well-known Khayyam quatrain:

> Ourselves, when young, did eagerly frequent,
> Professors of Law; and heard great argument.
> About it, and about, but evermore
> Came out by the same door as in we went.

Unconsciously – and he may not readily admit it – Twining's elegant essay on the antics of the Law Faculty of mythical Xanadu[2] neatly portrays how so many of our preoccupations about questions of 'access' are a game, almost a pastime: for immediate attention because the problem of numbers is on our door step; for leisurely disputation because it is an argument without end, *unless there is a public outcry*. Neither an ideal type nor a heuristic device – but, as with many stories, an exercise in (intended and unintended) persuasive definition – the discussion in Xanadu nicely portrays some of the dilemmas of rationalist discourse about law school admissions. While it succeeds as literary exposition, it fails as heuristic device precisely because it seems culture specific; and, the attempt to broaden its lesson results in the relativistic assurance that various legal systems encounter a large variety of problems which they resolve in a variety of ways. The only identifiable points of equivalence remain what we have earlier identified as: the problem of numbers, the quest for a socially and politically acceptable method of numbers reduction and the evolution of a system of communication to authoritatively pronounce upon the exchange value of a student as an entrant to the professional market.

All this must not be used to corrode confidence in the rationalist enterprise of finding solutions to this and other difficult problems. But, even if that enterprise seeks justification in its own logic, its solutions have to be vindicated as publicly acceptable, amidst a diversity of plural expectations which subject these solutions to private pressure, public disputation and 'irrational' policy making. Equally, philosophical justifications – never quite capable of providing an indisputably right answer; but never at a loss to stake a claim to objectivity – are invariably used in public debate to service the cause of private biases and interests with an enviable elasticity. Both these social facts – the need to find public acceptability for any justificatory argument and the controversial appropriation of such arguments as vehicles to advance private interests –

stress the need to contexualise who uses what argument for what purpose? And, this cannot be done without examining the law school and, indeed, the legal profession – as part of the social and political economy. For what is at stake in the discussion is not the academic resolution of moral arguments but the distribution of opportunities – and consequential advantages – which will determine important outcomes for particular individuals and society at large for many years to come. It is hardly surprising that in order to prevent disputes about the ordering of opportunities developing into full fledged social struggles, a concerted effort is made to keep decisions about admissions to law school and entrance to the profession as uncontroversial as possible. It is no less surprising that grievances about individual admissions and the criteria used slip through into public controversy – as law cases, in the media and even as violent expression, in the form of public riots.[3]

<h1 style="text-align:center">I I</h1>

Our tentative editorial consensus describing 'access' (to legal education and the legal profession) as the central problem discussed in these essays conceals incomplete arguments about the title of this volume and what it implies.[4] The term 'access' is lifted from a now dated problem-solving literature on legal aid.[4] The phrase 'access to justice' encapsulated a major remedial programme for those who could not afford the services of the private market economy of lawyering which collectively claimed a near monopoly of authoritative legal advice giving and assistance. While various versions of the programme provided 'access' to the legal profession (by putting money in lawyers' pockets) or corrected the market by creating some new institutional solutions (like law centres), the use of the word 'access' remained a neutral value affirmation of the 'rule of law'. 'Access' was part of an expanded procedural due process. In this affirmation, the State legal system was, indeed, the repository and custodian of 'justice'. 'Access' did not ensure a favourable (or even 'just') result but only a low level entry to the lawyering market to enable further 'access' to (designated State and other) legal process to affect the determination of the problem according to (or in the shadow of) the 'rule of (State) law'. Despite insightful critique that 'access' was only a 'sop' to give legitimacy to the legal system – and, in any event, identified the wrong problem to provide misleading solutions[5] – access had a charmed political existence. Governments did not want to be seen to guarantee more than 'access'; and, that too, to the disadvantaged on the basis of carefully designed means and merits tests. Nor did they want to antagonise the legal profession with too powerful an indictment of the latter's failure to service the public at large. The system as a whole (combining State justice and private lawyering) was deemed to work after the differential disadvantages which impeded 'access' for some were ironed out. 'Access' became the central problem, the minor wrong that had to be righted.

   The term 'access' cannot be transmuted into discussions about legal education and the legal profession without, at least, some intellectual agony about its antecedent pedigree. In our present discussion, too, there is public embarrassment that the system of education and professional selection consolidates the social reproduction of class privileges. 'Access' does not attack that process (unless demonstrably discriminatory) but holds out a promise of fairness. It does not guarantee – or, even, argue for – an assault on privilege, only asserts a willingness to affirm the need for due process. It does not seek structural changes in either the legal profession or legal education to identify a much wider range of 'legally qualified' persons who can use 'law' in a diversity of social situations and struggles, but tenaciously holds on to a particular view of the profession – limited in numbers, market oriented in style and elite in its operation. Better access to educational advantages and the profession is designed to give the system a face lift without foreshadowing any radical changes – an invitation to join the 'rat race' with a gentle reassurance that fairer criteria may afford a better chance.

The identifiable contours of the discussion about 'access to legal education and the legal profession' are determined by the manner in which legal professionalism has come to be defined by lawyers. Legal professionalism is presented as necessary in the public interest, thereby justifying elaborate 'long distance' training and careful and constant monitoring to ensure the attainment of legal competence and the preservation of public standards. Much of the wide ranging literature on the legal profession has to be reconstructed around an important distinction *between* legal professionalism as a self-defined and publicly identifiable market commodity or service *and* various critiques of legal professionalism as a social process and phenomenon.[6] As suppliers of a market commodity or service, legal professionals claim to be possessed of discrete, technical knowledge, available under non-discriminatory free market conditions (for the professions are not agents of the State or a group) and rendered in a (professional) non-partisan manner within an overall commitment to justice according to the 'rule of law'.

To recognise the manner in which legal professionalism is packaged as a market commodity or service is not to accept each ingredient or, indeed, the whole image at face value; nor does it obviate the need for further critique or analysis. Disarming confessions from Scottish and American lawyers that they hardly use their armoury of 'discrete' technical knowledge as part of their work,[7] an American's gentle – to the point of being sympathetic – portrayal of lawyers in Bangalore building clientele through image building,[8] and the partisan style of big Chicago law firms present empirical reality in ways that puncture the market and public portrayal of the legal profession.[9] But the disgruence between the marketed image and empirical reality does not disturb the salience of the legal profession as a market product. It continues to be presented as an attainable product, defended as necessary in the public interest and whose importance and integrity must be protected (including, perforce, by controlling entrance to their number).

Each ingredient of the market package is important to its self-definition. Many artisans possess discrete knowledge, but they are not a profession. This is partly because the social process of designating certain groups as professionals is arbitrary. It is also related to the analytic by which a professional is defined. Professionals claim to be independent both in the availability of their service as well as the style and modality of their operation. Claiming to be bound by the 'cab rank' first-come-first-served ethic they cannot normally refuse a case. Such a refusal can only take place for either mundane reasons of pressure of work or in the highest traditions of ethical commitment to the professional canons of ethics. The insistence on free market negotiations is linked to a somewhat archaic argument against any kind of regulation, on the basis that the latter compromises the independence of their judgment by juxtaposing financial pressures. But, in addition to possessing discrete knowledge which is allegedly to be used with fearless independence, the final claim to professional status rests on the overriding commitment to serve the ideals of justice according to law. The humble artisan cannot claim as much – freedom to negotiate any fee in defence of, and to preserve, the objectivity of his independent judgment or quite the same sense of divinity because of his unswerving professional adherence to the 'true' principles of righteous plumbing!

Legal professionalism achieves its distinguished purposes by what have been described as the four components of legal ideology: reification (through which 'law' re-defines and re-constitutes society), reverence (for the law, its votaries and what they do), righteousness (in being demonstrably fair) and rectitude (in acting according to predictable standards).[10] Yet, if these are the techniques through which legal professionalism is consecrated and preserved, it draws strength and social support from the need for class cohesiveness and because legal professionalism is a crucially important motif of governance in capitalist societies.

Let us examine both these elements further. In contradistinction to patron-client or master-servant relationships, capitalism unleashed new contractarian relations as ideal types for transactional arrangements. If the logic of these ideal types was followed through to its unintended conclusion, the result would have been a gift to chaos. Capitalism would have over-reached itself. Modern professionalism was a complex and imaginative response. As an intermediate non-governmental technique of governance, professionalism, with its claims to autonomy, universalism, independence of judgments and decision making and pursuit of the public interest, was a powerful instrument of social control. Permeating various aspects of civil and political society, professionalism helped to build and sustain systemic, ideological and decisional controls while formally distanced from any identifiable influence. While mavericks had to be tolerated, any indeterminacy inherent in its work was reduced by interstitial constraints structured into formal and informal understandings of professional discipline as well as the manner in which it had to be practised. Control through professionalism was comprehensive but indirect, cohesive but individuated into individual transactions, potentially highly interventionist in every sphere of life but more likely to be acceptable because of its claim to independence of judgment in the pursuit of the public interest. It was a slightly risky endeavour but one with far-reaching possibilities.

A crucial ingredient of control was maintaining class domination of the profession by ensuring a relatively homogenous social composition within the profession. This was, and remains, easier under conditions of controlled economic expansion and under circumstances when the egalitarian demands for equality of opportunity are suppressed or subdued. At the crucial early stages when modern professionalism came into being, entrance to the legal and other professions was not an expectation within the horizons of most people. Most professions hedged in the social reproduction of class by making social contacts and economic staying power as prerequisites for fulfilling professional career prospects. Social interlopers were co-opted by being made to operate within the modalities of a particular social and 'professional' style; or marginalised if perceived as a threat. Within large parts of the common law world, membership to the higher judiciary is still carefully modulated in this way. The kinds of causes of action, the emphasis on property law and commercial transactions and the economics of professional fee charging ensured a dominant middle-class use of professional services in civil matters whilst an aggressive criminal law, with an expansion of public order and other offences, imposed a savage control on the lower orders. In all this, none of the majesty of the law was lost, being given an extra layer of protection by a law of contempt of court which was dispensed on principles of strict liability.

It is a moot question as to whether those who possess real civil, economic and political power in society have allowed the professions to become autonomous repositories of power.[11] A recent study of the general practice of lawyers reminds us that the professional style of operation – as, indeed, I am sure intuitions about their social position, power and role as intermediaries – constrains lawyers who conduct themselves less as independent decision makers and more as translators who re-cast and conceptualise the claims of their clients.[12] It is important to bear this in mind in order to interpret the relative freedom from antagonism between the profession and other powerful interests in society.

However, if modern professionalism was a subtle method of governance, it was also fraught with alternative possibilities, many of which loomed over the horizon in different jurisdictional locations at different times. Spurred on by a more insistent egalitarian ideology, the pressure of numbers could – and did – expand and diversify the profession in ways that threatened its class cohesiveness, with further consequential effects on its style and modality of operation. New organisational forms of lawyering (including large megalaw firms) developed threateningly, institutionalising and stabilising precisely the kind of autonomous independent professional power which other powerful forces in society feared and, had hitherto, kept in relative abeyance. Conversely, powerful clients demanded a much closer relationship between themselves and their legal advisers, sustained the employment of in-house legal staff and forged stable preferential relationships with some lawyers and their firms. Similar developments took place within government. New forms of salaried lawyering were suggested for the disadvantaged, as salaried lawyers, albeit with higher turnover rates, identified emotionally with, and worked professionally in, law centres and social action groups. Alongside a de-mystification of law, exposure of aspects of law enforcement and investigative theory and research about lawyers and law practice did much to present 'law' as an expression of politics (no less immune from the corrupting influence and untidy vagaries of social and political life as any other activity) and lawyering as a business rather than a profession. These new images hardened as fratricidal competition within the profession has also accelerated further changes.

But, while the profession has allowed – and, was hardly in a position to prevent – deviations from the strict professional model, the latter has been retained as the marketed prototype with a continuing hold on the style and imagination of new entrants and the public. Recent studies of radical lawyering in the United Kingdom and of race discrimination lawyers show the extent to which the ideology of professionalism has imprisoned the professional mind and prevented the creation of newly devised forms of radical lawyering. At the same time, the professional model serves as a near total justification for the need for control of numbers and curricula. The emphasis of technical expertise was used to justify long periods of education and training and prevented, in varying degrees, multiple entry to the profession, except as a concession made under social and political pressure. The profession has also built hierarchical structures into their profession and entrenched forms of market-sharing on the basis of seniority, merit and specialisation. These are justified in the public interest on the basis that they are inspired by the allocative need for a rational division of labour. Above all, the professional model profoundly influences the educational curricula and the practice of law by emphasising the black letter law tradition which accords centrality to rules and court decisions and reifies legal reasoning. While the power struggle over defining the epistemological foundations of law continues, the profession model continues to hold sway influencing, in varying degrees, the perceptions of both lawyers and their public.

The 'professional' model – of which legal professionalism is a part – is historically specific to a particular epoch of development. An intriguing blend, combining ideological components with social class formation, it haunts contemporary society with a tenacity of purpose after obtaining a subtle appropriation of consensus for itself. Selective in its conferment of status – for example, intellectuals were too dangerous to be regarded as professionals and various groups like engineers and scientists denied designation to that status – it allowed a certain flexibility while taking the precaution of controlling too indeterminate a use. An American commentator on the English legal profession is surely right in detecting fundamental transformations which are just beginning.[13] In some countries, it is difficult to speak of the legal profession as anything more than a racket. More generally, fundamental structural changes are taking place in the manner in which the lawyers organise their work. New patterns of lawyer-client relationships are being developed, as part of the profession sees itself as a business concerned with obtaining measurable results. The staccato separation of law from politics and other instruments of social control is endorsed with much greater circumspection than before. Finally, the very notion of professionalism is being analysed as enmeshed in the political economy and not an independent variable outside it.

Despite all this, too much is at stake to permit an initiative to unwrap important motifs of governance (including 'law' and 'professionalism') so that – to borrow an analogy from the fairy tale about the Emperor's new clothes – the public may know how scantily dressed many of these instruments of control really are. 'Professionalism' remains important to governance. Too widely cast to be simply conspiracy, it profoundly influences the control of numbers and social composition of the legal profession, what, how and within what kind of schedule new entrants will be taught and how the subject matter of law and practice will be mythologised. It also prevents the growth of innovative legal education and lawyering. Yet 'professionalism' as an ideal is under considerable scrutiny both from within the profession and as a part of public critique.

By formulating our central problem as 'access to legal education and the legal profession', we may well have diverted public attention to resolving important but *limited*, matters of more immediate concern (about resolving the crisis of numbers, meeting the demand for a more diverse composition of the profession and responding to pressures to affect a more equitable share of the spoils of the market) in the light of strongly expressed egalitarian campaigns for equal opportunity.

I I I

The shadow of the numbers game hangs over the 'access' debate. This is not to suggest that there would be no 'access' questions if there were no problems of making a smaller selection from a large number. Amongst others, we would still be concerned with questions of competence. There are overriding arguments for not inflicting incompetent surgeons, doctors – or, for that matter, artisans, plumbers or motor mechanics – on an unsuspecting public even though there are obviously limits to the extent to which a free society can verify credentials and abilities in a cost effective and not unduly oppressive way. Our survey discloses jurisdictions where, at certain crucial junctures, there were few lawyers in the territory and an overall insufficiency of numbers was predicted with alarm. Reg Austin's moving account of how modern Zimbabwe[14] grappled with precisely such a problem, in the aftermath of a self-professed racist regime, exemplifies the range and complexity of questions that contend for attention. Too lenient a criterion would enable white professionals from South Africa and elsewhere to virtually capture and control the profession. The exclusion of whites would constitute a public act of direct discrimination subverting the very principle of racial justice on which the struggle for Zimbabwe was founded. Too strict criteria would result in incremental increases insufficient to meet anticipated need. Even after accepting citizenship as a prerequisite, there was an inevitable initial dependence on foreign law schools. But such a dependence created a caste system in favour of graduates from foreign law schools; and, simultaneous demands for both the abolition and retention of that route of entry. Developing an indigenous capacity to impart legal education and training had cost implications. In any event, predictions of the optimal number of entrants were themselves the product of a mixture of policy considerations about need and the social composition of the profession as well as privately held views by lawyers that expansion will affect the level of fees and the market distribution of work. Selina Goulbourne's study of Jamaica[15] portrays how these seemingly transitional problems continue for longer periods than would be normally anticipated. Desmond Greer's account[16] of the institutional re-location of control of professional legal education to a single Belfast-based institution contains important lessons about the tenacity with which the professional interest is protected; and, in our immediate context, how hopelessly misplaced well-planned calculations about numbers can be. Needless to say, the computation did not just misread the market demand but also sought to set unrealistic optimal limits. There is no dearth of stories about the struggle to find appropriate solutions to the problem of numbers.

The determination of numbers is influenced greatly by considerations of *demand, resources* and *need.* Each one of these is problematic. We can start at either end: begin with demand (in most cases assumed to be high), estimate educational training and professional resources (including excess capacity in the market at realistic fee levels) and either assume need (on the basis that lawyers, even if not necessarily a good thing, are, nevertheless, needed) or seek to predict it to and suggest an allocative distribution of manpower (including the manner in which it can be ordered or induced in particular directions). Alternatively, we could begin with need and work backwards to tailor demand. In *liberal versions* of this approach, there is a premium on the freedom to join the profession and to do what one likes after one has succeeded in doing so. In such circumstances, the major argument is over enabling resources (a matter of public finance) for training (assumed to be necessary) and over cautionary estimates of the possibility of a glut of professionals in the market. The converse approach of working backwards from need, to finding resources and filtering demand is overtly regulatory in nature, purporting to be a *planned developmental approach* to manpower needs. The choice of approach – often dictated by that jurisdiction's existential situation – is also a political choice of how one views individual choice, and the extent to which such choice and the market must be regulated or totally subordinated to developmental needs. Alongside, there are *pragmatic* mixtures of these *approaches*, not necessarily predicated on salutary quests for a sensible aristotelian mean but produced by untidy social and political policy compromises. These are, after all, not theoretical discussions about academically identified alternatives, but policies which will consequently affect a range of potentially expectant and vested interests and mould patterns of social mobility in any society for a long time to come.[17]

Need

Common to the public discussion and implementation of each approach is a discussion about needs, demands and resources. The concept of *need* is particularly tricky. It was especially important to an earlier 'access' debate about the provision of legal aid. An acute participant observer of that debate in England warned against formulating public policy on the basis of open-ended and malleable notions like 'need'[18] which could be made to arrive at diverse results derived at after taking into account a multiplicity of factors.

Where exactly would we begin if we try to identify the need for legal services as an exercise in manpower planning to determine numbers for 'access to legal education and the legal profession'? It would not take too long to enter into the well-trodden thicket of controversies exploring what legal services are available, the range and variety of service delivery and the overall social and other objectives of the programme. For convenience, we could begin with a demographic starting point to look at estimates of the number of lawyers per (say) 1,000 members of the population. Attempts to calculate lawyer/ population ratios within particular national jurisdictions have been made and compared with similar computations in others.[19] The results are often embarrassing, but obscure many important questions about what lawyers do and who uses them for what purpose? Do all persons have uniform needs for lawyers? Does the existence of a high ratio guarantee access? Are we concerned about geographic distribution? Do more lawyers stimulate more cases? Do lawyers kill other modes of dispute settlement? Many of these questions remain even after demographic ratios have been supplemented by considerations of geographic distribution and access. And, these questions become even more hugely complex when we link lawyer distribution with identifiable community needs, especially when such communities are identified by reference to ethnicity, religion, national and sub-national affiliation or caste.

Another method would be to try and gauge the litigational needs of the population. This could be done by looking at the docket of courts, longitudinally stretching over a period of time. Faced with an increasing docket expansion over many years, we might detect some curious results. Toharia's interesting study of litigation over a long period of time in Spain[20] showed a docket increase in the courts *but a relatively stable litigation pattern when averaged out against demographic increases*. This interesting research programme was replicated for various jurisdictions with similarly interesting results, portraying greater detail as to how the content of the docket changed from (often) one decennial epoch to the next.[21] All this, without even looking at the political economy, or the number and kinds of laws, lawyers and courts. While it is not necessary to restate theoretical objections to this longitudinal approach,[22] it is necessary to reject the hypothesis that the market determinant of the number of lawyers is satisfactory because the litigation rate remains constant in relation to demographic size. In truth, the literature points out that lawyering activity (as distinct from court centered litigational filing) increases in such societies. Toharia's Spain showed an increase in notarial activity. Lawyers appear to be busy in a huge number of ways as law increasingly imbricates each aspect of our lives; and, lest we think of lawyers as just waiting for cases to come to them, they encourage and discourage litigation to suit their convenience.[23] Their ability to create more work when it is in abundance is encapsulated in the marvellous metaphor of 'making rain while the sun shines'.

Looking at the size and variety of the docket may provide some limited insights into the manpower needs of the population required for litigational purposes. But, even such insights may be unsafe in as much as the decision to litigate is not the 'free choice' of lawyers or their clients but structured by the political economy. Litigation may be suppressed in some cultures and flower in others.[24] However, the need for legal services is not limited to litigation. A painstakingly devised project suggests that even in America which is 'alleged' to be going through a litigation explosion, a large number of people do not either convert their grievances into claims (designated as 'lumping') or, having made a representation or claim to the other side, convert claims into disputes (inelegantly, but expressively, called 'clumping'.)[25] Implicit in this argument is the policy suggestion that more rather than less support is needed in order that people might vindicate their rights or defend themselves against atrocities. Common sense insights derived from such research serve as a contrapuntal intuition to suggestions that there is a docket explosion, reminding us that many people simply suffer silently rather than use the law to claim even their legal entitlement. This is borne out by a number of studies in various parts of the world.[26]

All this complicates our efforts to quantify 'need' as part of the larger problem of estimating the number of lawyers needed in any society. If the estimate of 'need' requires us to go into far-reaching, but relevant, questions about the kind of support required to help people to sustain and ventilate legitimate grievances, a much more comprehensive exploration has to be undertaken about the kind of legal information and para-legal support needed by various persons, groups and communities for particular kinds of issues. Consideration also has to be given to various forms of service delivery for particular kinds of advice and assistance. And, as we proceed, we identify a greater multiplicity of educational tasks ranging from the education of the public to various other forms of training and support for lay people, informed activists, social workers and specialists. This is precisely the result of a recent comprehensive look at why the ethnic minorities in Britain do not use the anti-discrimination provisions of the Race Relations Act which was, ostensibly, designed for their use.[27]

There must be other ways of estimating need – as for example, quantitative surveys of what people think they need.[28] These are riddled with problems; and remain incomplete substitutes for any thorough democratic way of determining what people want. But is public demand the only determinant of public policy?

Finally, we cannot wholly foreclose the mischievous question as to whether we need lawyers and legal professionals at all. The social utility of lawyers has been the subject of innumerable vituperative and humorous comments. Shakespeare's injunction that we should kill all the lawyers is outmatched by Bentham's colourful diatribe against the profession – nicely recounted in Twining's essay earlier in this volume.[29] An eminent Indian historian is alleged to have commented that 'Mughal justice in India had one silver lining; it had no lawyers.' India's contemporary Ministry of External Affairs placed its own value on legal studies when it issued a circular that foreign exchange would not be available for students who wished to study tailoring and law.[30] While it would be interesting to look at the social implications of jokes about lawyers,[31] for our present purposes we are more directly concerned with the important question of the delegalisation of various aspects of the social and political economy. This is one additional variable in our examination of the kind of public need for particular kinds of lawyers and legal functionaries.

Any estimate of the number of lawyers and legal functionaries 'needed' in any jurisdiction cannot evade the responsibility of making important ideological choices about how and to what extent such an exercise should be undertaken. But these choices do not just emanate from ideological preferences but are conditioned by awkward pressures as the resultant policy tries to satisfy a range of reasonable and unreasonable demands pressed forward by powerful constituencies. Given the range of choices, it is theoretically and practically impossible to plan manpower needs with any non-controversial claim to accuracy. An honest effort to make 'need' the central consideration in evolving a public policy about 'numbers' must, perforce, be political; and even then – except in the most exceptional circumstances – the real dilemmas revolve around working out points of emphasis in discrete areas rather than pretending authoritatively to circumnavigate the universe of need. It may still be necessary to project some kind of predictable figure. But, it remains important to examine how this figure is arrived at. Numbers are not always fixed to match programmes with resources in order to enable the orderly development of tertiary, professional and other education. They are also part of concerted practices to keep the market small or fee levels high. That is hardly a reason to treat the exercise as socially fair, just or, for that matter, accurate.

Demand

How do we go about measuring demand? And to what end? An analysis of demographic patterns would give an age breakdown of the population to enable predictions of possible numbers of those ready for primary, secondary, tertiary or professional education.[32] Slightly more difficult is measuring numbers of late entrants who for some reason (including economic necessity, marriage and child rearing, disadvantage resulting in inability to reach competitive levels, etc) join the educational and training system outside normal predictable age levels. But, once this basic demographic information is available, political and ideological choices have to be made about demand. At the very outset, a decision in favour of universal educational opportunities at all levels is an ideological decision, pragmatically constrained by a great number of factors. These factors, too, do not just relate to overall resource constraints but more elaborate considerations of preserving the status quo, the pressure of resistant vested interests, supporting arguments for and against universalism and the nature of the existing system. And, even if the brave decision for universal opportunities at all levels is taken, selection for variants within categories is inevitable unless a decision for total uniformity is unequivocally taken and rigorously enforced. Even then, the possibility of creating an equality of opportunity and results remains largely theoretical. The facts would continue to belie egalitarian objectives. There are never enough resources. The political will to create enabling resources for universalistic educational programmes is enfeebled greatly by contrary demands to appropriate any emerging status quo to benefit some in preference to others.

More accurate pictures of the pressure for places for specific educational and training programmes and institutions can, and are, constructed out of the records of the actual choices made in any particular instance. These can be reinforced by showing trends showing the application success ratio. The higher the ratio, the greater the boast of the market-worthiness of the institution or programme. But, quite apart from status or 'public' standing on market evaluation, a closer look at the application might enable further information about the class, gender, ethnicity, religious, social and other background of the applicants; and, the relative failure and success rates in each category. Studied over a few years, important insights would be gained about the social composition of various educational institutions and professions.

Most manpower planning proceeds from looking at existing demand levels as displayed by actual trends. This is understandable. The head of an institution is perfectly entitled to argue that his predictions for Year II must, inevitably, be based on application success ratio in Year I, where success is the number of allotted places. From this would flow important decisional analyses for the future. Estimates could be made on whether expansion would be market led, the extent of public subsidy required and the places that should be allocated to particular classes of people as part of planned development. But, before we get bowled over by our seemingly successful attempt to put educational and professional manpower planning on a 'scientific' basis, the market demand figures need to be subjected to social analysis. Our various studies affirm patterns of class, gender and, where relevant, ethnic reproduction. Certain categories of persons are more likely to achieve successful levels of admission and attainment. This pattern may not just exist for particular educational programmes but prevail as dominant characteristics across the whole system or identifiably important parts of it.

More deeply delved into, the same information which shows the market trends may, and in all cases does, reveal continuing social patterns of entrenched advantage and disadvantage. To place faith in the market as a useful social barometer to plan numbers and to ignore the injustice of these entrenched patterns is intrinsically unjust, placing a premium on achieving just formal equality without looking at the social conditions under which patterns of unequal choices are constructed and sustained. Any contemporary reading of market trends which ignores these social dimensions invites hostile attack both for ideological reasons and because powerful constituencies in most societies fight strongly for equality of educational and professional opportunity. This is amply demonstrated in continuing demands made by blacks in America, untouchables in India, ethnic minorities in England, religious minorities and feminist lobbyists throughout the world. How are these demands to be accommodated? As an act of faith? Or, as pragmatic strategic exercises to quell disquiet?

In the mythical Xanadu with which this volume begins, centrality continues to be given to the market; but with the addition of some kind of corrective policy. Policies of positive action are devised so that candidates may reach the appropriate levels of market competition. The centrality of the market remains. The public policy objectives become more limited in their objective: to prepare disadvantaged groups to achieve the prescribed levels of market attainment. It is useful to note that the theory of positive action follows the market demand approach in emphasising the importance of attainment levels operated to sustain market selection at existing application success ratio levels. However, special programmes are devised in order to assist the disadvantaged to achieve market devised standards. Meanwhile, the market policy of assuming equality amongst unequals remains. Characterised in this way, the policy of market corrective positive action seems more like a sell out than a radical quest for social justice.

True levels of demand are difficult to determine. But, market demand is too skewed to represent these levels unless the precedential conditions of high social mobility can be assumed to exist. Creating such precedential conditions involves tackling entrenched disadvantage to achieve greater justice between generations.

Minority communities have always been a little sceptical about majoritarian plans for the uplift of those who are oppressed, discriminated against and disadvantaged. Going well beyond marginal solutions of providing marginal self-betterment plans provided by positive action schemes and 'access' courses, such communities have staked a claim to the right to set up their own educational and research institutions. Powerful examples of this can be found in the growth of religious schools in England and America. Muslim academies set up in the nineteenth century in India profoundly influenced the intellectual transformation of that community. But these institutional solutions are not just sought by minority communities but also by majority communities to remedy the effects of a disadvantaged past or to strengthen their social hold on a society. New programmes by the pro-Malay regime in Malayasia can be interpreted as such an initiative. Occasionally – as in the instance of Protestant and Catholic secondary schools in India – initiatives taken by a religious minority are appropriated by the middle class generally (including those from other faiths). Such institutions, though denominational in nature, acquire strength as the backbone through which the middle class sustain their power, influence and control of opportunities.

The advent of minority educational institutions has a profound influence on educational opportunities. Feared for perpetrating insular influences, where such institutions maintain high qualitative standards, they are also welcomed partly for the public finance reason that they assist and uplift in the national endeavour of providing good education and because they sustain patterns of class domination. They acquire an additional layer of protection because they arouse the sympathy due to a David in a game of Goliaths! At the same time, attempts to interfere with such institutions is widely protested against (in appropriate cases) as oppressing minorities. The predicament arising out of this mixed response to such educational institutions creates important dilemmas of public policy and constitutional jurisprudence. Where such institutions are religious institutions, providing funding for such institutions may have to satisfy 'separation of Church from State' doctrines in secular constitutions. Even in fundamentalist constitutions, the public policy issue of favouring the institutional solutions of some communities and discriminating against others can become an important issue of contention. Public funding for denominational schools became an important concern of American constitutional law;[33] and, remains a thicket of controversy in India. The Indian Constitution goes one step further in providing protection not just to religious but also other minorities 'whether based on religion and language ... (who) shall have the right to establish and administer educational institutions of their choice'.[34] Such institutions shall not be restricted to teaching just members of that minority, shall have the right to State funds as long as there is no compulsory religious education and cannot be discriminated against by the State in the dispensation of grants because the management of the institution is in the hands of members of a minority. If the establishment of minority institutions represents a significant triumph of threatened and disadvantaged peoples to find their own solutions to their historical predicament, they are also a weapon in the hands of the advantaged to consolidate continuing opportunities for themselves. Subject to class capture and often providing opportunities for the least disadvantaged within communities and the privileged of other communities, such institutions provoke a mixture of responses. Defended as an act of faith, they are often criticised for their elitism. To the extent to which they appeal to particular communities, they are seen as fulfilling aspects of the 'separate but equal' doctrine which took many years to dislodge in the United States.[35] The cultural separatism inherent in such institutions is resisted as inimical to a rational scientific secularism. While not ignoring the possibility of such institutional solutions being submerged in sectarianism or taken over by elitism, they remain more than relevant as community responses in societies where wide differentials exist and the quest for self-betterment is better located within one's own community rather than the patronage of business and government.[35] The danger of elite hi-jack or the dilution of egalitarian communitarian perspectives remains more than a theoretical possibility. The poor rely on support and resources from elsewhere. This is not always granted without some concession or compromise. Most governments resist the development of wholly autonomous educational institutions and seek to impose controls on them. To begin with, there is a default power to take over the administration of an institution in the event of mismanagement. To this are added powers of inspection. A range of controls are imposed in order to ensure uniformity of standards – not just to satisfy State imposed regulatory standards but because the job market supports the institution and verification of these standards as necessary both to discourage access as well as to make comparable assessments of candidates. The market casts its shadow on the whole process. Communitarian institutional solutions cannot evade regulatory control. But, they remain potentially interesting alternatives.

We have argued that certain limited notions of market demand are important for institutions to assess the pressure of places; but remain insufficient to gauge 'just' demand levels based on wider theories of social desert. Some corrective schemes give centrality to market demand while providing some opportunities for self-improvement. Other schemes fall prey to a mixture of market and State regulation, elite take-over, sectarian influence and other pressures. Eventually, the problem is not just one of individual equity amongst relatively equal competitors. It involves an investigation into the structure of inequality, including the long-term inter-generational social effect of unequal opportunities to education and professional mobility.

Resources

Resources in this context encompass all those financial or material resources which enable or disable equality of opportunity to education, training and professional mobility. This covers a wide ambit to include the resources that enable an individual to have a greater flexibility of educational and professional choice, the resources available through the charity market and in the private sector and the allocative possibilities within the public sector. At the *individual* level, we need not just dwell on the social advantages of wealth but on their effect on the capacity to enter into particular kinds of educational institutions and law school and, perforce, legal chambers. This is not just influenced by family background but the availability of public assistance, the possibility of easy loan finance facilities and the structure of the curricula whereby part-time courses allow a candidate to work in a gas station by day and law school at night! Many of these factors turn on decisions of public finance such as tax deduction for supporting children at certain levels of education or the availability of easy credit. They also depend on social attitudes which might earmark certain avenues as more socially acceptable than others. Equally, *social solutions* of providing scholarships, access schemes, educational and training institutions, traineeship or professional opportunities for new entrants are enmeshed in complex revenue decisions. In some societies, it is relatively easier to raise credit based on charity funds. India's charity laws, for example, are limited in scope. Accordingly, the possibility of creating new institutions outside State control are also limited. The Indian Law Institute, Banaras Law School and Delhi Law Schools owe a great deal of their development to support from a foreign foundation.[36] The end of that support has caused a relapse back into government control. The initiative of creating a new National Law School has been riddled with financial difficulties.[37] The shortage of law schools in Malaysia causes large numbers of principally minority community members to seek professional training abroad after considerable sacrifices are made by their parents and others.[38] No doubt the lack of charity funds arises not just because of the revenue laws of these countries but also because millionaires flounder to hide their black market economy money; and are, in any event, reluctant to invest in institutions whose future is made fragile by the ever increasing possibility of governmental interference and appropriation. *Public solutions* compete greatly for scarce resources.

Apart from tax concessions for charity efforts (which entail loss to the public exchequer), in our context, funds have to be distributed to provide enabling resources for individuals, institutions, schemes and programmes. In some African, South East Asian and West Indian countries, funds have been limited to create one or two professional law schools, thereby narrowing domestic opportunity while allowing the opportunity of getting recognised foreign qualifications to a privileged few. On the other hand, the Nigerian oil boom expanded legal education, drawing teaching talent transnationally from various quarters. The availability of public finance is not just limited by the biased intransigence of our rulers but other insistent problems which juxtapose, in some instances, the right to food against the right to middle-class professional opportunity. This only intensifies the scramble for professional opportunity; and – as Oliver Fulton points out – with a ceiling on an accommodating expansion as a remedy,[39] the threshold of solutions revolves around the tests used for selection and schemes and programmes to help certain classes of persons to overcome disadvantage.

Our examination of the numbers game is not to find solutions but to puncture the pretensions to infallibility with which numbers are presented in public discussions. It is easy to present demand as a mathematical sum based on the pressure of places or need as a variable of some measurable aspect of advice giving or litigation. Equally, the problems of access – as we have chosen to call them – are not just faced by individuals; but, are uncomfortably entrenched in the social structure as part of a collective predicament of some persons and groups. Justified on the basis of the scarcity of resources, the numbers game enables the creation of a system of control which often bears no relationship to the declared purposes for which they are allegedly created. These control systems need further justification and a thorough public critique in order to determine the extent to which they fulfil the egalitarian objectives of equal opportunity within an overall conspectus of social justice.

I V

At times, this essay seems to overstate the scepticism that the apparatuses to control 'access' to legal education and the profession are an end in themselves, of limited value as purposeful educational exercises and bearing a suspect relationship to the professional ends they seek to fulfil. This scepticism draws considerable strength from an almost universal fund of folk lore about successful lawyers and judges who were self-professedly bad, even lousy, students. Used to cast doubt on the usefulness of specific curricula as well as the enterprise of professional education as a whole, such stories are reinforced by further stories about those who acquired legal expertise without the benefit of legal education. Undoubtedly, these stories can be offset with hard data showing a positive correlation between educational performance and success; but, this does not destroy the value of these stories. In one sense, one example (if not in itself, complicated by exceptional circumstances) may be an example too many. If one person can achieve such success, so can others. And, if the highly selective, pointedly purposeful programme is not truly indispensable, what other factors (other than the purely idiosyncratic) contribute to success? And, if the measure of success is suspect, how is it to be measured? Before we get drawn into untidy explanations of these stories – too numerous to ignore – it might be useful to delve into the distinctness of legal knowledge; and whether our pedagogic endeavours lay the foundations of such knowledge.

Modern law is a direct expression of and is defined by politics. Part of a middle-class struggle for power, 'law' was appropriated to be redefined as authoritative rules declared or recognised by certain processes, with a self-sustaining claim to validity and social legitimacy, distinct and distinguishable from other instruments of control and enforced through special designated personnel, processes and institutions. Distinct from morality, modern law was clearly the product of political processes and not prior to them, even though the hermeneutic tradition through which law interpreted was anterior to law; and, was, in some instances, included and consecrated in the law itself. Developed in particular settings and supported by powerful constituencies, the hermeneutic tradition added ideological substance to the law. But, to elevate that tradition to an *ex cathedra* status is to obscure the political foundations of modern law and misunderstand the nature of the struggle over the meaning of law and the context in which it takes place. Consistent with the political definition of law, modern law can be characterised in the following ways:

(1) Law is distinct and autonomous.
(2) Law consists of rules authoritatively declared by particular institutions as well as practice.
(3) The practice is assimilated in concepts and doctrine.
(4) The practice seeks to adapt law to changing circumstances without sacrificing doctrinal consistency, where possible.

(5) A failure in the process of dynamic adaptiveness through practice can be corrected by declaring new rules, which would be doctrinally absorbed in the law.[40]

This statement conveys many important political messages about the distinctness of law, its source in political authority and the overriding primacy of authoritatively declared rules while acknowledging the capacity of the legal system to apply and adapt the rules through internal dynamic processes.

Legal education in the common law world reifies the form in which modern law is expressed. With its political origins eclipsed from view, the study of law becomes the study of rules and doctrine. These are to be found in statutes, judicial decisions and text books. And, so *sub silentio*, a form of presentation is elevated to the status of a science. No doubt law seeks to present the world in a different light – categorising and portraying social relationships in ways different from, but profoundly influencing, ordinary discourse, using particular theories of causation to explain conduct, truth and phenomena and adopting deductive and analogical forms of reasoning which seek, willy nilly, to be faithful to the political framework to which law owes its origins and within which it must operate. No less important for being so, it remains a style of discourse and not a form of knowledge. It is not a science but an art, a complex – often seemingly mystical – way of putting things across, with, at least, a formal claim to consistency. That the discourse must be learnt and decoded is unexceptional. But, is such an enterprise really a formal inquiry into the foundations of a new form of knowledge? Is the purpose of legal educational institutions to discipline the student to undertake such an inquiry? If so, do they attempt such a task? And, having attempted it, succeed? Or, is it just an exercise in learning, another political phenomenon expressed in a particular discourse created by and for particular locations? Setting aside its claim to be a science, the sceptics argue that to know it is to learn it.

Not surprisingly, these controversies have reverberated through the legal academy. Attempts to change the curricula to teach law as a phenomenon rather than an obscure science met with the kind of stiff resistance usually meted out by fundamentalist religious leaders to disbelievers and heretics.[41] Neo-empirical attacks on the significance of legal rules and doctrine continue. Such rules are featured as purely declaratory in nature, significant as 'bargaining endowments' in the hands of those who appropriate them rather than self-fulfilling determinants of social action.[42] This process of critical evaluation continues; and goes further to deconstruct law and legal institutions – no less legal educational and professional training institutions – as social phenomena and social processes.[43] The significance of these sharp divisions in the legal academy is often marginalised by showing these struggles as personality conflicts. Politically, there is a great deal at stake if law is demystified not just to expose the hiatus between declared norm and practice but to expose its political role and function in the political economy. This is the essential difference between the less threatening law-in-context approach which preserves the centrality of rules while providing information about the political origins and social consequences of particular rules and a more thorough going political sociology which critically evaluates the nature of modern law itself.[44]

However, the political struggle over the meaning and significance of law continues profoundly to influence legal education. Thus, some constituencies attack the political theory of law, arguing that law is not just a form in which our rulers express themselves but a set of values found either in the hermeneutic tradition developed by jurists and judges or drawn from rational discourse about fairness and justice. Those involved in legal education do not just make choices between competing theories, but are party to the political struggles themselves, sometimes anonymously through their curricula and sometimes in outspoken declarations detailing their point of view.

The growth of modern legal education as a distinct organised exercise is coterminous with the development of modern law and pressures to constitute the practitioners of law into a modern profession. Initially, legal education was expected to preach the new modern law as true doctrine and prevent too dramatic a change in the numbers, social composition and operational style of the profession. In all this, it had a significant but ancillary role, in that the new doctrine was unequivocally emphasised by political institutions and as court practice, and the numbers and composition of the profession were controlled by a combination of social methods. The role of law schools as 'gate keepers' of numbers and custodians of ideology was more systematically developed as the pressures to expand the profession reached threatening proportions and the utility of legal education to professional practice was seriously questioned.

By no means original, the 'Gower model' served as a brilliant archetypical response.[45] Legal education would be designed as a cumulative *linear programme*, with one stage leading into the next. The programme was divided into an academic stage, a professional stage, a training stage and market entry. Stretching over a long period of time, the linear programme was certainly daunting for all but the most courageous student. It sought justification in a planned sequentially ordered education which would lay the foundations of knowledge (academic stage), impart knowledge of practice and procedure (professional stage), provide experiential knowledge of how the system actually worked (through trained apprenticeship); and then permit market entry (sometimes with the requirement of further training, often for certain specialised kinds of practice). In some political economies, this package was wholly accepted, sometimes with additional requirements attached. For example, some countries allowed entry into the academic stage only to those who were already graduates. Chemistry, physics, history, literature, biology were all seen as equally relevant as a pre-requisite for academic legal education. Other political economies went to great lengths to ensure that all stages were completed before entry to the profession. Thus, where there were insufficient law schools in some third world countries, academic education in law schools in first world countries was recognised as a qualification even though the 'law' taught in the latter – although part of the family of common law systems – had little to do with the legal system of the former. In some countries, the full linear package was simply not accepted. Indian law students refused to go through the professional and training stage after they had been through law courses open only to graduates. In working out whether and which parts of a disaggregated linear model were acceptable, less depended on rational discussion, much more on the political support and will of the disputants. In some jurisdictions, the profession tenaciously clung on to the requirement of professional and training stages, seeking to administer these stages itself for fear that others might botch things up. In other jurisdictions, the profession has been happy to leave the control of numbers entirely to the academics, confident that the latter would be vigilant 'gate keepers'.

All this disturbs the logic of the linear model, deviations from which occur with no apparent loss of quality. But, faith in the logic of the linear model is also undermined in other ways. Let us begin by looking at the academic stage. What exactly does one teach at this stage? There is a lack of agreement about the epistemological basis of modern law. Even within a broad acceptance of modern law as an institutionalised political expression, there is a variance of emphasis between those who concentrate on the rules and those who dissolve the rules within the hermeneutic tradition of law.

Some law schools prefer not just to concentrate on legislative enactment and court judgments but look at law as a social phenomenon and examine the conditions and circumstances under which it is appropriated and by whom. Others teach law as a specialised political discourse, paying less attention to the doctrine except to deconstruct it as a part of an alternative, but not for that reason less rigorous, social explanation. All these approaches can be deemed to be academic. If academics remain divided about what the academic stage should consist of, they are under considerable pressure from students and the professional market to teach a more professionally relevant education and take greater notice of what takes place outside the doors of the law school.[46] This is both a plea for more relevant theory as well as for more about the practice. In the course of time, the academic stages display a diversity of approaches ranging from concentrating on reified doctrine to reflecting on law as social phenomenon and professional practice. Some schools even provide training programmes as part of academic curricula whilst professional education and training cannot ignore what may be regarded as academic. These untidy encroachments between various stages cast doubt on the need for a *linear* programme which requires one stage to neatly follow its predecessor. Attacked politically and with its various stages collapsed and fused to suit market demands and insufficient resources, the linear model is less of a programme and more of a heuristic device to *identify* various universal components of a legal (or for that matter any) professional education.

The linear model is threatened greatly by a competitor multi-entry model. This enables persons with varying working and other experiences to join the profession in different ways and at different stages, without the necessity of going through all stages prescribed by the linear approach. The significance of the multi-entry model is not trivialised by presenting it as a safety valve exception to 'lower order' legal functionaries (eg clerks, legal executives and others) whose claim to join the profession rests on the longevity of their experiences in legal offices. But, in recognising that professional expertise and competence can be acquired in ways outside normal courses of legal education and training, multi-entry systems can stake a theoretical claim to a much wider proposition which suggests that the knowledge of 'law' as a professional discipline can be acquired experientially (with some formal introduction to the subject). The multi-entry model is not just a supplement but a competitor to the linear model. It also has the benefit of being potentially more egalitarian.

Based on strongly theoretical premises that the knowledge of 'law' can only be acquired by a particular method of sequentially arranged formal education, the linear model finds itself subject to considerable pressures in evolving a method of selecting candidates for law schools. Problems of selection can also arise in a multi-entry system though by its very nature such a system permits a diversity of selection criteria. In a linear system, this problem usually arises at the stage of admission to law school. It is assumed that performance indicators at law schools are sufficiently accurate and relevant for being the major formal evaluating criteria for entry to subsequent stages. Problems of selection arise largely because of the pressures of numbers seeking entry although it is arguable that selection criteria should exist even where such pressures do not exist.

Formal criteria for assessment vary but can broadly be grouped into (past) achievement, assessment and aptitude.[47] The most widely practised tests concentrate on past academic achievement supplemented by overall assessment whether through references or interview. This is not done because there is some kind of positive correlation between pre-admission performance and subsequent career development, whether at law school or later on in the profession. But even though such a positive correlation cannot be established, these tests serve an important social purpose. They seek to design *a system which aims at projecting 'fairness' between candidates without asking whether any of them necessarily shows particular skills relevant to a legal education*. The assessment in such cases is a weak version to check out the candidates' ability (not aptitude) and, in some instances, make allowances for any social disadvantage they might have suffered. Some schools prefer to use achievement tests, refusing to muddy the clarity that such tests provide by adding on assessment features which allow discretion based on intuitive estimates. Others hold on to personal assessment procedures precisely because they enable a more considered view of candidates and give rise to the possibility of admitting disadvantaged and other minority students by using their social background to explain the non-fulfilment of normal achievement standards. Principles of fairness are supplemented by intuitions of social justice.

By contrast aptitude tests make clear assumptions both about the epistemological foundations of law and the manner in which knowledge of law can be acquired as well as that aptitude for such knowledge is sufficiently developed in candidates at certain stages in their life so that it can be equitably and fairly tested.[48] In one sense, if treated as an alternative to investigations into past achievement, aptitude testing seems egalitarian in that it allows candidates with poor past records to go for an aptitude test (even if this is done with the assistance of a crammer which promises to teach conquering aptitude tests in ten easy lessons!). But, whether we examine aptitude tests on the basis of relevancy ('do they really have any bearing on legal studies?', 'do people who do well in such aptitude tests do well at law school or in the profession?') or fairness ('is it uniformally applied?', 'they can redeem students with bad achievement records') or 'social justice' ('people with disadvantaged backgrounds get a better chance'), there is a paucity of convincing research on all three counts. Meanwhile, teachers and candidates alike remain scared of aptitude tests as capable of producing unpredictable results.

So far, we seem to have reached more puzzling results. Achievement tests are used even though definite correlations cannot be established between past achievements and future progress. Aptitude tests are being strenuously marketed as supplements and alternatives to achievement tests, although it is uncertain that aptitudes for law can be tested and whether these tests do so accurately. Multi-entry systems happily co-exist with linear systems without any loss of quality or danger to the public interest, suggesting that knowledge of law can be acquired with far less formal education than is commonly admitted. Clearly, these tests exist because the pressure of numbers is supplemented by the further ideological pressure requiring any process of selection to satisfy the requirements of equal treatment and fairness. Conceding that some minimal requirements must exist, any further tests are primarily attempts at 'fairness' rather than measurements of relevant ability. But even if they satisfy tests of fairness, they fail to deal with the problem of social differentials whereby certain classes of candidates are less likely to be successful at achievement, assessment and aptitude tests. It remains necessary to travel beyond fairness tests (primarily designed to protect examiners from allegations of bias and make the selection process less controversial) to tackle the more complex and more challenging problems of social justice.

The purposes of social justice are not sufficiently served by just the strong requirement of non-discrimination in selection, although principles of indirect discrimination go a long way to prevent the application of selection requirements or conditions which identifiable classes of persons cannot comply with. But in order that adherence to principles of indirect discrimination does not prevent the application of any selection criteria at all, it is generally agreed that it is permissible to create selection criteria which bear rational relevance to the purposes of selection. However the use of such criteria may be discriminatory against identifiable classes of persons who are not able to comply with them. This brings us back to the central question as to relevancy of criteria and tests for legal education. To impose tests which would predictably exclude classes of (disadvantaged) persons should satisfy the strictest tests of relevancy[49] rather than the more flexible test that most criteria are acceptable because they cannot be declared irrelevant. This would put far greater teeth into the law of discrimination and allow a much greater number of socially disadvantaged persons to satisfy selection criteria. But, the less elaborate the test, the greater the number of those who would qualify, rendering the final selection more difficult. It is necessary to stress that if many criteria alleged to be relevant were to be tested on the basis of strict relevancy tests, they would fail by virtue of being insufficiently relevant and indirectly discriminatory. Less demanding but more strictly relevant tests would allow for greater flexibility to accommodate the claim of socially disadvantaged people to a far greater extent than is normally permissible. This would enable the introduction of positive discrimination policies as a legitimate exercise of discretion in consonance with acceptable principles of social justice, to give priority to disadvantaged persons who otherwise meet criteria which have run the gauntlet of strict relevancy tests. But it seems highly unlikely that there would be majoritarian support for a strong anti-discriminatory policy whereby selection criteria would be subjected to a strict relevancy of purpose test to enable a large number of disadvantaged to make successful applications. The introduction of such tests may not just affect the majoritarian community adversely but also subvert the aims of selection tests, presently used in many jurisdictions to cut down the potential pool of applicants to exhaust and obviate the need for discretion.

How, then, is the social justice of providing equal opportunities for persons, drawn from disadvantaged backgrounds and unable to meet contemporary criteria for admission, to be achieved? To argue the case for self-betterment schemes is, by itself, unexceptionable provided they are linked to actual admission programmes, do not take an inordinate length of time and do not carry a stigma which the candidate wears throughout, at least, his educational career. There remains the difficulty of devising criteria by which we define socially and educationally disadvantaged persons and groups. India's long constitutionally incomplete quest to define its 'other backward classes' – that is, other than those specially designated as backward as a matter of consensus policy – shows how problematic such an enterprise can be.[50] Be that as it may, in our context, the real question is whether self-betterment schemes are enough? Or, do we need more aggressive and more focussed initiatives to achieve equality? These questions are of fundamental importance because strong arguments have been voiced that the quest for equality ends with the assurance of non-discrimination and providing opportunities to help themselves. Beyond that the standards set by the market hold their sway.

The retreat from the quest for equality begins with a distinction between positive action and preferential discrimination.[51] The distinction acquired popularity in England in the aftermath of the Scarman Inquiry into race riots in 1981, even though it is embedded in many public policy statements and the laws of many countries. Living in a hostile social environment and held back by continuing disadvantage imbricated in their lives, the black ethnic minorities claimed a right to preferential treatment as part of their claim to equality. What form could this preferential treatment take? The positive action of self-betterment training and educational schemes was readily conceded.[52] But, it was argued that there should be discrimination in favour of disadvantaged beneficiaries so that they were deemed to have a preferential claim to certain advantages or privileges (in, for example, apppointments or promotion to jobs) over similarly (or better) qualified persons who were not deemed to be disadvantaged. Rejected, *in limine*, largely because it would not be acceptable to the white majority, it was also argued that preferential discrimination was, itself, unfair. Seen more as a conspiracy rather than an argument, members of the ethnic minorities felt that their future was consigned to incremental development through self-betterment schemes rather than more direct access to opportunity and social mobility. Preferential discrimination means accelerated development by more direct entry to the opportunity itself rather than a chance to better oneself to reach competitive market levels. What gives rise for concern is not the rejection of preferential discrimination on the grounds that, for electoral reasons, politicians do not have the courage to stand up to majoritarian pressures but, that policies of preferential discrimination are projected as being inimical to equality rather than seen as a fulfilment of it.

The arguments against preferential discrimination are premised on several assumptions and arguments which merit further examination. In the *first* place, an impregnable sacrosanctity is attached to market criteria which – as we have argued earlier – are often made more stringent to deal with the problem of excessive numbers rather than constitute tests which are strictly relevant for the opportunity in question. *Secondly*, when there is a discretion, it is arguable that the discretion must be exercised so as to take into account the disadvantaged background or disability of any particular candidate. The case for taking disadvantaged backgrounds into account is stronger where the candidates are more or less of comparable ability.[53] It is not necessarily weakened where it is a factor to be taken into account even where some, though not wide, differences in ability may exist. *Thirdly*, in any planned development, it is reasonable to reserve some non-competitive categories exclusive to disadvantaged groups, subject to some minimal suitability test. Since such reservations will be part of a planned development, they are in addition to the normal competition based allocation and would not exist but for the need for creating further opportunities. *Fourthly*, the acceptance of one kind of preferential entitlement (to education and training for self-betterment schemes) and rejection of another kind of preferential entitlement (as, for example, a mainstream educational opportunity or a job) must rest on an arbitrary classification of opportunities. Even if advantaged persons and groups do not need a particular scheme, there is always a competition for resource allocation including, perforce, for self-betterment schemes for those amongst the advantaged who wish to make their chances more secure and water tight. *Fifthly*, candidates once admitted to an educational or job opportunity can be assisted to improve their abilities and sustain such improvements by in-house self-betterment schemes otherwise deemed to be acceptable as positive action. *Sixthly*, we must assume that the social desert of those for whom any preferential discrimination is designed is not in question in that their predicament was affected by factors outside their control, often the product of continuing discrimination or ostracism stretching back into the past.[54] The arguments in favour of preferential discrimination are not as illogical or weak as they are made out to be. They become stronger if there is an acceptance of schemes of positive action. The distinction between positive action and preferential discrimination rests more securely on the anvil of public (and electoral) acceptability.

The quest for a socially just equality seems to have been sacrificed to majoritarian bias and fear. Too high a premium seems to have been placed on fair conditions of competition; and, too low a priority seems to have been given to curing entrenched inequalities which afflict the disadvantaged and society itself.

Finally, before we leave the subject of criteria for assessment, it is necessary to examine the variety of purposes for which legal education and training is used other than as a device in the hands of various 'gate keepers' to control numbers. Apart from the not wholly convincing argument that legal knowledge can only be obtained through particular formal methods, professional education and training are designed to enable entry into the profession and alleged to help to maintain professional standards. It should be borne in mind that those who receive legal training do not always practise law as designated professionals but perform many similar tasks as in-house lawyers and the like. Such tasks are also performed by many lay persons and para-legals whose knowledge of law is derived from short-term courses and experience. Access questions cannot just be concerned with the uni-linear development of those persons who are formally admitted to practice. They must also be concerned with the much wider range of persons engaged in using law for a multiplicity of social tasks and how they can be trained to expand their social responsibility to perform their tasks better without getting trapped in elaborate curricula not entirely relevant to *their* objectives.

V

The profession is changing rapidly both within nations as well as trans-nationally. The various arenas in which law is *systematically* used has traversed well beyond lawyers' offices, the law courts and tribunals. Each one of these arenas has developed its own legal personnel so much so that the notion of a legal profession is too narrow to encompass the much expanded categories of legal persons engaged in a multitude of similar and dissimilar uses of the law. The proliferation of legal arenas, legal activity and legal institutions in late capitalism is reflected in the distribution of legal personnel. The legal profession is under pressure to change itself in ways that question the very basis of the professional model which has dominated legal education and the profession for many decades. Professional firms have expanded in size and the focus of their activity. New institutional methods of delivering legal aid have replaced earlier atomistic transaction-based legal aid programmes. The relationships between lawyers and clients have altered to include a variety of forms, sometimes treated as a business and sometimes held together in symbiotic association. There is an increasing in-house presence of legally trained personnel. Lay persons have also acquired legal knowledge and expertise requisite for their purpose. The age of the legal profession seems to have given way to an incoming era of legal personnel.

All this is further reflected in demands for a greater transnational mobility of legal personnel. Campbell Mclachlan's paper on patterns of mobility within the Commonwealth[55] shows how a new accommodating framework is being evolved so that lawyers of one jurisdiction can practise in another. This will not just affect the movement of lawyers across nations but also 'access' shopping by candidates who will seek qualifications in schools which are qualitatively better and/or a lesser strain on resources. Such movements are not just being encouraged within cognate systems belonging to a particular family of law but – as in the case of the European Economic Community – between civil and common law based systems. The claim for a specialised legal education within a particular jurisdiction must stand considerably diluted if such movement across relatively alien legal cultures is permitted unless the claim rests on some much more fundamental argument that knowledge of 'law' (as a generic form of knowledge) is sufficient qualification for making such a movement. Arguendo, a learned *dharmasasri* learned in ancient Hindu law (or his contemporary equivalent) must possess sufficient qualifications to practise in Sweden. Mclachlan does not take us into the discussions as to why these accommodating arrangements are made and who has reaped the benefit; nor, indeed, whether empirical evidence suggests it is a good thing. Many of these movements are invited by multi-national interests. The Japanese have found it makes more business sense to take their own lawyers to America but not allow foreign lawyers in Japan.[56] Business conglomerates in England use American and Australian lawyers.[57] The international movement of legal personnel is accompanied by associational relationships amongst legal personnel across jurisdictions. All this has to be set in a wider context of forum shopping and forum creation whereby certain kinds of disputes are resolved in particular kinds of favourable forums. The Bhopal litigation is a stern reminder both of the potential for the movement of lawyers throughout the world as well as how the global economy constrains the choice of forum and restricts such a movement.[58] There is much to be learnt from these developments which affect and challenge concepts of legal education as well as portend a much wider market of movement of legal personnel. Global access is not a matter for the future but is on our door-steps; and, it is being insidiously regulated in ways that merit further examination.

V I

Somewhere along the line, this essay has expanded the scope of its inquiry greatly. The use of the term 'access' suggests a much narrower problem. 'Access' to legal education and the profession is seen as being impeded by several difficulties. Providing 'access' means identifying the stumbling blocks and, where necessary, removing them or providing candidates with the support, facilities and opportunity of overcoming them. A similar use of the term 'access' was used in an anterior public controversy about the availability of legal services. It is readily assumed that a particular style and form of legal education is indispensable to enable and sustain legal 'professionalism'. The existence of brilliant legal professionals who did not have the benefit of legal education and training and the lack of positive correlation between those who excelled at law school and those did well in their professional career should make us pause. Is there really a systematic body of law which must be learnt in a particular way in order to produce a legal professional?

Rather than look at legal professionals as possessors of some discrete objective knowledge which they impart in a (professionally) distanced way, we have argued that modern professionalism is a motif and technique of governance which has acquired credence; and in which the public have been led to repose faith because it is projected as an autonomous and independent mechanism whereby, in our context, an overtly political modern law is seen to be administered by an identifiable high status group who 'objectively' apply recognised (seemingly universal) standards with no ulterior motive other than the determination and application of these standards in the public interest. As a technique of governance, professionalism is a brilliant self-regulatory response to the needs of expanding political economy to obtain legitimacy and ensure some predictable standards. As long as professional groups retain some social cohesion, their own behaviour remains as manageable as it is crucial. As egalitarian pressures to change the social composition of the profession and upset the 'fee' market become more imminent, there is a counter pressure to mystify the foundations of legal knowledge and make courses in legal education and by way of training prerequisites for attaining the status of a lawyer. No doubt there is a great deal about the law that needs to be learnt; but the diversity of legal personnel (who may not have had the benefit of, or even the full extent of, the prescribed legal education or training) competently discharging a variety of law jobs in many national and transnational locations, suggests that prescribed educational and training schemes are both inadequate and go well over the top.

Legal education and training must be seen as a social device to discourage and restrict numbers and ensure only incremental changes in the social composition of the profession. And, even if that is not intended, it is certainly the most demonstrable effect of virtually all such educational and training schemes. Schemes of legal education and training are under a considerable pressure, not just to be fair between competing claims but to work towards more substantial objectives of social justice. Law schools and legal professional organisations have gone out of their way to demonstrate that the criteria that they have used are non-discriminatory and otherwise fair. If the disadvantaged cannot meet these criteria, they must – with or without the assistance of public support (to which they are deemed to be entitled) – evolve self-betterment schemes in order to improve their abilities to obtain success in open competition. The cause of the disadvantaged will not go further for fear of upsetting majoritarian fears although the stated reason for policy restraint is that further preferential treatment would itself be unfair and discriminatory. As the schemes to resolve the dilemmas of the numbers game become more complex, they are more likely to have a far greater adverse effect on the disadvantaged. And, if such elaborate schemes are not really indispensable for professional development, the fact that they are indirectly discriminatory against the interests of less fortunate persons is an additional reason for taking a much closer look at entrance tests, legal curricula and training programmes. It is also a reason for allowing a far wider range of mechanisms by which entry to the profession is possible. But, if the disadvantaged are to break out of their cycle of deprivation, self-betterment schemes are not enough. Indeed, if it is honestly believed that self-betterment schemes will help the disadvantaged, why is it wrong to exercise a preferential discretion in favour of candidates who are otherwise equally competent or can achieve levels of competence, given half a chance? The distinction between positive action and preferential discrimination is political and directly linked to the numbers game.

But, there are other reasons as to why elaborate schemes of legal education and training need to be reviewed. In recent years, we have seen a vast proliferation of legal personnel, not quite trained in the same way as those formally designated as legal professionals. By all accounts, such legal personnel display satisfactory, if not exemplary, levels of competence. Lawyers, too, traverse from one legal system to another without the need for extended induction courses. It is simpler to think of lawyers as legal personnel. The concept of legal professionalism clouds our understanding and persuades us to convert an educational enterprise into a concerted practice.[59]

NOTES

[1] The term 'gate keeper' for those in charge of formulating and implementing admission criteria is taken from William Twining's essay (Chapter 1) and draws from my more comprehensive term 'power filter' used in the Commonwealth Legal Education Association meeting on this subject in 1984. The use of the term should not convey the impression that each 'gate keeper' acts independently of the systemic constraints of which their own 'gate keeping' is a part.

[2] W Twining 'Access to Legal Education and the Legal Profession: A Commonwealth Perspective' supra chapter 1.

[3] Litigation concerning the universities is increasing throughout the world. In common law systems, the view that disputes within universities should be settled by the Visitor without recourse to courts, is giving way to a much more expanded use of courts. More specifically, litigation on admissions has increased. In India and America a special species of such litigation concerns the application of non-discrimination criteria and the implementation of preferential discrimination schemes.

   Recently, there were riots in Gujarat, India, over the preferential discrimination policies of the government. Earlier, in the sixties India's requirements of professional law examinations and legal training were abolished after public demonstrations (including burning of buses) in protest of their inacceptability.

[4] See generally M Cappaletti, B Garth (and J Weisner) *Access to Justice: A World Study* (Sijthoff, Alphen Aan Den Rijn, 1978–9, in four volumes).

[5] For example M Galanter 'The duty not to deliver legal services' (1976) 30 University of Miami Law Quarterly 929; D Trubek 'Book Review' (1977) Wisconsin Law Review 303.

[6] For a provocative review of the literature see R Abel *The Legal Profession in England and Wales* (Oxford, Blackwell, 1988) 3–31; ibid 'Lawyers' in L Lipson and S Wheeler (ed) *Law and the Social Sciences* (New York Russell Sage Foundation 1986) 369.

[7] Eg C Campbell 'Lawyers and their public' (1976) Juridical Review 20 at 34; J Carlin *Lawyers on Their Own: A Study of Individual Practitioners in Chicago* New Brunswick (NJ), Rutgers University Press 1962, 41. I was refreshingly redirected back to these by Abel (supra n 6) 12–13.

[8] R Kidder 'Formal Litigation and Professional Insecurity: Legal Entrepreneurship in South India' (1974) 9 Law and Society Review 11–37.

[9] For example J P Heinz and Edward O Lauman *Chicago Lawyers: The Social Structure of the Bar* (New York, Russel Sage, 1982).

[10] M Cain 'Necessarily out of touch: Thoughts on the organisation of the bar' in P Carlen (ed) *Sociology of Law* (London, Sociological Monograph 23) 223.

[11] Eg T Johnson *Professions and Power* (London 1973).

[12] M Cain 'The general practice lawyer and the client: Towards a radical conception' (1979) 7 International Journal of the Sociology of Law 331.

[13] R Abel (supra n 6) 308.

[14] R Austin 'Access to Legal Education and the Legal Profession in Zimbabwe' supra chapter 13.

[15] S Goulbourne 'Access to Legal Education and the Legal Profession in Jamaica' supra chapter 9.

[16] D Greer 'Access to Legal Education and the Legal Profession in Northern Ireland' supra chapter 10.

[17] For an interesting exercise on how numbers can be estimated see Association of University Teachers, United Kingdom: *The Real Demand For Student Places* (London, 1983).

[18] P Lewis 'Unmet legal needs' in P Morris, R White and O Lewis *Social Needs and Legal Action* (London, Martin Robertson, 1973).

[19] For a comparative survey see R Abel 'Comparative Sociology of Legal Professions: An exploratory essay' (1985) American Bar Foundation in Research Journal 1 esp Tables at 58–79; M Galanter (infra n 21) Table 3 at 52.

[20] J Toharia 'Economic development and litigation: The case of Spain' presented to the Conference on the Sociology of the Judicial Process, University of Bielefeld, West Germany, 1973.

[21] For a survey see L Friedman 'Courts over time: A survey of theories and research' in K O Boyum and L Mather: *Empirical Theories About Courts* (New York, Longman 1983) 9; and, for a political use of these theories see M Galanter 'Reading the landscape of disputes: What we know and don't know (and think we know) about our allegedly contentious and litigous society' (1983) 31 University of California Los Angeles Law Review 3.

[22] See R Dhavan *Litigation Explosion in India* (New Delhi, Indian Law Institute, 1986) chapter 1 'Understanding the Terrain of Litigation' (3–22).

[23] Toharia (supra n 20).

[24] Note, for example, the more recent view eg J Haley 'The myth of the reluctant litigant' (1978) 4 Journal of Japanese Studies 359, questioning the 'Kawashima' thesis that the Japanese are culturally non-litigious but that litigation is suppressed in Japan; for other comparisons see Galanter (supra n 21) 51–61.

[25] D Trubek et al *Civil Litigation Research Project* (Madison, Wisconsin 1983); ibid 'The costs of ordinary litigation' (1983) 13 University of California Los Angelos Law Review 72.

[26] For example, J Fitzgerald 'Grievances, disputes and outcomes: A comparison of Australia and the United States' (1983) 1 Law in Context 15; see further Galanter 'The day after the litigation explosion' (1986) 46 Maryland Law Review 3.

[27] R Dhavan *So Why Are So Few Cases? On the Uses and Non-Uses of the Race Relations Act 1976* (A two volume report submitted to the Commission for Racial Equality, London 1988).

[28] Eg B P Pashigian 'The market for lawyers: The determinants of the demand for and supply of lawyers' (1977) 20 Journal of Law and Economics 53; R Badger 'Prediction and Selection of law school admissions' (1985) 31 University of Chicago Law Record 16.

[29] Twining (supra n 2) at pp 8 and 34, nn 11 and 12.

[30] Taken from S S Dhavan 'The role of the bar and the judiciary in the modern state' in Allahabad High Court Centenary Celebrations Volumes (Allahabad High Court, Allahabad, 1968) II, 303 at 303–4.

[31] My friend Christie Davies, Professor of Sociology at the University of Reading rightly urges a systematic study of legal jokes as a means to learn more about the profession.

[32] See Association of University Teachers (supra n 17); and more generally several contributions in O Fulton (ed) Access to Higher Education (Guildford Society for Research into High Education 1981).

[33] This is a long-standing controversy which has moved to a more meaningful response in giving denominational schools right to public support subject to certain conditions; see for example, *Board of Education v Allen* (1968) 392 US 236.

[34] The right of religious and linguistic minorities to establish education institutions is enshrined in Articles 29 and 32 of the Constitution of India; for a review of some of the literature see R Dhavan 'Religious freedom in India' (1978) 35 American Journal of Comparative Law 209 at 231–41. As the Indian government seeks to assimilate more and more educational programmes within the State system, a much greater control is being exercised on these institutions. Not surprisingly, a greater number of constitutional controversies remain unresolved.

[35] One of the less discernible consequences of any community self-reliance programme is the 'separate but equal' doctrine which is regarded as constitutionally pernicious if enforced by the State as policy (see *Brown v Board of Education* (1954) 349 US 294).

[36] For aspects of American influence on Indian legal thinking and education see R Dhavan 'Borrowed Ideas: On the impact of American scholarship on Indian Law' (1985) 33 American Journal of Comparative Law 505.

[37] The National Law School is expected to operate within the climate of a new educational plan for education on which see S P Sathe 'Access to Legal Education and the Legal Profession in India' supra chapter 8 generally: and J Cottrell '10 + 2 + 5: A change in the structure of Indian education' (1986) 36 Journal of Legal Education 331–57.

[38] It is a matter of regret that we did not receive a report on the Malaysian Bar. Discussion of some aspects of legal education in Malaysia may be found in S Yoong 'The Bar in Malayasia' (Undergraduate Dissertation, Brunel, the University of West London, 1988).

[39] See further O Fulton 'Access to Higher Education: A Review of Alternative Policies' supra chapter 2.

[40] Adapted from R Dhavan 'Judging the Judges' in R Dhavan et al (ed) *Judges and the Judicial Power* (Bombay, N M Tripathi, 1985) 5 at 13.

[41] The disputes were more forceful and pointed than they are made out to be. Cf W Twining *Karl Llewellyn and the Realist Movement* (London, Weidenfeld and Nicolson, 1973).

[42] The phrase 'bargaining endowment' is taken from Mnookin and Kornhauser 'Bargaining in the shadow of the law: The case of divorce' (1979) 88 Yale Law Journal 950. There are wide ranging epistemological implications of treating 'law' as a 'bargaining endowment', that is, a centrifugal message being sent out and differentially appropriated by society (see M Galanter 'Justice in many rooms: Courts, private ordering and indigenous law' (1981) 19 Journal of Legal Pluralism 1). The term 'neo-empiricists' is used to describe contemporary scholarship in sociology of law which seeks to examine the manner and conditions under which 'law' is appropriated by society (see further R Dhavan supra n 40) 5 at 16–20.

[43] There appears to be an extremely volatile contemporary controversy concerning the rise of critical legal studies in the limited studies. For a slightly dated but affectionate account see J Schlegel 'Notes towards an intimate, opinionated and affectionate history of the conference on Critical Legal Studies' (1984) 36 Stanford Law Review 391. While it remains eclectic in composition its central thrust is to re-examine the epistemelogical basis of law and deconstruct its theory and practice.

[44] Thus, law-in-context did not really produce a new epistemology of law but simply created a model for research whereby the policy background of any law was investigated along with general information about its social use while continuing to treat rules as central. This view was exemplified in the W Twining and R Stevens edited *Law-in-Context* series published by Weidenfeld and Nicolson. As the series has expanded, it is producing a richer methodology which goes beyond the over-simplified law-in-context model.

[45] See generally L C Gower *Independent Africa: The Challenge to the Legal Profession* (Cambridge, Mass, Harvard University Press, 1967). The 'Gower' model has been adapted in England (see Ormrod) Report on the Committee on Legal Education (London, Her Majesty's Stationery Office, 1971) Cmnd 4595. Indeed, it is a common sense portrayal of what is already happening in many common law countries and elsewhere.

[46] The attempt to provide a more professionally relevant education has led to an increase in courses on procedure or particular aspects of contemporary law deemed to be useful in future practice. The interior contents of courses have also been changed to reflect this preference. Finally, the expansion of sandwich legal education has enabled students to divide their time between academic courses at the university (or other educational institutions) and practical experience in various kinds of law-related work locations.

[47] See further O Fulton 'Access to Higher Education: A Review of Alternative Policies' supra, chapter 2.

[48] For a review of the literature see generally T Cannon 'Admission Tests for Law Schools: Some Cautionary Remarks' supra, chapter 4.

[49] Much of this discussion is set in context of the definition of 'indirect discrimination' in section 1(1)(b), the United Kingdom Race Relations Act 1976. However, the broad point of tightening the relevancy criteria remains. It is crucial to allowing more disadvantaged persons to make it and enlarge the discretionary power within which preferential discrimination schemes can be devised.

[50] See generally M Galanter's incisive essay 'Who are the other backward classes? An introduction to a constitutional puzzle' (1978) 13 Economic and Political Weekly 1812–28.

[51] For a review of the literature, including the more limited controversy see generally J Edwards *Positive Discrimination: Social Justice, and Social Policy: Moral Scrutiny of a Policy Practice* (London, Tavistock Publications, 1987) a wide ranging survey but unsympathetic to taking a forceful stance in favour of preferential discrimination; see also The Scarman Report: *The Brixton Disorders 10–12 April 1981* (London, Her Majesty's Stationery Office, 1981, Cmnd 8427).

[52] See N Kibble 'Race, class and access to legal education' Paper to the Eighth Commonwealth Conference, Ocho Rios, Jamaica 1986; S Brown and H Vasquez *Pluralism in the legal profession: Models for minority access* (San Francisco, Maldef, 1980); University of Toledo Law Review 'Symposium on disadvantaged students and legal education' (1970) University of Toledo Law Review Nos 2 and 3 ...; and more generally S Lucas and P Ward (ed) *A Survey of Access Courses in England* (University of Lancaster 1985). N Kibble's paper in this volume addresses itself to some of these issues; see N Kibble, Chapter 7 above.

[53] R Dworkin 'Reverse discrimination' in his *Taking Rights Seriously* (London Duckworth, 1978 edn).

[54] For observations on the social debt owed to communities which are disadvantaged for no fault of their own see M Galanter *Competing Equalities: Law and the Backward Classes in India* (Delhi, Oxford University Press, 1984) 552–9.

55 C McLachlan 'Legal Practitioner Mobility in the Commonwealth' supra chapter 14.
56 See K Rokumuto in R Abel and P S C Lewis (eds) *Lawyers in Society* (1988) vol 2 ch 4.
57 See generally M Galanter 'Larger than life: Megalaw and Megalawyering in contemporary United States' in R Dingwall and P Lewis (ed) *The Sociology of the Professions* (London 1983) 152–76; E Spangler *Lawyers for Hire* (New York 1986); R Nelson 'Practice and Privilege: Social Change in the structure of large firms' (1985) American Bar Foundation Research Journal 109; ibid 'The changing structure of opportunity: recruitment and careers in large law firms' (1985) American Bar Foundation Research Journal 95. There is no significant study on megalawyering in England but see S Morgan *Megalawyering in England* (Undergraduate dissertation, Brunel the University of West London, 1986) – and, more importantly on the new large firms and in-house lawyering see R Abel *The Legal Profession in England and Wales* (supra n 6) 111–113, 210–217; D Campbell-Smith 'The rise and fall of a new breed of lawyer' (1983) *Financial Times* (May 13); R Davies 'Overseas lawyers in the United Kingdom' (1985) *Financial Times* 15 July. Clearly, more research needs to be done on (i) changing patterns in the legal profession; (ii) the variety and range of legal personnel other than legal professionals strictly so-called; and (iii) the international mobility of legal professionals and legal personnel.
58 For an early account of the influx of American lawyers see M Galanter 'Legal torpor: why so little has happened in India after the Bhopal tragedy' (1985) Texas International Law Journal 272. However, the implications of Bhopal on the lawyering needs and convenient forums for international dispute resolution of this nature need to be evaluated.
59 I have argued that there is a distinct shift from the era of the legal professional to a much more differentiated and less cohesive collection of people called legal personnel. For our present purposes, the expansion of legal personnel necessitated that the monolithic unilinear model of legal education (supra) needs to be re-examined and replaced by a genuinely wide based multi-entry model. But, this paper suggests that professionalism is itself a historical limited technique of governance. The full implications of this need to be elucidated further.

Appendices

Introduction

These appendices bring together a small selection of extracts from public documents which illustrate the application of some of the approaches and ideas that have been discussed in previous chapters. These are presented as examples rather than as models. Some of them, such as the presentation of statistics by race and gender and aptitude tests, have been the subject of controversy. Others may be suitable in some contexts, but not in others.

   I *Admission bulletin* of the Faculty of Law of the University of Windsor.

  II Survey of minority group students enrolled in JD programs in approved law schools.

 III *Cautionary policies* concerning use of LSAT and LSDAS (1985).

  IV A Part-time Access Course: University of London, Department of Extra-Mural Studies, Certificate in Legal Method. Extract from *Course Handbook 1988–89*.

   V A Full-time Access Course: Vauxhall College of Further Education/South Bank Polytechnic Law Access Course. *Course Handbook 1988–89* (edited extracts).

I   Admission bulletin of the Faculty of Law of the University of Windsor

The objective of the admissions policy is not only to select from among the many applicants those students who will excel in the study of law but also to select those students who, while doing well in the study of law, have the potential to contribute creatively and meaningfully to the Law School and the community.

Criteria

The majority of applicants are considered by the Admissions Committee in the framework of the following criteria:

(a) University program

This category includes such considerations as averages and performance trends in light of relevant considerations; awards and prizes; the nature and content of the program taken (if particularly relevant to the study of law); the level of any degree(s) obtained.

(b) Work experience

Part-time, summer, and/or full-time work experience will be analysed for its indication of organisational and administrative skills and initiative. Vocational, professional or other special qualifications will also be considered.

(c) Community involvement

Contribution to the community (city/town; university; religious; etc) will be assessed for indications of talent demonstrated by the applicant, and commitment to the community. Factors examined include the nature of the applicant's participation in service clubs, community service organisations, religious, athletic and social organisations.

(d) Personal accomplishments

Factors considered in this category includes extracurricular activities; hobbies and special accomplishments (including activities outside regular academic programs in high school and university); artistic and athletic accomplishments; communication skills and languages spoken.

(e) Career objectives

The applicant's career objectives, including how and where the legal education will be employed, are considered.

(f) Personal considerations

Personal factors affecting the applicants are recognised in this section. Any personal factors such as illness, bereavement, unusual family responsibilities or other such circumstances which may have some bearing on the applicant's qualifications will be noted.

(g) Law school admission test scores

The Admissions Committee has decided that LSAT scores written more than three years prior to the academic year of application will not be considered. Applicants who have not written the LSAT within the last three years should write the next available test.

It must be emphasised that no one factor is solely determinative of admission to the Law School. The Admissions Committee assesses applications in light of all the above criteria. It should also be noted that the chief source of the Admissions Committee's information about applicants is the information provided by the applicants themselves in their personal profiles. Therefore, it is very important that an applicant take care to present a full and rounded view of himself or herself to the Admissions Committee.

Admissions committee

Approximately 1,500 applications were received for admission into the 1987–88 first-year class. The Admissions Committee is charged with the duty of establishing admission policy and criteria and, further, the Admissions Committee establishes the procedures for assessment of completed application files. The Committee is composed of 15 members including the Dean of the Faculty of Law, the Associate Dean as Chair, nine professors, three students and one representative from the Admissions Office.

Admission procedures

A candidate for admission to the first year of the program leading to the degree of Bachelor of Laws must follow the procedures and submit to the documentation established for the year in which the applicant wishes to enter. The procedures and documentation established by the Admissions Committee for the entering class of 1988–89 are as follows:

(1) All requests for, or submission of, application forms must be made to the Law School by February 1st, 1988.

(2) All applications for admission to the Law School must be submitted directly to the Faculty of Law, University of Windsor, Windsor, Ontario, Canada N9B 3P4.

(3) In order to complete the application file an applicant must submit the following required materials preferably by the recommended submission dates:

    (a) The Personal Profile: February 1st, 1988.

    (b) The current official LSAT report. (Reminder: LSAT scores prior to October 1984 will not be considered.)

    (c) Official transcripts of all grades achieved in post-secondary institutions prior to February 1st, 1988.

    (d) Official transcripts subsequent to February 1st, 1988 as soon as they become available.

    (e) Two letters of reference: Those applicants who have attended a post-secondary institution during the three years prior to the application (ie, since September 1984) are required to submit at least one letter of reference from a member of the teaching staff who taught them at such institution.

    (f) Data card indicating names of referees and LSAT scores.

    (g) If the applicant has attended university but has matriculated from secondary school, a matriculation certificate.

    (h) List of current courses: February 1st, 1988.

All application files must be completed by the applicant by May 2nd, 1988 otherwise the application may not be considered.

(4) Applicants who have applied in a previous year, are required to provide all new documentation. Transcripts, reference letters, Personal Profiles, LSAT scores, etc from a previous application will not be used for this application.

(5) Applicants will be notified as soon as possible whether or not they have been accepted. Applicants who are notified that they have been accepted must signify their intention to attend within two weeks of the date of the mailing of the notification of their acceptances. Failure to do so will result in withdrawal of acceptance. Information regarding deposit of tuition will accompany an acceptance. This deposit is non-refundable after June 15th. The balance of the first semester tuition is required by August 5th.

Some applicants (for example, those in the work force) may require early consideration of their application for reasons of possible family relocation, notice to employers, etc. Such persons should write the Admissions Office specifically requesting early consideration and setting out in detail the reasons for the request. In order to receive early consideration, the application must be complete. It is nonetheless in the applicant's best interest to complete the application as early as possible.

All inquiries regarding admission should be addressed to:

Admissions Office
Faculty of Law
University of Windsor
Windsor, Ontario
N9B 3P4

Due to the limited number of places in Law I, all applicants who meet the minimum requirement may not receive acceptances.

Retention of Materials:
All material submitted by or on behalf of applicants will be used solely for Admissions purposes and will be kept confidential. The materials will be the property of the University and may be destroyed following the year for which the application is made.

Law school admission test

All applicants to the first year of study at the University of Windsor Faculty of Law (except Native Canadians, see page 4) must write the Law School Admission Test (LSAT). It is not necessary that application be made to the Faculty of Law, University of Windsor prior to registration for the Law School Admission Test.

Reminder:
An LSAT written more than three years prior to the academic year of application will not be considered.

The Law School Admission Test is given several times each year at convenient locations in Canada and the United States. For detailed information applicants are referred to the LSAT Bulletin of Information which is available to all candidates who apply for admission to the Faculty of Law of the University of Windsor. In the alternative applicants may obtain information about the LSAT by writing directly to Law School Admission Services, Box 2000, Newtown, Pennsylvania 18940.

Admission to the practice of law

A Bachelor of Laws degree does not in itself entitle one of practise. Applicants who propose to enter the practice of law in any province of Canada are expected to consult directly with the Law Society of such province to determine its requirements for admission. Every provincial Law Society, in the Common Law provinces, requires some period of articleship within the province as a condition of being admitted to practice. Some provinces may require that, in addition to the LLB, a student have an undergraduate university degree before being admitted to the period of articleship; other provinces may require that, in addition to the LLB degree, a student has successfully completed a minimum of two years' university work after senior matriculation or its equivalent.

In Ontario, the Law Society of Upper Canada, in the report of the Special Committee of law schools, stated that the admissions requirements are:

> The minimum requirements for admission to a law course should be: (a) successful completion of two years' in an approved University after senior matriculation; or (b) successful completion of three year approved course in an approved University after junior matriculation.

In 1972, the report of the Special Committee on Legal Education to the Law Society of Upper Canada recommended as follows:

> The law schools and the law societies should recognise a category of 'mature student' applicants, who have not met the normal pre-law school requirements of university work. Law schools should waive the normal requirements and admit those mature students who on the basis of age, experience, maturity and outstanding qualities as evidenced in their previous careers merit an opportunity to study law.

Applications from Native Canadians

The Faculty of Law of the University of Windsor has approved a special admissions policy in order to encourage Native Canadians to pursue legal studies, since they do not have meaningful representation within the legal profession. Any Native Canadian applicant who has successfully completed, and is recommended by the Director of, the eight week Program of Legal Studies for Native People offered each summer by the Native Law Centre at the University of Saskatchewan at Saskatoon gains automatic admission to the Windsor Faculty of Law.

A Native Canadian applicant who wishes to be considered under this special admissions policy, rather than under the general admissions criteria, must apply to the Law School in accordance with the admissions procedures set out above and include with the application a letter advising of his or her intention to complete the Program of Legal Studies for Native People. The Law School Admissions Test is waived and in special circumstances the Faculty of Law may, upon application, waive other requirements.

An applicant under the special admissions policy who does not gain automatic acceptance may be further considered under the general admissions criteria if he or she has satisfied all of the general admissions requirements, including completion of the Law School Admissions Test.

The integrated MBA/LLB program

This Program is designed to enable a student to obtain both an MBA and an LLB within four years. Successful applicants will pursue first-year studies separately in the Faculty of Business Administration and the Faculty of Law. Years III and IV of the Integrated Program will involve work in both Faculties.

Prospective Integrated Program students must gain admission independently to both Faculties; the GMAT and LSAT are both required. To facilitate Program planning, interested students are urged to seek admission to both Faculties simultaneously. Candidates are approved by the Committee of Directors of the Program; those admitted are granted a Deferred Admission to the Faculty whose first-year studies are to be pursued in the second year of the program.

Applicants seeking to enter the integrated Program should so signify in the space designated on the application for admission, and return the Application Form before February 1st. Such students should also make simultaneous application to the Faculty of Business Administration.

Further questions concerning the Integrated Program should be directed to: Chair, Committee of Directors, Integrated MBA/LLB Program, Faculty of Law, University of Windsor, Windsor, Ontario N9B 3P4.

Joint JD/LLB program

This program has been designed to enable University of Windsor law students to obtain a JD from the University of Detroit simultaneously with the LLB from the University of Windsor. The degree requirements of the two institutions must be separately met. The University of Windsor has agreed to allow its students to use a total of 19 semester hours taken at the University of Detroit towards satisfaction of this LLB requirement. The University of Detroit has agreed to grant University of Windsor students the equivalent of 2 years' advanced standing with regard to obtaining a JD. American Bar Association rules require that a student receive at least 29 semester hours credit from the University of Detroit as a pre-requisite to granting a degree.

It becomes possible for a student at the University of Windsor to obtain both degrees in three calendar years (as opposed to academic years, ie 6 semesters) through the following program:

(1) Completion of the 1st year at Windsor.
(2) Taking 5–6 hours at the University of Detroit during the summer following their first year at Windsor.
(3) During the second and third years at Windsor, taking a total of 19 hours at the University of Detroit. Those credits would count towards their LLB.
(4) During the summer between their second and third year at the University of Windsor, taking a total of 4–5 hours at the University of Detroit (so that a total of 29 hours at the University of Detroit is completed by the end of the students' third year at the University of Windsor).

Correspondence should be directed to: Faculty Director, Joint JD/LLB Program, Faculty of Law, University of Windsor, Windsor, Ontario N9B 3P4.

Advanced standing

Applicants who have attended a foreign law school or who are qualified to practise in a foreign jurisdiction may be considered for advanced standing. Applicants who wish to be considered for advanced standing should indicate which year of the LLB program they are applying for in the appropriate space on the Application for Admission. Such applicants are also required to submit with their applications a letter of recommendation for advanced standing from the Canadian Joint Committee on Accreditation. Information concerning the Canadian Joint Committee on Accreditation may be obtained by writing to:

Professor V Krishna
Executive Secretary
Joint Committee on Accreditation
Faculty of Law,
Common Law Section
University of Ottawa
Ottawa, Ontario
K1N 6N5

Advanced Standing applicants are required to complete all documentation as described on page 2.

Entrance awards, bursaries and scholarships

The following entrance awards, bursaries and scholarships are available to incoming students for the next academic year. The decision as to recipients will be made on the recommendation of the Dean in consultation with the Admissions Committee.

Entrance award

One or more awards valued up to full tuition are available to students entering first year with superior admissions qualifications.

University of Windsor scholarship

One $500 scholarship to a student, resident of Essex, Kent and Lambton counties, with a minimum 'A' average.

Blake, Cassels and Graydon scholarship

Two scholarships of $1,250 each to students entering first year based upon academic performance and community service.

II Survey of minority group students enrolled in JD programs in approved law schools*

Minority Classification	No of Schools Reporting†	Academic Year	1st Year	2nd Year	3rd Year	4th Year	Year Not Stated	Total
Black American	171/174	1984–85	2,214	1,878	1,686	177	0	5,955
	170/173	1983–84	2,247	1,813	1,711	196	0	5,967
	169/172	1982–83	2,217	1,827	1,623	185	0	5,852
	169/172	1981–82	2,238	1,793	1,596	162	0	5,789
	168/171	1980–81	2,144	1,684	1,531	146	0	5,506
	166/169	1979–80	2,002	1,647	1,438	170	0	5,257
	164/167	1978–79	2,021	1,565	1,572	192	0	5,350
	160/163	1977–78	1,945	1,648	1,508	203	0	5,304
	160/163	1976–77	2,128	1,654	1,488	233	0	5,503
	160/163	1975–76	2,045	1,511	1,452	119	0	5,127
	154/157	1974–75	1,910	1,587	1,329	145	24	4,995
	147/151	1973–74	1,943	1,443	1,207	101	123	4,817
	144/149	1972–73	1,907	1,324	1,106	74	12	4,423
	142/147	1971–72	1,716	1,147	761	55	65	3,744
Mexican American	171/174	1984–85	607	538	486	30	0	1,661
	170/173	1983–84	642	558	511	33	0	1,744
	169/172	1982–83	628	573	491	47	0	1,739
	169/172	1981–82	665	490	541.5	59	0	1,755.5
	168/171	1980–81	659	500.5	498	32	0	1,689.5
	166/169	1979–80	642	517	471	40	0	1,670
	164/167	1978–79	606	471	510	62	0	1,649
	160/163	1977–78	588	519	421	36	0	1,564
	160/163	1976–77	591	465	463	69	0	1,588
	160/163	1975–76	535	480	407	21	0	1,443
	154/157	1974–75	568	439	338	17	0	1,362
	147/151	1973–74	539	386	271	63	0	1,259
	144/149	1972–73	480	337	238	17	0	1,072
	142/147	1971–72	403	262	170	11	37	883
Puerto Rican†	171/174	1984–85	132	137	123	15	0	407
	170/173	1983–84	166	152	120	12	0	450
	169/172	1982–83	171	130	105	12	0	418
	169/172	1981–82	149	120	116	11	0	396
	168/171	1980–81	158	135	141	8	0	442
	166/169	1979–80	172	153	107	9	0	441
	164/167	1978–79	184	126	104	9	0	423
	160/163	1977–78	138	92	106	14	0	350
	160/163	1976–77	118	95	105	17	0	335
	160/163	1975–76	113	121	96	3	0	333
	154/157	1974–75	119	91	59	3	0	272
	147/151	1973–74	96	47	32	5	0	180
	144/149	1972–73	73	40	25	5	0	143
	142/147	1971–72	49	25	18	2	0	94

* In March, 1983, the Office of the Consultant issued revised minority JD statistics based on a review of every law school questionnaire received between 1974 and 1982. Discrepancies were the result of inconsistent reporting of Hispanic students by some law schools. Appropriate adjustments were made, and some minor errors in transcription corrected. The data collected between 1971 and 1973 were compiled for the Consultant's Office by the Educational Testing Service and were not refigured.

† Puerto Rican students enrolled in the three ABA-approved law schools located in Puerto Rico are not included in these statistics. For the 1984–85 school year, enrolment in ABA-approved law schools in Puerto Rico totalled 1,633 students.

© AB 'Section on Legal Education. reproduced with permission.

Survey of minority group students (*continued*)

Minority Classification	No of Schools Reporting‡	Academic Year	1st Year	2nd Year	3rd Year	4th Year	Year Not Stated	Total
Other Hispano	171/174	1984–85	537	427	426	49	0	1,439
American	170/173	1983–84	458	432	370	42	0	1,302
	169/172	1982–83	520	367	326	36	0	1,249
	169/172	1981–82	452	307	254	24	0	1,037
	168/171	1980–81	359	272	226	25	0	882
	166/169	1979–80	261	236	187	22	0	706
	164/167	1978–79	288	218	194	16	0	716
	160/163	1977–78	257	193	142	25	0	617
	160/163	1976–77	244	152	132	10	0	538
	160/163	1975–76	170	146	81	9	0	406
	154/157	1974–75	187	101	94	10	0	392
	147/151	1973–74	94	70	59	4	34	261
	144/149	1972–73	96	72	60	3	0	231
	142/147	1971–72	74	62	35	3	5	179
American Indian	171/174	1984–85	173	135	111	10	0	429
or Alaskan	170/173	1983–84	169	126	134	12	0	441
Native	169/172	1982–83	154	134	110	8	0	406
	169/172	1981–82	160	112	124.5	5	0	401.5
	168/171	1980–81	163	137.5	107	7	0	414.5
	166/169	1979–80	171	110	100	11	0	392
	164/167	1978–79	145	110	124	11	0	390
	160/163	1977–78	137	130	90	6	0	363
	160/163	1976–77	133	87	75	6	0	301
	160/163	1975–76	118	88	84	5	0	295
	154/157	1974–75	110	90	65	0	0	265
	147/151	1973–74	109	65	44	3	1	222
	144/149	1972–73	79	48	4	42	0	173
	142/147	1971–72	71	46	18	2	3	140
Asian or Pacific	171/174	1984–85	766	610	600	50	0	2,026
Islander	170/173	1983–84	711	610	578	63	0	1,962
	169/172	1982–83	731	593	562	61	0	1,947
	169/172	1981–82	650	579	486	40	0	1,755
	168/171	1980–81	641	485	473	42	0	1,641
	166/169	1979–80	577	487	452	31	0	1,547
	164/167	1978–79	557	435	398	34	0	1,424
	160/163	1977–78	509	409	423	41	0	1,382
	160/163	1976–77	484	439	378	23	0	1,324
	160/163	1975–76	436	343	287	33	0	1,099
	154/157	1974–75	429	322	288	21	3	1,063
	147/151	1973–74	327	297	202	19	5	850
	144/149	1972–73	298	218	144	20	1	681
	142/147	1971–72	254	142	72	7	5	480
Group not	171/174	1984–85	0	0	0	0	0	0
stated§	170/173	1983–84	0	0	0	0	0	0
	169/172	1982–83	0	0	0	0	0	0
	169/172	1981–82	0	0	0	0	0	0
	168/171	1980–81	0	0	0	0	0	0
	166/169	1979–80	0	0	0	0	0	0
	164/167	1978–79	0	0	0	0	0	0
	160/163	1977–78	0	0	0	0	0	0
	160/163	1976–77	0	0	0	0	0	0
	160/163	1975–76	0	0	0	0	9	9
	153/157	1974–75	0	0	0	0	23	23
	147/151	1973–74	6	5	1	0	0	12
	144/149	1972–73	1	2	2	2	0	7
	142/147	1971–72	0	23	25	0	0	48

‡ Puerto Rican students enrolled in the three ABA-approved law schools located in Puerto Rico are not included in these statistics. For the 1983–84 school year, enrolment in ABA-approved law schools in Puerto Rico totalled 1,720 students.
§ This classification refers to students reported as being members of a minority group but not identified further.

Survey of minority group students (*continued*)

Minority Classification	No of Schools Reporting¶	Academic Year	1st Year	2nd Year	3rd Year	4th Year	Year Not Stated	Total
Total Minority	171/174	1984–85	4,429	3,725	3,432	331	0	11,917
	170/173	1983–84	4,393	3,691	3,424	358	0	11,866
	169/172	1982–83	4,421	3,624	3,217	349	0	11,611
	169/172	1981–82	4,314	3,401	3,118	301	0	11,134
	168/171	1980–81	4,124	3,215	2,976	260	0	10,575
	166/169	1979–80	3,825	3,150	2,755	283	0	10,013
	164/167	1978–79	3,801	2,925	2,902	324	0	9,952
	160/163	1977–78	3,574	2,991	2,690	325	0	9,580
	160/163	1976–77	3,698	2,892	2,641	358	0	9,589
	160/163	1975–76	3,417	2,689	2,407	190	9	8,712
	153/157	1974–75	3,323	2,630	2,173	196	50	8,372
	147/151	1973–74	3,114	2,313	1,816	195	163	7,601
	144/149	1972–73	2,934	2,041	1,619	123	13	6,730
	142/147	1971–72	2,567	1,707	1,099	80	115	5,568

¶ Puerto Rican students enrolled in the three ABA-approved law schools located in Puerto Rico are not included in these statistics. For the 1983–84 school year, enrolment in ABA-approved law schools in Puerto Rico totalled 1,720 students.

Legal education and Bar admission statistics 1963–84

Year	Total	Enrolment Women	First Year	LSAT Administrations	JD or LLB Awarded	Admissions to the Bar
1963	49,552	1,883	20,776	30,528	9,638	10,788
1964	54,265	2,183	22,753	37,598	10,491	12,023
1965	59,744	2,537	24,167	39,406	11,507	13,109
1966	62,556	2,678	24,077	44,905	13,115	14,644
1967	64,406	2,906	24,267	47,110	14,738	16,007
1968	62,779	3,704	23,652	49,756	16,077	17,764
1969	68,386	4,715	29,128	59,050	16,733	19,123
1970	82,041	7,031	34,713	74,092	17,183	17,922
1971	94,468	8,914	36,171	107,479	17,006	20,485
1972	101,707	12,173	35,131	119,694	22,342	25,086
1973	106,102	16,760	37,018	121,262	27,756	30,879
1974	110,713	21,788	38,074	135,397	28,729	30,707
1975	116,991	26,737	39,038	133,546	29,961	34,930
1976	117,451	29,982	39,996	133,320	32,597	35,741
1977	118,557	32,538	39,676	128,135	33,640	37,302
1978	121,606	36,808	40,479	125,757	33,317	39,086
1979	122,860	38,627	40,717	111,235	34,590	42,756
1980	125,397	42,122	42,296	112,750	35,059	41,997
1981	127,312	44,902	42,521	111,373	35,598	42,382
1982	127,828	47,083	42,034	118,200	34,846	42,905
1983	127,195	47,980	41,159	111,118	36,389	41,684
1984	125,698	48,499	40,747*	104,621	36,687	42,630†

NOTES: Enrolment is that in American Bar Association-approved schools as of October 1. The LSAT candidate volume is given for the test year ending in the year stated. Thus, 104,621 administrations occurred in the test year June, 1983, through February, 1984. JD or LLB degrees are those awarded by approved schools for the academic year ending in the year stated. Thus, 36,687 degrees were awarded in the year beginning with the fall, 1983, term and ending with the summer, 1984, term.

Total new admissions to the bar are for the 1984 calendar year and include those admitted by office study, diploma privilege, and examination and study at an unapproved law school. The great bulk of those admitted were graduated from approved schools.

* Of the 40,747 first-year students, 16,233 are women.

† Represents 41,951 admitted by examination, plus 679 admitted by diploma privilege. It does not include admissions on motion by a jurisdiction of attorneys from other jurisdictions, which totalled 3,401.

III Cautionary policies concerning use of the LSAT and LSDAS

These Cautionary Policies are intended for those who set policy and criteria for law school admission, interpret LSAT scores and LSDAS reports, and use other LSAC/LSAS services. The Policies are intended to minimise unwise or indefensible uses of these services by law schools, and to protect applicants from inappropriate treatment and unfair decisions based on improper use of the services.

1 The Law School Admission Test

Because LSAT's are administered to all applicants under standard conditions and each test form requires the same or equivalent tasks of everyone, LSAT scores provide a standard measure of abilities. Comparison of a law school's applicants both with other applicants to the same school and with all applicants who have taken LSAT's thus becomes feasible. However, while LSAT scores serve a useful purpose in the admissions process, they do not measure all the elements important to success at individual institutions. LSAT scores must be examined in relation to the total range of information available about a prospective law student. It is in this context that the following restraints on LSAT score use are urged:

Do not use the LSAT score as a sole criterion for admissions

The LSAT should be used as only one of several criteria for evaluation and should not be given undue weight solely because its use is convenient. Admissions officers should always keep in mind the fact that the LSAT does not measure every discipline-related skill necessary for academic work, nor does it measure other factors important to academic success.

Do not rely on the LSAT without testing its predictive utility at your school: use of validity studies

The LSAT scores should be used only when there is a demonstrated relationship between scores and actual performance in the user law school.

Cautionary Policies Concerning Use of the LSAT and LSDAS reprinted with permission of Law School Admission Council/Law School Admission Service.

Quantitative data used in the selection process should be validated regularly so the law school can use LSAT scores and other information most effectively. For this purpose Law School Admission Council/Law School Admission Services annually offers validity studies to member schools at no charge. Only by checking the relationship between LSAT scores, undergraduate grade-point average and law school grades will schools be fully informed about how admission data, including test scores, can be used most effectively by that school.

Do not use LSAT scores without an understanding of the limitations of such tests

Admissions officers and members of admissions committees should be knowledgeable about tests and test data and should recognise their limitations. Such limitations are set forth in the Operations Reference Book and are regularly discussed at workshops and conferences sponsored by Law School Admission Council/Law School Admission Services.

Avoid improper use of cut-off scores

Cut-off LSAT scores (those below which no applicants will be considered) are strongly discouraged. Such boundaries should be used only if choice of the particular cut-off is based on a carefully considered and formulated rationale (for example, one based on clear evidence that those scoring below the cut-off have substantial difficulty doing satisfactory law school work). Note that the establishment of a cut-off score will often involve distinctions based on score differences not substantial enough to be reliable. Significantly, cut-off scores may have a greater adverse impact upon applicants from minority groups than upon the general applicant population. Normally, an applicant's LSAT score should be combined with the undergraduate grade-point average before any determination is made of the applicant's probability of success in law school.

Do not place excessive significance on score differences

Scores should be viewed as approximate indicators rather than exact measures of an applicant's abilities. Distinctions on the basis of LSAT scores should be made among applicants only when those score differences are reliable.

Do not misapply an LSAT score requirement to handicapped applicants

Many disabled applicants are unable to take the LSAT; they should, without prejudice, be considered on the basis of other information available. Some other persons may furnish LSAT scores which, because of testing conditions adapted to particular disabilities, may not be fully comparable to the scores of other applicants. Both of these matters are considered in some detail in the Operations Reference Book.

Do not misuse repeater scores

LSAC/LSAS research indicates that when an applicant has taken the LSAT more than once, the average of the scores has more predictive validity than any one of the separate scores unless special circumstances are present. In the absence of such circumstances, a decision to use one of the separate scores rather than the average is probably unwise.

Avoid encouraging use of the LSAT for other than admission functions

The LSAT was designed to serve admission functions only. It has not been validated for any other purpose. LSAT performance is subject to mis-understanding and misuse in other contexts, as in the making of an employment decision about an individual who has completed most or all law school work. These considerations suggest that LSAT scores should not be included on a law school transcript, nor routinely supplied to inquiring employers (without the student's specific authorisation, the Buckley Amendment would preclude the latter, in any event).

2 The Law School Data Assembly Service

The LSDAS summarises undergraduate academic records in uniform fashion. It does not reflect differences in grading patterns or overall student body ability from college to college. LSDAS Reports therefore provide only generalised information, the specifics of which must be probed in the decision-making process.

Do not rely on the grade average reported by LSDAS without examining necessary additional information

Decisions should not be based on cumulative averages as they appear on the LSDAS Report alone. Rather, the following kinds of information should be considered in order to interpret LSDAS grade-point averages:

○ the undergraduate institution at which the averages were earned, and (when known) the colleges or departments within the institution;
○ the distribution of grades at the institution, and the applicant's approximate rank in that distribution;
○ the applicant's performance from year to year; and
○ types of courses in which the applicant excelled or did poorly.

Do not treat the one-page LSDAS Report as a substitute for the actual transcript

Interpretive information about college transcripts and grades can be obtained by consulting the Guide to Undergraduate Colleges (furnished by LSAC/LSAS) and the transcript(s) which accompany each LSDAS Report. The transcript tells much more than the LSDAS Report alone, and should always be examined.

Do not misuse the predictive index available on the LSDAS Report

LSAC/LSAS will produce an index calculation on the LSDAS Report to the law school. The index calculation is unique for each law school. The index is a convenient starting place for the evaluation of each applicant. It is based on a combination of LSAT score and undergraduate grade-point average (UGPA), as specified by the law school. A law school should base its index formula on evidence of the predictive value of LSAT and UGPA for that particular law school. The validity study available annually to each law school by LSAC/LSAS provides a formula for the statistically optimal combination of these two predictors. A law school should have a carefully considered justification if it uses any other index formula.

The simplicity and seeming precision of the index figure poses a risk that excessive weight will be placed on it. Admissions officials should remember that the index is derived using methods that are subject to limitations discussed in the Operations Reference Book.

For application deadline purposes, a transcript's receipt at LSAC/LSAS should be considered timely by the law school if the receipt date at LSAC/LSAS is at least four weeks before the school's deadline

Processing and mail delays can occur in the LSDAS system, particularly during peak periods; applicants should not be disqualified or disadvantaged thereby.

3 The Law School Candidate Referral Service

The Candidate Referral Service enables eligible law schools to search the LSDAS file to identify registrants who have characteristics specified by the schools (and who have given their permission to be in the Candidate Referral Service). While this provides LSDAS-registrants an opportunity to be made aware of educational and scholarship possibilities that they might not otherwise have considered, it places a concomitant responsibility on the schools to be sensitive and realistic in their encouragement of applications. Accordingly,

○ Law schools using Candidate Referral Service data to initiate communications with prospective applicants should identify this source.
○ Law schools should attempt to recruit only those persons who appear to have a reasonable chance for acceptance if they apply, and who, if admitted, would have a reasonable chance to succeed academically.
○ Persons contacted should be provided with information about admissions procedures and standards, so they may understand their chances of being accepted.
○ Candidate Referral Service information should be used for recruiting purposes only by the law school to which the information has been released.

4 Law School Admission Test and Employment

○ Employers of law school students or graduates should not seek or use LSAT scores of individual students.
○ Law schools should neither include LSAT scores on student transcripts nor supply individual LSAT scores to employers.

5 General Statement on Confidentiality of Law School Admission Council/Law School Admission Services Data

Law schools that use LSAT scores, LSDAS Reports, and related data should maintain a system for protecting the privacy of applicants. In particular, they should:

○ treat such data confidentially;
○ release such data to persons not associated with the admissions process only with the consent of the applicant (except where the data may be aggregated in a form not identifiable with individuals); and
○ use summary and other aggregated data with discretion and for the purposes intended.

IV A Part-time Access Course –
University of London, Department of Extra-Mural Studies Certificate in Legal Method, *Course Handbook 1988–89* (extracts)

Introduction

This one-year course of study is intended to provide a preparation for studying law at degree level. The emphasis will be almost entirely on the *methods* of reading, analysis and reasoning appropriate to the discipline of law. The course is not concerned with learning legal facts and rules, it is about learning legal skills and methods.

The Certificate meets the general entrance requirements of the University of London for those over 21. Students holding the Certificate will be able to enrol for the External LLB of the University of London.

The Certificate comprises two courses which will run concurrently and complement each other. Students will be expected to attend classes two nights a week from September until May, together with a number of Saturday seminars.

Scheme of study

The objective of the Certificate's two courses is to introduce students to a range of materials of law study and to provide them with a basic set of tools (in the form of questions) to apply to any law-related text.

Both courses may involve active learning by students through classroom discussion of text and film, written exercises, debates and simulated arguments.

Course 1: Legal Reasoning and Analysis

This course will concentrate on problems of interpretation of rules in general and legal rules in particular, especially those based on legislation and reported cases. Interpretation and application of rules; who interprets rules for what purposes; rules and language; how doubts about interpretation arise; the nature of reasoning; and what is involved in reasoning about competing interpretations of cases, statutes and rules of all kinds. (It will also deal with algorithms, flow charts and other tools for analysing, organising and communicating complex rules.)

Course 2: Reading Law

Using a range of legal and non-legal texts, the core of the course will involve reading, analysing and discussing concrete examples of each kind of text.

This course will deal with methods of reading, analysing and using a wide range of material of law study for different purposes, reading, for example, the law reports to find out what the law is on a given point or to trace the historical development of a particular topic or to study the style and approach of an individual judge.

Regulations

No formal academic qualifications are required, but candidates will be expected already to have sufficient study skills and command of English to be able to read on their own, to write essays and to do prescribed exercises. Those entering the course will be expected to be capable of beginning degree studies at the end of a year's study.

Assessment

Assessment on the course is by examination and the submission of course work and those candidates successful in *Course 1* and *Course 2* are awarded the certificate.

Candidates will be required to prepare written and other work, normally twelve pieces of work. The folder of course work being submitted to the Department through the course lecturers will be made available to the examiners. (Students will be asked to indicate the three best pieces of work and place them at the front of their folders.) Assessment of the work will constitute forty per cent of the overall assessment (twenty per cent for each course).

There will be two unseen three-hour examination papers, one for each course. Each paper will count for thirty per cent of the overall assessment together with assessment of work produced during the course, twenty per cent for each course. The overall course marks will consist of sixty per cent for examinations and forty per cent for course work.

V   A Full-time Access Course –

Vauxhall College of Further Eduction/South Bank Polytechnic Law Access Course, *Course Handbook 1988– 89* (edited extracts)

Introduction

The Vauxhall College/South Bank Polytechnic Law Access Course is a one year full-time course. It started in 1983 and has now operated successfully for six years. In that time over 100 students have entered higher education from the course. The Access Course is a partnership between Vauxhall College and the Polytechnic, with students attending four days a week at the College, and one at the Polytechnic. Polytechnic law lecturers share responsibility for recruitment, teaching and assessment on the course.

The Access Course

The Access Course is not a foundation course introducing legal subjects to students, but is based on skills development. Students are encouraged to develop:

(a) *study skills:* personal organisation, research/library skills, note-taking, examination preparation and writing;
(b) *communication skills:* reading and language skills, essay writing and oral presentation;
(c) *reasoning skills:* understanding and critically analysing arguments, relevance and the use of evidence, constructing clear and persuasive arguments, presenting oral and written argument.

Students are also introduced to the particular skills and exercises that form the basis of assessment on the Law degree – the interpretation and application of rules, reading complex legal texts, case analysis and problem-solving.

The course is continuously assessed through a variety of exercises and assignments.

– written and oral exercises set by the members of the course team;
– a research paper of 5,000 words;
– mock examinations.

Most work will be graded. *All* work will receive detailed individual comments to help students to identify their strengths, weaknesses and measure their progress. Comprehensive and careful individual feedback is a central feature of the course. Individual and class-based feedback, individual and group tutorials, and individual half-termly progress reports all help to guide the student's development.

In order to complete the course successfully, the course team must be satisfied that the student has acquired the academic skills necessary for entry onto the Law degree. The course team must also be satisfied that the student has sufficient maturity, motivation and self-discipline to cope with the demands of Law degree study. A high level of attendance and punctuality are required of all students. Students are encouraged to take responsibility for their own work.

Recruitment/entry requirements

There are no formal entry requirements. All people interested in the course are invited to attend an Open Evening where they will have an opportunity to speak with both staff and students. All applicants are required to take an English comprehension and writing test to ensure that entrants have a sufficient level of communication skills to cope with the work required of them. All those who meet this standard are invited for an interview to discuss their experience, interests and aspirations. The course admits approximately 24 people per year.

Progression

Students who *successfully* complete the Access Course have a guaranteed place on the LL B at South Bank Polytechnic, ie they do not have to go through the standard application procedure and compete for the limited available places.

Select bibliography

Abel, R *The Legal Profession in England and Wales* (1988) Blackwell.

Abel, R and Lewis, P (eds) *Lawyers in Society* Vol One: *The Common Law World*, Vol Two: *The Civil Law World* (1988) University of California Press.

Acker, S and Piper, D W (eds) *Is Higher Education Fair to Women?* (1984) SRHE.

Acker, S, Megarry, J, Nisbet, S and Hoyle E (eds) *World Yearbook of Education: Women in Education* (1984) Kogan Page.

Adam, B 'Stigma and Employability: Discrimination by Sex and Sexual Orientation in the Ontario Legal Profession' (1981) 18 Canadian Bar Review of Sociology and Anthropology 216.

Adam, B and Lahey, K 'Professional Opportunities: A Survey Of The Ontario Legal Profession' (1981) 59 Canadian Bar Review 674.

Adler, C, Kahane, R and Avgar, A *The Education of the Disadvantaged In Israel: Comparisons, Analysis and Proposed Research* (1975) Hebrew University of Jerusalem School of Education.

Agnew *Women in the Professions* (1987).

Ahmed, K 'Towards Equality: Consequences of Protective Discrimination' (1978) 13 Economic and Political Weekly 69.

American Bar Association Section of Legal Education and Admissions to the Bar. *A review of Legal Education in the United States, Fall 1984: Law Schools and Bar Admission Requirements* (1985) ABA, Chicago.

Anderson, D S and Western, J S 'Social Profiles of Students in Four Professions' (1970) 3(4) Quarterly Review of Australian Education 1.

Anderson, D S, Western, J S and Boreham, P R 'Law and the Making of Legal Practitioners' in Tomasic R (ed) *Understanding Lawyers* (1978).

Anderson, D S, Boven, R, Fensham, P J and Powell, J P *Students in Australian Higher Education: A study of their social composition since the Abolition of Fees* (1980) Australian Government Publishing Service.

Arthurs, H W, Weisman, R and Zemans, F H 'Canadian Lawyers: A Peculiar Professionalism' in Abel, R and Lewis, P (eds) *Lawyers In Society* Vol One: *The Common Law World* (1988).

Association of Graduate Careers Advisory Services (AGCAS) *Becoming a barrister in the 1980's: A survey of law graduates who took the Bar final course in the years 1979, 1980 and 1981* (1984) AGCAS.

Solicitors' finals 1983: A detailed report on how candidates fared at the College of Law and the Polytechnics (1984) AGCAS.

Becoming a trainee solicitor: A report on the experiences of law graduates of 1982 (1984) AGCAS.

Astin, A *Minorities in American Higher Education* (1982) Jossey-Bass.

Auerbach, J L *Unequal Justice, Lawyers and Social Change in Modern America* (1976) Oxford University Press.

Badger, R I 'Prediction and selection in Law School Admissions' (1985) 31 U of Chicago Law School Record 16.

Bailey, J B and Marsh, S B 'Law teaching at colleges of further education' (1981) 15 Law Teacher 83.

Bailey, R L *Minority Admissions* (1978) Health.

Balmford, R (ed) *Legal Education in Australia* (1978) Australian Law Council Foundation.

Bankowski, Z and Mungham, G 'A political economy of legal education' (1978) 32 New Universities Quarterly 448.

Barton, L and Walker, S *Race, Class and Education* (1983).

Bastedo, T G 'Law Colleges and Law Students in Bihar' (1986) 3 Law & Society Review 269.

Baxter, S 'An Analysis of the Social Backgrounds of the Justices of the High Court of Australia' (1983) Unpublished paper, Sydney University.

Beed, T W and Campbell, I G *Supply and Demand Factors Associated with the Legal Profession in New South Wales* (1979) University of Sydney Sample Survey Centre.

Beed, T W and Campbell, I G 'Supply and Demand Factors Associated with the Legal Profession of New South Wales' (1977) University of Sydney Sample Survey Centre (Occasional Paper No 1).

Bell, Jr D A 'Black Students in White Law Schools: The Ordeal and the Opportunity' (1970) University of Toledo LR 539.

Bell, Jr D A *Race, Racism and American Law* (1973) Brown and Co.

Bell, Jr D A 'In Defense of Minority Admissions Programs: A Response to Professor Graglia' (1970) 119 U Pa Law Rev 364.

Black, J (ed) *Radical Lawyers: Their Role in the Movement and in the Courts* (1971) Avon.

Blackstone, W T and Heslep, R D (eds) *Social Justice and Preferential Treatment: Women and Racial Minorities in Education and Business* (1977) University of Georgia Press.

Bradsen, J R and Farrington, J A 'Student Selection and Performance in the Faculty of Law, The University of Adelaide' (1986) 29 (i) Australian Universities' Review 25.

Briere, G 'Les Conditions d'Admission Dans les Facultés de Droit du Quebec' (1980) 11 Revue Generale de Droit 359.

Brooks, R 'Affirmative Action in Law Teaching' (1982) 14 Columbia Human Rights Law Review 15.

Brown, C *Black and White Britain: The third PSI survey* (1984) Heinemann.

Brown, S and Marenco, E *Law School Admissions Study*, MALDEF (1980).

Brown, S and Marenco, E 'Innovative Models for Increasing Minority Access to the Legal Profession' in White D (ed) *Towards a Diversified Legal Profession* (1981) National Conference of Black Lawyers (NCBL).

Browning, B G 'Admissions Criteria Research Project' (1976) University of Manitoba (unpublished).

Boxill 'The Morality of Preferential Hiring' (1978) 7 Philosophy and Public Affairs 246.

Carter, J 'University of Saskatchewan: Program of Legal Studies for Native People' (1980) 4 Can Community LJ 28.

Clement, W 'Inequality of Access: Characteristics of the Canadian Corporate Elite' (1975) 12 Canadian Review of Sociology and Anthropology 33.

Cohen, M, Nagel, T and Scanlon, T (eds) *Equality and Preferential Treatment* (Princeton: Princeton University Press, 1977).

Cohen, P 'Bar Racism on Trial' (1982) LAG Bulletin 6 (April).
'Racial Discrimination among Solicitors' (1982) LAG Bulletin 11 (May).

Colchester, T 'Views of the Numbers Game from the Sidelines: The New South Wales and Ontario Enquiries' (1984) 37 CLEA Newsletter.

Commission for Racial Equality 'Code of Practice for the Elimination of Racial Discrimination and the Promotion of Equality of Opportunity in Employment' (1984) CRE.
'Chartered Accountancy Training Contracts: Report of a formal Investigation into Ethnic Minority Recruitment' (1987) CRE.
'Medical School Admissions: Report of a formal Investigation into St George's Hospital Medical School' (1988) CRE.

Cooray, M *Changing the Language of the Law: The Sri Lankan Experience* (1985) Les Presses de l'Universite Laval, Quebec.

Cormack, R J and Osborne, R D (eds) *Religion, Education and Employment: Aspects of Equal Opportunity in Northern Ireland* (1983) Salem House.

Cottrell, J '10 + 2 + 5: A Change in the Structure of Indian Legal Education' (1986) 36/3 J of Legal Education 331.

Council of Legal Education, Jamaica *Legal Education in the West Indies 1963– 1972* (1972).

Council of National Academic Awards *Future Development of CNAA's Academic Policies of Undergraduate Level* (1983) CNAA.

Craft, M and Craft, A 'The Participation of Ethnic Minority Pupils in Further and Higher Education' (1983) 25/1 Education Research 10.

Cunningham, S 'Women's Access to Higher Education in Scotland' in Acker, S, Megarry, J, Nisbet, S and Hoyle, E (eds) *World Yearbook of Education: Women in Education* (1984).

Deloria, S 'Legal Education and Native People' (1973–74) 38 Saskatchewan Law Review 22.

Derham, D 'Legal Education – University Education and Professional Training' (1962) 36 Australian Law Journal 209.

DES (Department of Education and Science) 'Higher Education in the 1990's' Government Green Paper Cmnd 9524 (1979) DES.

DES (Department of Education and Science) 'Projections of Demand for Higher Education In Great Britain 1986–2000' (1986) DES.

DES (Department of Education and Science) 'Higher Education: Meeting the Challenge' Government White Paper Cm 114 (1987) HMSO.

Dias, C, Luckham, R, Lynch, D O and Paul, J C N *Lawyers in the Third World: Comparative and Developmental Perspectives* (1981) International Center For Law In Development.

Duncan, M 'The Future of Affirmative Action' (1982) 17 Harvard Civil Rights and Liberties L Rev 503.

Duncan, N and W-Kibble, N 'Excellence and Diversity: admissions policies in law schools' (1986) 20 Law Teacher 36.

Dworkin, R 'Reverse Discrimination' in *Taking Rights Seriously* (rev ed 1978) Duckworth.
A Matter of Principle (1985) Harvard University Press.

Edwards, E G 'Higher Education for Everyone' (1982) Spokesman.

Edwards, J *Positive Discrimination, Social Justice and Social Policy* (1987) Tavistock.

Eggleston, S J, Dunn, D K and Anjali, M *Education for Some, The Educational and Vocational Experiences of 15–18-year-old Members of Ethnic Minority Groups* (1986) Trentham Books.

Ely, J H 'The Constitutionality of Reverse Racial Discrimination' (1974) 41 U Chi L Rev 723.

Evans, N *Curriculum Opportunity. A map of experiential learning in entry requirements to higher and further education award bearing courses. A Project Report* (1983) FEU.

Farrant, J 'Trends In Admission' in Fulton, O (ed) *Access to Higher Education* (1983).

Feldthusen, B 'Are There Too Many Lawyers?' (1982) 2 The Windsor Year-book of Access to Justice 224.

FEU *Changing the focus: Women and FE* (1985) FEU. *Black Perspectives on FE Provision: A Summary Document* (1985) FEU.
Access to Further and Higher Education (1987) FEU.
Black Students and Access to Higher Education (1987) FEU.

Finch, J and Rustin, M (eds) *A Degree of Choice? Higher Education and the Right to Learn* (1986) Penguin.

Fiss, O 'Groups and the Equal Protection Clause' (1976) 5 Philosophy and Public Affairs 107.

Fleming, J, Gill, G and Swinton, D *The Case of Affirmative Action for Blacks in Higher Education* (1978).

Fuchs, C E 'Reworking the Latent Agenda of Legal Education' (1986) 10 Nova LJ 449.

Fulton, O 'Principles and Policies' in Fulton, O (ed) *Access to Higher Education* (1983).

Fulton, O (ed) *Access to Higher Education* (1983) Society for Research Into Higher Education.
'Elite Survivals? Entry "Standards" and Procedures for Higher Education Admissions' (1988) 13/1 Studies in Higher Education 15.

Galanter, M *Competing Equalities* (1984) Oxford University Press.

Gardner, J W *Excellence: Can we be Equal and Excellent Too?* (1961) Harper Colophon.

Gifford, T *Where's the Justice?* (1986) Penguin.

Ginger, T J 'Affirmative Action: Answer for Law Schools' (1985) 28/3 Howard Law Journal 701.

Glasser, I 'Affirmative Action and the Legacy of Racial Injustice' in Katz, P A and Taylor, D A (eds) *Eliminating Racism* (1988).

Glazer, N *Affirmative Discrimination: Ethnic Inequality and Public Policy* (1975) Basic Books.

Goldman, A H *Justice and Reverse Discrimination* (1979) Princeton University Press.

Goldring, J 'An Updated Social Profile of Students Entering Law Courses' (1986) 29/2 Australian Universities Review 38.

Goodlad, S *Education for the Professions* (1984) Society for Research Into Higher Education and NEPR.

Goolsby Jr, T M 'A Study of Criteria for Legal Education and Admission to the Bar' (1967) 20 J Legal Education 175.

Goulbourne, S 'Minority Entry to the Legal Profession: A Discussion Paper' (1985) Centre for Research in Ethnic Relations, University of Warwick.

Gower, L C B *Independent Africa: The Challenge to the Legal Profession* (1967) Harvard University Press.

Graglia, L A 'Special Admission of the "Culturally Deprived" to Law School' (1970) 119 U Pa Law Rev 353.

Greenwalt, K 'Judical Scrutiny of "Benign" Racial Preference in Law School Admissions (1975) 75 Columbia L Rev 559.

Gross, B R *Reverse Discrimination* (1977) Prometheus Books.
Discrimination In Reverse: Is Turnabout Fair Play (1978) New York University Press.

Grove, J D 'A Test of the Ethnic Equalisation Hypothesis; A Cross National Study' (1978) 1 Ethnic and Racial Studies 175.

Guest, S and Milne A (eds) *Equality and Discrimination* (1985) Franz Steiner Verlag.

Halliday, T 'Six Score Years and Ten: Demographic Transitions in the American Legal Profession, 1850–1980' (1986) 20 Law & Society Review 53.

Halsey, A H, Heath, A F and Ridge, J M *Origins and Destinations* (1980) Oxford University Press.

Hamlar, P V T 'Minority Tokenism in American Law Schools' (1983) 26 Howard Law Journal 443.

Hansen, O 'Black Cloud Over Law Society' (1985) *Guardian* (5 June).

Hathaway, J C 'The Mythical Meritocracy of Law School Admissions' (1984) 34 Journal of Legal Education 86.

Henderson, W J and Flores, L 'Implications for Affirmative Admissions After *Bakke*: Preliminary Analysis of Academic and Bar Performance of Council on Legal Education Opportunity Program Fellows, 1968–1978' in White D (ed) *Towards a Diversified Legal Profession* (1981) NCBL.

Hazell, R (ed) *The Bar on Trial* (1978) Quartet.

Hester, D 'Attempting to Compensate for Socio-Economic Disadvantages by Manipulation of University Selection Methods' (1987) 30/1 Australian Universities' Review 42.

Hilliard, A 'Ethnic Participation in Higher Education: Philosophical, Economical, and Political Perspectives, USA' in 'Multi-Ethnic Higher Education in Inner City Areas: Report of the 1986 Joint Conference South Bank Polytechnic and City College of New York' (1986) South Bank Polytechnic.

Hinds, L S 'The Rutgers Report: The White Law School and the Black Liberation Struggle' in Lefcourt, R (ed) *Essays to Demystify Law, Order and the Courts* (1971).

Hurst, W *The Growth of American Law: The Law-Makers* (1950) Barton.

Huxter, M T 'Survey of Employment Opportunities for Articling Students and Graduates of the Bar Admission Course in Ontario' (1981) 15 Law Society of Upper Canada Gazette 169.

Imam, M 'Reservation of Seats for Backward Classes in Public Services and Educational Institutions' (1966) 8 J of the Indian Law Institute 441.

Inner London Education Authority (ILEA) *Race, Sex and Class 3. A policy for equality: Race* (1983) ILEA.
Race, Sex and Class 6. A policy for equality: Sex (1985) ILEA.
We Meet the Challenge: ILEA Response to Meeting the Challenge (1987).

Inns of Court School of Law *Comparison of Degree and Bar Examination Results. Academic Session 1986–87* (1987) Council for Legal Education (CLE).

International Council for Educational Development *Access Policy and Procedures and the Law in US Higher Education* (1978) ICED.

International Legal Center *Law and Development: The Future of Law and Development Research* (1974) ILC.

International Legal Center *Legal Education in a Changing World* (1975) ILC.

Jamdaigni, L, Philips-Bell, M and Ward, J (eds) *Talking Chalk. Black Pupils, Parents and Teachers speak about Education* (1982) AFFOR.

Jeffcoate, R *Ethnic Minorities and Education* (1984) Harper & Row.

Jenkins, R and Solomos, J 'Racism and Equal Opportunity Policies in the 1980s' (1987) Cambridge University Press.

Jones, J 'Access to University Education in New Zealand' (1982) 7/2 Studies in Higher Education 159.

Kairys, D (ed) *The Politics of Law: A Progressive Critique* (1982) Pantheon Books.

Karabel, H and Halsey, T H *Education and Inequality* (1977) Oxford University Press.

Katz, P A and Taylor (eds), D A *Eliminating Racism* (1988).

Kaye, D M 'Searching for the Truth about Testing' (1981) 90 Yale LJ 33.

Kennedy, H 'Women at the Bar' in Hazell, R (ed) *The Bar on Trial* (1978).

Kennedy, R 'Persuasion and Distrust: A Comment on the Affirmative Action Debate' (1986) 99 Harvard L Rev 1327.

Keon-Cohen, B A 'Community Legal Education in Australia' (1978) 4 Monash Law Review 292.

Kibble, N W 'Race, Class, and Access to Legal Education' (England) Paper delivered at the 8th Commonwealth Law Conference, Ocho Rios, Jamaica, 1986 (forthcoming).

Kinoy, A 'The Rutgers Minority Student Program: Commitment, Experience and the Constitution' (1976) Rutgers Law Journal 857.

Kirpal, V 'Higher Education for the Scheduled Castes and Scheduled Tribes' (1978) 13 Economic and Political Weekly 165.

Labour Party *Education After Eighteen: Expansion with Change* (1982) Labour Party.

Larson, M S *The Rise of Professionalism: A Sociological Analysis* (1977) University of California Press.

Lawrence III, C R 'Minority Hiring in AALS Law Schools: The Need for Voluntary Quotas' (1986) 20 U San Francisco L Rev 429.

Law School Admission Council *Law Schools Admissions Research 1949–83* (microfiche, 4 vols) LSAC/LSAS.

Law Society 'Final Examination Statistics' (1986) Law Society Gazette 3499 (19 Nov).

'Ethnic Monitoring Statistics' (1988) Law Society Gazette 38 (27 July).

'Equal in the Law: Report of the Working Party on Women's Careers' (1988) Law Society.

'The Recruitment Crisis: Report by the Training Committee' (1988) Law Society.

Law Society of New South Wales Composition of the Profession. (1978) Law Society of NSW (submission to NSW Law Reform Commission).

Law Society of Upper Canada 'The Report of the Special Committee on Numbers of Lawyers' (1983) 17 LSUC Gazette 222.

Lee, R G 'A Survey of Law School Admissions' (1984) 18 The Law Teacher 165.

Lefcourt, R (ed) *Essays to Demystify Law, Order and the Courts* (1971) Vintage Books.

Leonard, W J 'Bakke: Extending the Dream Deferred' in White, D (ed) *Towards a Diversified Legal Profession* (1981) NCBL.

Letwin, L 'Some Perspectives on Minority access to Legal Education' (May 1969) 2 Experiment and Innovation 10.

Linke, R D, Oertel, L M and Kelsey, N J M 'Participation and Equity in Higher Education: A Preliminary Report on the Socioeconomic Profile of

Higher Education Students in South Australia, 1975–1984' (1985) 11(3) Australian Bulletin of Labour 124.

London, J R 'The Admissions and Education Committee: A Perspective on Legal Education and Admission to Practice in the Province of Manitoba, Past, Present and Future' (1978) 8 Manitoba LJ 553.

Loo, C M and Rolison, G 'Alienation of Ethnic Minority Students at a Predominantly White University' (1986) 57/1 Journal of Higher Education (USA) 58.

Lucas, S and Ward, P *A Survey of 'Access' Courses in England* (1985) School of Education University of Lancaster.

Lyon, E S 'Unequal Opportunities: Black Minorities and Access to Higher Education' in 'Multi-Ethnic Higher Education in Inner City Areas: Report of the Joint South Bank Polytechnic and City College of New York Conference' (1986) South Bank Polytechnic.

Lyon, E S and Gatley, D A 'Black Graduates and Labour Market Recruitment' (1988) Higher Education and the Labour Market (HELM) Working Paper No 5.

Mabey, C 'Black Pupils' Achievement in Inner London' (1986) 28/3 Educational Research 163.

MacDonald, R A 'Law Schools and Public Legal Education: The Community Law Programme at Windsor' (1979) 5/3 Dalhourie LJ 779.

Maczko, F and McKenna-Kay, E S 'Criteria for Admission to the Bar and Articles' in Matas, R J and McCawley, D J (eds) *Legal Education in Canada* (1987).

Manning, W 'Diversity and Due Process in Admissions' (1979) 22 Howard Law Journal 317.

Marks, P G 'A statistical summary of the solicitors' profession' (1984) 81 Law Society Gazette 2607.

Marks, P G 'Annual Statistical Report 1985' (1985) 82 Law Society Gazette 2903, 2913.

Marks, P G 'Annual Statistical Report 1986' (1986) 83 Law Society Gazette 3257.

Marks, P G 'Annual Statistical Report 1987' (1987) Law Society Gazette 2446 (2 Sep).

Marsh, S B 'The Last Twenty Years' in Slade M (ed) *Law in Higher Education into the 1980's* (1980).

Marsh, S B 'The CNAA Law Degree' (1983) 17 Law Teacher 73.

Martin, L 'From Apprenticeship to Law School: A Social History of Legal Education in Nineteenth Century New South Wales (1986) 9(2) University of New South Wales Law Journal 111.

Matas, R J, Mr Justice and McCawley, D J (eds) *Legal Education In Canada* (1987) Federation of Law Societies of Canada.

Mathews, J 'The Changing Profile of Women in the Law' (1982) 56 Australian Law Journal 634.

McCrudden, C 'Changing Notions of Discrimination' in Guest, S and Milne, A (eds) *Equality and Discrimination* (1985).

McCrudden, C 'Rethinking Positive Action' (1986) 15 Industrial Law J 219.

McDonald, P 'The Class of '81 – A Glance at the Social Class composition of Recruits in the Legal Profession' (1982) 9 Journal of Law and Society 267.

McKennirey, J *Canadian Law Faculties* (1983) Social Science and Humanities Research Council.

McKenzie, D 'The Changing Concept of Equality in New Zealand Education' (1975) 10/2 New Zealand Journal of Educational Studies 93.

McLachlan, C *Admission of Commonwealth Lawyers* Commonwealth Secretariat, London, 1985.

Millar, W M 'The Role of Women in the Profession' (1985) 30 Journal of the Law Society of Scotland 86.

Millins, P K C 'Access Studies to Higher Education (September 1979–December 1983): A Report' (1984) Roehampton Institute of Higher Education.

Molyneaux, P 'Association of Women Solicitors-Membership Survey' (1986) 83 Law Society Gazette 3082.

Montoya, R 'The Myth of Reverse Discrimination' (1978) Health Pathways No 3 (September).

Morris, L *Elusive Equality: The Status of Black Americans in Higher Education* (1979) Howard University Press.

Morton, J 'Discrimination in the Legal Profession' (1985) New Law Journal 573 (14 June).

Nairn, A 'Standardised Selection Criteria and A Diverse Legal Profession' in White, D (ed) *Towards a Diversified Legal Profession* (1981) NCBL.

Ndulo, M 'Legal Education in Zambia: Pedagogical Issues' (1986) 2 Lesotho LJ 75.

Neave, G 'Elite and Mass Higher Education in Britain: A Regressive Model?' (1985) Comparative Education Review 29.

Neave, G *Patterns of Inequality* (1976) NFER.

National Advisory Board For Local Authority Education *A Strategy for Higher Education In the Late 1980's and Beyond* (1984) NAB.

Nyerere, J *Education For Self-Reliance* (1967) Government Printer, Dar-es-Salaam.

Older, J 'Reducing Racial Imbalance in New Zealand Universities and Professions' (1984) 20/2 The Australian and New Zealand Journal of Sociology 243.

O'Neil, R M 'Preferential Admissions: Equalizing the Access of Minority Groups to Higher Education' (1971) 80 Vale LJ 699.

O'Neil, R M *Discriminating against Discrimination: Preferential Admissions and the DeFunis Case* (1975) University of Indiana Press.

Osborne, R D et al 'Class, Sex, Religion and Destination: Participation and Higher Education In Northern Ireland' (1984) 9 Stud Higher Education 123.

Osborne, R D (ed) *Education and Policy In Northern Ireland* (1987).

Palmer, F (ed) *Anti-Racism – An Assault on Education and Value* (1986) Sherwood Press.

Parker, K E 'Ideas, Affirmative Action and the Ideal University' (1986) 10 Nova LJ 761.

Pashigan, B P 'The Market for Lawyers. The Determinants of the Demand for and Supply of Lawyers' (1977) 20 J of Law and Economics 53.

Patchett, K 'The Role of Law in the Development Process' (1987) 48 Commonwealth Legal Ed Assoc Newsletter 33.

Paterson, A 'The legal profession in Scotland' in Abel, R and Lewis, P (eds) *Lawyers in Society*, Vol 1: *The Common Law World* (1988).

Pearce, D, Campbell E, Harding, D *Australian Law Schools: A E and Discipline Assessment for the Commonwealth Tertiary Education Commission* (1987).

Pearson, R and Sachs, A 'Barristers and Gentlemen: A Critical Look at Sexism in the Legal Profession' (1980) 43 MLR 400.

Podmore, D *Solicitors and the Wider Community* (1980) Heinemann.

Purich, D J 'Affirmative Action in Canadian Law Schools: The Native Student in Law School' (1986–87) 51 Sask LR 79.

Purvis, J *Gender, Race and Education* (1984) Open University.

Quicke, J 'The "New Right" and Education' (1988) 36/1 British Journal of Educational Studies 5.

Ramsey, Jr H 'Affirmative Action at American Bar Association Approved Law Schools 1979–80' (1980) 30 J Legal Education 377.

Read, B 'Exit from law schools: Possibilities and actualities' (1984) 18 Law Teacher 175.

Ripps, S R 'A Curriculum Course designed for Lowering the Attrition Rate for the Disadvantaged Law Student' (1986) 29 Howard Law Journal 457.

Roderick, G W, Bell, J M, Dickinson, R and Wellings, A *Mature Students in Higher and Further Education: A study in Sheffield* (1981) University of Sheffield.

Roderick, G W and Bell, J M ' "Unqualified" Mature Students at the University of Sheffield' (1981) 6/2 Studies in Higher Education 123.

Rosen, S J 'Equalizing Access to Legal Education. Special Programs for Law Students who are not Admissible by Traditional Standards' (1970) U Toledo Law Review 321.

Ruhela, S P (ed) *Social Determinants of Educability in India* (1969) Jain Brothers.

Rudd, E *The Educational Qualifications and Social Class of the Parents of Under-graduates entering British Universities in 1984.* (1986) Royal Statistical Society.

Sachs, A and Wilson, J H *Sexism and the Law: A Study of Male Beliefs and Judical Bias* (1978) Martin Robertson.

Samuels, G 'Control of Admission to Practice – Its Effect on Legal Education' in Balmford, R (ed) *Legal Education in Australia* (1978).

Sandalow, T 'Racial Preferences in Higher Education: Political Responsibility and the Judical Role' (1975) U Ch L Rev 653.

Sargisson, H 'Women in the Legal Profession: A Discussion of their Changing Profile' (1982) LLB (Honours) dissertation, Auckland Law School.

Saunders, N 'Legal Education in a Multi-Racial Society' (1988) Unpublished M Phil Thesis, University of Warwick.

Sear, K 'The Correlation Between A-level grades and Degree results in England and Wales' (1983) 12 Higher Education 609.

Sedlacek, W T 'The Aftermath of Bakke: Should We Use Race in Admissions' (1979) 22 Howard Law Journal 327.

Senate of the Four Inns of Court and the Bar 'Quality of Entry: Report of the Executive Committee Working Party' (1985).

Senate of the Four Inns of Court and the Bar 'Report of the Race Relations Committee 1984–85' (Chairman, The Hon Mr Justice Scott) (1985).

Senate of the Four Inns of Court and the Bar 'Report of the Race Relations Committee Committee 1985–86' (1986) Law Society Gazette 2482 (27 Aug).

Sharma, G S (ed) *Educational Planning: Its Legal and Constitutional Implications In India* (1967) N M Tripathi.

Sindler, A P *Bakke, Defunis and Minority Admissions* (1978) Longman.

Singh, P ' "Equal Opportunity" and "Compensatory Discrimination": Constitutional Policy and Judicial Control' (1976) 18 J of the Indian Law Institute 300.

Slocum, A A 'CLEO: Anatomy of Success' (1979) 22 Howard Law Journal 335.

Smith, D H *Admission and Retention problems of Black Students at Seven Predominantly White Universities* (1980) National Advisory Committee on Black Higher Education and Black Colleges and Universities.

Smith, D and Tepperman, L 'Changes in the Canadian Business and Legal Elites 1870–1970' (1974) 11 Canadian Review of Sociology and Anthropology 97.

Smith, L, Stephenson, M and Quijano, G 'The Legal Profession and Women: Finding Articles in British Columbia' (1973) 8 UBC Law Review 137.

Smith, M G *Culture, Race and Class in the Commonwealth Caribbean* (1984).

Smith, P. 'Race Relations Survey. A Survey of Ethnic Minority Recruitment to the Bar in England and Wales' (1989) Bar Council.

Smithers, A and Griffin, A 'Mature Students at University: Entry, experience and outcomes' (1986) 11/3 Studies in Higher Education 257.

Smithers, A and Griffin, A *The Progress of Mature Students* (1986) Joint Matriculation Board, Manchester.

Stager, D 'The Market for Lawyers in Ontario: 1931 to 1981 and Beyond' (1982) 6 Canada-United States Law Journal 113.

Stevens, R B *Law School: Legal Education in America from the 1850's to the 1980's* (1983) University of N Carolina Press.

Thomas, G E *Black Students in US Graduate and Professional Schools in the 1980's: A National and Institutional Assessment* (1987) Spencer Foundation.

Thomas, G E (ed) *Black Students in Higher Education: Conditions and experiences in the 1970's* (1978) Greenwood Press.

Tomlinson, S 'Black Women in Higher Education – Case Studies of University Women in Britain' in Barton, L and Walker, S (eds) *Race, Class and Education* (1983).

Tomasic, R (ed) *Understanding Lawyers* (1978) The Law Foundation of New South Wales and George Allen & Unwin.

Tomasic, R 'Social Organisation Amongst Australian Lawyers' (1983) 19 Australia and New Zealand Journal of Sociology 447.

Traynor, R B 'Who should be a lawyer, but why?' (1960) 13 J Legal Ed 157.

Troyna, B (ed) *Racial Inequality in Education* (1987) Tavistock.

Troyna, B and Williams, J *Racism, Education and the State* (1985) Croom Helm.

Twining, W 'Legal Education Within East Africa' in East African Law Today (1966) British Institute of International and Comparative Law.

Twining, W and Uglow, J (eds) *Legal Literature in Small Jurisdictions* (1982) Canadian Law Information Council and Commonwealth Secretariat.

University Grants Committee *A Strategy for Higher Education into the 1990's* (1984) HMSO.

University of Saskatchewan Native Law Centre *Programme of Legal Studies for Native People* (1981) Univ of Saskatchewan Native Law Centre.

US Commission on Civil Rights *Toward Educational Opportunity Affirmative Admissions Programs at Law and Medical Schools* (1978) Clearinghouse Publications.

Wang, B L C 'Positive Discrimination in Education: A Comparative Investigation of its Bases, Forms and Outcomes' (1983) 27/2 Comparative Education Review 191.

Warren-Piper, D (ed) 'Is Higher Education Fair?' Papers presented to the 17th Annual Conference of the Society for Research Into Higher Education (1981) SRHE.

Wasserstrom, R A 'The University and the Case for Preferential Treatment' (1976) 13 American Philosophical Quarterly 165.

Weil, S W 'Non-traditional learners within Traditional Higher Education

Institutions: Discovery and Disappointment' (1986) 11/3 Studies in Higher Education 219.

Weisbrot, D 'The Australian Legal Profession: From Provincial Family Firms to Multinationals' in Abel, R and Lewis, P (eds) *Lawyers In Society* Vol One: *The Common Law World* (1988).

White, D M (ed) *Towards a Diversified Legal Profession* (1981) National Conference of Black Lawyers.

Williams, J 'Education and Race: The Racialisation of Class Inequalities' (1986) 7/2 British Journal of the Sociology of Education 135.

Williams, J. Cocking, J and Davies, L 'Words or Deeds? A Review of Equal Opportunity Policies in Higher Education' (1989) CRE.

Williamson, W 'Class Bias' in Warren-Piper, D (ed) *Is Higher Education Fair?* (1981).

Wilson, J F 'A Survey of Legal Education in the United Kingdom' (1966) 9 Journal of the Society of Public Teachers of Law 1.

Wilson, J F and Marsh, S B 'A Second Survey of Legal Education in the United Kingdom' (1975) 13 Journal of the Society of Public Teachers of Law 239.

Wilson, J F and Marsh, S B 'A Second Survey of Legal Education in the United Kingdom', supplement No 2 (1978) Institute of Advanced Legal Studies.

Wilson, J F and Marsh, S B 'A Second Survey of Legal Education in the United Kingdom', supplement No 2 (1981) Institute of Advanced Legal Studies.

Wood, R 'Aptitude Testing is not an engine for equalizing Educational opportunity' (1986) 34/1 British Journal of Educational Studies 26.

Yates, J and Davies, P *The Progress and Performance of Former Access Students in Higher Education 1984–1986* (1986) Roehampton Institute of Higher Education.

Yens, D P, Benenson, T F and Stimmel, B Recruitment of under-presented Student Groups: A Controlled Study (1986) 57/1 Journal of Higher Education (USA) 44.

Symposia

(1970) University of Toledo Law Review 227. Symposium on disadvantaged students and legal education – programs for affirmative action.

(1975) 4 Black LJ 453. Edited Transcripts of Proceedings of the American Association of Law Schools Section on Minority Groups.

(1979) 31 Rutgers Law Review 857. Rutgers Law School Minority Student Program: Documents from the Faculty Debates.

(1979) 22 Howard LJ 299. CLEO Symposium.

(1984) 34 J Legal Ed 343. Law School Admissions in the 21st Century.

(1986) 20 University of San Francisco Law Review 383. The 1985 Minority Law Teachers Conference.

(1987) 12 Thurgood Marshall Law Review 299. Minority Legal Pedagogy: Foundation for Participation in the Legal Profession: A Symposium.

Government Reports/Official Reports

Armitage Report Report of the Committee on Legal Education in Northern Ireland (Cmnd 579) (1973) HMSO.

Arthurs Report Law and learning: Report of the Consultative Group on Research and Education in Law (1983) Social Sciences and Humanities Research Council.

Bowen Report Legal Education in NSW: Report of Committee in Inquiry (1979) Government Printer NSW.

Bromley Report Report of the Committee on Professional Legal Education in Northern Ireland (1985).

Leverhulme Report Excellence in Diversity. Towards a New Strategy for Higher Education: Report of the Society for Research into Higher Education (1983).

Martin Report Report of the Committee on the Future of Tertiary Education in Australia (1964) Australian Universities Commission.

McNally Report Committee of Inquiry into the Qualifications for Registration as a Legal Practitioner (1985).

Ormrod Report Report of the Committee on Legal Education (Cmnd 4594) (1971) HMSO.

Rampton Report Committee of Inquiry into the Education of Children From Ethnic Minority Groups: West Indian Children In Our Schools (Cmnd 8723) (1981) HMSO.

Robbins Report Report of the Committee on Higher Education (Cmnd 2154) (1963) HMSO.

Swann Report Committee of Inquiry into the Education of Children from Ethnic Minority Groups: Education For All (Cmnd 9453) (1985) HMSO.

Wooding Committee Report Report on Legal Education in the West Indies (1967) Institute of Commonwealth Studies.

Wran Report Report of the Committee on Higher Education Funding (1988) Government Printer.

Bibliographies

Amin, K, Fernandes, M and Gordon, P *Racism and Discrimination in Britain*. A Select Bibliography 1984–87 (1988) Runnymede Trust.

Lulat, Y G-M 'International Higher Education Bibliography' Instalment No 1, Parts 1 and 2 (1987) 16 Higher Education 659. 'International Higher Education Bibliography' Instalment No 1 Part 1 (1988) 17 Higher Education 417.

Swanson, K *Affirmative Action and Preferential Admissions in Higher Education* (1981) Scarecrow Press.

Wheat, C 'Selected Bibliography: Minority Group Participation in the Legal Profession' (1970) Toledo Law Review 935.

Index

Access
  access courses
    full-time course (Vauxhall College/South
      Bank Polytechnic) 323–324
    part-time course (London University)
      321–322
    Scotland 222–223
  Admission Bulletin (University of Windsor)
    305–311
  critique of term 'access' 275–276
  excellence versus access 28–30
  global access 296
  linear model of legal education 290–292
  multi-entry model 291–292
  problems generally 1–3
  resources 286–288
  social desirability 9, 10
Admission criteria
  aptitude/achievement tests 32, 47–48, 292–
    293
  Law School Admission Test (USA), 60, 63,
    78–83, 117, 316–320
  preferential discrimination 20–25, 294–295
  problems 1–3
Affirmative action
  positive action, as 20
Arenas of law
  proliferation of 295–296
Australia
  Aboriginal lawyers 95, 96
  age and experience 89–90
  areas of employment 87–88
  disadvantaged groups 100–108
  elitist nature of profession 88–89
  ethnic identification 95–97
  financial support of students 106–108
  history of profession 85
  law schools 85, 90, 100–105
  market control by profession 87
  mobility of profession 100
  numbers of lawyers 86–87
  religious institutions and lawyers 94–95
  routes of entry to legal profession 85–86, 100
  socio-economic backgrounds 88–89, 97–
    100
    disadvantaged groups 100–108
  women lawyers 90–94

Barriers to access
  discrimination 17–20
  generally 5–7
  language 13–15
  length of period of full qualification 15–17
  positive action opposed 20–28
Bentham, Jeremy
  attack on legal profession 8

Canada
  Admission Bulletin (University of Windsor)
    305–311
  articles of clerkship 126
  civil law system 114, 116
  common law system 114, 117–118
  financial barriers to study 128
  half-time legal study 120, 129
  lack of information 129
  language factors 125
  law school admission criteria 115–118
  lawyers from foreign jurisdictions 125–126
  mature students 128, 129
  mobility of lawyers 125–126
  native Canadians 122–125, 129
  nature of legal system 114–115
  numbers of law students and lawyers 127–
    128
  professional qualification 126
  Quebec 114, 116
  routes of access 115
  traditionalism 128
  women lawyers 120–122
Commonwealth
  legal practitioner mobility
    admission rules, function of 258
    bias towards UK qualifications 262
    Carribbean experience 263
    citizenship requirements 264
    diversity and inconsistency of regulations
      261, 265
    EEC experience 259, 260–261
    emergence of transnational law 259–260
    freedom of movement, for and against
      258, 265–269
    general admission requirements 261–263
    Law Ministers discussion paper 269–270
    multi-national law firms 259

339

Commonwealth – *continued*
  legal practitioner mobility – *continued*
    national/domestic nature of legal practice
      259
    nature of Commonwealth 259
    reform proposals 269–270
    retraining requirements 263–264
    special admission for particular case 264–
      265
Control of market
  legal professionalism, through 276–279
Criteria, assessment
  aptitude/achievement tests 32, 47–48, 292–
    293
  Law School Admission Test (USA) 60, 63,
    78–83, 117, 316–320
  preferential discrimination 20–25, 294–295
  problems 1–3

Demand
  legal services, for 283–286
Disadvantaged groups
  aptitude testing 32, 47–48, 292–293
  minority community institutions 285–286
  older students 51
  remedial education 31
  self-betterment schemes 293–294, 297–298
  survey of students enrolled in JD programs
    312–314
  United States, in 56, 61–63
  women. *See* Women
Discrimination
  barriers to access 17–20, 293
  Law School Admission Test (USA) 60, 63,
    78–83, 117
  removal of 41–42

England
  black students under-represented 132, 136
  composition of professions 132–135
  demographic changes and higher education
    135, 143–144
  discrimination 133–134, 153–154, 155
  legal education
    access courses 141–142, 147–148
    admissions policies and A-level standard
      137–138
    class composition of student body 136–
      137
    expansion of 135–136
    financial barriers 139, 150
    financial support of students 145–146,
      148, 150, 156
    flexible provision 147
    government policy 135, 142–148, 156
    graduate entrants to professsions 135,
      148–149
    mature students 140–141
    part-time degrees 140–141
    polytechnics 135–137, 144–145
    racial and class exclusivity 139–140, 153–
      154, 155, 156

England – *continued*
  legal professions
    apprenticeship by articles or pupillage
      152
    criteria for recruitment 153–154
    finals courses 150–152
    financial barriers 139, 150
    future for entry 155
    non-law graduate entry 149–150
    qualification process 148–149
    recruitment crisis 150, 153
    restrictive practices crumbling 148
    skills required 153
    stratification within professions 154–155
  proposals for improved access 155–157
  racial discrimination 133–134, 153–154, 155
  women 133, 136
  working class students under-represented
    132, 136
Equality of opportunity
  assessment of policies 44–46
  expansion of places as a remedy 43–44
  financial aid 42–43
  inequality or participation in higher
    education 40–41
  removal of discrimination 41–42
  resources 286–288
  self-betterment schemes 293–294, 297–298
European Economic Community
  transnational legal practice 259, 260–261

Financial factors
  equality of opportunity through financial
    aid 42–43
Freedom of movement
  arguments against
    interests of host society 266–267
    protection of host legal profession 266
    protection of local legal education 266
  arguments for
    development of common legal heritage
      268
    development of Commonwealth legal
      cooperation 268–269
    non-discrimination principle 268
    right to choose counsel 267–268
  justification of 258, 265
  legal practitioners in Commonwealth. *See
    under* Commonwealth

Government reports
  bibliography 337

Higher education
  achievement/aptitude dilemma 32, 47–48,
    292–293
  alternative entry criteria 46–48
  equality of opportunity 41–46, 293
  equality of results 49–50
  expansion of places 43–44
  first line of control of profession, as 39–40
  inequality of participation 40–41
  older students 51
  policy decisions 53

Higher education – *continued*
 regulation and selection by 39–40
 retention of selected students 52–53
 selective and mass systems 5–6
 targets or quotas 50
 under-represented groups 40–41

India
 case study on positive discrimination 25–28
 higher education, availability of 164
 inaccessibility of legal services 166, 167, 169, 170
 law colleges 162–163, 164
 lawyers' role in social transformation 162
 legal aid 165, 166, 167, 168–169, 170
 legal education
  access to all graduates 164, 169
  cost of 169–170
  eligibility requirements 164, 165
  five-year course 163–164
  neglect of 163
  quality of 165–166, 169
  reforms of 163–166
  rote learning 162–163, 166
  socio-economic background of students 164–165
 legal profession
  access to 168–169
  difficulties facing entrant to 167–168
  inadequacies of 166–168
  nature of lawyering 166–168, 169–170
  profile of 166–168
  socio-economic backgrounds 168
  women lawyers 168
 National Movement 162
 people's courts 169
Interests of lawyers
 Bentham's analysis 8
 legal professionalism 276–279, 296–297
 private biases and interests 274–275

Jamaica
 barriers to access 174
 education system, generally 182–183
 legal education
  1971 Treaty on entry requirements to law schools 179–181
   impact of reforms, 181–185
   problems arising from 184–185
  background to reforms 177–179
  clinical/practical training 181–182
  composition of student body 179
  consultants' proposals (1981) 184–185
  financial support of students 183–184
 legal profession
  access to 185–187
  entry removed from control of profession 181, 185
  historical development 175–177
  increase in numbers 182
  length of period of training 183, 185
  location of legal firms 188
  recruitment policies of firms 185–186, 187–188

Jamaica – *continued*
 legal profession – *continued*
  resistance to reforms 187
  rural areas 188
  status symbols 186
 nature of course 184–185
 social and economic conditions 174
 women lawyers 179, 180, 186–187
Justice
 access to 8, 9

Law firms
 changing nature of 295
Law lecturers
 gatekeepers, as 3–7, 273–275
Law schools
 admission policies 10–13, 31
 gatekeepers, as, 3–7, 273–275
 management of 274
Legal personnel
 transnational mobility 296
Legal professionalism
 control mechanism, as 276–279, 296–297
Legal services
 need and demand for 281–286

Merit
 selection on basis of 29–30
Minority groups
 educational institutions set up by 285–286
 survey of US students 312–314
Mobility of legal practioners
 Commonwealth, in. *See under* Commonwealth
 transnational mobility 296

Need
 Legal services, for 281–283
Northern Ireland
 education system 199–200
 emigration of students to Great Britain 198
 legal education
  admission and A-level performance 199–200
  law degree requirement 197–198
 legal profession
  admission of Institute students into profession 209–211
  alternative courses 202–203, 207
  Armitage Report 195–196, 197
  Bromley Report 196, 197
  control over admission 203–205
  financial support during training 211–213
  Institute of Professional Legal Studies 195–197, 201–209
  law degree requirement 197–198
  Law Society 191–192
  nature of 191–194
  non-law graduates and non-graduates 200–201
  numbers seeking admission 201–203
  office training 210–211
  professional training and admission 194–197

Northern Ireland – *continued*
Institute of Professional Legal Studies –
continued
  religious composition 192, 194
  selection of Institute students 205–209
  social composition 192, 194
  social economic and political context 190–191
  unionist/nationalist divide 190–191
  women lawyers 192, 193–194, 200
Number of lawyers
  control of 10–13
  demand 283–286
  manpower planning 10–13, 281
  need 281–283
  problem of 274, 279–281
  resources 286–288

Politics
  law as product of 288–290
Positive action
  opposition to 20–28
  species of 20–21
Preferential treatment
  direct preferential treatment 20, 22–25
  species of 20–21, 294–295
Professionalism, legal
  control through 276–279, 296–297

Racial prejudice
  barriers to access 17–20
Resources
  equality of opportunity, for 286–288
Reverse discrimination
  direct preferential treatment 20–25
Routes of entry
  linear or multi-entry model, 290–292
  policy of flexibility 31
  single and multiple routes 6
  Xanadu examples 5–8

Scotland
  legal education
    access courses 222–223
    Diploma in Legal Practice 223–225
    ethnic background of students 221
    law school applications and admissions 220, 221–222
    mature students 221, 222
    social background of students 220–221, 231
    vocational training 223–225, 232
    women students 221
  legal profession
    admissions to 219, 225–226, 227
    alternative routes in to 222, 231–232
    historical background 218–219
    nature of 217–218
    sectors of practice 229
    supply control of entry to 226–229, 232
    women lawyers 221, 226, 228, 229–231
  population of 217
Sri Lanka
  language factors 13–15

Standards of legal profession
  access, and problem of 28–30

Teachers of law
  gatekeepers, as 3–7, 273–275

United States of America
  admission statistics 315
  colonial and revolutionary period 57–58
  composition of profession 59–61
  current law school admissions 59–61
  establishment of formal legal education 58–59
  Law School Admission Test (LSAT) 59–60, 63, 78–83, 316–320
  minority group students, enrolment survey 312–314
  post-revolutionary period 58–59
  racially and culturally biased testing 62–64
  racism 55, 56
  sexism 55, 56
  subordinate groups 55
  Urban Legal Studies Program 64–72, 83
  women's law school admissions 61–62

Women
  Australia 90–94
  Canada 120–122
  discrimination 1–2
  England 133, 136
  India 168
  Jamica 179, 180, 186–187
  Northern Ireland 192, 193–194, 200
  older students/returners 51
  Scotland 221, 226, 228, 229–231
  United States 55, 56, 61–62
  Zimbabwe 249

Xanadu
  mythical jurisdiction of 1–28

Zambia
  Citizen's Advisory Bureau 241
  demand for legal services 241, 243
  factors affecting access 238–239
  legal education
    admission to professional training 236–237
    bursaries 238
    drop-out rate 236, 237
    quota allocation 235–236, 238, 243
    recruitment 235–237
    School of Law, 234–235, 235–236, 237, 238–239
  legal profession
    access routes into 237–238, 239
    articles of clerkship 237, 238, 239
    Law Association 239–240
    Law Practice Institute 234–235, 236–237
    rural areas 240, 241
    size of, and distribution 239–241, 242, 243
  proposals for improved access 244
  television law programme 241, 243

Zimbabwe
entry routes to profession considered 246–248
legal education
access since independence 249–252
access to professional training 250–251, 254–255, 256–257
criterion for admission 249
current admission practice 250
curriculum 252–254
failure rates 251
law in context 252–253
lecturers 253
mature students 250
part-time and extra-mural study 251–252
social background of students 249–250

Zimbabwe – *continued*
legal education – *continued*
Southern Rhodesia legal profession 245, 249–250
University College of Rhodesia 249–250
white students 250
women students 249
Legal Practitioners Act 1981 246, 253, 255
legal profession
access to 250–251, 254–255, 256–257
practical training 255
legal services, distributions of 256
McNally Committee Report 246–248
political and idealogical developments 257
post-independence transition 245–246